Speculative Modernism

CRITICAL EXPLORATIONS IN SCIENCE FICTION AND FANTASY
a series edited by Donald E. Palumbo and C.W. Sullivan III
Earlier Works: www.mcfarlandpub.com

57 *Wells Meets Deleuze: The Scientific Romances Reconsidered* (Michael Starr, 2017)

58 *Science Fiction and Futurism: Their Terms and Ideas* (Ace G. Pilkington, 2017)

59 *Science Fiction in Classic Rock: Musical Explorations of Space, Technology and the Imagination, 1967–1982* (Robert McParland, 2017)

60 *Patricia A. McKillip and the Art of Fantasy World-Building* (Audrey Isabel Taylor, 2017)

61 *The Fabulous Journeys of Alice and Pinocchio: Exploring Their Parallel Worlds* (Laura Tosi with Peter Hunt, 2018)

62 *A Dune Companion: Characters, Places and Terms in Frank Herbert's Original Six Novels* (Donald E. Palumbo, 2018)

63 *Fantasy Literature and Christianity: A Study of the Mistborn, Coldfire, Fionavar Tapestry and Chronicles of Thomas Covenant Series* (Weronika Łaszkiewicz, 2018)

64 *The British Comic Invasion: Alan Moore, Warren Ellis, Grant Morrison and the Evolution of the American Style* (Jochen Ecke, 2019)

65 *The Archive Incarnate: The Embodiment and Transmission of Knowledge in Science Fiction* (Joseph Hurtgen, 2018)

66 *Women's Space: Essays on Female Characters in the 21st Century Science Fiction Western* (ed. Melanie A. Marotta, 2019)

67 *"Hailing frequencies open": Communication in Star Trek: The Next Generation* (Thomas D. Parham III, 2019)

68 *The Global Vampire: Essays on the Undead in Popular Culture Around the World* (ed. Cait Coker, 2019)

69 *Philip K. Dick: Essays of the Here and Now* (ed. David Sandner, 2019)

70 *Michael Bishop and the Persistence of Wonder: A Critical Study of the Writings* (Joe Sanders, 2020)

71 *Caitlín R. Kiernan: A Critical Study of Her Dark Fiction* (James Goho, 2020)

72 *In* Frankenstein's *Wake: Mary Shelley, Morality and Science Fiction* (Alison Bedford, 2020)

73 *The Fortean Influence on Science Fiction: Charles Fort and the Evolution of the Genre* (Tanner F. Boyle, 2020)

74 *Arab and Muslim Science Fiction* (Hosan Elzembely and Emad El-Din Aysha, 2020)

75 *The Mythopoeic Code of Tolkien: A Christian Platonic Reading of the Legendarium* (Jyrki Korpua, 2021)

76 *The Truth of Monsters: Coming of Age with Fantastic Media* (Ildikó Limpár, 2021)

77 *Speculative Modernism: How Science Fiction, Fantasy and Horror Conceived the Twentieth Century* (William Gillard, James Reitter *and* Robert Stauffer, 2021)

78 *English Magic and Imperial Madness: The Anti-Colonial Politics of Susanna Clarke's* Jonathan Strange & Mr. Norrell (Peter D. Mathews, 2021)

Speculative Modernism
How Science Fiction, Fantasy and Horror Conceived the Twentieth Century

WILLIAM GILLARD, JAMES REITTER
and ROBERT STAUFFER

CRITICAL EXPLORATIONS IN
SCIENCE FICTION AND FANTASY, 77

Series Editors Donald E. Palumbo *and* C.W. Sullivan III

McFarland & Company, Inc., Publishers
Jefferson, North Carolina

This book has undergone peer review.

ISBN (print) 978-1-4766-8333-1
ISBN (ebook) 978-1-4766-4495-0

LIBRARY OF CONGRESS AND BRITISH LIBRARY
CATALOGUING DATA ARE AVAILABLE

Library of Congress Control Number 2021045603

© 2021 William Gillard, James Reitter *and* Robert Stauffer. All rights reserved

No part of this book may be reproduced or transmitted in any form or by any means, electronic or mechanical, including photocopying or recording, or by any information storage and retrieval system, without permission in writing from the publisher.

Front cover illustration by Tithi Luadthong (Shutterstock)

Printed in the United States of America

*McFarland & Company, Inc., Publishers
Box 611, Jefferson, North Carolina 28640
www.mcfarlandpub.com*

To Susan, Ann, and Becky

Should the wide world roll away
Leaving black terror
Limitless night,
Nor God, nor man, nor place to stand
Would be to me essential
If thou and thy white arms were there
And the fall to doom a long way.
　　　　　　　　—Stephen Crane (1895)

Acknowledgments

No book like this ever comes together without the support and sage advice of many people. The three of us agreed to meet at the Northeast Modern Language Association annual conference in 2019 to dream about a book we'd write together. We'd like to thank the two people who came to our paper session that weekend to listen to us spout off about Robert E. Howard and M.P. Shiel. You were small in number, but you inspired us! It was at that conference that we first met Gary Mitchem, senior editor at McFarland. We owe him a debt of gratitude for encouraging us that day and for giving us a purpose and structure for our ideas. We'd like to thank academic librarians everywhere. Bill would especially like to thank Ane Carriveau, Kelly Johnson, and Rebecca Durbin at the UW Oshkosh Fox Cities Library for their immense help in allowing him to request every book in the world at one time or another during the writing and revision process. We could not have done it without you! Speaking of gathering the shelves and shelves of books necessary for a project of this scope, we'd like to thank independent booksellers everywhere, particularly those in Dutchess County, New York, and Appleton, Wisconsin, and also Barbara and Gary Alexander of Alexander Books in Lafayette, Louisiana. We'd like to thank our families and friends for being patient with us, for being sounding boards, and for allowing us the time and space to write this book. Finally, we'd like to thank our peer reviewers for taking great care in reading our manuscript closely and providing us with invaluable feedback on the content and our process. Our book is much, much better because of you fine readers.

Contents

Acknowledgments	vi
Preface	1
Introduction	5

1. Utocalypse — 15
  All Will Be Well: The Utopian Roots of Speculative Modernism — 17
  The Screw Turns: Bleak Reality Murders Optimism — 22
  Anti-Utopians: The Individual Versus Society — 31
  Conclusion — 40

2. Shadows at the Turn — 42
  Gothic Origins of Speculative Modernism — 46
  Gothic Extensions: Doppelgängers to Vampires — 50
  Ghosts and the Unexplained — 55
  Conclusion — 73

3. This Island Earth: Nature vs. Speculative Modernists — 75
  Science Will Bend Nature to Serve Humanity: The Utopian Perspective — 79
  There Are Things We Can Never Know: The Purple Cloud and the Limits of Science — 86
  Beyond This Place and Time: The Natural World Will Outlast Us — 90
  Weaponizing Nature: Understanding the Non-Human World in Order to Destroy It — 96
  Conclusion — 100

Contents

4. Worlds Beyond	102
What Do We Really Have to Offer?	106
They Want What We Want	114
"We're Down; We're Beat": Humanity's Defeat	121
Conclusion	130
5. Machinocracy	132
A Species in Distress: Machines Will Save Humanity	135
Sand in the Gears: Machines Can't Save Us	139
Building the Perfect Gun: Machines Will Kill Us All	146
Conclusion	156
6. Divine Secrets	157
The Benevolent Universe: Spiritual Rewards for the Speculative Modernist	161
Cruel Reality: Monsters Lurking Beyond the Veil	172
The Neutral Universe: Our Truth Lies Within Ourselves	180
Conclusion	185
7. We Are Fortunately Flawed	187
Sherlock Holmes: Ego and Ultra-Rationalism	190
Tarzan: Natural Law and the Laws of Man	194
Buck Rogers: Future Perfect	198
King Kull: Governing by Axe	199
Conan the Cimmerian: Blood on Steel	201
Jirel of Joiry: Darkness and Light	204
Conclusion	206
Epilogue	209
The Editorial Tastemakers	209
The Book Publishers Who Made the Old New Again	212
Conan as Chronicle	214
Chapter Notes	217
Works Cited	225
Index	239

Preface

The year is 1928.

Summer.

Imagine you are a fan of science fiction and weird stories and you are sitting on your front porch waiting for the mail to arrive. Finally, there it is—the August issue of *Amazing Stories* is in your hands. Your parents just don't understand why you love this stuff so much. The magazine is always good, you think, but they just can't relate. At first, when you scan the table of contents, you might be interested in the new story by H.G. Wells, "The Moth," a fascinating short without the social theory baggage that weighed down so much from Wells in those days. You read that story to learn of a mean-spirited public battle between rival lepidopterists that turns strange when one of them dies and the other, feeling intense guilt for how poorly he treated his late colleague, is driven insane by a strange moth that only he can see. Turn back a few pages, and you'll read part one of a story you have never heard of, by two authors named Lee Hawkins Garby and Edward Elmer Smith. This was Smith's first story sale, and it changed science fiction forever. *The Skylark of Space* is the ur-text of the space opera genre and remains one of the most famous science-fiction series ever. Between Wells and Smith in that August 1928 issue of *Amazing Stories*, you'll find a story called "Armageddon 2419 A.D." by Philip Francis Nowlan. This story birthed perhaps the most famous science-fiction character of all time, Buck Rogers, whose popularity has endured for nearly a century. No less a figure than Donald A. Wollheim, influential author, editor, publisher, and founding member of the Futurians, said, "The role of Buck Rogers in the rise and popularization of science fiction can scarcely be overestimated" (Wollheim). What linked all of these stories was the intense love of science and the promise of human innovation.

Those were wonderful times to be a reader of speculative fiction.

But these are wonderful times to be reading the literature of that era, too. In the first quarter of the twenty-first century—as the incredible pace of change makes our heads swirl, with immense pressure coming at us from climate change, pandemics, racial injustice, and political conflict—the speculative fiction that was written and eagerly devoured by our great-great-grandparents provides enjoyment, insight, and, perhaps, solace in these times. If they were able to survive what they did, then maybe we can survive this most challenging era, too. After all, what do we know about our present moment? I feel as if we are probably missing some very important things. I do know that writers of speculative fiction continue to ask the right kinds of questions about who we are and where we are headed, and those are the questions that fascinate me the most. Young dreamers of all ages—dreamers like me—will continue to be drawn to these stories, and this book might provide an entry point for some of it. I hope that you enjoy reading it as much as we enjoyed writing it!

—**Bill Gillard**

I was a latecomer to the field of literature but was always obsessed with horror, fantasy, and science fiction through films and television. Growing up with Saturday morning cartoons, the Universal Monsters, and Godzilla broadcasts on television prior to cable, I was always drawn to the dark and the fantastic—but I hated reading! Nothing, not even the great works of Tolkien, would hold my adolescent/teenage attention span.

Once cable came to the masses, I discovered Conan and was completely overtaken by Arnold Schwarzenegger's portrayal, James Earl Jones as the villainous Thulsa Doom, Mako's narration, and especially that Basil Poledouris score. *Night Flight* and *USA Up All Night* were viewing staples. It was only through the movies and syndicated shows like *Star Trek* and *The Twilight Zone* that I began to scratch the surface of the Speculative Modernists. Still, I found myself more intrigued by the cover art of these books rather than the actual words on the page.

Despite my getting older, I was (and still am) obsessed with cartoons. In complete honesty, I habitually watched afternoon animation of the 1980s—and I loved the villains. In fact, I only grew tired of those shows because I wanted the bad guys to be more powerful than they were portrayed to be and for the "good guys" to be not so good. Villains were always defeated, and I wanted them to win. My teenage attitude (informed greatly by heavy metal music) was simple: give me darkness; I had no love for rainbows, unless they were in the dark. Horror films, accessed through cable or rental video stores, were my outlet, but I discovered fantasy could have that darkness too. Maybe, just maybe, I should give reading these books another shot, as it seemed the latter often informed the former.

Edgar Allan Poe and Washington Irving fit that bill, but I also kept on encountering H.P. Lovecraft's name. So came Cthulhu and the like. These were books I could get into! I also discovered the literature of Robert E. Howard through my obsession with the Conan film. It was time to give Tolkien another go, especially since I loved the animated Rankin & Bass adaptations as well as the Bakshi films. Science fiction could do the trick, too, inspired by the 1981 film *Heavy Metal*.

When I attended college, I settled on being an English major, but I enrolled in the writing track and barely read any literature. It wasn't until my graduate coursework, especially during my PhD, that I developed a true love of reading and literature. I caught up very quickly but didn't abandon my love of films or television. Instead, I tried to build bridges between the two—which has informed my professional and personal interests and is one of the main reasons I wanted to write this book with Rob and Bill (Rob and I currently work in the same department, and Bill is a colleague from a former stint; Rob and Bill grew up together).

—James Reitter

Sometime in the early 1990s, I wandered down West 47th Street in search of a bookstore I had only just heard about called Gotham Bookmart. There was no sign outside that indicated that it was a bookstore, and the main entrance was slightly below street level as I recall, so it was not the most obvious of booksellers. I found my way inside with an article I had found (I'm afraid I have not been able to locate it again) that gave a history of fantasy writers who wrote before J.R.R. Tolkien's *The Hobbit* had been published and had possibly some influence over his work. I found where James Branch Cabell was supposed to be on the shelves. There was one copy of *Jurgen*, but there was also a note inviting me to come to the counter if I was looking for other Cabell titles. When I approached the counter, holding the copy of *Jurgen*, the bookseller looked excitedly at me, anticipating my question. He led me behind the counter to a bookshelf filled with all of his various titles: *Hamlet Had an Uncle*, *The Cream of the Jest*, the many books in the *Biography of the Life of Manuel*, which tells all about the doings in Poictesme. Over time, I returned to the Gotham Bookmart to buy what I could afford, and I now have a good collection of Cabell's books.

Part of the charm was that I had found this seemingly secret load of books that somehow belonged to me. I expanded my knowledge of early fantasy to Dunsany, Eddison, Machen, Clark Ashton Smith, Robert Howard and all of the great fantasy writers of the early part of the twentieth century. I had already discovered Lovecraft and Tolkien, but all of these amazing works filled in the corners of my fantasy fandom, even though it would be many years before I could find the really obscure books on eBay, Vialibri, and other bookselling sites.

I found these works, thanks to this one lost article, and now I feel I need to return two favors. First, to the authors, I'd like to do my part to bring them back into the light of day, by bringing out their literary merits and showing how important they are both to our studies of literature and to our studies of culture. Second, I feel that it is important to the readers going forward. I'd like to help construct and expand that list of writers, so that a whole new group of fans can find them, and not just in those vanishing bookstores. While working on this book, I have found many other authors that my lost article didn't mention: Marie Corelli, Mary Elizabeth Counselman, Evelyn Underhill, and so on. None of these authors is perfect, but they have helped me learn a lot about *fin de siècle* culture and the origins of the genre works I do love so much. I hope that you'll find here, if nothing else, a list of authors to go dig up to see if they hold any merit for your understanding of Speculative Modernist literature.

—**Rob Stauffer**

Introduction

In the summer of 1905, the Salon d'Automne in Paris presented a gallery of paintings, among them Henri Matisse's "Woman in a Hat," that was so unsettling the art critic Louis Vauxcelles dubbed the artists "Les Fauves"—"the wild beasts." In the autumn of the same year, in New York, a production of George Bernard Shaw's *Mrs. Warren's Profession* was interrupted by the police who arrested the cast and crew for indecency. In May of 1913, back in Paris, the Ballet Russes's premiere of Igor Stravinsky's ballet *The Rite of Spring* was heckled to the point that the dancers could not hear the music being played only a few feet away. These moments in the world of painting, drama, and music ushered in a chaotic new age where everything that went before, all the foundations of these arts, was blown apart and put back together in radical new ways. Violent arts to match the violent, changing times. Changes in literature, however, while just as radical and disquieting, found a more insidious path in a form so innocuous seeming that it was often thought of as children's literature or pure fantasy. This path is what we now call speculative fiction.

The span of roughly half a century between the 1880s and 1930s was a time of great upheaval and radical change in virtually all facets of Western life. Intellectual shifts were often mirrored by rapid changes that impacted everyday life. One of the most significant developments of the time was the pioneering efforts of Sigmund Freud and his development of psychoanalysis that brought theories of the subconscious to the forefront. This had a tremendous impact on not only the intellectual but artistic world, giving rise to movements such as Cubism, followed by Dada and Surrealism. Music also shifted away from traditional tonality with Arnold Schoenberg and standard rhythm through Stravinsky. The reconfiguring of aesthetics—governing of representations of truth, reality, and beauty—was spearheaded by Walter Pater and bled into architectural design, coming to fruition with the Bauhaus movement and followed up by Frank Lloyd Wright, which blended aesthetics with function and brought theoretical revolutions into common living.

Architecture was not the only tether between intellectual philosophies and everyday life. Mass populations were introduced to technological inventions at a breakneck pace. Innovations in transportation such as the bicycle and motorcar were rapidly replacing the horse and buggy as a means to travel and traveling farther and farther away from a home to a place of employment became much more feasible. The evolution of the bicycle also had a great impact on fashion, particularly for women. The fashion world began to reconsider the practicality of lengthy Victorian dresses and slowly replaced them with "rational clothing" like bloomers and flexible corsets (Ostroff).

Science also underwent incredible innovations that impacted the mass populace. Edison brought the world electric light. Guglielmo Marconi introduced the first radio. Count Ferdinand von Zeppelin created machines that could be steered through the skies above. Politics, too, was undergoing monumental change with the death of Queen Victoria and the assassination of President William McKinley, both occurring in 1901. Modernism was not only a philosophical or artistic revolution; it was a new cultural era for the Western world.

The best-known authors of what came to be called the Modernist era responded with radical experiments in form and style, a reconsideration of humanity's place in the cosmos, and a fresh focus on language, its limits and possibilities. Modernist giants such as William Carlos Williams, Virginia Woolf, Ezra Pound, Gertrude Stein, and T.S. Eliot blew up the universal creed of the Victorian literary age: that in writing we could find Truth and Beauty, and that in language we could attach names to Reality. These great Modernist writers smashed and reassembled the tools of their predecessors—poetry, the various forms of fiction, and even memoir—into weapons that they used to annihilate formerly sacred institutions of literature. When they were finished, very little of the old faith in language and our ability to comprehend the objective Truth of the world remained.

Before the most well-known Modernists were in their primes, another, very different story was being told, a story that creeped and oozed its way into the 1900s. The cataclysmic changes of the late nineteenth and early twentieth centuries spawned several new literary genres. Although the earliest examples of science fiction, horror, and fantasy predate the Modernist era, the three genres grew in popularity during these years. Long before the great Modernists arrived at the party, writers of speculative fiction, as these genres are now known collectively, had already been exploring the same cultural forces as their canonical counterparts. The best-known literary Modernists innovated, there is no denying that. However, the work of literary Modernism began long before Pound—who was not even born until 1885—draped petals on a wet, black bough, and long before Stein announced that the difference is spreading. It was in the burgeoning genres of speculative fiction that American and British writers offered weird and frequently terrifying reasons for hope amid the chaos.

Modernism has been defined in many ways. Common among nearly all of the definitions is that the old world was dying, and reliance on the way things had always been done had led us all to a profoundly violent and bleak dead end. Literary Modernists embraced the desire to abandon obsolete institutions that had led humanity to ruin. They searched for—and frequently did not find—a new way of being in the world, a way that made sense and could be sustained for future generations. Modernism was an era of cataclysmic change in art, literature, science, and philosophy that dismantled the certainties of the Enlightenment and deflated the airs of societal sophistication of the Victorian Age. As J.M. Roberts articulates in *The Twentieth Century*, Modernism was "a shift in the focus of the arts to the subjective, from the object depicted or the story narrated to a vision, a state of mind and primal reaction, above all to the state of mind of the artist, whether it was comprehensible or not to anyone else" (324). The comforts of cultural, economic, and spiritual norms gave way to an impending tidal wave of skepticism and pessimism that began in earnest in the mustard gas-filled trenches and ended with the twin hellfires of Hiroshima and Nagasaki. Rebuilding the world using fragments of the shattered old world is a frequent theme in Modernist literature. Eliot's speaker in "The Waste Land" (1922) asks:

> What are the roots that clutch, what branches grow
> Out of this stony rubbish? Son of man,
> You cannot say, or guess, for you know only
> A heap of broken images... [660].

Especially as World War I ground an entire generation of men and women into blood-soaked mud, the survivors, like those at the heart of H.G. Wells's *The Shape of Things to Come* (1936), cast about in the ruins of civilization for some way to rediscover meaning. They use the broken remnants of the old order to begin to rebuild something new. Ezra Pound's dictum of "make it new" (inspired by writings of Confucian philosophy) became the calling card that symbolized the era. Unlike in earlier literature of this type, Modernism is marked by the idea that humanity might have lost the right to survive, that humans have worn out their welcome on a fragile and finite Earth.

When one looks in august encyclopedias or literary guidebooks on Modernism, one will almost never find a mention of the role speculative fiction played in the creation of this movement. Sometimes H.G. Wells or Sir Arthur Conan Doyle might make their way into the notice of the academic seeking to understand the Modernist period, but rarely is any intrusion into the genres made to chronicle the effects each had on the other. Lately, there has been an awakening to the importance of speculative fiction literature among academics, but generally even then the literature is rarely studied the way canonical works from the early twentieth century are. The lens of Modernism demonstrates the impact these speculative fictions had on the world, an impact that was often not felt for a generation as the works were mostly gobbled up by young minds who encountered these books in dime-store paperbacks and magazines. Just as the disruptions described above in the worlds of painting, drama, and music, seeds were being buried deep in the minds of a generation who would later fight wars with jet planes and rockets, who would fly to the Moon, build artificial brains, and push the arts to their limits. Our book, therefore, seeks to fill that gap left in the description of the Modernist arts and to acknowledge speculative fiction's rightful place as both creation and creator in the turbulent opening to the twentieth century.

This book examines the relationship between speculative fiction and the Modernist movement in American and British literature, a synergy we call "Speculative Modernism." Although detective, adventure, Western, and romance stories were immensely popular during this era, our study focuses only on horror, science fiction, and fantasy. Our focus will be on the years 1880–1939, a period that includes the rise of literary Modernism until its gradual transition to Postmodernism in the 1940s. Speculative fiction provides an alternative to the bleakness of Modernism, but we may not like the answers we find there. Yes, human civilization seems to be breaking down violently and completely, but these genres provide possible alternatives to simple despair. Perhaps from our endless wars and godless nature will arise something new, something unlooked for—maybe Yeats's "rough beast"—will bring us new diversions for the next twenty centuries. Our book looks at speculative fiction of both Britain and the United States during this period. We focus exclusively on fiction because that is where the genres were born and where they find their earliest, most vibrant expression. We look for common ground among these genre works and their much better-known Modernist counterparts and investigate how the themes of Speculative Modernist authors such as H.P. Lovecraft, William Hope Hodgson, H.G. Wells, Robert E. Howard, and others align with Modernist giants like T.S. Eliot, Stephen Crane, and Ezra Pound. While canonical authors often reach bleak conclusions, Speculative Modernists provide the next steps in the existence of the universe.

With recognized acknowledgments to *Journey to the Center of the Earth* (1864) and *From the Earth to the Moon* (1865) by Jules Verne, the stories of Sheridan Le Fanu, and the like, we will be focusing entirely on

British and American writers. In similar fashion, literary predecessors such as Edgar Allan Poe, Washington Irving, Wilkie Collins, and other celebrated nineteenth-century writers have created many of the conceptual and thematic foundations to be discussed in this book, but they have been largely excluded as individual entries from our investigation and exploration because, according to the definition of Modernism we stipulated above, they are not Modernists.

Instead of wallowing in society's collective destruction, Speculative Modernists imagined what might come next. Their new world emphasized how unreachable a unified perfection really is, how unrealistic that dream is. Instead of striving for that perfection, they argued that the focus should be on making old forms new in order to fit the times. This also comes with the realization that the universe (as we construct it) is no longer egocentric; there are other realms of existence outside of what is apparent. As such, writers have to negotiate those realms and other possibilities of reality. Additionally, there must be a balance between technology and humanity and caution over innovation outpacing wisdom. The human form creates its own reality, but there is another reality that runs deeper, a larger truth to things. However, that realization comes with the freedom to cast off the weight of cultural and societal expectations. These are the concepts of the Speculative Modernists, radical and unsettling though they may be.

We acknowledge that this study does not include the comprehensive catalogues of the authors selected. As can be readily determined by their individual bibliographies, many of these authors were rather prolific in their careers, especially in regard to publications in a variety of popular magazines and serials, not just "pulps." We could not use every text written in this era, of course, but in the texts we have explored in this book, we see Speculative Modernism as a separate literary accomplishment that is worthy of discussing alongside canonical Modernism.

Our idea of Speculative Modernism, then, is built on the concept that each of the speculative genres—science fiction, horror, and fantasy, as conceived early in the twentieth century—represent how the godless, unfeeling universe that the literary Modernists were so depressed about could be seen in other ways: as a hope for human ingenuity and survival ability as seen in science fiction, as a recognition that humans are not the single hope for life in that cold, grim place we call home as seen in horror, and as a chance for renewal in the decay of empires and civilization itself in fantasy. We address these basic principles by examining seven main Modernist themes in speculative literature, and they each inform the chapters in this book.

In our opening chapter, "Utocalypse," we look at literary utopians who delved into the idea of human perfectibility during the final decades of the nineteenth century and helped to build a speculative-fiction audience.

In the early decades of the Industrial Revolution, the first stirrings of the science-fiction genre did not seem to be much changed from where literature had been up to that point. The emphasis on both sides of the Atlantic was on the collective future: how society might be organized in ways that could prevent war, feed the hungry, reward talent and hard work, and create greater equality and fairness for all. These utopians were all the rage both in America and Britain during the late stages of the nineteenth century. World War I marked a clear divergence in science fiction between the American and British approaches. While writers in Britain continued to flip utopian ideas into dystopias—their individuals finding it hard to survive in anyone's depiction of a universally good society—American writers focused on the power of the individual to build a future worth living in. Conservative and progressive politicians began to see how the "rugged individual" could live autonomously with nature as an ally rather than an opponent. The dreams of taming the wild frontiers instead of destroying them offered solutions to the terrors modern man was facing. Perfect society became something to flee. We begin to get glimpses of utopias gone awry in such works as Max Beerbohm's "Enoch Soames" (1916) which hints at how individuality has been surrendered a hundred years hence. Charlotte Perkins Gilman's *Herland* (1915) completes the notion of how society could only be saved by rendering men obsolete. The bleak solitude at the end of time in William Hope Hodgson's *The Dream of X* (1912) shows us society at its end, serving the only purpose for which society ever seems to be useful: keeping the monsters at bay.

Utopian stories were not the only tropes that transcended the nineteenth century and were reinterpreted during the Modernist era. Speculative Modernist writers engaged with the older forms of Gothic literature and created something new out of the old and tired forms. Although not new to the canon of literature, the questioning of the nature of death through phantasms, ghosts, apparitions, and the like began to take a rather grim turn with the likes of Ambrose Bierce. The "life beyond life," which Bierce characterized and Bram Stoker's seminal work *Dracula* (1897) built upon, elevated the stories of the undead used to terrify children to become veiled critiques of the failing institutions such as religion and social class. These texts, along with the ghost stories of Edith Wharton and others, use the spiritual and supernatural to undermine the social, cultural, and religious norms that had been in place for centuries. While these stories portray pessimism and perhaps even evil (according to a general morality), they do indicate a further step in our existence, and that this next step may even be a natural one if we allow it to be. Speculative Modernism adapts these once religious myths into something more concrete, warnings that could be used in the temporal world as well as the one hereafter. "Shadows at the Turn" examines how these supernatural stories around the turn of the century are really about the horrors we put in our own way; the ghosts are only shadows of the institutions of the past keeping us from achieving our goals.

Thomas Hardy wrote in his poem "Hap" (1898) about "crass Casualty" and "purblind Doomsters" who toss "blisses" and pain almost as if at random (Hardy "Hap" 1868–69). This exemplifies the Modernist idea that the callous and cold non-human world cares not at all for humankind. Speculative Modernists moved past this idea and crafted depictions of the Earth rebelling against humanity; they began to see mankind as a temporary caretaker that could be replaced if he continued to ravage the non-human world. The chapter "This Island Earth" wrestles with humanity's position to and in opposition with the non-human world in stories that offer a different path of existence beyond our anthropocentrism. *After London* (1885) by Richard Jefferies depicts a flawed future human race, one that is held back by all of the old and familiar jealousies and violence. Other stories appeared that explored the limits of human knowledge even given the best science. Humanity is blinded by its egocentrism into feelings of invulnerability that their science provides, evidenced in seminal texts like H.G. Wells's *War of the Worlds* (1898). Apocalyptic stories generally conclude with the end of humanity, but Speculative Modernists recognized that the Earth could and would likely continue long after human extinction. Clark Ashton Smith's descriptions of an Earth at the end of her days (the Zothique stories) make clear that humanity is the problem, and nature, whether it be through cataclysms, toxins, extraterrestrial influence, or even the re-emergence of once dominant primordial life, will correct course. Stories arose, especially between the world wars, that depicted humanity willingly seeking its own end, looking for a brutal and definitive surrender in its war against the non-human world.

Modernists were anxious about the fall of empires and dreaded the chaos that would ensue. Speculative Modernists did not restrict themselves to the crumbling of the civilized world, but rather dreamed of worlds where it had not existed in the first place. Alongside the ersatz magic of the bazaar in Joyce's "Araby" (1914), Edgar Rice Burroughs, among others, takes us to exotic places both on this earth and beyond, and while there is much vanity in the travels of his characters, love gives them meaning regardless of what they find. The fantasy genre continued to develop with the meticulous efforts of J.R.R. Tolkien, the acclaimed author who created Middle Earth. By giving us new realms to dream of, Speculative Modernism provided an escape hatch out of the doom of industrialization and impending war. Modernism struck down the failing institutions of society and religion, but the speculative-fiction writers reimagined societal institutions as if starting all over again. The chapter "Worlds Beyond" guides us into these worlds and what they come to signify for the reading public. These authors discussed what we might find whether we went to other planets or if the inhabitants of other planets came here.

Humanity would need a new kind of partner if we were to survive these other worlds that lay just out of reach, a new partner that only innovation and technology could supply. Anxiety about developments in technology, especially instruments of war, consumed Modernist thinking. It was natural that machines and the wonders of the future became the subjects of Speculative Modernism. One of the earliest science fiction novels, *Ralph 124C 41+* by Hugo Gernsback, follows a well-trod path laid out by William Morris, Wells, Edward Bellamy, and William Dean Howells in their popular and influential utopian novels of the late nineteenth century. A naïve traveler arrives to experience an advanced civilization. In this case, though, the centerpiece is the wonders of the advanced technology of New York City in the year 2660. This novel marks a new beginning for American Modernism in the genres. Technology takes center stage, for better or worse, and matters of society and history slough off like scabs. Writers like Gernsback showed readers the wonders of invention, but other writers were more skeptical. Some wrote stories about the limits of machines to save us from ourselves, while others created characters building weapons of mass destruction. Our chapter titled "Machinocracy" explores the meaning behind attitudes and anxieties of the future in Speculative Modernism in relation to the perspectives of Modernism.

The Modernists embraced Nietzsche's death of God and fragmented in search of something with which to replace him. Speculative fiction writers saw it the other way around, trading the "reality" of the nineteenth century for a "true" world that lay beneath. They created a mythology that looked both backward, before the building of worshipful institutions, and forward to how the new sciences could be incorporated to find deeper meanings. They shaped a new kind of fantasy that saw the entire world—our wars, our troubles, and joys—as mere distraction from the broader mystical universe or perhaps simply a front for it. These authors shone a light into the Dark Ages and brought back the mystical interests that were buried by those who sought out answers to the universe in more concrete terms. The chapter "Divine Secrets" investigates how these fantasy authors rekindled interest in the medieval period as they recaptured and recast ideas that the Industrial world dismissed as frivolous. There were still a few who were unwilling to let go of the realm of gods and the power of the supernatural. Yeats and his Golden Dawn are products of this New Mysticism that looks at man's relationship with God, or the gods, or the Great Old Ones, or The Things That Came Before. C.S. Lewis rewrites the mythology of Christianity in his

Narnia and Perelandra series and delves into serious questions that center around the Christian principles of the divine savior. The mystical forces introduced in all of these works are the driving forces behind their respective hopes and fears for the future.

In our final chapter, "We Are Fortunately Flawed," any optimism for the perfectibility of humanity has been lost. We are who we have always been: broken, selfish, vain, dishonest, and violent. World War I clinched it. The recognition that everything we do is in vain had a significant impact on Modernist writers. It led to, among other things, the despair of Eliot's "The Love Song of J. Alfred Prufrock" (1915), but in the speculative fiction of the time period, the hopelessness of humankind became an opportunity. Sherlock Holmes, Tarzan, and Conan do not harbor the responsibilities of Prufrock. Instead, they take advantage of the void of morality and purpose. Humans were not the saviors of the universe, nor was there a collective moral/ethical consistency of character. Therefore, individuals were not ascribed the burden of ultimate responsibility for the universe's well-being. The flaws of the individual mean absolutely nothing to the unimaginably cold, eternally indifferent universe, thus providing the opportunity to seize the day free of social and cultural restrictions.

Canonical Modernists took the shattered tools of their predecessors and made literature possible again. Their experimentation and openness to new forms and new ideas in writing rose out of the despair and nothingness of the trenches of World War I. Their pessimism about humanity's future and our ability to connect with one another remained profound. It was in the genres of speculative fiction—science fiction, horror, and fantasy—that a new sort of future began to take shape. These popular genres asserted that the universe contained more than just us in it, and that our downfall meant only that something new was on the horizon. Darwin's theories imply a universe where humanity is not the end of evolution. Though civilizations fall, all will not be lost. There would be a few survivors, and from the ruins of that once-great being would rise another dominant species, perhaps hideous to us. Nature does not resent the failure of the human experiment, but instead will adjust to champion a new race of beings and the story will go on. That the center cannot hold is perhaps the end of *our* story, but not the end of *the* story.

This then is the story of Speculative Modernism.

1

Utocalypse

> They constantly try to escape
> From the darkness outside and within
> By dreaming of systems so perfect
> that no one will need to be good.
> But the man that is will shadow
> The man that pretends to be.
> —T.S. Eliot, *The Rock* (1934)

From the middle of the nineteenth century through the first decade of the twentieth, the themes and ideas in speculative fiction did not seem to be much changed from where non-genre literature had been up to that point. The literary focus in both Britain and the United States was decidedly on communities and the individual's role in them. The most popular speculative stories of the era were about experiments in the organization of society that might serve to amplify or mitigate society's negative elements, especially those that came about as a result of the Industrial Revolution and the rise of urbanization. The emphasis on both sides of the Atlantic was on the collective future: how human society might be organized in ways that could prevent war, feed the hungry, reward talent and hard work, and create greater equality and fairness for all. These utopias were all the rage during this era. Initially, the idea of utopia was as a clever thought experiment that would examine how curing the ills of society would change it and whether that would be tolerable or not. The utopians of the late nineteenth century however took that thought experiment to the extreme, measuring out how society could cure all the ills of humanity, but in the process forsook the individual. Modernism—after the years of civil war in America and European wars in Britain—realized that there was no society that could cure all of the ills of mankind, because the individual was becoming more empowered, not less.

As the twentieth century opened, traditional literary utopias fell out of favor. This Atlantic divergence was slow in developing during the late stages of the nineteenth century, but it really picked up momentum between the wars. Speculative Modernism emerged in Britain as genre writers, especially after World War I, depicted individuals trapped in dystopias. On the American side of the Atlantic, stories of individuals who triumphed by wit, brawn, or technological wizardry became much more common. These American writers increasingly placed a fully-formed individual character at the center of their stories, a character whose "utopia" was personal and subjective. Frequently, these individuals clashed with their societies, and in this conflict, the limits of utopian thinking were revealed. The American ideal of the rugged individual became the central national narrative, especially during the Depression. Speculative Modernist writers responded by creating the genre archetype of the lone hero—Flash Gordon, Buck Rogers, Conan—who triumphed no matter what society tried to throw their way. In the first section of this chapter, "All Will Be Well: The Utopian Roots of Speculative Modernism," we'll look at the stories that laid the groundwork for Speculative Modernism. The wide popularity of the utopians—who were not all that Modern given our definition—nevertheless created a ready audience for what was to come.

In 1983, Darko Suvin pinned an exact date for the start of science fiction in the UK: May 1, 1871. It is true that there had been works—some of them incredibly influential, such as *Frankenstein* (1818)—that had appeared long before this date, but Suvin rests that argument on a confluence of events that brought us works such as *The Coming Race* (1871) by Edward Bulwer-Lytton, *The Battle of Dorking* (1871) by George Tomkyns-Chesney, and *Erewhon* (1872) by Samuel Butler. Suvin argues that proximate causes for the outpouring of this new genre included a "crisis in confidence" (148) in the British Empire at the time. The economy was "gloomy" (148) and pessimism began to take root, even at the height of the reach and influence of the Empire (Suvin). Writers of speculative fiction—especially the burgeoning field of science fiction—looked closely at the state of society in the rapidly growing United States and Britain at the height of its empire. These writers projected the changes and challenges they were witnessing into a fictional future filled with wonders—and sometimes horrors. This inclination is familiar now in the era of Netflix's *Black Mirror* (2011–2019) and the like, and it made for popular literature back then, as well. Few writers sold more books, for example, than Edward Bellamy during his heyday in the 1880s. In the second section, "The Screw Turns: Bleak Reality Murders Optimism," we examine how the Speculative Modernists use this concern to extrapolate what the society of the future will look like.

In the third section of the chapter, "Anti-Utopians: The Individual Versus Society," we explore the authors who narrowed their focus from the future of society as a whole to what effect this will have on the individual.

As societies become stronger and people focus on not only their survival but their perfectibility, Speculative Modernists ask what room will be left for the individual. The rugged explorer and the swashbuckling sea captain have their place in an expanding world, but these individuals will find it tougher to be who they are in a society in which everyone has their place.

Whatever the date, speculative fiction began in earnest sometime in the late nineteenth century. No longer was the world of the parent or the grandparent fit for the child and grandchild. Some new world needed to be imagined, and these late nineteenth-century writers began what would grow into the Speculative Modernist movement in horror, science fiction, and fantasy. First came the utopians, with work such as *Erewhon* by English novelist Samuel Butler and *Mizora* (1880–81) by the American author Mary E. Bradley Lane. These novels were very much conjectures about alternatives to the present day, strange parallel civilizations where the social structure has been profoundly changed. Novels like these—and there were many of them during these years—formed the foundation for what was to come during the Speculative Modernist era. This chapter looks at works by utopian writers—the precursors to Speculative Modernism—to show how these writers, none of whom were distinctly Modernist, nevertheless sowed the seeds of Modernism in the genres. The utopians offered a vision of human perfectibility that Speculative Modernist writers recognized as an impossibility.

All Will Be Well: The Utopian Roots of Speculative Modernism

There are many studies of utopian literature as such. Lyman Tower Sargent defines utopia as "a non-existent society described in considerable detail and normally located in time and space that the author intended a contemporaneous reader to view as considerably better than the society in which that reader lived" (Sargent *Utopianism* 6). In Sargent's definition of utopianism, it is difficult to find anything that sounds very much like the themes and attitudes of Modernism: "Literary utopias have at least six purposes, although they are not necessarily separable. A utopia can be simply a fantasy, it can be a description of a desirable or an undesirable society, an extrapolation, a warning, an alternative to the present, or a model to be achieved" (8). In his summary of the entire history of the genre, Sargent identifies three major areas of focus for these late nineteenth- and early twentieth-century utopians. Those three themes are the creation of an equitable economic system, the purpose and utility of communal living, and the position of women in a utopian (or dystopian) society (Sargent

"Themes" 278). Given the themes and purposes of these novels along with the audience's expectations for them, it is difficult to argue that the wide and deep popularity of utopian fiction during this era constitutes a movement toward Modernism. Instead, these massively popular utopians on both sides of the Atlantic were plowing the fields where something different would take root. Utopians set up the conflicts between individuals and society that Speculative Modernism addresses. Most important, how will a wide variety of individuals fit into a single society? These utopians helped to create an audience that craved an escape from the world they lived in. Utopians captured the imagination of the reading audience, but the reality of the mechanized world crushed any hope that utopias could be anything but a cruel fairy tale. They also built a firm foundation of ideas about other worlds, other possibilities for humanity and, in doing so, fed a ravenous audience that transitioned easily to science fiction, fantasy, and horror.

In the United States, one of the most popular speculative-fiction novels of the era was the bestseller *Looking Backward* by Edward Bellamy, which was published in 1888. Given the economic hardships of the late 1800s in America and the rest of the world, books like this one became more common. With the exception of the haunting and emotionally charged ending, *Looking Backward* is similar to many utopias of this era: it is an economic and social argument masquerading as fiction. In this novel, our hero, Julian West, a well-to-do young Bostonian who needs the help of an "Animal Magnetist" to sleep at night, goes a little overboard with the treatment one evening and sleeps for 113 years. He wakes in Boston surrounded by caring people who gradually—through hundreds of pages of explanation—inform him about the changes to the world he has awoken to. West's guide, Dr. Leete, shows him a world that is filled with societal wonders that create a socialist utopia, but the changes to the technological prowess of the civilization are scant. In Bellamy's book there are telephones and they are used mostly for transmitting religious services or the live musical performances that occur around the clock with musicians working in shifts to keep the music coming all day and all night so that it is available for whomever wants to open up the line. However, Bellamy does not depict the use of the telephone for individual communication. He is focused on the community purpose of the tool and not on the liberation of the individual from traditional constraints. In this utopia, advances in science that augment human capability show up here and there, but they are not crucial to the design and survival of the society.

An early example of post-apocalyptic Speculative Modernism is *After London* (1885) by British author Richard Jefferies. It posits an undefined catastrophe that causes the depopulation of the island of Britain. It might have been a sea-level change or the passing near to Earth of a large celestial body that affected the Earth's "magnetic currents, which, in an imperceptible manner, influence the minds of men" (Jefferies 28). People with the means to do it fled the impending disaster on ships. They departed across the sea, leaving the poor and uneducated behind. Nothing was heard from those departing rich folks again; they vanished without a trace. It was not long before agriculture and trade stopped and the few surviving people dispersed into the now-wild countryside. The end result was that civilizations around the world failed in much the same manner as Britain did. Much of the island of Britain, including the entire city of London, now lies at the bottom of a giant lake. The utopians argued that human society was perfectible, that we were on the brink of great things, if only we could put our ideas in order. Jefferies, however, created a world where even the best ideas of humanity matter not at all if the Earth decides to wipe humanity away. There are forces arrayed against the characters in *After London* in the climate, geography, and wildlife that make human efforts seem puny and ineffectual. Under this stress, humanity would have no choice but to abandon those lofty ideas:

> Even among the ancients, when every man, woman, and child could exercise those arts which are now the special mark of nobility, i.e., reading and writing, there was a degraded class of persons who refused to avail themselves of the benefits of civilization. They obtained their food by begging, wandering along the highways, crouching around fires which they lit in the open, clad in rags, and exhibiting countenances from which every trace of self-respect had disappeared [35].

Reduced to subsistence, the idea of human perfectibility and utopia become dim, distant fantasies.

The second part of the novel, the section titled "Wild England," is an adventure story set in this new, wild world. The new world is quasi-medieval, with warring despots making life miserable for the rest of the population. The Bushmen, the descendants of Victorian civilization, live nomadically and primitively in what was once a flourishing world capital. The focus of the novel is decidedly on the social aspects of human culture. There is very little of late nineteenth-century technology that survives this apocalypse. War, famine, and ignorance, however, thrive. The protagonist, Felix Aquila, is much like the rest of the survivors. He is a negligible noble who is in love with a woman, a baron's daughter named Aurora, who is just out of his reach according to the antique, pre-apocalypse rules about such things. In despair, he builds a canoe and explores his world, finally settling with a shepherd tribe and continuing his mild adventures. He finds a gift for Aurora and vows to return home to give it to her. The end.

What *After London* lacks in riveting plot elements, it more than makes up for in excitingly original ideas. In this novel, we hear the first note of what would become full-throated Speculative Modernism three decades and more in the future. Jefferies creates a dystopian fantasy that presents a profoundly bleak vision of the potential of human social organization, especially under duress. Like his contemporaries, Jefferies is focused on the structures of human civilization and society. Unlike the utopians, however, Jefferies shows himself to be a Speculative Modernist in his depiction of the Earth swallowing the polluted and corrupt human civilization whole. Jefferies depicts a society that is not perfectible; humanity cannot transform present-day into something ideal. This is not just an attack on urbanization or the aristocracy. Felix clearly prefers the rural areas to the city, and yet the countryside is filled with narrow-minded, violent people. There is no redemption for humanity to be found in Jefferies's dystopia, and that is the one element that makes this novel one of the earliest examples of the Speculative Modernist outlook on life and humanity. Jefferies's theme would be echoed nearly fifty years later by Walter Benjamin, an influential German philosopher between the world wars, in his 1931 essay, "The Destructive Character": "The destructive character sees no image hovering before him. He has few needs, and the least of them is to know what will replace what has been destroyed. First of all, for a moment at least, empty space—the place where thing stood or the victim lived. Someone is sure to be found who needs this space without occupying it" (Benjamin). Felix Aquila can be seen as that destructive character. He is present in ruined England but glides above it in his canoe. He goes about his work but is not a fixer. Although Benjamin was an influential Modernist thinker, it is worth noting that Jefferies wrote his novel fifty years earlier.

William Morris used ecological dystopias in general and *After London* in particular, Jed Mayer argues, to build a foundation for his irrepressibly optimistic novel, *News from Nowhere*, which was published in 1890. In the article "A Darker Shade of Green: William Morris, Richard Jefferies, and Posthumanist Ecologies," Mayer contends:

> Jefferies's vision of a future ecology and its social consequences is almost unremittingly pessimistic, yet in this dystopian vision William Morris found the roots of his own ecological and social utopia. [...] The discovery of hope in a portrayal of ecological catastrophe helped to make more vivid for Morris the limits of anthropocentrism, and offered greater possibilities for advancing a mode of environmental criticism which would regard humans as only one strand of a diverse web of organic life [80].

Mayer's assertions places Morris's novel squarely within the boundaries of Speculative Modernism. Humanity is not the whole story, and the end of humanity is not the end of Earth's story.

Like his utopian contemporaries, the main character in *News from Nowhere*, a cipher named William Guest, exists to explore the many varieties of economic thinking that were current in that time. He falls asleep after a wild night of debate at the Socialist League and awakes to find himself transported to an uncertain future time where all of the ideals he had been advocating as a staunch socialist have come to fruition. Morris uses Guest to answer the many questions people have posed about socialism and, partly, to answer Edward Bellamy's much less joyful *Looking Backward*. Admittedly, there are few obviously Modernist elements present in Morris's utopian novel. Throughout *News from Nowhere*, there are brief mentions of small advancements in technology in the future, but nothing much has changed in any real way from the late nineteenth-century present day. Transportation, medicine, manufacturing, weaponry—any of the areas in which science fiction posits the world to come—show no development whatsoever despite the decades that have passed between when Guest fell asleep and when he awoke. The preferred mode of transportation in 2003, for example, is the horse and buggy. As a piece of Modernist science fiction, this novel comes up short. Because of its popularity, as social commentary germane to 1890 in England, it is a must-read. This novel is typical of what was popular on both sides of the Atlantic before World War I. The focus is squarely on social institutions and the individual's place in them. Some mark this as a bit of an artistic cul-de-sac: "Its influence on later utopian writing has been negligible, and on genre sf [science fiction] still less, since [Morris's] vision is so relentlessly pastoral, looking back to an idealized Middle Ages" (Clute and Nicholls 833). This perspective might not tell the whole story, however. Morris would go on to publish his novel, *The Well at the World's End* (1896), a story that also looks backward toward medieval themes, which might very well be the first example of the "high fantasy" genre. In any case, Morris's inclination to ignore the vast social and technological changes of the late nineteenth century is an idea that others, including E.R. Eddison and J.R.R. Tolkien, among many others, would run with decades later.

One of the most well-known utopians of the era was William Dean Howells, whose novel *A Traveler from Altruria* was published to great acclaim in 1894. This novel became the first in a trilogy that includes *Cosmopolitan* (1894) and *Through the Eye of the Needle* (1907). In *A Traveler from Altruria*, a select group of the American elite hosts a visitor from the distant land of Altruria who has come to learn about America. These elites are proud of the social order in the United States and are eager to brag about it. Throughout the course of the novel, however, Americans are revealed to be obsessed with wealth, class, the accumulation of money, and selfishness. The Altrurian, through leading questions and gradual revelations about Altruria itself, offers an indictment of American Gilded Age society. This novel posits an alternative realm, a hidden world, that causes readers in their familiar world to question their assumptions about culture and humanity.

Utopian literature was characterized by a boundless optimism that the many ills of the present day could be fixed with the right application of social theory, technology, and community spirit. Although utopian stories have been around for centuries and continue to be popular, the era where stories were filled with hope for the future did not last very long. In its place, a literature of lowered expectations and pessimism came to the fore. There might be better alternatives to what the present offers, but the path between here and there is forever blurred.

The Screw Turns: Bleak Reality Murders Optimism

The real change to all of this utopian thinking came with the great H.G. Wells, whose ideas fundamentally altered how humanity thinks about the future of our species, civilizations, and the planet we inhabit. The degradation to the agencies of human will and communal initiative is what distinguishes Wells from his utopian predecessors; these are the ingredients that make him a Speculative Modernist, especially in some of his most well-known novels. Humanity is not the master of its future. Some combination of happenstance and luck will determine where we are all headed. Sarah Cole argues in *Inventing Tomorrow: H.G. Wells and the Twentieth Century* that Wells's early science fiction shows two possible paths toward the future. In one case, humanity brings together its brightest minds to chart a path into the collective future. These are Wells's utopias, stories that range from mildly fictional to outright social treatise. On the other path, humanity lurches forward into the future "consumed by the twin processes of happenstance and decay" (Cole 151). Readers see this dynamic at work most clearly in three of the giant novels in Wells's oeuvre: in the bifurcation of the human species that we see in *The Time Machine* (1895), the invasion by an overwhelming enemy in *War of the Worlds* (1898), and in the irrationality of the decades-long global war depicted in *The Shape of Things to Come* (1933). Utopians such as Bellamy and Howells presented worlds that could be tamed by humanity using tools they invent to bend the natural world to its service. Wells, the Speculative Modernist that he is, blew all of that up and began with much less optimistic assumptions about humanity's power to control its fate.

John S. Partington, who has published prolifically on Wells, argues that the depiction of the year 802701 that is found in Wells's *The Time Machine* shows that Wells is disinterested in projecting a future filled with technological advances, even hundreds of thousands of years down the road. Instead, we get the trappings of Victorian culture depicted in what is left of human civilization (Partington *The Time* 58). *The Time Machine* presents a stable, two-tier society organized around a particular idea. Nevertheless, the focus is not at all on society or on planned organization of human interactions. In fact, there seems to be nobody paying much attention at all to how Eloi and Morlock interact. The two races are running along well-worn grooves with no possibility for abstract consideration of the state of society. The Eloi have arrived at this moment in time seemingly without intention. They evolved and vanished during the course of the novel as if by accident.

More or less at the same time, a parallel narrative was running through Wells's writing. Perhaps humanity could, after all, tame those elements of chaos and destruction that seemed always to be just outside of the door. Partington argues that in *A Modern Utopia*, curiosity and initiative are not weapons to be used by one class against another, but instead are tools used by the human race to direct its own evolution through educational, cultural, and biological competition on its own terms (Partington *The Time* 62). Partington's idea implies that even though technology advances in the later utopias of Wells, it does so in service of and subject to human impulses and is subjugated completely by social ideas. Progress, Wells seemed to argue, does not come about simply through advances in technology or any sort of significant and measurable technological progress—the showpieces of many utopias from the previous generation—nor will it come without inspired human effort and intention. At times, as if to provide a counterweight to chaos, Wells echoes the utopians by arguing that the right ideas backed by the right people cause the conditions for society to move forward rapidly. Central planning by government is the key to all of this. A minimum standard of living—including health care, education, housing, and elderly care, managed economic competition, procreation and child rearing, and protection for the vulnerable—is the foundation of what amounts to a perfected Victorian England. Wells marks a transition point between the utopian past and the Speculative Modernist future in that he seemed to be of two minds when it came to humanity's collective future. On one hand, humans are powerful; on the other, the universe will do whatever it does.

By 1911, building on the ideas of Wells, the utopian impulse had fully mutated into something strange and totally Modern. *Ralph 124C 41+* by American editor Hugo Gernsback, was published serially in 1911 and 1912 in Gernsback's own monthly, *Modern Electrics*, a magazine devoted to amateur radio that he began in 1908. By 1926, Gernsback abandoned nonfiction and hard science to dive into science fiction, which he called "scientifiction,"[1] full time with his groundbreaking monthly, *Amazing Stories*.

Gernsback is a seminal figure in the history of science fiction, an editor and author that Gary Westfahl[2] said "achieved for science fiction what had never been done for the scientific romance, the necessary work in establishing a literary genre" (Westfahl *Mechanics* 43). Gernsback was the founder of *Modern Electrics* (1906), the first magazine devoted exclusively to science fiction and then as the founder of such foundational and popular magazines such as *Amazing Stories* (1926) and many others. It is difficult to underestimate Gernsback's formative influence on the genre. He is not without his detractors, however. As a businessman, his ethics were questionable. After paying H.P. Lovecraft only $25.00—"a ridiculous price" (de Camp 282)—for "The Colour Out of Space," Lovecraft began referring to Gernsback as "Hugo the Rat" (de Camp 282). In *the Mechanics of Wonder*, Westfahl gathered a collection of writers and critics who panned Gernsback's prose as "illiterate ... sorry ... deficient ... preliterate" and many other negative extremes. He went on to say that "If aesthetic quality is the only reason for reading, no one should read *Ralph 124C 41+*" (Westfahl *Mechanics* 92). Nevertheless, as Westfahl continues, this is "the one essential text for all studies of science fiction, a work which anticipates and contains the entire genre" (Westfahl *Mechanics* 93).

The themes and structure of this novel follow a well-trod path laid out by Morris, Wells, Bellamy, and Howells in their popular and influential utopian novels. One of the areas where it bridges the gap between Modernists and their predecessors is that it shares the wide-eyed optimism of the utopians but places that optimism into a twentieth-century hard science fiction context. Gernsback does not present any kind of clear path toward perfecting human society through technological innovation or ideas. Instead, he shows readers the familiar scenes of future social and technical triumph mixed with a host of familiar human failings: greed, jealousy, deception, and murderous depravity, to name four. The optimism of the utopian age has ebbed by this point, and Speculative Modernism is well underway.

Ralph 124C 41+ is not a stylistic triumph. Gernsback scholar Gary Westphal states that Gernsback "recognized well enough that he was not a particularly talented writer, as evidenced by numerous self-deprecating comments about the quality of his own work" (Westphal 24). There really is no plot to speak of, and the characters have all the vitality of CPR manikins. The year is 2660. The title character is an employee of the government due to his rarity and utility as the smartest guy in any room. He is one of the dozen most intelligent people on Earth (hence the + at the end of his name), an inventor, and a humanitarian with a strong romantic streak. His first action in the novel is to hurriedly improvise an avalanche-melting microwave ray that he uses to save Alice, an exquisitely beautiful Swiss stranger whose video phone had connected to his through some glitch just as she was staring at an Alpine avalanche that was about to bury her alive. She then travels from her home to New York City to thank Ralph. The novel proceeds much as utopian novels did, with a tour through the wonders of the futuristic world. He tutors her on the electric roller skates that they use to get around town. They see solar power plants, artificial lighting, massive sports palaces that include lighting for night games, television, the electric power grid, synthetic foods, commercial air travel, spaceflight, tape recording, and several other predictions by Gernsback that are familiar in our world. Interestingly, Gernsback's utopia is not under the polar ice cap like *Mizora* or one hundred years hence as in Bellamy's novel. Instead, the utopia is in New York City in the present day of the novel.

Ralph 124C 41+ lacks anything resembling the explicit social commentary so prevalent in utopian fiction of the nineteenth century. In fact, this novel is a sure sign that we have arrived in the Speculative Modernist era. Ralph is unconcerned with humanity, economic fairness, a woman's role in society, or any of what Lyman Tower Sargent argued were the central tenets of utopian literature. This is an ideal society where the strong rule the weak and people succeed according to their innate abilities. In Ralph's world, his fellow New Yorkers are free to move about and live the lives they choose, more or less. People still work in the stores and perform in circuses. There are two dreadful men who are pursuing Alice trying to win her love through kidnapping and threats of murder. (Gernsback was no enlightened soul, unfortunately. Proceed into this miasma of bigotry with caution.) One of the antagonists, who is referred to as "black" several times, has a "mouth that betrayed cunning and had a touch of viciousness" (Gernsback 45). The other, a Martian, is seven feet tall and has red skin. Alice is afraid of both of them and does what little she can, being a helpless woman, to discourage them. It falls to Ralph to end the threat to Alice's safety and good name. Complicating Ralph's utopia are laws that prevent intermarriage between Martian and Earthling, which makes the Martian's murderous infatuation more complex. The novel adds up to an affirmation of American rugged individualism, and so it is an implicit repudiation of the social utopias that came before it. The individual is glorified. Individualism and meritocracy add together to create the next step in the American story as that literary culture diverges from its counterpart across the Atlantic.

Just as utopias existed before Modernism, horror has antecedents in medieval literature. It can be argued that horror has existed in our creative consciousness, lurking in dark corners dating back to our earliest methods of storytelling. However, Speculative Modernists advance the notion with what Lovecraft coined "cosmic horror," the idea that the universe itself is the horror we are all born into. Elements of this type of horror dominate the first third of William Hope Hodgson's chaotic work, *The Dream of X* (1912), which is a greatly truncated version of his extended work, *The Night Land* (1912). This "highly individualistic and idiosyncratic novel of the dying Earth" (Clute and Grant 471) depicts the remaining glimmers of civilization trapped in a protective force field of sorts called "the Earth Current." Beyond the force field await terrible dangers, punctuated by "watchers" from the North-West, North-East, South-West, and South-East. These watchers are constantly monitoring the condition and veracity of the force field, eager to spot any points of weakening. In terms of work habits and social sensibilities, Timothy S. Murphy names Hodgson as "Lovecraft's most important predecessor" (Murphy 225). One does not need to travel a great distance between Hodgson's "watchers" and Lovecraft's many flavors of "old ones." Indeed, Lovecraft was among Hodgson's first critics, and he became a champion of Hodgson's reputation, calling Hodgson "one of the few who have captured the illusive inmost essence of the weird" (Lovecraft "On the Trail" 5).

The horror in *The Night Land* arrives at the realization that They have always been watching and waiting, even before the advent of man. Horror, it seems, is intrinsic to existence itself. As the narrator explains:

> Of the coming of theses monstrosities and evil Forces, no man could say with much Verity; for the evil of it began before the Histories of the Great Redoubt [the human Sanctuary] were shaped; aye, even before the sun had lost all power to light; though, It must not be a thing of certainty that even at this far time the invisible, black heavens Held no warmth for this world[....] The evil must surely have begun in the Days of the Darkening (which I might liken to a story which was believed doubtfully, much as we of this day believe the story of Creation) [Hodgson *Night* 45].

Hodgson's horror is natural, but unearthly, and is undergirded by the knowledge that the Earth Current, although vast, is not inexhaustible. Murphy points out that "someday the Earth-Current preserving the Great Redoubt will run out, just as the current of the Lesser Redoubt ran out, and there will be no one to rescue the remnants of humanity as the narrator has rescued his beloved" (Murphy 231). Although Hodgson's novel traffics in the weird and unquantifiable, there is also a strong foundation that is reliable, even if hidden: "As in the fantastic cosmological vision at the heart of *The House on the Borderland*, here thermodynamics is the foundation of materialist cosmology as well as ontology, and entropy is the ultimate fate of the material universe and all its contents, including the human spirit" (Murphy 231). The idea that humanity is powerless to alter the immutable forces of the physical world is what sets Hodgson's work—and that of later Speculative Modernist horror writers—apart from writers of ghost stories and other strange tales of earlier eras. Hodgson's watchers, and the lesser Monsters and Ab-human creatures that serve as their minions, are part of nature. They belong. However, they are not part of human existence. Hodgson explains how "Outward Powers" have kept a barrier in place between humanity and these Others, but that barrier is slowly being eroded and humanity will soon be overtaken. The reason for the erosion is not quite clear, although Hodgson writes that "the world [became] full of lawlessness and degeneracy" (46), hence the reason for the sanctuary of the "Last Redoubt" and the protection of the Earth Current. They were here first and will remain after. Humanity never has been nor never will be anything of particular importance.

By the start of World War I, even popular literature was turning away from idealism and faith in human potential. "Enoch Soames," a 1916 short story by Max Beerbohm—author of *Zuleika Dobson* and a well-known English drama critic, essayist, caricaturist, and bon vivant—depicts the futility of utopian thinking given man's limits, the inability to create anything of worth, including language. The title character, named perhaps for Cain's son and founder of cities, is an offensive fop and truly horrific poet and is offered a self-serving and destructive deal by the devil himself. If Soames gives up his future and agrees to accompany the devil to hell that day, he would be granted an hour in London one hundred years hence. He accepts the offer and uses his time to look himself up in the Reading Room of the British Museum and does nothing else. He fails to look for anything except himself in the distant future. The world he sees that day presents the kind of utopian thinking that Beerbohm railed against. In this story, he describes faceless drones under the thumb of an all-encompassing bureaucracy, all wearing the same kind of clothes and sporting numbers instead of names. The big "innovation" in the future is that writing was now done phonetically, and that arrogant writers have finally been put in their place. In the snippet of writing Soames brings back to the 1890s, we can find the future's condemnation of them: "Nou that th littreri profeshn haz bin auganized az a department of publik servis, our riters hav found their levvl an hav lernt ter doo their duti without thort ov th morro" (690). Beerbohm lampoons utopian writing, and, at the same time, creates what can be recognized as a Speculative Modernist protagonist in Soames, who is alienated, self-absorbed, and thoroughly pessimistic about humanity writ large. His pitiful efforts at poetry get him nowhere, neither in the present nor the future, and his big decision amounts to suicide. He recognizes that nothing of any meaning can be accomplished, and so he volunteers to die. This character is completely without hope, and, as such, represents a true Modernist way of thinking about the future of humanity. Soames wisely chooses hell over the soulless future, knowing that serving the devil in Hell will be better than living in a world where writers are condemned to "publik servis." The fact that Beerbohm, a "fine miniaturist" cloaks his particular brand of modernism in "polished prose" (Clute and Grant 102), indicates his skill in presenting not only Soames but also the entire London literary scene of the 1890s—as well as the London of 1997—as modern subjects, buffeted by the same winds of despair that other characters from this era are subject to. Beerbohm's "enduring toughness" (Clute and Grant 102) that lurks beneath the veneer of light-hearted fantasy is the Speculative Modernist surprise at the heart of this story.

Although the devil is not the main character of Beerbohm's narrative, his role is rather revealing about the nature of humanity and its relationship to the sinister or evil. If the devil is a human creation, then he belongs to humanity. If the devil came first, then humanity is at least in part modeled after him. At his lowest point, Soames enlists the devil's aid. After he travels in time and returns to the restaurant, he simply awaits his self-imposed fate, much to the chagrin of Beerbohm who wants Soames to attempt an escape of his "inevitable ending" (691), however futile that may be. Resolute, he offers no such resistance when the devil comes to take him away per their pact. He is resigned to his fate, offering to Beerbohm that it's just his luck. He is betting his soul that he will be remembered by literary posterity. Soames fervently wants to make an impact, but his trip to 1997 reveals that he will be completely forgotten. He is in hell either way.

This exchange between Soames and the devil is a familiar one. It is a motif that predates even Marlowe's *Doctor Faustus*. However, things become very interesting after Soames's fate is sealed. Beerbohm goes on to explain that he has seen the devil again in various situations out and about and states how a "great cold wrath" (694) fills him whenever he is reminded of Soames's interaction with the devil and how a myriad of others similarly suffer at his dominion. The devil, indeed, is among us. What makes matters worse is that when Beerbohm comes face to face with the devil, he does not chastise, argue with, or berate him. Instead, he simply nods and smiles. Afterward, he is haunted by his shame. It can be argued that he is actually haunted by his realization that we are friends with the devil. Therein lies the true horror of this short story. As discussed in the next chapter, "Shadows at the Turn," this comfort with the evil and sinister provides Speculative Modernists with a new twist to the existing genre of horror fiction.

Society has many ways to show this comfort as well, especially in the devil of racism that plagues humanity. In W.E.B. Du Bois's "The Comet" (1920), the destruction of New York City by a comet provides a moment for one African American man, who finds himself suddenly released from the oppression of society. Du Bois is known for his more important works, like *The Souls of Black Folk* (1903), but this story shows that he was a Speculative Modernist as well.

Du Bois does not, at first, give us a description of his protagonist, Jim

Davis, beyond the fact that he is sent to do the jobs for a bank in which he works that are too risky for "valuable men" (5) to do. This is his salvation, though, in that while he is sent to go search for company records in a dangerous vault in a deep basement, he misses the passing of the comet, and is therefore saved from the death everyone else faces. He climbs out of the vault only to find everyone dead. Tellingly his first thought is not concern for his life or for the lives of the others at the branch, but a fear of what it might look like should he get caught by the police here: "Then a new thought seized him: If they found him here alone—with all this money and all these dead men—what would his life be worth?" (7). Jim has been trained by his society to think not of his own life first, but of the possible trouble he could be in with those higher up the hierarchy.

The first time Du Bois mentions that Jim is Black is when he finds the rich, white woman who was saved because of her hobby. Because she was in a darkroom developing pictures, she, too, was not affected by the comet. Without the presence of their usual oppressors, they are not sure how to react to each other:

> They stared a moment in silence. She had not noticed before that he was a Negro. He had not thought of her as white. She was a woman of perhaps twenty-five—rarely beautiful and richly gowned, with darkly-golden hair, and jewels. Yesterday, he thought with bitterness, she would scarcely have looked at him twice. He would have been dirt beneath her silken feet. She stared at him. Of all the sorts of men she had pictured as coming to her rescue she had not dreamed of one like him. Not that he was not human, but he dwelt in a world so far from hers, so infinitely far, that he seldom even entered her thought. Yet as she looked at him curiously he seemed quite commonplace and usual [9].

Du Bois takes us back and forth between their two points-of-view as they each begin to recognize the humanity of the other, and the servitude that each has been forced to endure, each in their own station. Ytasha Womack, in her book *Afrofuturism: The World of Black Sci-fi and Fantasy Culture*, places their negotiations in terms of race, stating that, at the time, "race imbalances were so entrenched that only a catastrophe could bring equity" (119–120). Likewise, the story's calamity brings the sexes closer to a power balance.

Jim joins forces with her in order to help her find her father, but when they are confronted with the idea that they may be the only two people left in the entire world, they begin to think of loftier goals, a new Adam and Eve. For the first time, they both see beyond their places in the world and the place the other has occupied and they imagine themselves the founders of a new order, a new world. Du Bois draws the line between Jim and this woman, at least as far as their class, but then erases it as they realize that class has no more meaning. As the two are drawn into each other's embrace, they realize that they are one race, and the only hope for humanity. The moment is reminiscent of M.P. Shiel's *The Purple Cloud* (1901). Jeffson and Leda seem like incompatible parents of a new human race, but not more so than the pairing of Du Bois's two opposites who have each been trained by the former civilization. His story gives readers a moment in which all of the ills of society, all that divides these two people, are shed, and they become simply two people at the beginning of a new world:

> She was no mere woman. She was neither high nor low, white nor black, rich nor poor. She was primal woman; mighty mother of all men to come and Bride of Life. She looked upon the man beside her and forgot all else but his manhood, his strong, vigorous manhood—his sorrow and his sacrifice. She saw him as glorified. He was no longer a thing apart, a creature below, a strange outcast of another clime and blood, but her Brother Humanity incarnate, Son of God and great All-Father of the race to be [Du Bois 15].

Du Bois is not the utopian of the previous century, though. He was participating, at least in part, in a different tradition altogether. Stories about interracial romance were well-known and became popular during the Harlem Renaissance, which reached its height during the 1920s. Jim knows that nothing can be as simple as getting a fresh start, a chance to remove all that devastates the relationships among the people of this world. The optimism of the brave new world is dashed to pieces when the flares he has sent out into the night to alert any other survivors who might be left in New York City only draws the attention of the woman's father and his young employee, Fred, who also happens to be a future son-in-law. Fred is the first character in the story to call the female character by her name, Julia; until this point, she is simply "the woman" or, in the note she finds from her father, "Daughter." She is, like Jim, defined only by the relationship she has to powerful white men. Du Bois spends some time in her point of view, but even then she is only known as "she" or "her."

When these men of power and wealth return to New York, Jim is treated the way he always has been by the types of people her father and boyfriend are. He is handed some money, only after Julia explains how Jim had helped her, and the two men quickly dismiss him and go back to their world of luxury. They too had been saved by their wealth and privilege, as they had been out of the city in Fred's new Mercedes. Jim is left to return to Harlem on his own. In the end, Jim's only consolation is that he is found by a woman, presumably his wife, carrying their dead child. Julia returns to her life of luxury, and Jim returns to his place of servitude. Du Bois recognizes that it would take the destruction of the whole world to make Jim and Julia equals in this crazy society they live in, not just the devastation of New York City. He saw the bleak relationships among the races and knew that it would take the near ending of the world to rectify them.

In the aftermath of World War I, Speculative Modernists abandoned the possibility that human social and technological ingenuity could create the means to transform human society into a paradise. In the place of utopian thinking came a wave of literature that featured utopians as the villains, where the lone individual stood as bulwark defending liberty while the forces of conformity and control threatened on every side. As individuals began to realize that their place in society has been determined by others, the new realities that were created by the chaos and pessimism of the early twentieth century—whether caused by natural disaster, war, discrimination, poverty, or obsolete ways of thinking[3]—gave them the opportunity to redefine themselves.

Anti-Utopians: The Individual Versus Society

In the aftermath of World War I, one of the most important developments in the history of American science fiction occurred: the founding of *Amazing Stories* by Hugo Gernsback. It was the first magazine devoted solely to science fiction. Starting with the April 1926 issue and continuing monthly, this magazine was filled with short stories and serialized novels about scientific wonders and space exploration whose heroes were often young American men bent on taming the universe and spreading American can-do optimism wherever they went. Indeed, the post–World War I period marked a clear divergence in speculative fiction between American and British approaches. While writers in Britain flipped utopian ideas into dystopias after the horrors of war—thereby maintaining a tight focus on social issues—American Speculative Modernists focused on the power of the individual to build futures worth living in.

The American business leader and politician, Herbert Hoover, began his rise into prominence that resulted in him being elected president of the United States in 1928. Starting in 1919—at the conclusion of the War and with peace talks still continuing at Versailles—Hoover began advocating for low taxes, limited-government, and minimum regulations, policies that arguably contributed to the stock market crash and the worldwide Great Depression.[4] In his book *The Politics of American Individualism* (1975), Gary Dean Best argues that Herbert Hoover drew positive national attention in the confident, happy, postwar American era because he advocated the belief that America was characterized by "rugged individualism," a term Hoover coined. Best writes that Hoover's outlook provided a very appealing alternative to "the destructivist, collectivist philosophies that were creating havoc" in postwar Europe (26). A symbol of this rugged individualism was folk hero, Davy Crockett. Hoover rose to fame in part by elevating figures such as Crockett, who represented the "less than a thousand men, inspired by the urge of freedom" whom Hoover lionized in his speech dedicating the memorial at Kings Mountain in 1931 (Hoover).

By the end of the Modernist era in the late 1930s, the stark thematic difference between American and British speculative fiction becomes impossible to miss. British writer Aldous Huxley's dystopian novel, *Brave New World* (1932), continues the familiar conversation of how an individual situates themselves in the larger "perfect" society. *Brave New World* exemplifies the transatlantic split by focusing on social "advancements" above individuality or new technologies. Adam Roberts argues that "the greatest achievement of *Brave New World* is not portraying dystopia; it is portraying dystopia as utopia" (162). Huxley's text indeed is utopian in nature but creates a rather sinister world that is utterly intolerant of other "impure" races or even biological impulses. His Londoners—the civilized—are little more than passive, manufactured entities that believe they are enlightened. In his book-length study of *Brave New World*, Peter Edgerly Firchow argues that Huxley's Londoners are Americans projected into the future, their extreme individualism amplified by their complacency: "One of the most ominous portents of the American way of life, Huxley went on to say, was that it embraced a large class of people who 'do not want to be cultured, are not interested in the higher life'" (Firchow 34). Despite their advanced technology and social structures, they prove themselves to be rather naïve and close-minded through the guise of sophistication and mind-numbing drug dependence. Even though this novel depicts flashy new gadgets and all kinds of advances in technology, Londoners are all in service and subject to human impulses and are subjugated completely by social ideas.

Taking a more sociological approach to the possibilities of utopia, Huxley focuses more on social equalities, challenging social institutions, and even reproductive rights among "citizens." However, he also makes clear distinctions between the "haves" and the "have-nots" based not on economic success but more on the allegiance to the new social norms compared to the "savages" that conform to old (and outdated) social institutions. Acting in many ways as a precursor to George Orwell's *1984* (1949), Huxley's work proposes a division of population based on education, physical prowess, and thinly veiled segregation of races, but stops short of becoming Orwellian in its population and thought control. However, this "brave new world" makes a strong case for dismantling previously held sacred beliefs and institutions such as marriage, monogamy, procreation, and even traditional concepts of parenthood. Romance and courtship become an archaic and pointless endeavor. Movement between the social/intellectual class is prohibited and futile, according to the structure designed to keep the society intact and stable. There is no room for variation here, only production in accordance with one's prescribed status and position.

By most, if not all accounts, this system works for its citizens. Being conditioned to accept and even revel in this stability from being hatched—humans are no longer born but emerge and are conditioned in "hatcheries"—no one challenges their status. No one has an impulse to develop into something more than what they are assigned. If, for some reason, citizens become upset over something, there is always the mind-numbing "soma" drug that is taken with alarming frequency in order to regulate and stabilize moods. Civilization cannot afford anyone making waves. Huxley recalls the ancient past per Modernist literary tendencies with this not so casual reference to the Greek lotus-eaters. Where Huxley induces this passivity through drug use,[5] Wells calls attention to this through evolution with the Eloi in *The Time Machine*. It is easier (and better) to not think or question; utopian society will provide all that is needed or wanted. Everything is going to be all right. There's nothing to worry about here.

The first half of the novel establishes the utopian society, known as the "World State." The second half portrays the disruption of that society following the arrival of the outsider, John, the "Savage," who comes from the "Savage Reservation" which is beyond the borders of the World State. Bernard, the protagonist, is an employee at one of the hatcheries. He is an imperfect member of the "Alpha" population who continually attempts to engage in intimacies with Lenina, a friendly but inferior Beta, who is not interested due to Bernard's shortcomings. Nonetheless, they become close friends. Lenina has struggles of her own and wants the experience of true love with one person, despite passionate and logical arguments for promiscuity from her best friend, Fanny. The two set out on an adventure beyond the borders of the World State of Europe and visit the forbidden lands of a "Savage Reservation"[6] in America where the old social institutions of free will, monogamy, and natural childbirth are still present.

Where Alice in *Ralph 124C 41+* is threatened by Martians, *Brave New World*'s Lenina and the rest of the World State are confronted by a transplanted member of the "uncivilized," referred to as "the Savage" or even "Mr. Savage." Through a purposefully thin veil that alludes directly to the treatment of Native Americans, Huxley illustrates a blatant racism toward the savage from the perspective of Lenina and Bernard. There is no room for the individual in the brave new world. As a result, John is banished from society but not from the World State, as he is still a subject of public fascination; he still serves a purpose. Likewise, Helmholtz Watson, a disillusioned Alpha-plus scholar, is banished to the Falkland Islands, a prison state for nonconformists. The message of Huxley's novel is clear: utopian society cannot exist with the individual. Everyone must serve everyone else and the system is what's most important. Yet, we clearly see the flaws of the system at work and become more and more sympathetic to the individual despite the practicality of the utopia.

Lyman Tower Sargent labeled the "woman question" as one of the central elements of late nineteenth-century utopian fiction. The question of how women would take their place in a future society became even more problematic as the focus of British writers turned toward dystopia following World War I.[7] The *Science Fiction Encyclopedia* praises the British author John Collier's *Tom's A-Cold* (1933) as "a remarkably effective post-holocaust novel" that "can be seen, in its atmosphere of almost loving conviction, as a genuine successor to Richard Jefferies's *After London*" (Clute and Nicholls 243). Collier's novel shows us the almost total absence of women, a fact that causes disaster for the men at the center of the novel and is the main driver of the plot. This grim novel, which was written and published during the early years of the Great Depression, is set in the 1990s after an unnamed but hinted-at catastrophe saw cities burn and millions die. Unlike many other speculative works, it is not a foreign enemy or aliens from another planet who have shattered civilization and scattered people into tiny, primitive, warring enclaves comprised almost exclusively of men. Instead, *Tom's A-Cold* depicts humanity as devolving into jealous and lazy people, a situation that smothers any happiness that might spark in this future world.

The hero of the story, Harry, bristles under the leadership of the aging and crusty chief who leads their valley stronghold, which is comprised of a few dozen men. Interestingly, about half of the men are in their fifties and sixties. There are no men who are in their thirties and forties. The next generation, embodied by Harry and his trusted sidekick, Crab, have greater ambitions than the stagnation offered by the chief and his generation. They raid a neighboring stronghold to kidnap women, as many as they can manage, and bring them back to their valley to become wives to the lonely men. Harry's selected mate at first loves him but then her affections are flipped after Harry unwittingly kills her brother, who was hunting in the forest. From that event springs her plan to stage her own death, escape back to Swindon, and rally those men to revenge against Harry. Harry's leadership collapses even as they successfully repel the invaders and he is destroyed.

Interestingly, Collier promises in his introduction that his book "contains no sociological interest at all" (5). While previous visions of the future by English authors, such as those found in Wells, Morris, and even Jefferies, put forth ideas about the organization of future society, Collier might be selling his novel short as an expression of and a response to utopian thinking. In *Tom's A-Cold*, he gives us a band of men loosely united under an all-powerful chief. At one point, the gang (as they call themselves) votes to maintain this absolute monarchy. They continue to talk about their society and seem at times to believe that they can create rules and structures that would lead to their happiness, but their hearts are not in it. Social structures are not the answer, and British Speculative Modernists demonstrated again and again in dystopias like this one that utopian thinking is at a dead end. Instead, and this places Collier firmly into the camp of fellow Speculative Modernists, Collier's focus is on the inner life of Harry as he comes of age, falls in love with the wrong person, rises to great power, and then is ruined. The focus is on the rise and fall of a single man in a dystopian context. This is the British difference. After World War I, British writers continued to focus on communities, as seen in *Brave New World* and *Tom's A-Cold*, social structures that negate the individual. In the United States, however, Speculative Modernists wrote stories about the triumph of individuals despite civilization.

American Speculative Modernists sought solutions outside of society, often in the individual who no longer abides by rules and behaviors dictated by social norms. Their sense of utopia, or at least of the civilization most built for survival, is a much darker one. H.P. Lovecraft, known more for his "cosmic horror" short stories, gives us a glimpse of a society perfectly working together to solve their own impending destruction in "Shadow Out of Time" (1936). The Great Race of Yith has already escaped their own planet's destruction by switching places with an ancient race of tree-like creatures that lived on the Earth millions of years ago. They recognize that all things must come to an end, and so are constantly on the lookout for their next situation. Together they compile a great library of all the beings that will ever rule the Earth and with this information they choose their next switch:

> This [...] was the greatest race of all; because it alone had conquered the secret of time. It had learned all things that ever were known or ever would be known on the earth, through the power of its keener minds to project themselves into the past and future, even through gulfs of millions of years, and study the lore of every age [Lovecraft "Shadow" 232–33].

They do not fear giving up their temporal forms, nor do they consider the fate of the victims they leave behind. Lovecraft examines our own need for temporal identity and our inability to sever ties with a failing temporal reality. Nathaniel Wingate Peaslee's horror at having to live among the Yith, while his own body is used for reconnaissance, is nothing compared to the realization that the Yith—in their infinite wisdom—overlook the human race as a suitable solution for survival. Lovecraft's story is the true endgame of utopia, condemned as a horrifying world where all work to contain the evils that have been suppressed and trying to find a way out of the coming predicament. Evil will escape at some point, and the utopia is sacrificed for survival. All the Yith do is look at the future of planet earth to determine where they can send their souls, leaving behind all that was their civilization. From greatness and dominance to simple survival, the Great Race leave their forms behind to settle not in the self-destructive failing humans, but in the insect creatures that will take over the world when man destroys himself. Utopias fail simply because everything must, and survival will call for the sacrifice of one's very nature—a solution that no human being can condone to their own destruction.

This story was published just a year before Lovecraft's death in 1937 and just three years before the beginning of the World War II. Like "Enoch Soames" on the other side of the Atlantic, the question of whether having a perfect society is worth the cost to the individual is answered by the madness of Peaslee's self-destruction. The Americans saw this universal notion of people working together as completely as the Great Race of Yith as being utterly horrific.

Fellow contributor to *Weird Tales* and Lovecraft's frequent correspondent Robert E. Howard holds the "generally acknowledged position as the founder of 'Sword & Sorcery' fantasy" (Kauffman 35) and took readers back to the core impulses of uncivilized humanity with his most beloved hero, Conan, who first appeared in "The Tower of the Elephant" (1933). As Howard scholar Patrice Louinet discusses, Howard admitted that it is a reworking of a King Kull story called "By This Axe I Rule!" written in 1929 and published in 1967, well after Howard's death via suicide at the age of thirty. It has been well documented that Conan is an embodiment of the fantasies and desires of Howard himself—in many ways, it is who Howard wished he could be. According to the author himself, the character of Conan came to him fully formed. The stories of the barbarian that Howard penned were essentially told to him by Conan himself, and that Howard merely wrote them down as a recollection from the hero's memory, hence they are non-chronological (Louinet "Hyborian" 430, 432).

In H.P. Lovecraft's famous, genre-defining essay "The Supernatural Horror in Literature" (1939),[8] he describes the cosmic fear that is pervasive during the Hyborian Age. As Lovecraft explains:

> The true weird tale has something more than secret murder, bloody bones, or a sheeted form clanking chains according to rule. A certain atmosphere of breathless and unexplainable dread of outer, unknown forces must be present; and there must be a hint, expressed with a seriousness and portentousness becoming its subject, of that most terrible conception of the human brain—a malign and particular suspension or defeat of those fixed laws of Nature which are our only safeguard against the assaults of chaos and the daemons of unplumbed space [Lovecraft "Supernatural" 1043].

Conan encounters the "unexplainable dread of outer, unknown forces" that Lovecraft describes as part of his definition of the true weird tale. In many ways, Conan experiences this chaos and the circling demons. As Howard writes:

> Conan felt his soul shrivel and begin to be drawn out of his body, to drown in the yellow wells of cosmic horror which glimmered spectrally in the formless chaos that was growing about him and engulfing all life and sanity. Those eyes grew and became gigantic, and in them the Cimmerian glimpsed the reality of all the abysmal and blasphemous horrors that lurk in the outer darkness of formless voids and nighted gulfs [Howard "Phoenix" 25].

Civilization does not have the capacity to deal with such forces—hence the distress and anxiety found in Yeats's poem "The Second Coming" (1920), where "mere anarchy is loosed upon the world, / the blood-dimmed tide is loosed, and everywhere / the ceremony of innocence is drowned" (2036). Yet, through Conan, Howard provides us with a new, but changed survival. Conan becomes the safeguard in its most primal form. Related to this, an interesting aspect of Howard's prehistory universe is the evolution and consequent de-evolution of the human species. Referring back to his Pre-Cataclysmic Age, pre-humans rose up. According to "The Tower of the Elephant," "We say men grow from the ape and build the shining cities [...] We saw them reel before the thrusts of the heathen Atlanteans and Picts and Lemurians. We saw the oceans rise and engulf Atlantis and Lemuria, and the isles of the Picts, and the shining cities of civilization" (Howard "Tower" 78). A great cataclysm had occurred and new continents emerged. There were beings that survived such an upheaval, but they actually regressed in their physical and intellectual development. As the god-like Yag-kosha continues to explain to Conan, "We saw the survivors of Pictdom and Atlantis build their stone age empires, and go down to ruin, locked in bloody wars. We saw the Picts sink into abysmal savagery, the Atlanteans into apedom again. We saw new savages drift southward in conquering waves from the arctic circle to build a new civilization" (78). Conan comes out of this new race as a Cimmerian, descendant of Atlanteans. In the southern regions of the world, evolution once again moved forward and civilizations emerged from these "new savages." Yet, Conan, now an evolutionary outsider, remains as conqueror and even King. By being fixed and static in the evolutionary process, Conan is apparently more equipped and better able to negotiate and succeed in this post-cataclysmic world. Howard gives us an unrefined, uncivilized hero in Conan. It is no wonder that he has endured for almost a century, despite our fascination with technology and sophistication. When those artifices are stripped away, we still have Conan.

In his own essay charting the Hyborian Age, Howard writes of his own creative process: "In writing about [Conan] and his adventures in the various kingdoms of his Age, I have never violated the 'facts' or spirit of the 'history' here set down, but have followed the lines of that history as closely as the writer of actual historical-fiction follows the lines of actual history. I have used this 'history' as a guide in all the stories in this series that I have written" (Howard "Hyborian" 381). Headlong into Modernism and the aftermath of World War I, Howard looked to a different world from the one that existed—the one that had seemingly failed. He blended ancient histories (influenced largely by H.G. Wells's *The Outline of History* [1920]) with even more ancient mythologies (influenced by *Bullfinch's Mythology* [1881] and Lewis Spence's Atlantean writings [1924–27]) to create an alternative: familiar, yet different from the current world at the time. As a friend and contemporary, H.P. Lovecraft was an ardent admirer of Howard's Hyborian Age, but is famously quoted as saying that "'the only flaw in this stuff is R.E.H.'s incurable tendency to devise names too closely resembling actual names—names which, for us, have a very different set of associations'" (qtd. in Louinet "Introduction" xxii). Indeed, there is familiarity. Realms from Norse mythology such as Asgard and Vanaheim become physical countries in the Hyborian Age, as do geographical regions such as Zimbabwe. However, Howard uses this familiarity as a foundation for something new. As Jeffrey Shanks articulates in "Hyborian Age Archaeology," "The term *mythopoesis*—'myth-making'—is sometimes used in conjunction with Howard's creation of the Hyborian Age. The term is not inaccurate, but perhaps it does not go far enough; a better term might be '*cosmopoesis*,' the creation of a new world, a new epoch, a new universe" (29). This is one of the clear narrative pillars of the Conan stories, one which was painstakingly purposeful in its craft and execution. By giving Conan a mythology to dwell in, Howard creates connection to the world in which Howard is living.

As the Hyborian Age offers an alternative to the apocalypse of Modernism via the fall of civilization and pre-existing order, Conan seems to embody both the anxiety of the age, and a solution to it—even though we may not like it. From the first submitted draft of "The Phoenix on the Sword" (1932):

> His mirth fell away from him like a mask, and his face was suddenly old, his eyes worn. The unreasoning melancholy of the Cimmerian fell like a shroud about his soul, paralyzing him with a crushing sense of the futility of human endeavor and the meaninglessness of life. His kingship, his pleasures, his fears, his ambitions, and all earthly things were revealed to him suddenly as dust and broken toys. The borders of life shrivelled and the lines of existence closed in about him, numbing him. Dropping his lion head in his mighty hands, he groaned aloud [Howard "Phoenix draft" 360–1].

Conan's perspective here embodies the anxieties and attitudes of Modernism and echoes the bleakness of T.S. Eliot's *The Waste Land* as well as Yeats's "center" that will not hold in "The Second Coming." However, there is the spark to come in the very next lines:

> Then lifting his head, as a man looks for escape, his eyes fell on a crystal jar of yellow wine. Quickly he rose and pouring a goblet full, quaffed it at a gulp. Again he filled and emptied the goblet, and again. When he set it down, a fine warmth stole through his veins. Things and happenings assumed new values. The dark Cimmerian hills faded far behind him. Life was good and real and vibrant after all—not the dream of an idiot god [Howard "Phoenix draft" 361].

Out of despair, Conan emerges renewed. He is renewed not because the world has changed and everything is back to "normal." He is renewed because he no longer has to think or be civil. He can be barbaric in a now barbaric world. Unlike British Speculative Modernists, Howard, a Texan, creates a way for society to accommodate the individual. As a consistent trait, Conan is not one for civility or civilization. As a general principle, he does not understand it and it only frustrates him. Once the veil of civility is lifted, Conan finds happiness—real and vibrant. Conan's realization is what Modernism lacks, and what Speculative Modernism provides: new methods for a new world. Howard creates this world for us, along with its conquering hero. Conan replaces the promise (and failure) of civilization with more primal inclinations. When Bêlit, Conan's Queen in "Queen of the Black Coast" (1934), asks him what he believes in, Conan replies:

> I have known many gods. He who denies them is as blind as he who trusts them too deeply. I seek not beyond death. It may be the blackness averred by the Nemedian skeptics, or Crom's realm of ice and cloud, or the snowy plains and vaulted halls of the Nordheimer's Valhalla. I know not, nor do I care. Let me live deep while I live; let me know the rich juices of red meat and stinging wine on my palate, the hot embrace of white arms, the mad exultation of battle when the blue blades flame and crimson, and I am content. Let teachers and priests and philosophers brood over questions of reality and illusion. I know this: if life is illusion, then I am no less an illusion, and being thus, the illusion is real to me. I live, I burn with life, I love, I slay, and am content [Howard "Queen" 133].

If the prevailing winds of Modernism sing of the crumbling of civilizations and the doom of sanity and meaningfulness, Howard's Hyborian Age offers the readers of speculative fiction in popular literature an "Age undreamed of" (Howard "Phoenix" 7). Emerging out of "Cimmeria, land of Darkness and deep Night" (Howard "Cimmeria" 1), comes Conan, a hero of this new world, but an antihero to the world we once knew and thought of as the pinnacle of mankind with our sophistication and advances in technology.

Howard reminds us that civilized man does not fit in with the natural world. Civilized man produces unnatural things, such as Huxley's World State. Through the artifice of civility, we, humanity, ignore what is natural in us. That very same civility also destroys what is natural around us. The world is not at odds with us; we are at odds with it. Conan reminds us of a part of ourselves long forgotten. It is part of why he has endured for almost a century when other fictional characters have come and gone. The Hyborian Age reminds us of what the world could be again. It is interesting to make the correlation between the Hyborian Age rising after the Great Cataclysm, and Howard's forgotten age sprouting up after World War I.

What was held so dear—so necessary—is now rendered voiceless and useless. Gone are the laws of governments, the guidance of religious belief, the stability of economic growth, the comforting notions of family and loyalty, and the knowledge of scientific discovery. These concepts are irrelevant to Conan. He does not trust science, or anything to do with civilization, as evidenced in "Beyond the Black River" (1935): "That's the way with civilized men. When they can't explain something by their half-baked science, they refuse to believe it" (Howard "Beyond"). Conan even considers the civilized man as an affront to his natural state. As he explains in the first chapter of "The Tower of the Elephant," "Civilized men are more discourteous than savages because they know they can be impolite without having their skulls split, as a general thing" (Howard "Tower" 63). Civilization is false, and even worse, reduces its citizens to being cowards who hide behind laws and social norms. Conan does not see the sense is such behaviors, and he has a point. In times that see a dismantling of such things, Conan's perspective runs against the very notion of Empire and its expansion. He will not be conquered.

Conclusion

One of the hallmarks of Speculative Modernism is its movement away from the idea of human social perfectibility. The nineteenth-century utopians had faith in their ability to formulate the right social ideas so that all needs were satisfied and lasting peace blanketed the world like a tranquilizing fog. As the century turned, that faith crumbled. In Britain, Speculative Modernists turned toward stories of social institutions run amok. Dystopias reigned. In America, Speculative Modernists raised up the liberated and powerful individual, armed with a ray gun or sword, as the cure for society's ills. In 1905, English satirist and social commentator G.K. Chesterton wrote:

And the weakness of all Utopias is this, that they take the greatest difficulty of man and assume it to be overcome, and then give an elaborate account of the overcoming of the smaller ones. They first assume that no man will want more than his share, and then are very ingenious in explaining whether his share will be delivered by motor-car or balloon [Chesterton 73–74].

Speculative Modernists recognized Chesterton's truth. This realization preceded World War I—and the advent of mainstream literary Modernism—by at least a decade if not two. By the time trench warfare had crushed the utopian hope for a bright future for humanity based on creativity and community spirit, this optimism had already been abandoned in speculative fiction. Modernism arrived between the world wars and brought with it the characteristic pessimism of that movement. Speculative Modernists, however, perhaps because it was their business to imagine possible futures no matter how unsavory, were there first.

The nineteenth century's optimistic use of the concept of utopia does indeed help to set up the world of speculative fiction. Technology will allow access to the endless universe, and social order will strengthen our resolve to conquer, even if it takes centuries. The notion of the generation ship, born in the early part of the twentieth century, is perhaps the greatest carry over from the utopic visions of the nineteenth century—the idea that humans will begin a voyage that they will never see the end of, all for the love of the continuation of the human race as a whole. Speculative Modernism, however, saw how the "savage," "the rugged individual," "the loner" would all defy this utopic vision and bring it crashing down in one way or the other. British writers saw how utopia would quickly become stifling to the individual, and either the character has to break down the carefully constructed utopia or go mad. American writers reveled in the loner and the potential of the individual who is willing to risk everything. For who would not risk everything knowing that it will all come to an end anyway by war or by natural disaster?

It was not only utopian thinking that was upended during this era. Ghost stories and their relatives had been popular for centuries at that point. Speculative Modernists, however, took the elements familiar to readers and turned them inside out. What used to haunt us became quaint and narrow, the terror drained from them. In their place were things that did not just go bump in the night. Instead, these monsters predicted the end of humanity and of the universe. Our next chapter, "Shadows at the Turn," looks at the changes that Speculative Modernism brought to those stories.

2

Shadows at the Turn

> It was as if, at moments, we were perpetually coming into sight of subjects before which we must stop short, turning suddenly out of alleys that we perceived to be blind, closing with a little bang that made us look at each other—for, like all bangs, it was something louder than we had intended— the doors we had indiscreetly opened.
> —Henry James, *The Turn of the Screw* (1898)

Ghosts and monsters are nothing new to human narrative constructs. They can be traced back to our earliest myths and have always been with us. These nonhuman entities have been our companions throughout history, the manifestations of imagination coexisting with intellect. Whether it be the monstrous Tiamat of Babylonian creation myths or the incarnation of the devil in the legend of Johann Georg Faust, the concept of the sinister Other has been the shadow by our side throughout history. From the dawn of the Speculative Modernist era, these entities transformed from beings created and inspired by cultural and social anxieties to manifestations that provide a glimpse of something more than what we are supposedly confined to. They offer us alternatives of the future, however malignant they may be.

Existing in oral forms via myths and folktales, the nonhuman Other has served multiple purposes in assisting how we situate ourselves within what we know (or imagine) of the world. They can represent all that remains mysterious to us, the repression of primal instincts, or power beyond our grasp. These figures or creations (to evoke Mary Shelley's monster) seem to have answers that we are unable to attain for ourselves, and they aren't very willing to share. This makes them at once terrifying and fascinating, an ideal figure to carry literary audiences into the twentieth century and this new era of Modernism, a time that features radical developments in science, technology, aestheticism, and psychology.[1] As John Paul Riquelme discusses in his article "Oscar Wilde's Aesthetic Gothic: Walter Pater, Dark Enlightenment, and *The Picture of Dorian Gray*":

As a Gothic revisionary interpretation of Pater's late Romanticism, this particular instance of excess [in *The Picture of Dorian Gray* (1890)] marks a turning point in literary history toward literary modernism. The reliance on doubling as a symptom of a darkness within both culture and the mind follows Robert Louis Stevenson's *The Strange Case of Dr Jekyll and My Hyde* (1886) and anticipates Bram Stoker's *Dracula* (1897) and Joseph Conrad's writings, especially *Heart of Darkness* (1902) and *The Secret Sharer* (1910). The conjoining of light and dark occurs as the narrative of a doubling that becomes visible through acts of aesthetic making and aesthetic response. The collaborative act of creating the painting brings into being something apparently new, original, and masterful that turns out to be not only beautiful but also atavistic and terrifyingly at odds with the public values of the society that applauds its beautiful appearance ["Aesthetic Gothic" 611].[2]

One will note that each of the texts named is considered well known and well respected. They are, indeed, benchmarks, but do not quite fit into the Modernist canon. However, it can be argued that they set up the foundations for what is to come in the decades that lead up to the turn of the century.

Monsters, whether external like Frankenstein's creature, internal like Jekyll/Hyde's doppelgänger split, or a combination via contamination as seen in the vampire, grew into fabulous, terrifying, and profitable forms during the nineteenth century. Vampires, in particular, have an enduring presence as a literary terror and metaphor for the anxieties and secret desire of culture. Although by no means the first literary vampire, Bram Stoker's *Dracula*, another work of canonical literature, extends the monster into Modernism as well. Although predating Sigmund Freud's Oedipal Complex by two years,[3] *Dracula* is a novel that "successfully manages a fantasy which is congruent with a fundamental fantasy shared by many others" and what Maurice Richardson, author of "The Psychoanalysis of Ghost Stories," calls "'a kind of incestuous, necrophilous, oral-anal-sadistic all-in wrestling match'" (qtd. in Roth 411). Phyllis Roth continues this argument as she identifies how Stoker manages to "transform horror into pleasure" and that "much of the novel's great appeal derives from its hostility towards female sexuality" (Roth 411). Riquelme strengthens this connection between the vampire double and Modernism with Oscar Wilde and Bram Stoker, linking the literary era by way of Irish nationalism:

> The anthropological issues concerning the character of the human are as evident in this [Stoker's *Dracula*] modernist form of the Gothic, written in this case by an Irish colonial author, as they are in postcolonial literature. Those issues come forward most obviously in Stoker's short story when the events turn toward infanticide and patricide. In this strange, blatantly violent story, the dynamics of the double involve the hybridity of colonial identity in representations that expose the destructive character of antagonistic oppositions. As is the case

with all the other modern Irish writers who present doubling emphatically in their works, including Wilde, Yeats, and James Joyce, Stoker's sensibility arises from a cultural situation characterized by oppositions of a violent, destructive kind. Like these other Irish writers, he presents at times the destructive and self-destructive character of conflictual doubling, and at times the possibility of a hybridity that might transform conflict into a disquieting, risky merger, whose results are unpredictable ["Dark Modernity" 592].

Here, we see a type of symbiotic relationship between forms. The Gothic, at least in part, gives rise to Modernism, but also manages to coexist and adapt with the changing times. The vampires of Speculative Modernism too extend the conversation between desire, instinct, and cultural anxiety, but manage to widen the notion and definition of the vampire beyond nineteenth-century notions.

Nineteenth-century British culture and society witnessed a desire for sophistication and an emphasis on social status, despite the massive gaps between rich and poor, educated and non-educated, respectable and detestable. Gone were the genialities of the Romantic Age. In America, the tumult was that much greater as the Civil War tore the country in two and the economic dependency on forced labor became nullified as slavery was abolished. Although the anxieties were different, those anxieties managed to manifest themselves in the Gothic. As Michael Cox and R.A. Gilbert discuss in their introduction to *Victorian Ghost Stories: An Oxford Anthology*, the Victorian ghost becomes familiar in its terror:

[T]he Victorian ghost story turned to the prosaic detail of modernity to establish a credible context for supernatural violation. […] Everyday detail abounds in the Victorian ghost story; details of décor and dress, food and drink, furniture and transport, landscape and architecture, as well as the realities of social and sexual relationships. Despite the pace of change, there were still plenty of apparently settled social structures; marriage, the law, landed and aristocratic society, the Church, the universities, the colonial experience. Any of these could provide an ordered microcosm into which the supernatural could intrude [Cox and Gilbert xvi–xvii].

Yet, Victorian writers in England and Romantic writers in America felt the need to update their ghosts and monsters. Science was becoming more and more fashionable with each new development (technological, biological, zoological, psychical, etc.). Just as scientific knowledge continued to evolve in the mind of popular and intellectual culture, so too did its monsters.

Henry James's *The Turn of the Screw* (1896) capitalized on this, and such concerns were in the forefront of the author's creative process. According to Francis X. Roellinger's article "Psychical Research and 'The Turn of the Screw'":

James's interest in psychical phenomena is well known to his readers, and is the subject of frequent mention in the recollections of his friends. Although he was not a member of the [Psychical] Society, founded in 1882, several friends were active in its affairs, two of them—F.W.H. Myers and Edmund Gurney—being founders. William James was a corresponding member from 1884 to 1889, vice president from 1890 to 1893, and president from 1894 to 1896. [...] That James had read and studied the reports of the Society is evident from the Preface [to *The Turn of the Screw*], in which he refers frequently to the "new" ghost, "the mere modern 'psychical' case," and to the "today so copious psychical record of cases of apparitions" [Roellinger 134–5].

James was well aware of the popularity of ghost stories over the previous century but wanted to create something new within the form. This links directly to Pound's Modernist dictum. Elizabeth Gaskell, Charles Dickens, and James catapulted the ghost into canonical literature, but the sensational writings of Wilkie Collins continued on through the short story in popular magazines of the time, the breeding ground for Speculative Modernists.

Gothicism does not disappear toward the end of the century. For our purposes, Gothicism slowly merges into speculative fiction, or "fantastique," along with the emerging genres of science fiction and fantasy. The nonhuman entities of Speculative Modernism are an untapped part of us, and always have been. Although these nonhuman Others have long predated the late-nineteenth and early-twentieth centuries, during the Modernist era they take on different forms. They fill the void that is rendered by the meaninglessness of that world. Instead of anxieties, they represent an additional "something" that is beyond our scientific or religious comprehension. In this chapter we will examine Gothic origins of Speculative Modernism and explore four different kinds of monsters: doppelgängers, vampires, and ghosts and the unexplained that defy categorization. Each of these archetypes construct the sections of this chapter, set up by a transition from nineteenth-century Gothicism to Speculative Modernism. Doppelgängers, typically seen as the double, allow readers to reimagine themselves. Similarly, vampires are at once ourselves and what we could be turned into. Finally, ghosts and the unexplained are equal remnants of the past, an undefinable present, and a future yet to be reconciled or fully understood.

The monstrous Other has always occupied a space in our imagination, taking form in art, drama, and literature (both oral and written). However, it can be argued that the writers of the late-nineteenth and early-twentieth centuries portray the figures, these manifestations in a unique and more ominous way than their predecessors. While it is true that the likes of Bierce, Algernon Blackwood, and Mary Wilkins Freeman stood on the cantilever of Edgar Allan Poe, Shelley, and Washington Irving to peer into the darkness, these writers became giants in their own right by allowing us to peer into the abyss of terror created by the crumbling of the world as the century turned and world war was on the horizon. Modernists could not hear the joyful song of Thomas Hardy's beruffled thrush, as

>   at once a voice arose among
>   The bleak twigs overhead
>   In a full-hearted evensong
>   Of joy illimited;
>   An aged thrush, fail, gaunt, and small,
>   In blast-beruffled plume
>   Had chosen thus to fling his soul
>   Upon the growing gloom [Hardy "Darkling" 1050].

As a Modernist, Hardy's speaker cannot hear the joy, the "blessed Hope" of such a song. The Speculative Modernists, however, hear something different in the "growing gloom." They hear terrible roars, the melancholy clanking of ancient chains, rumbles of unseen forces, and gurgles from unimagined beings. These writers find a degree of joy, however twisted, in that.

Gothic Origins of Speculative Modernism

Speculative Modernism is impossible to understand without exploring its Gothic origins. Typically understood to begin in earnest with Horace Walpole's *The Castle of Otranto* (1764), Gothic literature has remained with us as a prominent genre for centuries. However, it can be argued that its peak was reached in the 1800s. Undeniable literary classics such as *Frankenstein* (1818), *The House of Seven Gables* (1851), *The Strange Case of Dr. Jekyll and Mr. Hyde* (1886), and *Dracula* (1897) span the entirety of the nineteenth century. As has been purported by many scholars, the antagonists of these texts tend to represent various anxieties of the respective eras, including (but not limited to) economic/social class distinction, sexuality, familial sins, scientific progress, and global expansion.[4] However, the nonhuman Other—either spiritual or physical—takes on different significance on the precipice of and into Modernism. Ghosts, vampires, the unexplainable all manifest to fill the void that Modernism creates. The advances and expansions of the nineteenth century bring into possibility the dawn of a new world, but what if that new world is devoid of meaning? Readers can turn to the Speculative Modernists for the answers, but what they find is often horrifying.

Gothicism has a rich and celebrated history. As Fred Botting explains in his study of the tradition, *Gothic*,

> imagination and emotional effects exceed reason. Passion, excitement and sensations transgress social proprieties and moral laws. Ambivalence and uncertainty obscure single meaning. Drawing on myths, legends and folklore of medieval romances, Gothic conjured up magical tales of knights, monsters, ghosts and extravagant adventures and terrors. Associated with wildness, Gothic signified an over-abundance of imaginative frenzy, untamed by reason and unrestrained by conventional eighteenth-century demands for simplicity, reason or probability [3].

Walpole's seminal work is recognized as the first to bring these motifs together in a template of sorts that subsequent texts rely on such as the dark and gloomy castle, the underground labyrinth, the wildness of nature and weather, the life-threatening pursuit, and the nonhuman and mysterious Other as monstrous and malignant entity. The most common forms of the latter are criminals/deviants on the rational end of the spectrum and ghost and vampires on the metaphysical/spiritual side. Gothic motifs inspired the Speculative Modernists, as characters exhibiting these forms would serve as the basis of a new brand of horror.

Gothic literature keeps its sense of morality intact in Ann Radcliffe's *The Mysteries of Udolpho* (1794). Despite the convoluted machinations of the antagonist the Marquis Montoni and a sinister family secret, order (both domestic and moral) is restored as Montoni is revealed to be in league with criminals, not demons. Emily, the heroine of the narrative, regains control of her sensibilities and Montoni suffers the loss of his, succumbing to greed and corruption as the main conflict of the novel. Radcliffe advances the genre not by content but by style. Her sense of tension and suspense through the perspective of Emily's imagination are what makes this story a benchmark of the genre. Fancy gives way to reason, and the mysteries of the castle of Udolpho and all that lies therein are explained. As Robert Miles explains, "The device of the explained supernatural is given its fullest, most sophisticated expression in *The Mysteries of Udolpho*, Radcliffe's most famous novel" (82).

The deviant physical and malign spiritual Other can be traced back to Matthew Lewis's infamous novel *The Monk* (1796). The basic premise is how a celebrated and revered monk, Ambrosio, falls victim to his pride and abandons social and professional responsibilities in service to lust and desire. Through several convoluted entrapments, Ambrosio ultimately commits murder and incest, finally relinquishing his soul to the devil in order to escape from earthly torment only to be betrayed by the devil. Although still considered a Gothic Romance, Lewis's novel "offers a far more unbuttoned version of Gothic than the mix of sentimental romance and explained supernaturalism which had defined the genre under Radcliffe[....] Incest, and incestuous rape, murder, matricide and sororicide, all feature, together with a blasphemous identification of Satan and the Madonna, and of sexual temptation with religious devotion" (Trott 54). What makes Lewis's work so important for the Speculative Modernists, beyond the sheer audacity of it, is the inclusion of both secular and sacred abominations.

Perhaps no one in the history of Gothic literature has done more to create the terror, horror, and doom than the undeniable master of the macabre, Edgar Allan Poe. One needs to simply scan through the titles of his fiction to grasp his influence, one that exists in Speculative Modernists and current writers alike. Many of his stories can be viewed as foundational texts in terms of style and narrative to the Speculative Modernists, but "The Facts in the Case of M. Valdemar" (1845) is arguably the most significant to changes that will take place in these weird tales a half century later. Gothic scholar Elisabeth Bronfen discusses how Poe's story serves as a primary example of the "rhetorical gesture" of how "the reader is drawn into a phantasy scenario that hesitates between mastery over and submission before the irrevocable law of death" (114). Recalling the ambiguities of ventriloquism and mesmerism first brought to the literary public by Charles Brockden Brown via *Wieland* (1798), *Ormond* (1799), and *Arthur Mervyn* (1800), Valdemar posits a life suspended in death. As an act of scientific experimentation, Valdemar instructed physicians and narrator to mesmerize him on his death bed, but before expiration. In so doing, Valdemar becomes trapped in a state of suspension, although his body expires. However, he remains in existence for seven months, where he continually communicates through a disembodied voice that he is dying. Finally, the narrator agrees to "wake" Valdemar, only to have him disintegrate:

> As I rapidly made the mesmeric passes, amid ejaculations of "dead! dead!" absolutely bursting from the tongue and not from the lips of the sufferer, his whole frame at once—within the space of a single minute, or even less, shrunk—crumbled, absolutely rotted away beneath my hands. Upon the bed, before that whole company, there lay a nearly liquid mass of loathsome—of detestable putridity [Poe "Facts" 728].

Not only do we see a gruesome description of bodily decay here that writers like H.P. Lovecraft will build upon in their strange tales, but we also arrive at an ending that offers more questions than answers. In Poe, narratives are often unresolved, at least to the moral satisfaction of readers. With "resolutions" such as what we see in "Valdemar" and "The Cask of Amontillado," readers are not offered a feel-good ending. The lasting effect of these horrors is one that is not easily shaken. These shadows do not readily disappear in the morning light. Instead, these horrors endure, and the shadows always accompany us. The ambiguous and rather abrupt ending would come to be a calling card of sorts for the Speculative Modernists to come.

American poet and fiction writer Emma Frances Dawson continues the motif established by Poe's Valdemar with her own suspensions between life and death with her short story "An Itinerant House" (1897). Dawson's tale provides a rather convenient bridge to the Gothic past by paying homage to the likes of Shelley and Poe. Yet, it tantalizes readers with advances in technology such as the study and investigation of magnetism as a science.[5] The latter is what situates Dawson as a Speculative Modernist, situating familiar Gothic tropes in with the modern world at the turn of the century. Felipa the housekeeper was pronounced dead by a doctor upon confronting her lover about an affair. Another tenant, a doctor-in-training, Dering, wished to perform more thorough tests, including electric shocks (recalling *Frankenstein*). As he explains, "'Every corpse [...] can thus be excited soon after death, for a brief time only, and but once. If the body is not lifeless, the electric current has power at any time'" and that "'the nerve which hears is the last to die'" (Dawson 239). With that, Volz, a family friend, begins to play "gypsy music" that would be "'like holding wild flowers to her nostrils'" and reasons that, according to the narrator, "Time, space, our very identities, [are] consumed in this white heat of sound" (240). We see a blending of science (electricity) and sensation (in this case, music) here in order to rouse the spirit—if such a thing exists. Revived from death after two days, Felipa once again spoke, and communicated her great displeasure, referring to the threesome of well-doers as "idiots":

> Better dead than alive! True. You knew I would be glad to die. What right had you to bring me back? God's curses on you! I was dead. Then came agony. I heard your voices. I thought we were all in hell. Then I found by your evil cunning I was to be forced to live. It was like an awful nightmare. I shall not forget you, nor you me. These very walls shall remember—here where I have been so tortured no one shall have peace. Fools! Leave me! Never come into this room again [241].

With that, Felipa follows the Gothic trope of the cursed house and evokes the torturous lingering of Poe's Valdemar. Dawson's literary allusions continue with the inclusion of English novelist T.A. Trollope (brother of Anthony Trollope) and theories of passionography (the imprint of emotions on physical objects or surroundings), which occur throughout the tale. The exact phrase of "better dead than alive" and "the nerve which hears is last to die" repeats verbatim from different characters separated by time, not space. The narrative ends with an affirmation of the paranormal science of magnetism that was initially purported by Dering. The story concludes: "'The magnetic man *is* a spirit!'" (254). Not only do readers see the classic Gothic characteristics of the haunted house/room and the living death akin to somnambulism, but also the disembodied spirit attaching itself to an unfamiliar science—something we cannot yet understand.

Gothic Extensions: Doppelgängers to Vampires

The spirit is not always separate from the body but can inhabit it as well. However, it is not at all necessary for the spirit to align with its biological, conscious host. In 1886, Robert Louis Stevenson published *The Strange Case of Dr. Jekyll and Mr. Hyde*. He had already gained wide acclaim for his novel, *Treasure Island*, which was a bestseller in 1883. Jekyll and Hyde astounded the reading public, who consumed it voraciously. The novella—dismissed by some as one of the many penny dreadfuls (sensational stories that were widely available)—was all people wanted to talk about. Sermons were delivered about the novel and stage adaptations soon followed. Although the field of psychology was still in its infancy, the novel seemed to touch a live wire in the minds of a ready audience.[6] It tapped into ideas about good and evil that had percolated through the culture for centuries. Such connections persist today. Psychologists Angela M. Griffin and Judith H. Langlois argue that the idea that beauty and good are linked in the same way that ugliness and evil are linked has been a constant theme throughout Western culture since the ancients.

As much as the novel wants to show that we are all created with two sides to us that compete for supremacy, there are signs early in the novel that show that perhaps our personalities and behavior are more complex than the battle between good and evil. Jekyll's old friend, Dr. Lanyon, notices Jekyll's increasingly strange and antisocial behavior. Even before Jekyll seemingly splits himself into two halves, one misshapen and evil while the other handsome and good, there is trouble. Something inside Jekyll is struggling to get out, something that drives a wedge between himself and his closest friends.

The struggle between what Jekyll labels "dualities" is where the narrative ends. The doctor, what the reader perceives as the pure and good version of the man, attempts to expunge the evil within him, to separate fully his own, true self from that evil. His great scientific and ethical transgression—the desire to indulge his vices under the guise of Hyde while maintaining an unblemished reputation as Jekyll—spins out of his control when he loses the ability to change from one to the other at will:

> It was on the moral side, and in my own person, that I learned to recognise the thorough and primitive duality of man; I saw that, of the two natures that

contended in the field of my consciousness, even if I could rightly be said to be either, it was only because I was radically both; and from an early date, even before the course of my scientific discoveries had begun to suggest the most naked possibility of such a miracle, I had learned to dwell with pleasure, as a beloved daydream, on the thought of the separation of these elements. If each, I told myself, could be housed in separate identities, life would be relieved of all that was unbearable; the unjust might go his way, delivered from the aspirations and remorse of his more upright twin; and the just could walk steadfastly and securely on his upward path, doing the good things in which he found his pleasure, and no longer exposed to disgrace and penitence by the hands of this extraneous evil. It was the curse of mankind that these incongruous faggots were thus bound together—that in the agonised womb of consciousness, these polar twins should be continuously struggling. How, then were they dissociated? [Stevenson 59].

Readers see in Stevenson's masterwork the changing nature of the establishments of Gothic literature as the Speculative Modernist era rises. The uncanny Other no longer comes from elsewhere, no longer frightens because it is a stranger. Instead, as the horrified Jekyll found out, the evil Other—as well as the pure and upright Other, the side of the self most civilized—exists in all of humanity. Turning one half or the other loose will bring about destruction, yet they are both there, speaking as humanity finds its way, broken and directionless, into the twentieth century.

The doppelgänger has allowed the animalistic Other to enter into human behavior, but that animalistic Other can also be cast into a far more terrifying and ancient entity. One of the most enduring and impactful representations of the nonhuman Other is the vampire. Although Bram Stoker's *Dracula* proves the benchmark of the vampire, according to Leonard Wolf's introduction to the collection *Blood Thirst: 100 Years of Vampire Fiction*, the concept dates back thousands of years in folk narratives and is even seen as far back as the second century via *The Golden Ass* (Wolf 4). However, the vampire truly takes its recognizable form in the nineteenth century with texts like John Polidori's *The Vampyre* (created alongside Shelley's *Frankenstein* as part of Byron's famous horror story challenge), first published in 1821, James Malcolm Rymer's *Varney the Vampire* (1847), and Sheridan Le Fanu's *Carmilla* (1872). As Wolf explains, Polidori's humanlike creature named Ruthven is based on Byron himself, and the text centers more on keeping the nature of the vampire a secret instead of focusing on the vampire itself. Wolf goes on to explain how Rymer's vampire is rather comedic and extreme in its descriptions (4–5). Varney would become the inspiration for F.W. Murnau's cinematic vision for *Nosferatu* (via Max Schreck) in 1922. Le Fanu's *Carmilla* moves the tradition toward a more recognizable archetype, albeit through a female rather than a male. Le

Fanu adds homosexuality to the vampire template, but as Wolf argues, the novella concerns itself more with the complexities and consequences of love rather than the social taboo of lesbianism. Stoker's *Dracula* continues this tradition.[7]

Although the novel didn't become a bestseller until after his death, Stoker's villain has become a fixture in the public consciousness and takes his shape across the globe. This is largely due to the success of Tod Browning's 1931 film starring the mesmerizing Bela Lugosi in the lead role. Unlike Carmilla, Stoker's vampire is a rather one-dimensional character. He is the embodiment of evil, a servant of Satan. However, what he represents is often argued to be much more complex. Many scholars and critics have claimed that Dracula epitomizes our repressed desires and impulses (deviant sexualities, primal violence, etc.) as well as social and domestic anxieties (advancing technologies, changing gender roles, expansion/dilution of the Empire, etc.).[8] Added to this is the position that Dracula occupies in the turn-of-the-century understanding of where humanity, or lack thereof, stands in the grand scheme of things. Dracula is not human. He is not an animal. He is not a god. He is Other, and readers are constantly drawn to him. He endures. Dracula signifies the solution to the growing fear over meaninglessness. The vampire remains enigmatic. The creature exists out of time, immortal.

While *Dracula* and *Carmilla* are iconic, the vampire (or derivations thereof) can be seen in shorter fiction as well at the turn of the century. Mary E. Wilkins Freeman's "Luella Miller" (1902) is much more subtle than the sensual Carmilla or the satanic Dracula. Winner of the first William Dean Howells medal for Distinction of Fiction from the American Academy of Arts and Letters, Freeman's short story speaks to a draining of good will instead of literal blood. Luella Miller uses the kindness of others for her own sustenance and can even be seen as a precursor of sorts to Blanche DuBois from Tennessee Williams's *A Streetcar Named Desire*, almost fifty years later. Presented in the form of Lydia Anderson's memory years after Luella's death (reminiscent of Poe's unreliable narrator trope), the tale examines her history as a "survival of the wild horror and frenzied fear of their ancestors who had dwelt in the same age with Luella Miller" (Freeman "Luella" 69). Luella is cast as a rare yet nontraditional beauty with unique powers of persuasion and magnetism. She "'used to sit in a way nobody else could if they sat up and studied for a week of Sundays [...] and it was a sight to see her walk. If one of them willows over there on the edge of the brook could start up and get its roots free of the ground, and move off, it would go just the way Luella Miller used to'" (70). Soon after her husband's untimely death, Luella, who always seems to be in need of assistance, receives aid from her sister-in-law. Despite being a picture of robust health and youth at the start of her caregiver tenure, the sister-in-law ultimately dies as well. This pattern would continue even through blood relations like Luella's aunt, Abby. Eventually, neighbors catch on to this pattern and rumors start to spread. Everyone becomes afraid of even entering the residence. However, there are those who want to care for her out of sympathy, or moral/professional responsibility. Unfortunately, they suffer the same fate. With no one left to help her, Luella expires after an abnormally long life, but is seen that night under a full moon leaving the forbidden house along with all of her supposed victims.

One of the aspects that should not be ignored about the tale is the gender of the author. As one of the first of the subgenre to be written by a woman,[9] "Luella Miller" stands out from the traditional vampire we are accustomed to. She is not animalistic, sinister, or sexualized. She is vulnerable, and that vulnerability is her most dangerous characteristic. Luella is an emotional vampire; she drains the vitality from people's goodwill and compassion. There is no blood that trickles from the necks of victims or from the lips of monsters here. Remarkably, Freeman actually gets us to sympathize with her. She presents Luella as hysterical, often "laughin' and cryin' all together" (Freeman "Luella" 72) that recalls Charlotte Perkins Gilman's "The Yellow Wallpaper," published ten years prior.[10] Although Lydia paints a rather sinister picture, as readers, we question how much Luella can really help herself from her actions. In fact, Freeman makes it rather clear that we are not to see Luella as an evil entity. She even goes so far as to include a minister who condemns "the sin of superstition" about Luella, and her neighbor Lydia Anderson feels anger toward Luella, not horror. As Lydia explains, "but sometimes I wondered lately if she knew it—if she wa'n't like a baby with scissors in its hand cuttin' everybody without knowin' what it was doin'" (76). Freeman's tale subverts but is also subversive. Just as the characters in the story, we succumb to Luella's appeal of helplessness as well.

Luella not only appears to be unwilling to perform domestic tasks, but incapable. In one of the most chilling episodes of the story that foreshadows Ira Levin's *The Stepford Wives* (1972), an exchange between Lydia and Luella underscores a recoil of female domesticity:

> "Aunt Abby ain't got up yet?"
> "No, she ain't," says I [Lydia], pretty short.
> "I thought I didn't smell the coffee," says Luella.
> "Coffee," says I. "I guess if you have coffee this mornin' you'll make it yourself."
> "I never made coffee in all my life," says she, dreadful astonished [Freeman "Luella" 73].

The implication is clear. Making coffee is not so much beneath her as it is utterly foreign to her. She is incapable of doing these things, *anything*, for herself. This is not a matter of social or economic hierarchy. However, Luella's helplessness is not a mere matter of gender either. In another scene, Luella explains to Lydia that she cannot do domestic tasks, that her caregivers—in this case, Maria Brown—have to do the work for her. This removes gender from the dynamic. Instead of focusing on gender roles here, it becomes apparent that Luella is Other. Similar to Gilman's troubled protagonist in "The Yellow Wallpaper," Luella's gender is a symptom, not a cause.

"Luella Miller" belongs in the subgenre of vampire fiction and inhabits the void created by *fin de siècle* meaninglessness. Her supernatural departure, walking along with her "victims" on the night of a full moon, implies an incomprehensible existence for both characters and readers. As the story concludes, "nothing is now left of it [Luella's forbidden and subsequently abandoned house] except a few old cellar stones and a lilac bush, and in summer a helpless trail of morning glories among the weeds, which might be considered emblematic of Luella herself" (Freeman "Luella" 79). Luella occupies something out there that is undefinable. No answers are offered. Yet, knowing that the undefinable something is out there provides some type of assurance. In tales such as "Luella Miller" where the vampire becomes a sympathetic figure and is released from her ethical complications and continues on to a better existence, Speculative Modernists like Mary E. Wilkins Freeman create a hope out of hopelessness, an undefined meaning out of meaninglessness.

Francis Marion Crawford, a celebrated novelist of literary realism and author of the influential *The Novel: What It Is* (1893), reclaims the "traditional" vampire in his story "For the Blood Is the Life" (1905), whose title is a direct quote from *Dracula*. This tale features descriptions such as "an upturned throat, over which a very thin red line of blood trickled, down into his collar" and "dead eyes that saw in spite of death—upon parted lips redder than life itself—upon two gleaming teeth on which glistened a rosy drop" (Crawford "Blood" 300) and is a narrative of supernatural love. The vampire is never given a name—only the "Thing": "that Thing which is neither alive nor dead, that Thing that will abide neither above ground nor in the grave" (300). What makes Crawford's vampire so haunting is not the biological horror of a fanged woman draining the life of her lover through gleaming teeth and red lips, but the mystery of her. Crawford is very careful to not identify the Thing as a vampire. As a point of order, Crawford describes her as a shadow and an unidentifiable body resting on top of a burial mound, dismissed as "an effect of moonlight" (287). Extending Stoker's narrative stance of reporting the tale through journals or letters and thereby layering narrative,[11] Crawford tells the story of the botched robbery of a deceased man of wealth's inheritance and the subsequent death of Cristina (a servant caught in the middle between the thieves). In death, Cristina preys on the vain Angelo, who was in line for the inheritance. However, this story is told to a priest from an eyewitness, Antonio. All of this is buried with the narrative of the narrator relating the story to Holger, a friend.

Outside of the core narrative of Cristina and Angelo, the narrator relates the story to Holger due to his curiosity being sparked by seeing the outline of a body lying atop a burial mound spotted in the light of the moon from an overlooking tower. At the end of the tale, Holger asks his friend about the lingering outline on the burial mound, glowing in the moonlight. Despite the narrator explaining the Thing's "death" at the bloody hands of Antonio and his driftwood stake, Holger wonders if it is "quite dead yet" (Crawford "Blood" 301). As the last paragraph in the narrative states, "I wonder too. But whether it be dead or alive, I should hardly care to see it, even in broad daylight" (301). Similar to *Dracula*'s rather ambiguous ending concerning the fate of the vampire, Crawford's Thing may not have come to her ultimate end. The doubt lingers, just like her outline atop the grave. The doubt lingers because one needs the mystery, the unexplained.

The vampire, a seemingly eternal character, rises from the tomb in the nineteenth century and replenishes its thirst in the social and literary contexts of Modernism. Vampire characters such as Luella Miller and Crawford's Thing are essential to the story of horror created by the Speculative Modernists. The appeal is intimacy in addition to immortality. Readers develop a very personal relationship with vampires, a relationship that is simultaneously appalling and irresistibly attractive. Victims of the vampire willingly succumb to its spell, whether that be through charisma, sympathy, wealth, or status. There is a quality about vampires that draws readers again and again.

Ghosts and the Unexplained

Tales of ghosts, spirits, and apparitions enjoyed incredible popularity during the Romantic and Victorian eras with canonical writers like Dickens, Emily Brönte, Gaskell, Poe, and Irving. However, new forms of such ethereal entities emerge. Alongside these reimagined incarnations, an unknowable threat emerges among Speculative Modernist writers, one that defies definition and categorization. Such a threat can be found in Francis Marion Crawford's "The Upper Berth" (1886). In the story, Crawford presents an impossibility in the setting of the mundane. Additionally, the victims are trapped within the confines of a ship on a voyage across the Atlantic. Instead of a vampire tale, readers engage with a haunting in Room 105 of the *Kamtschatka*, a ship once favored by the narrator, Brisbane, as he made regular trips across "the duck pond." Reminiscent of the investigative powers of Poe's detectives, Brisbane is at a loss for how to explain the mysteries of the upper berth of his room. He is obsessed with the open portal and pervasive smell of saltwater death that envelops the room. This is only made worse by a mysterious, uncommunicative stranger assigned to the bunk who suddenly disappears in the middle of the night, presumed to have committed suicide via an overboard jump.

After running a series of experiments with the security of the portal window that continually opens despite being securely latched, Brisbane suffers his first gruesome encounter with an unexplainable entity: "I laid hold of something that had the shape of a man's arm, but was smooth, and wet, and icy cold. But suddenly, as I pulled, the creature sprang violently forward against me, a clammy, oozy mass, as it seemed to me, heavy and wet, yet endowed with a sort of supernatural strength" (Crawford "Upper" 221). Being the rational and reasonable narrator that he is, Brisbane quickly dismisses the recollection as caused by indigestions from a previous disagreeable meal of Welsh rarebit (a mixture of eggs and cheese). Simply put, the experience was reduced to a mere nightmare—rational and logical. Unfortunately, such an encounter was not meant to be singular for Brisbane.

Haunted by the experience and still determined to solve the mystery, Brisbane appeals to a man of science, a fellow passenger that is also a surgeon. Unfortunately, the doctor is just as determined to leave the ship as Brisbane is to uncover its mystery. As the doctor explains:

> "It is my business to keep my wits about me—not to go off fiddling with ghosts and things. [...] Have you [Brisbane] any reasonable explanation of these things to offer?" he asked.
>
> "No; you have not. Well, you say you will find an explanation. I say that you won't, sir, simply because there is not any."
>
> "But my dear sir," I retorted, "do you, a man of science, mean to tell me that such things cannot be explained?"
>
> "I do," he answered stoutly. "And if they could, I would not be concerned in the explanation" [Crawford "Upper" 223].

The surgeon outright refuses to follow his professional worldview and ignores science and curiosity in light of terror and fear of the unknown. He is well aware of the limits of human understanding and comprehends the position of humanity against unexplainable nature. It is clear that he does not want to know, that he is better off as an individual in blissful denial. In this way, he personifies much of what Speculative Modernism posits.

Undeterred, Brisbane ultimately enlists the help of the captain (despite warnings and pleas from those aware of the room and its curse) to trap the creature and resolve the situation. After setting the trap in the berth, Brisbane and the captain finally encounter the thing described as "the body of a man long drowned [...] the slippery, oozy, horrible thing—[with] dead white eyes" (Crawford "Upper" 227). Brisbane attempts to capture it, but it thrashes him violently. The captain manages to land a blow. He is shaken, "an inarticulate cry of horror" (227) across his face. The thing vanishes through an aperture far too small for its size, and the story ends with Brisbane, the doctor, and the captain all vowing to never sail the ship again. The mystery remains unresolved and unexplained. The lack of any reasonable explanation for the monstrous nonhuman entity becomes a feature of Speculative Modernists, as can be seen with almost incomprehensible Others in H.P. Lovecraft and William Hope Hodgson a few decades later.

Around the turn of the century, ghost stories had become somewhat commonplace and were attracting critical attention as a genre form. This is due to the extreme popularity of the form, especially from Victorian England: "Ghost stories were something at which the Victorians excelled. They were as typically part of the cultural and literary fabric of the age as imperial confidence or the novel of social realism[....] [A]ll subsequent practitioners have been indebted to the Victorian achievement in one form or another" (Cox and Gilbert x–xi). However, the form became so popular that satires began to crop up, such as Oscar Wilde's "The Canterville Ghost" (1887). As such, genre writers often felt the need to justify the seriousness and quality of ghost stories, especially since "much of the output [of ghost stories] was hack commercial fiction of the weakest sort" (Cox and Gilbert x). Olivia Howard Dunbar is the author of an essay defending horror stories, "The Decay of the Ghost in Fiction" (1905),[12] and numerous short tales. One of the most successful of these works is her story, "The Shell of Sense" (1908). Dunbar pens her story from the point of view of a deceased spirit, which she refers to as "the shadow-folded transition" (Dunbar 326). The tale progresses as Frances (the ghostly narrator) learns her capacities in the corporeal world that her sister, Theresa, and her husband, Allan, still inhabit. What complicates the plot is the repressed affections between Allan and Theresa. As an invisible spirit, Frances is exposed to the now undeniable connection between the two, a connection that had existed for years, but never acted upon until her passing.

Through the exploration of her abilities (and limitations), Frances learns that she can, in fact, affect things around her. Frances credits her return to the strength of her love for Allan. "It was for him that I made this first lonely, frightened effort to return, to recover" despite Allan's propensity to dismiss anything irrational or unprovable by confirmation of sight (Dunbar 328). Frances discovers that her presence can be felt by both Allan and Theresa, although they both characterize her efforts as "strange sensations." Allan even goes so far as to dismiss these feelings as trivial mentalities, often relating to gender inferiority: "'What I mean, [...] is a special, an almost ominous sense of cold. Upon my soul, Theresa,'—he paused—'if I *were* superstitious, if I *were* a woman, I should probably imagine it to seem—a presence'" (328). The message, recalling Gilman's dismissive husband (who is also a medical doctor) yet again, is that women are irrational figures and that men, driven solely by empirical evidence and not distracted by trivialities such as superstitions or ambiguous sensations are the ones who stabilize the uncertain and ground the flights of fancy. Theresa responds with desperate pleas. "Don't think it, I beg of you! I've tried so hard not to think it—and you must help me. You know it is only perturbed, uneasy spirits that wander. With her [Theresa] it is quite different. She has always been so happy—she must still be" (329). Dunbar's Theresa acknowledges the conventions of the subgenre in a moment of self-awareness. Relying on the well-established tradition of Gothic ghost stories, she believes that ghosts are manifestations of disgruntled or wronged spirits. However, Dunbar subverts this perspective with Frances. She only becomes "perturbed" when she discovers the affection shared between her now-available husband and her seemingly conniving and predatory sister. A disastrous blow is rendered by Allan, who then labels "the presence" as not merely a spirit, "but something much more terrible" (329) within earshot of the ethereal Frances.

Although Frances writhes in the agony of apparent betrayal by her sister and her husband, she also experiences a sense of relief over the release from the confines of the body:

> Then in the anguish of it all I remembered, awkward, untutored spirit that I was, that I now had the Great Recourse. Whatever human things were unbearable I had no need to bear. I ceased, therefore, to make the effort that kept me with them. The pitiless poignancy was dulled, the sounds and the light ceased, the lovers faded from me, and again I was mercifully drawn into the dim, infinite spaces [Dunbar 330].

This is what makes Dunbar's text Speculative Modernist. This world, our world, is filled with the unbearable. However, escape from it is not death, but something else—something that Frances herself does not yet understand. Where the Modernists stop and circle in despair and meaninglessness like vultures riding air currents in order to target carrion, Speculative Modernists like Dunbar travel those air currents to something more, perhaps better. They don't know where those currents lead, but they are moving beyond what is known and accepted. They offer not stagnation, nor solution. They just present an unknown alternative.

Frances has options in front of her. She can either remain with the anguish of the unbearable or detach and embrace the newness of her ethereal existence. Unfortunately for all involved, she chooses to stay anchored to her hell in the name of justice and revenge. As she confesses, "Of the efficacy of my own vigilance, so long as I might choose to exercise it, I could have no doubt, for I had by this time come to have a dreadful exultation in the new power that lived in me" (Dunbar 330). It is the ability to choose that is what is most important to her. Her love for Allan dictates that choice, but it is hers to make.

Continuing her experiments of transfiguration, Frances eventually achieves visibility, however brief. Yet her moment of personal triumph results in the very actions she was trying to prevent. As she confesses, it was her brief moment of visibility after corporeal death that drove Allan and Theresa into each other's arms for the very first time. With their suspicions confirmed and flustered with horror and guilt, the pair begin to theorize what future they might have together in light of Frances's lingering. Eventually, Theresa comes to the decision that it is Frances's right to keep her and Allan apart if she so wishes. Witnessing such heartbreak while back in her ethereal form, Frances begins to change her perspective and motivations:

> As I remembered that extraordinary speech, and saw the agony in her face, and the greater agony in Allan's, there came the great irreparable cleavage between mortality and me. In a swift, merciful flame the last of my mortal emotions—gross and tenacious they must have been—was consumed. My cold grasp of Allan loosened and a new unearthly love of him bloomed in my heart [Dunbar 334].

Seeing the sincere and honorable affections between Allan and Theresa, Frances reverses her course and actually works toward keeping the two together and allowing for their happiness. She proceeds to visit both Allan and Theresa in dreams, urging them to stay together and thwart Theresa's planned departure. As each partner confesses their dream to the other, they realize that they have Frances's blessings. Upon the decision to stay together, Frances is released from her confinement of mortal emotions. To conclude her tale, Frances explains that "theirs is the fullest joy that the dwellers in the shell of sense can know. Mine is the transcendent joy of the unseen spaces" (336). As alluded to earlier, Frances enters into a new, undefined existence, those "unseen spaces." Through her first-person point of view from the Other, Dunbar provides "transcendence" beyond the known. She is also careful to stop well short of qualifying what that means. An explicit example of this can be seen in Allan's response to Theresa's question about whether her thought that Frances visited him in his dream: "'I can never understand, but I know'" (336). That sentiment is apropos to the Speculative Modernists and what they offer the literary world. During the turn of the century, rationalism often coexisted with spiritualism and the acknowledgment of existence after death.[13]

This acceptance of apparitions, simultaneously unnerving and uplifting, continues with Freeman's "The Shadows on the Wall" (1903). Through the death of their brother, the surviving siblings—three sisters (Emma, Rebecca, and Caroline) and one brother (Henry, a doctor)—obsess over what is to come next. However, a mysterious shadow, presumably a resonance of the departed Edward, lingers on in the study of their house. The existence of this shadow defies any manipulations of light or objects and infiltrates the fragile psyches of the siblings. Emma describes that shadow as "awful" despite making the obvious connection, thanks to Caroline's logic, to her deceased brother. Rebecca experiences a "frenzy of fear" (Freeman "Shadows" 257). In this light, Freeman's story can be seen as a forebearer of Virginia Woolf's first published story, "The Mark on the Wall" (1917). However, Henry dismisses the supernatural as he explains "there is no accounting for shadows" and that "a man is a fool to try to account for shadows" (259). Yet, Henry later falls prey to the classic Gothic trope of attempting to use reason and logic to explain the unexplainable. This would prove to be his downfall. After failing to devise any explanation for the shadow on the wall (and refusing to acknowledge that it has any connection to Edward, even though the shadow only appeared after his death), Henry gets called away on mysterious business. Three days pass—the same amount of time that the shadow has lingered after Edward's passing—and Caroline and Emma finally go back into the study, while Rebecca answers a ring at the front door of the house. As the two sisters discover that there are now two shadows in the study, Rebecca learns via delivered telegram that Henry has suddenly died. There is an interesting purpose to Freeman's story of apparition. Whereas Luella Miller stipulates the existence of the Other as something innocent and unexplainable, the shadows of Edward and, consequently, Henry, portray the Other as something inexplicable. They exist beyond comprehension.

M.R. James was known more for his medieval scholarship than for his fiction writing, but he demonstrates precisely what we mean by the term Speculative Modernist. His ghost stories, largely written to amuse himself and his colleagues, represent the Modernist movement in a surprising way. His ghosts, rather than recall that all of human history is but a ghost to the coming state of affairs, demonstrate that there is no anchor to the present as much as there is to the past. In some ways, James makes medievalism the perfect outcome of Modernism—a fact that would play out among the great fantasy writers of the early twentieth century, like J.R.R. Tolkien and C.S. Lewis.

James himself writes in the preface to his second collection of ghost stories, *More Ghost Stories of an Antiquary* (1911), that he sees two requirements in a modern ghost story: that they happen in mundane places to mundane people, and that their ghosts are terrible and monstrous rather than pleasant or helpful. He worries, in his preface, that he has foregone his authorly duties of creating what he calls a "psychical theory" for his ghosts (James *More*). His concern is that occultists seek to find a scientific reason for ghosts, to pin them down somehow to be dissected and studied. He warns that his stories are just that and nothing more. He even ties his work to the great stories of the previous century and assures us that they are mere Christmastime amusements (James *More*). However, S.T. Joshi, in his introduction to *Count Magnus and Other Ghost Stories* (2005), suggests that James's tales "generally set only a few decades prior to their date of writing, establish a continuity between past and present in which the present is entirely engulfed and rendered fleeting and ineffectual in the face of the heavy cultural burden of prior centuries" (Joshi Introduction *Count*). Readers also see this in the terrors presented by H.P. Lovecraft in "The Shadow Out of Time" (1936) where the past seeks not to haunt the present, but rather subdue it for colonization. James is not quite as direct as his successors will be, but perhaps his story "The Ash-Tree" (1904) conveys this weight most clearly.

The main story is straightforward: at a time in the distant past, a man who lived in a particular house condemned to death a local woman for being a witch. She dies promising vengeance, and sure enough the man is killed by some terrible poison that turns his body black. The room in which he slept is closed up for fifty years, until his grandson decides to sleep there, after making renovations to the house that include digging up the local woman's grave, which is found empty. He also dies in the same horrible way after a night in which he is kept awake by something scratching at the window. In the end, local men summoned to take down the ash tree near the window discover a family of enormous poisonous spiders with strangely familiar looking eyes, and the missing body of the declared witch. The story is clearly the old-fashioned sort with ties to the distant past, but what makes the story fit alongside the Speculative Modernists is the narrator of this story.

To begin with, the narrator describes these ancient houses that inhabit a particular region of England and talks about how they are generally the same: "I like the pictures, of course; and perhaps most of all I like fancying what life in such a house was when it was first built, and in the piping times of landlords' prosperity, and not least now, when, if money is not so plentiful, taste is more varied and life quite as interesting" (James "Ash-Tree"). He describes a time in which people, while much more superstitious, at least believed in something, and while he can't understand the witch-burning craze of the time, he appears to have some reverence for the time and the men who built these houses. This is reminiscent of Hawthorne as a nineteenth-century Gothic writer recreating the world of his Puritan forebearers a century earlier.

The narrator then clinically recites the history of one particular house and the tree that grows nearby. He lists each story as recounted in various documents citing very particular references as any good antiquarian should. When he gets to the police report of the first man's death, he reports another superstitious moment in which the coroner taken up by the strange death of the owner of the property, takes up a bible found on the man's nightstand and performs a ritual—which is related to the history of the Blessed Martyr King Charles, tying it to not only the history of the place, but to the history of the religion of the place. The coroner randomly opens the bible in three places creating a prophecy that seems to warn them of the spiders that live in the tree, an idea that is not obvious until the revelation at the end of the story. The narrator then reports that the sermon given at the man's funeral ties his death to the Popish plots of earlier days to overthrow good Anglican men. Again, the narrator points to the depth of belief these men have and how their beliefs helped to define their world.

As a preface to the second man's death, the narrator states, "Sir Richard was a pestilent innovator, it is certain. Before his time the Hall had been a fine block of the mellowest red brick; but Sir Richard had travelled in Italy and become infected with the Italian taste, and, having more money than his predecessors, he determined to leave an Italian palace where he had found an English house" (James "Ash-Tree"). While he never comes out and says that the new proprietor had a disregard for the history and custom of the place and the arrogance to throw all of that away in favor of a foreign ideal, it is clear that Sir Richard draws upon himself the vengeance not only of the deceased witch, but the ghosts of the history of that land and building. After choosing the accursed room to sleep in, he even performs the same ritual with the bible as a joke. When he opens the bible to "Thou shalt seek me in the morning, and I shall not be," Sir Richard mocks, "Well, well! Your grandfather would have made a fine omen of that, hey? No more prophets for me! They are all in a tale" (James "Ash-Tree"). He is found dead the next morning. Ultimately, the spiders provide a logical reason for the two horrifying deaths. Their poison is what did the men in, but after the tree is burned down and the spiders are all destroyed, they find the missing body, presumably of the old witch, who got her revenge in the end after all. The narrator's voice tells us so clinically about the horrible doings, as if it is merely something to be reported, and yet his details seem to keep with a wonder that has gone missing in the new century and the new ideas of men. Modern men don't believe in such things as witches, yet it is difficult to escape the narrator's immediacy of description without supernatural implication.

Similar to the reinvention of the ghost per James and others, the vampire also gets reimagined, even transcending the humanoid form so popular in the previous century. Casting the vampire as non-definable Other, Algernon Blackwood penned "The Transfer" in 1912, but his work as a Speculative Modernist was much more far reaching. None other than H.P. Lovecraft states in his essay "Supernatural Horror in Literature" that in Blackwood's work

> may be found some of the finest spectral literature of this or any age. Of the quality of Mr. Blackwood's genius there can be no dispute; for no one has even approached the skill, seriousness, and minute fidelity with which he records the overtones of strangeness in ordinary things and experiences, or the preternatural insight with which he builds up detail by detail the complete sensations and perceptions leading from reality into supernormal life or vision. Without notable command of the poetic witchery of mere words, he is the one absolute and unquestioned master of weird atmosphere; and can evoke what amounts almost to a story from a simple fragment of humourless psychological description. Above all others he understands how fully some sensitive minds dwell forever on the borderland of dream, and how relatively slight is the distinction betwixt those images formed from actual objects and those excited by the play of the imagination [Lovecraft "Supernatural" 1091].

Similar to Stoker's *Dracula*, Blackwood's capitalization on the association between vampirism and modern technologies is readily apparent in multiple texts with his inclusion of the newness of motor cars, photography, and the electricity inherent in living things. However, Blackwood's "vampire" is devoid of the good/evil paradigm. In fact, it is explicitly stated that Mr. Frene (senior), an implied social vampire (recalling Freeman's Luella), is portrayed as gregarious and charismatic, not predatory: "In the man's immediate neighborhood you felt his presence draining you; he took your ideas, your strength, your very words, and later used them for his own benefit and aggrandizement. Not evilly, of course; the man was good enough" (Blackwood 84). There is a threat from Mr. Frene, and everyone involved knows it. Yet, Frene is not the primary concern. In a unique twist, it is the forbidden corner of the estate that is responsible for the true uneasiness in the tale. The corner is barren of vegetation despite lush flora surrounding it. The gardeners dismiss the bald corner by means of sloping land and poor soil, yet it is responsible for a sinister feeling; the occasional dead animal or bird found on the spot doesn't help matters. Blackwood's dialogue among the narrator, the governess Miss Gould, and her charge Jamie reveals an emerging trope of Speculative Modernism—the implication that being different (or unknowable) is not tangential to something negative: "It's bad, Miss Gould," he told me. "But Jamie, nothing in Nature is bad—exactly; only different from the rest sometimes." (Blackwood 83) The last segment of Miss Gould's response is emblematic. "Different" is not necessarily "bad"—especially in regard to Nature. Likewise, ghosts, vampires, inexplicable phenomena are not *unnatural*—only unfamiliar to what we understand about Nature. Over and over again, characters attempt to understand the mysterious through conventional logic and reason. These efforts, time after time, prove fruitless. Yet, the unexplainable persists, and that is the core of these Speculative Modernist writers. They stabilize William Butler Yeats's center that cannot hold through the nonrational and unidentifiable.

In addition to providing readers with supernatural horror, Blackwood also offered up a bit of a solution, introducing readers to the character of John Silence in 1908. Capitalizing on the success of Sherlock Holmes in the late 1890s,[14] John Silence is a detective of the supernatural and his adventures consist of transfiguration, lycanthropy, Satanism, and elemental spirits. This is also true for William Hope Hodgson's ghost-finder detective, Carnacki (1910–1912). However, unlike Holmes, Silence and Carnacki do not always "solve" their mysteries with logic and science. Although these collections are short—five stories of Silence and nine of Carnacki—they portray not only the supernatural, but a sincere investigation of it. That investigation does not always reveal rational or explicable solutions. Silence and Carnacki demonstrate that the traditional understanding of the universe is quite limited.

While Blackwood and Hodgson are among the most renowned authors of the Speculative Modernists to locate the unknown not only in the corporeal, but in the topographic as well (as seen in the vampiric "barren spot" in "The Transfer"). More famous for her novels and feminist perspective (often mentioned alongside Gilman), Gertrude Atherton offered up the brief but haunting story "The Striding Place" in 1896. What is most remarkable in this story of the search for a missing companion in the borderland wilderness of a castle and the sinister oddity of the Strid, a geological crack of earth and water that became "the home of the eyeless things which had devoured all that had covered and filled that rattling symbol of man's mortality" (Atherton 235), is the declarative speech made by Gifford, the traveling companion to the protagonist, Weigall:

> "I cherish the theory," Gifford had said, "that the soul sometimes lingers in the body after death. During the madness, of course, it is an impotent prisoner, albeit a conscious one. Fancy its agony, and its horror! What more natural than that, when the life-spark goes out, the tortured soul should take possession of the vacant skull and triumph once more for a few hours while old friends look their last? It has had time to repent while compelled to crouch and behold the rest of its work, and it has shrived itself into a state of comparative purity. If I had my way, I should stay inside my bones until the coffin had gone into

its niche, that I might obviate for my poor old comrade the tragic impersonality of death. And I should like to see justice done to it, as it were—to see it lowered among its ancestors with the ceremony and solemnity that are its due. I am afraid that if I dissevered myself too quickly, I should yield to curiosity and hasten to investigate the mysteries of space" [234].

Gifford's philosophy epitomizes the attitudes of writers that delve into the "supernatural" entities at the turn of the century. There is something more than the mortal life we are accustomed to, and there is much that has yet to be explained by our science and rational, logical thought. As Gifford suggests above, we are inclined to agonize and be horrified over things that don't readily fit into the categories of our world.[15] However, there is also an undeniable appeal of those things as well, an odd comfort that humans—their existence, knowledge, technological advancements—are not the apex of existence. Nature has more in store. It is not terribly concerned with humanity.

At the same time as these tales of horror were being widely read, there were also stories that poked fun at the genre. Stephen Crane's "The Black Dog: A Night of Spectral Terror" was first published in *New-York Tribune* on July 24, 1892. Upon first reading the story, the familiar elements of a ghost story steam and bubble on the page. Travelers lost in the forest in a thundering downpour fear for their lives. They stumble upon a mysterious house and ask for shelter. The man inside talks about his unseen "ol' uncle, Jim Crocker" who is upstairs "sick ter death." The "slate-colored man" who owns the house speaks ominously about the black dog who will howl when his uncle is on the brink of death. That story is enough to spook the visitors, who react with bravado and skepticism to cover their fear. Sure enough, a "strange cry" arises in the tumult outside and the men bound up the stairs in terror to see if the black dog is coming for Uncle Crocker. They find the old man at death's door in the shabby upstairs room. Outside, they hear and then see the black dog howling. The slate-colored man resigns himself to his uncle's death, while the visitors become alarmed. One of them begins to throw things out the window at the dog who, mysteriously, just keeps howling ominously. Howling, that is, until the desperate man hurls the bowl of soup out the window. Only then does the spectral dog stop howling. Finally, the men work up the courage to look outside the window again. What they see is a hungry, abandoned dog hungrily lapping up the soup. So much for a ghost dog. By the end of the story, Uncle Crocker died and the dog had a decent meal.

"The Black Dog" features a realistic setting for human fears to run amok during a dark and stormy night. Although the story seems light and not worthy of close study, this and his other early tales show us a young Crane moving toward the themes that would characterize his later fiction.

According to Paul Sorrentino's biography on Crane, "Of particular note, however, is Crane's concern with what will become a hallmark of his writing: a blurring of lines between fact and fiction as he incorporated fact, folklore, and legend into his narrative" (137). Crane's early stories "reflect major forces that transformed American culture in the last part of the nineteenth century" (135).

In a letter to publishers Crane wrote in an attempt to get some of his early stories into print, he referred to them as "eight little grotesque tales of the woods which I wrote when I was clever" (Crane "Letters" 59). "The Black Dog" was among these eight, and this story shares the same parodic elements as the others in the collection. Crane takes elements from the Gothic and ghost story traditions and recasts them as ridiculous. In "The Black Dog," a reader encounters so many ominous elements that he cannot help but explode into laughter when the mundane ending is revealed. The four bumbling travelers who are lost at the start of the story populate the other stories, as well. As Stephen Solomon states in his book, *Stephen Crane from Parody to Realism*, they "constantly overrate the importance of natural events that take place in the woods" (2) so that everything they encounter, be it normal weather events, unexpected people, the howling of a hungry dog, and many other elements, seems supernaturally terrifying. Crane here is skewering the traditional stories about apparitions and other numinous spectral things that go bump in the night.[16]

Oscar Wilde's *The Picture of Dorian Gray* (1890) stands beside the phantasmic stories of Stevenson and Stoker as an undeniable classic and has transcended the general dismissal of such stories as mere popular whimsy. However, being the clever wit that he is, Wilde found a new audience with ghost story readers. In light of such attitudes, Wilde crafted "The Canterville Ghost" in 1887, three years before his blockbuster novel.

The story begins with an explicit self-awareness of the standards of the late Victorian ghost story and presents an excessively wealthy American family that is searching for the authenticity of old country (since the United States doesn't have a lengthy history) and an escape from the prioritized economics of urban life. They find it in an old castle for sale in England. The castle, however, is haunted by a ghost. Instead of being dismayed by such information, the Otis family is enthralled by the possibility of such an entity, instantly thinking of fame and fortune such an attraction would garner.

Indeed, the castle is inhabited by the ghost of Sir Simon de Canterville, an ancient ancestor who was starved to death inside the castle walls by his brothers. The ghost proceeds to make his presence known through mysterious blood stains, clanking chains, and howling sounds. Unfortunately for the ghost, none of these trappings engage the family as intended.

In a pointedly sarcastic reflection of American salesmanship and materialism, the sinister blood stain from Lady Eleanor de Canterville's murder can be removed by "Pinkerton's Champion Stain Remover and Paragon Detergent" (Wilde 195) and the horrible clanking of chains can be silenced by applying "Tammany Rising Sun Lubricating Oil," (197) as the pragmatist Mr. Otis recommends.

The twin boys from the Otis family take their flippancy even further, purposefully setting traps for and tormenting the ghost. Neither the twins, nor Mr. or Mrs. Otis are in any way frightened over the shenanigans of the Canterville Ghost. It is only Virginia, the fifteen-year-old daughter, that treats the ghost in any type of serious fashion, and it is through her that Wilde's story turns from an outright satire of the entire subgenre and into more of a sympathetic version of the classic Gothic form. Giving up the "responsibility" of terrifying the residents, the ghost begins to confide in Virginia, garnering our sympathies as well. The ghost resolves to finally (after three hundred years) sleep in the Garden of Death, but to do so, Virginia must weep for him so that the Angel of Death will have mercy on his soul. The true villains of the story are clearly the unworthy American parents and their disrespectful obnoxious twins. Virginia's love and forgiveness are the ghost's salvation.

One of the iconic writers within all three subgenres discussed (vampires, ghosts, and the unexplained) is American writer Ambrose Bierce. Arguably most known for his civil war story "An Occurrence at Owl Creek Bridge" (1890) and his satiric reference text *The Devil's Dictionary* (1906), Bierce was a regular contributor to speculative fiction during his short but extensive career.[17] In his introduction to the Bierce ghost story collection *Can Such Things Be?* (1893), prominent author and editor Clifton Fadiman aptly characterizes Bierce as bitter and uncompromisingly nihilistic. He argues that

> it is pertinent that Bierce, who disliked human beings and scoffed at social relationships, should have written so much and on the whole so well about ghosts, apparitions, revenants, were-dogs, animated machines, extra-sensory perception, and action at a distance. It is as though the man's inability to stomach the real world forced him to try to establish citizenship in the country of the occult. [...] Rather, must we think of his interest (not necessarily his belief) in the supernatural as part and parcel of his general misanthropy. He was so obsessed by the horror of real life that he had to call in the aid of another dimension in order to express it [11].

We indeed find a large degree of hopelessness in Bierce. Through his stories, it becomes rather evident that humanity is "out of our element." The world is not ours to control any longer. Yet, Bierce is not utterly fatalistic. Similar to the writers mentioned throughout this chapter, Bierce does not provide any answers or conclusions to the horrors we encounter in these tales. No other story of his captures this theory better than "The Damned Thing" (1893). For such a short and compressed tale, it is one of the most anthologized short stories of the horror genre, and one of the few Speculative Modernist narratives that has actually entered into the literary canon.

"The Damned Thing" is a mystery concerning the sudden death of Hugh Morgan. Eight men gather in an attempt to piece together the events that lead to and ultimately caused Morgan's death. These men include a coroner, local residents, and an eyewitness, William Harker. Relying on his own notes, Morgan's journal, a report submitted by him to the newspaper concerning Morgan's demise, Harker argues his theory about what actually killed his friend. In his recounting, Harker explains that he and Morgan encountered a phenomenon of sorts while quail hunting, labeling it "the Damned Thing"—an inexplicable and invisible force observed through the strange movement of wild oats, "as if stirred by a streak of wind, which not only bent [them], but pressed [them] down—crushed [them] so [they] did not rise" (Bierce "Damned" 142). In his account to the coroner and peers, Harker also offers his personal philosophies based on this experience: "We so rely upon the orderly operation of familiar natural laws that any seeming suspension of them is noted as a menace to our safety, a warning of unthinkable calamity" (143). Of course, these interjections are met with stern disapproval and dismissal akin to madness from the seven "jurors." The horror that Fadiman alludes to above is not in the Thing itself, but in his inability to explain it through rational or scientific means. What remains inexplicable and unidentifiable becomes uncontrollable, and ultimately challenges both intellect and ego. People would rather be wrong than admit that they don't know.

In his explanation of what transpired, he reasons that the Damned Thing is a creature invisible *to us*. He theorizes that there are "colors which we are unable to discern" and that the "human eye is an imperfect instrument; its range is but a few octaves of the real 'chromatic' scale. I am not mad; there are colors we cannot see [...] the Damned Thing is of such a color" (Bierce "Damned" 147). It is not, as Harker reasons, that the Damned Thing does not exist. Nor is it a matter of him being "mad." Instead, it is simply beyond our physical capacity to see it. Therefore, it does not exist (despite empirical evidence). Such closed-mindedness is the culmination of the human ego, and of our inherent egocentrism. According to the jurors (and even the coroner), there cannot possibly be anything that exists beyond our understanding. Such things are relegated to tricks of light or sleight of hand, as often seen in the fruitless attempts at explanation in strange tales. The closed-minded jurors fight against other alternatives with every fiber of being. However, that is exactly where the Speculative Modernists force their way into the consciousness of the era.

The question of consciousness is at the core of Bierce's micro-story "One Summer Night" (1893). In one of the more audacious beginnings since "Call me Ishmael," Bierce begins, "The fact that Henry Armstrong was buried did not seem to prove that he was dead: he had always been a hard man to convince" ("Summer" 36). Although this story is a quirky combination of Poe's "The Premature Burial" (1844)—a common motif for Poe—and Stevenson's "The Body Snatcher" (1884), Bierce's story is remarkable for its beginning. The idea that life and death can be willed attributes an immense power to human life, a power that we might not fully be aware of or understand. However, within our confines of understanding, this power remains out of our grasp. Such a concept would continue with Bierce's "Haïta the Shepherd" (1891). The story unfolds with a shepherd who is having difficulty maintaining his flock of sheep, and worries that he has offended his god, Hastur. Deep in melancholy, Haïta isolates himself from society. In his isolation, he encounters a beautiful but highly secretive maiden. All forms of contact with her are fleeting, and the reason for her seemingly random disappearances remain a mystery. Finally, Haïta encounters a hermit, who reveals that he knows the maiden's history:

> "My Son, I have attended to thy story, and I know the maiden. I have myself seen her, as have many. Know, then, that her name, which she would not even permit thee to inquire, is Happiness. Thou saidst the truth to her, that she is capricious for she imposeth conditions that man can not fulfill, and delinquency is punished by desertion. She cometh only when unsought, and will not be questioned" [Bierce "Haïta" 152].

The hermit then asks about Haïta's history with Happiness, and he confesses that he had only had her for a moment at a time before driving her away. The hermit concludes that "but for thine indiscretion, thou mightst have had her for two," indicating that happiness can never be more than fleeting. If Happiness (personified in the story) is so fickle, what does that leave Haïta (i.e., the reader) with? Perhaps, as Bierce and other Speculative Modernists suggest, there is more beyond the grasp of the intellect than is immediately apparent.

These Speculative Modernists found an audience ready to believe, to throw themselves into stories of the otherworldly Other. Arthur Machen was a well-known Welsh writer and mystic whose short story "The Bowmen" was first published in 1914 soon after World War I began. Machen, reportedly, was influenced by the events of the Battle of Mons, during which a greatly outnumbered British force inflicted huge casualties on the advancing German army, despite the unexpected retreat of French allies that exposed the British flank ("Battle"). Machen read accounts of the battle, one that proved to be much more difficult than the British public expected it would be, and he quickly wrote his story.[18] Six days after the battle, when Machen's story was published in London's *The Evening News*, it gained an instant wide readership. In fact, due to its narrative structure and first-person point of view, many readers of the newspaper mistook it for a news report and believed that the events of the story actually happened during that bloody battle on the border of France ("Battle"). There seemed to be an appetite on the part of the British reading public, at least in some quarters, to embrace the idea that supernatural forces would rally to the aid of the British military in their hour of need.

The story tells of the frightening advance of tens of thousands of German soldiers against the British line. The "heathen horde" (16) of "grey bodies" (15) came in wave after wave as the British troops ran low on ammunition and healthy soldiers to man the line. One soldier remembers some Latin from a vegetarian restaurant in London where he recently ate lentils that "pretended to be steak" (15). The Latin is an invocation to St. George, the patron saint of England, asking that the soldier-saint come to the aid of the English forces. The German hordes started dropping dead all over the battlefield: "'Look at those grey ... gentlemen, look at them! D'ye see them? They're not going down in dozens, nor in 'undreds; it's thousands, it is. Look! look! There's a regiment gone while I'm talking to ye'" (16). By the end of the story, the German commanders were making excuses, accusing the British of using chemical weapons against them because there were no wounds on their dead soldiers. However, the British soldiers—and the reading public—knew that it had been St. George leading the ghosts of the Agincourt bowmen, made famous by Shakespeare in *Henry V*. This dream team for England's glorious past made quick work of the German horde, and the public steeled themselves for a long and difficult war. Machen's ghosts are not complex creatures. They do not interact with the living, except to kill German soldiers who have already been dehumanized as a "grey advancing mass" (15) and "a grey world of men" (15). These ghosts are summoned by the living to carry out a task that concerns only the living. Even in death, they are still British soldiers with a duty to fight.

By the time Fascism was rising in Europe and the worldwide economic depression was in full swing, the old ideas about spirituality and the afterlife had been questioned by Speculative Modernists, some of whom achieved great fame and literary acclaim. Edith Wharton is best known for her stories of high society life in New York City near the turn of the century, with novels such as *The House of Mirth* (1905) and *The Age of Innocence* (1920). In addition to these novels which earned her literary immortality, she was a prolific short story writer. Some of her shorter works, notably the novella, *Ethan Frome* (1911), delved deeply into themes of repressed sexuality and the confinement of marriage. However, Wharton also cast her shadow into the realms of ghosts and the supernatural. As Catherine A. Lundie articulates, "Wharton's ghost stories, among the finest of her time, provide chilling investigations of gender roles and relations" as evidenced in "The Lady Maid's Bell," published in 1902 (27). However, the idea of physical and metaphysical transcendence is at the core of Wharton's famous short story "Afterward," first published in 1910. Continuing in the vein of self-awareness seen in Wilde's "The Canterville Ghost" and the secrets locked inside a domicile akin to Poe's "The Fall of the House of Usher" (1839), Wharton's ghost is the wronged Robert Elwell. The Boyle family is eager to settle into a life of leisure after a fortuitous (and nefarious) business deal. One of the great disappointments, however, is that they won't be exposed to a traditional ghost (something they were looking forward to), but that the Lyng Ghost—named after the estate—will only be understood after the fact of its involvement, not during. As Ned cries out in frustration, "'Life's too short for a ghost who can only be enjoyed in retrospect'" (Wharton "Afterward" 387). Once again, we see an acceptance of ghosts into the everyday. In fact, the ghosts aren't something to be feared, but sought after. However, it is only the thrill-seeking "new money" Americans that become ghosthunters, and the acquisitions of or encounters with ghosts become a sort of status symbol for them. The self-awareness of apparitions and the like is on full display in Wharton's text:

> It was the house itself, of course, that possessed the ghost-seeing faculty, that communed visually but secretly with its own past; if one could only get into close enough communion with the house, one might surprise its secret, and acquire the ghost-sight on one's own account. Perhaps, in his long hours in this very room, where she never trespassed till the afternoon, her husband had acquired it already, and was silently carrying about the weight of whatever it had revealed to him. Mary was too well versed in the code of the spectral world not to know that one could not talk about the ghosts one saw: to do so was almost as great a breach of taste as to name a lady in a club ["Afterward" 390].

Ghosts have become familiar to Wharton's Americans. The "code" that is referred to indicates an almost institutional knowledge, but per Modernist tendencies, those institutions become dismantled. Mary Boyle's efforts are frustrated despite her familiarity.

Mary Boyle finally learns of how her husband Ned came into the financial deal that allowed the family to move into the Lyng estate. She discovers that Elwell had subsequently died shortly after a botched suicide attempt due to financial ruin caused by Ned Boyle's closing of a local mine. The ghost of Robert Elwell finally absconds with Ned Boyle, leaving Mary to grasp the foreshadowed warnings from earlier in the narrative. Per the legend, the ghost is only realized after the fact, hence the title of the story. As Monika Elbert explains in her article "Mirrors, Sickrooms, and Dead Letters: Wharton's Thwarted Gothic Love Plots":

> Wharton dispels the myth of the Victorian model of Gothic womanhood in her ghost stories, which span the period between 1891 and 1937 and thus bridge the gaps between late Victorian, Realistic, and Modernist depictions of the Gothic heroine. There is no vestige of sentimentality left in Wharton's heroine by the end of her typical Gothic narrative: she is forced to encounter the rational within herself to decipher the madness around her, or she is made to look like a fool by the servant class [805].

Mary Boyle is left to her own devices, resigned to the doom that is to come as a result of the madness and chaos of her domestic role in marriage. She no longer has the structure of being a wife and now struggles with the anxieties over living as a widow.

Though the Modernists were generally known for their serious and bleak outlook on life, *Topper* by Thorne Smith, published in 1926, took quite a different turn with ghosts, injecting humor, albeit with quite a sarcastic bite, but humor nonetheless. In this novel (and its sequel, *Topper Takes a Trip*), ghosts serve a very different function from being remnants of things that were. In fact, their sole purpose seems to be to drive the living away from the dangerously humdrum existence they had created for themselves in the post–World-War-I world.

The plotline is fairly simple. Staid banker, Cosmo Topper, tired of his middle-class life and dyspeptic wife, buys a car that once belonged to a wild couple, George and Marian Kerby, and in so doing rouses the spirits of the former owners, who taunt him into having adventures. They are so bored in the afterlife that they have returned to try to drag poor Topper out of his miserable existence into one of excitement. Sure enough, his wife is humiliated by him, he loses his job, and is forced to flee his middle-class life. In the process, though Marian Kerby falls in love with her slightly plump refugee and tries to help him find his happiness.

While the novel is filled with hilarious adventures—an invisible woman drinking and driving high speed automobiles down quiet country roads, trying on newfangled undergarments, robbing department stores, and breaking into summer cottages while their owners are away—the book also reminds us of the trials of modern life. Though we are surrounded by wealth, good cheer, high adventures, and love, the world prefers to grind us down with commutes, nine-to-five work life, and Puritan fantasies of repression. The ghosts of those who broke the rules and defied society are doomed to watch as the repression grows ever more powerful.

Topper spends the whole first half of the book trying to keep himself from falling into the Kerby's web, and to keep himself believing that there was another life, if he'd just let go of the old one. He tries everything to explain away the craziness being followed around by ghosts who want to help him escape his miserable existence causes: "He had preferred to accustom his mind to the fact that he had gone mad, mildly mad, and, as he fervently hoped, temporarily so. The best way to combat this madness, he concluded, was to give in to it, to make no effort to regain sanity, but gradually to feel his way back to his normal state like a man delicately shaking a leg that had fallen asleep" (Smith *Topper* 32–33). The madness takes him, but he begins to enjoy it.

The Kerbys take bewildered Topper to the places where they loved to party, but are not there anymore. He felt a desire to break out of his humdrum life and live in their world, though it took him far from his own:

> Mr. Topper stood on the back veranda of the inn and gazed into the woods. A breeze, fresh and soothing, filled with a lonesome fragrance, brought peace and a strange excitement to his heart. He felt happy and almost young. He had forgotten about his stomach. It was as if he had withdrawn from his old life and was digging with his toes in new and magic soil. How unreal and far away Mrs. Topper seemed. How delightfully remote from him was everyone he knew [Smith *Topper* 55].

In the end, though, he realizes that the Kerbys lived and died in a world that never really existed. No escape from his normal life truly exists, because he is a creature of that world—missing his wife, missing his cat, missing his normal life. He crashes into the same tree that killed the Kerbys while escaping more misadventures but is saved by the incorporeal Marian Kerby breaking his fall. As he is taken away to the hospital, he realizes that a little of the Kerbys still lingers on with him. "In a little while, he would be leaving the hospital, going home, going back to the distractions and obligations of life, going back to desks, schedules, commutation tickets, legs of lamb and familiar eyes. But things would never be the same. Topper was sure of that. Life would never get him. He would use it differently now. He himself was a different man" (219). In this case the ghosts were not of what was. They were not demanding retribution or trying to fulfill things left undone. They were simply trying to break the humdrum world the twentieth century had created.

Conclusion

By the end of the nineteenth century, tales of ghosts and monsters were becoming more in demand—and readily available in the growing number of periodicals of the era—but also less and less original. During this time, Speculative Modernists breathed new life into Victorian apparitions that had grown stale. The intangible anxieties over the turn of the century and the very tangible ramifications of industry and war unlocked the doors to the unknown and unexplained, manifested in the imaginations of writers living on the fringes of the literary world. These writers reinvented the supernatural Other of the nineteenth century. Gone were the shackles of tradition and expectations. In their place emerged a unique, unidentifiable nonhuman entity that at times rings familiar with the past but offers new motivations and comprehension. At other times, the entity is entirely new, and we don't know what to make of it—much like the world of the initial decades of the twentieth century.

These manifestations modernized some of the archetypal monsters of the human imagination. Doppelgängers called attention to the duplicitous nature of *fin de siècle* culture transitioning out of stable cultural structures and into political, sexual, and technological upheaval. Vampires took on many different forms, ranging from horrid Gothic incarnations to voids of space that drain the vitality of everything around it, a sort of human black hole. Ghosts became familiar and even benevolent—so much so that they were at times even exploited for human gains. The unexplained forced us to put our own ego in perspective and gave a much larger context to what we thought we knew of the world around us.

As is the case with century marks in human history, the transition from the nineteenth century into the twentieth century is simultaneously an opportunity to look back and recall, but also to look forward and wonder. What has the world taught us, and how can that help us for today and tomorrow? Our previous chapter, "Utocalypse," addresses this question on a societal level. Speculative Modernists grasped the past, but didn't merely repeat it or regurgitate what was familiar. They let it churn inside them until they were ready to give birth to something more fitting of a new world. This new world, one that will be discussed in "This Island Earth," would struggle to comprehend meaning when everything known and relied upon turned meaningless and unstable. The house of cards was collapsing, and it was time to replace the deck. Sure, the new deck would have its familiar face cards. W.B. Yeats, T.S. Eliot, Gertrude Stein, and Ezra Pound weren't being replaced, but this new game would include wild cards: M.R. James, Thorne Smith, Arthur Machen, Mary E. Wilkins Freeman, and the like. These authors cast eerie shadows, both familiar and foreign, around every corner and every turn.

3

This Island Earth: Nature vs. Speculative Modernists

> You say nature is always nature, the sky is always the sky. But sit still and consider for one moment what sort of nature it was the Romans saw on the face of the earth, and what sort of heavens the medievals knew above them, and your sky will begin to crack like glass.
> —D.H. Lawrence, "Review of a Second Contemporary Verse Anthology" (1923)

The Romantic and Transcendental eras in literature exalted the role of the non-human[1] world in human affairs. The ills of early Industrialization, they argued, could be cured if only we moved out of the crowded and dirty cities, even for an afternoon, to merge with the pastoral world and to rediscover a less blighted, more authentic version of ourselves. Poets such as Wordsworth and Coleridge urged readers to abandon their cramped urban homes to find their true selves in the wilderness. These Romantics were hugely popular and influential during the first half of the 1800s, a time when populations in vast numbers moved from rural areas to cities, when children for the first time were growing up, in places where the non-human world was not the idyllic countryside that the Romantics championed. On the American side of the Atlantic, Transcendentalists such as Emerson and Thoreau were championing similar ideas:

> Our village life would stagnate if it were not for the unexplored forests and meadows which surround it. We need the tonic of wildness[....] At the same time that we are earnest to explore and learn all things, we require that all things be mysterious and unexplorable, that land and sea be indefinitely wild, unsurveyed and unfathomed by us because unfathomable. We can never have enough of nature [Thoreau *Walden* 557].

This late nineteenth-century generation's experience of the urban landscape combined with philosophical changes brought about by Darwin's idea caused a sharp break with the idealization of the natural world advocated by their parents and grandparents. Industrialization surprised and discomfited the generation that had seen their world change profoundly. The children of those Romantics had grown up in a world of both trees and smokestacks reaching skyward.

For them, the boundary between the human and non-human living world could not easily be described. The early literary Modernists began to equate the built environment with the non-human world, and the idea of nature as being wholly separate from humanity became a quaint notion from a bygone generation. The lines between man-made industry and nature blurred and distinctions became less clearly defined. Nicholas Daly argues that "modernism incorporates technological change as historical content ... and at times it self-consciously drew on the machine for aesthetic models" (Daly 404). Previous generations of writers looked to the non-human world for inspiration, while literary modernists, Daly asserts, looked at the world they had built for transcendent meaning. By the late nineteenth century and during the first few decades of the twentieth, humanity gained the ability to manipulate the environment in ways previously unthinkable; what had once been wild and mysterious was now there to be hacked, using the twenty-first-century term. Romanticism and Transcendentalism had run their course and no longer spoke to the experience of readers who lived during the Age of Steam, those for whom Thoreau's "unexplored forests and meadows" had been clear-cut, mined, built up into cities, or turned into landfills. Generations had lived off the land and by the skills of artisanship. No more. In the developed world, personal incomes were rising fast during the second half of the nineteenth century (Bairoch 95), and the possibilities for one's life expanded rapidly. A literary response was inevitable.

Scholars who study this era of speculative fiction have taken notice of this profound shift in the lived experience for the audience of American and British speculative fiction. In fact, it was during this era that a majority of these populations became urban and not rural. In about 1920, for example, the population of the United States became, for the first time, more than fifty percent urban, a number that was steadily and quickly rising (Greenfield). In the UK, "the greatest overall change in settlement was, in fact, the massive urbanization that accompanied Britain's early industrial development" ("Urban Settlement"). Not only that, but after World War I, once the demand for heavy industry to support the war effort dropped precipitously, population centers around mining towns dropped quickly in favor of the much more cosmopolitan London ("Urban Settlement"). As the lived experience of writers changed from the rural and non-human worlds to the built environment, their fiction changed, too. The most well-known utopian fiction of the late nineteenth century concerned itself with agrarian matters. Speculative Modernists embraced machines and the built environment as the new normal. The divorce from the countryside was quick and complete. In fact, as Brian Stableford notes in his entry on Ecology in *The Encyclopedia of Science Fiction* (1999), "[e]arly sf writers were often oblivious to the simplest matters of ecology" (Clute and Nicholls 365), ignoring even basic ideas such as carnivores need herbivores, and herbivores need plants. It is true that even in the agrarian utopias of the nineteenth century there was often a profound misunderstanding of natural systems and the interdependence of all species in life on Earth. Nevertheless, while there was a lack of understanding of the new field of "ecology" among early writers of Speculative Modernism, the tension between the non-human world and humanity's ability to impact that world became more and more of a central theme of speculative fiction as the twentieth century turned.

From about 1880 onward, Modernist writers broke away from their Romantic and Transcendental predecessors by stepping back from idealizing the non-human world in their writing. Whereas at an earlier point, writers drew sharp lines between the human experience and the much more authentic "natural" world, these early Modernists saw the boundaries between worlds blurring. Influential editor and artist Wyndham Lewis argued in "Manifesto" (1914) that the industrial era "has reared up steel trees where the green ones were lacking; has exploded in useful growths, and has found wilder intricacies than those of nature" (Lewis 36). Anne Raine makes the argument that "for both [Virginia] Woolf and [William Carlos] Williams, the goal of modernist innovation is not greater fidelity to nature [...] but rather a richer apprehension of human consciousness or the construction of aesthetic objects with their own autonomous life" (100). Writers used to go out into the world to find things to write about. In the Modernist era, what happened inside one's own mind sufficed as subject matter and the objects of the exterior world came to include written texts, as well.

Alfred North Whitehead was one of the most important thinkers on Mathematics, Philosophy, and Science during the Modernist era. Whitehead's interests ran wide and deep, and the historical perspective he provides about the state of science at the turn of the century is essential in understanding how Modernist ideas diverged from what had come before. In his book *The Concept of Nature* (1920), Whitehead argues that humanity's knowledge of nature—or what he calls "the machinery involved in the development of nature" (Whitehead *Science* 111)—is forever incomplete. There is just no way, given our meager tools and the immense complexity of the natural world, that we can grasp the totality of it. This throwing in the towel by a prominent natural philosopher is striking in light of the changes in social thought and in literary culture. Whereas the world once had made sense through religion or through science in the years since the Enlightenment, now, nothing connected conclusively. Nothing could be stated equivocally.

Whitehead became the most important figure in what became known as Process Philosophy. Whitehead argued that the material world as previously conceived is actually an innumerable series of interconnected processes. These processes might resemble discreet events or material objects, but things are not as they always have been or will be. They were something else and are on their way to becoming something entirely different. The universe is unstable; nothing is as it appears because our ability to grasp the universe is limited by our senses. Wordsworth's "natural" world, a place where humans can find communion with something permanent and true, just does not exist for Modernists like Whitehead: "The simple security of old, orthodox assumptions has vanished[....] The eighteenth century opened with the quiet confidence that at last nonsense had been got rid of. To-day, we are at the opposite pole of thought. Heaven knows what seeming nonsense may not to-morrow be demonstrated truth" (Whitehead *Science* 113–114). Modernist writers took the burgeoning ideas of the turn of the century and ran with them. If the subject is fundamental change in how people perceive the world and how they can learn the truths of things, what better writers than those in the genres of science fiction, fantasy, and horror to fully explore the ramifications of these fundamental changes? These genre writers projected their new ideas into every aspect of human endeavor. Farming, for example, had been from the beginning of agriculture a collaboration between humans and the natural world, but early Speculative Modernists saw new possibilities in mastery of the food-growing process. Improvements to food production became an important focus of some early Speculative Modernist fiction. It wasn't just agriculture. Every aspect of life to that point was in play, and genre writers explored all of it.

This chapter looks at how Speculative Modernist writers depicted humanity's changing relationship with the non-human world. The stories from this era generally fall into four categories. At the start of this era, there was much optimism that humanity could use the tools of science to "tame" the non-human world, to make the Earth better serve its human masters. The section "Science Will Bend Nature to Serve Humanity" explores this idea. The optimism of the utopians pushed up against the lived experience of the Industrialization Age of both writers and audiences at the turn of the century. The pendulum then swung in the other direction, and stories depicted a non-human world that is far, far more powerful than humanity ever could be; catastrophes await humanity at every turn. "There Are Things We Can Never Know" looks at the Speculative Modernist stories that emerged about the limits of humanity's ability to control the non-human world, how human ingenuity has its limits. In horror and fantasy, the message during the era is that no matter what humanity thinks about its ability to control the non-human world, nature will endure even beyond the human species, an idea discussed in the section titled "Beyond this Place and Time." Finally, in the section titled "Weaponizing Nature," the pessimism at the heart of Modernism reveals itself in stories about characters who use the tools of science, ideas that for a previous generation meant liberation and progress from the forces of the non-human world, for destructive purposes, sometimes on a large scale.

This chapter begins with the observation that for readers and writers of speculative fiction, possibilities for their world were shrinking quickly. Industrialization had reached an inflection point in the United Kingdom as, especially in London, living conditions for the working class were becoming intolerable. In the United States, frontiers were closing up one by one, and a typical American's relationship with the once wide-open spaces of the vast continent was changing rapidly. It is no wonder that writers of speculative fiction mixed their creativity into the brew of culture and philosophy and found themselves on the cresting wave of something new and strange.

Science Will Bend Nature to Serve Humanity: The Utopian Perspective

Speculative Modernists recognized the potential of the Industrial Age to remake humanity's relationships with the non-human world. Nineteenth-century utopians saw the possibilities for a new kind of agriculture, one based on science and the mastery of processes and forces that were once the realm of the wild world. *Mizora* (1880) by Mary E. Bradley Lane—a book called "the first feminist technological Utopia" (117) by the historian of American technology, Howard P. Segal—tells the story of the first woman in literature to reach the North Pole. Vera Zarovitch is a Russian princess who speaks her mind, and for that she is exiled to Siberia, where she expects to live out her days. Growing restless, Zarovitch leaps at the chance to escape on a ship going north, but the ship meets a disastrous end. Zarovitch is the sole survivor, and she is rescued by Arctic natives, who adopt her as one of their own. She works like any other member of the group, as a hunter, most notably, and finds some happiness there, but she continues to be restless and stocks a boat for a solo journey north, an idea her friends try to talk her out of. Nevertheless, she follows through on her plan, and, upon paddling to the North Pole, finds herself sucked into a vortex and down into a strange realm. There she meets amazingly beautiful women who inhabit a land called Mizora. This man-free world has used science to solve the problems of the outside world. More than a century after *Mizora* was published, it is clear that Lane's vision of a feminist utopia has some serious problems. The novel's solution for the post–Reconstruction America seems to be to eliminate anybody who is not Caucasian and blonde. Katherine Broad, in her article "Race, Reproduction, and the Failures of Feminism in Mary Bradley Lane's *Mizora*," takes on the many challenges this text presents. Broad concludes that "while Mizora is predominantly read as a feminist utopia, these two terms must be historicized to make visible the repressive foundations of Lane's ideal society and of the scholarship that celebrates Mizora as a progressive feminist text" (248). Despite the fact that *Mizora* is widely acknowledged as the first feminist utopia, this novel belongs here because it does not focus on economic systems or dazzling technology. Instead, this novel focuses on the Mizoran society's relationship to the earth and to ecology, with long discussions about food production and renewable energy.

The Preceptress, reacting in horror to the idea that there are still men in the outside world, argues that men and the problems they bring are a characteristic of the distant past, an era when women were subject to forces outside of their power, including the production of what the Mizorans label "adulterated food" (Lane 49). She summarizes the organizing philosophy of the Mizorans by asserting: "We are a people who have passed beyond the boundary of what was once called Natural Law. But, more correctly, we have become mistresses of Nature's peculiar processes. We influence or control them at will" (90). All manner of diseases had been prevented in Mizora by the cultivation of "perfect" foods. Zarovitch is taken on a tour of the grape arbors and flower gardens, all of which a thoroughgoing knowledge of science had transformed into powerhouses of managed agricultural productivity. In food production, the Mizorans use sophisticated technology and knowledge to remake their relationship with the natural world. They are after nothing less than a perfected version of agriculture, a method of producing foods in their original, unadulterated forms, a diet that helps give them the mental acuity necessary to make great advances in all fields of study:

> "Science discovered that mysterious and complicated diseases often had their origin in adulterated food. People suffered and died, ignorant of what produced their disease. The law, in the first place, rigidly enforced the marketing of clean and perfect fruit, and a wholesome quality of all other provisions. This was at first difficult to do, as in those ancient days, (I refer to a very remote period of our history) in order to make usurious profit, dealers adulterated all kinds

of food; often with poisonous substances. When every state took charge of its markets and provided free schools for cooking, progress took a rapid advance. Do you wonder at it? Reflect then. How could I force my mind into complete absorption of some new combination of chemicals, while the gastric juice in my stomach was battling with sour or adulterated food? Nature would compel me to pay some attention to the discomfort of my digestive organs, and it might happen at a time when I was on the verge of a revelation in science, which might be lost. You may think it an insignificant matter to speak of in connection with the grand enlightenment that we possess; but Nature herself is a mass of little things. Our bodies, strong and supple as they are, are nothing but a union of tiny cells. It is by the investigation of little things that we have reached the great ones" [49].

The more nineteenth-century agricultural industrialization remakes the production of food, the greater the risk that we will create unintended consequences. Indeed, the tension between innovation and danger runs through the descriptions of many of the utopian elements of the Mizoran society, and it is a conflict that Speculative Modernists would explore with much greater depth in future works.

The natural world, one that had been to this point in history deeply connected to human survival especially through agriculture, had been rendered less relevant by advances in science. No longer did pestilence, blight, and climate unpredictability cause the Mizoran civilization stress. No longer did farmers and food processors need to go to great lengths to cultivate and preserve their foods, thereby introducing poisons into one's diet. In fact, the Mizorans were attempting to establish processes that removed any trace of "earthly matter" (Lane 45). They were not there yet, but their goal was to somehow remove the idea that the earth participated in the growing of food, the conversion of the sun's energy into plant life. The Preceptress mixes frustration and optimism in her explanation of the current state of Mizoran food production: "But there is always more or less earthy matter in all food derived from cultivating the soil, and the laboratories are now striving to produce artificial fruit and vegetables that will satisfy the palate and be free from deleterious matter" (47). This contradiction is at the heart of the environmental philosophy advocated by the Mizorans. They'd like to think of themselves as mistresses of their world, as people not subject to the unpredictability of disease and disorder, but even their much-advanced science has not yet found a way to disentangle humans from the non-human world. No matter how they try, they are still tethered.

The final complication in the vision of Mizora as a utopia where the tension between unpredictable and unmastered non-human world impinges upon the idea that humanity can overcome disease and death comes at the end of the novel when the main character, for whom the world of men was oppressive and alienating, nevertheless chooses to return to it. She brings with her a Mizoran friend named Wauna, who exclaims:

> How grand [...] are the revelations of nature in your world! To look upon them, it seems to me, would broaden and deepen the mind with the very vastness of their splendor. Nature has been more bountiful to you than to Mizora. The day with its heart of fire, and the night with its pale beauty are grander than ours. They speak of vast and incomprehensible power [Lane 144].

The Mizorans are confident that their science and ingenuity will solve all of their problems; they are Modernists through and through. It is also clear that, in her return from Mizora, Zarovitch has realized that human knowledge and skill in manipulating the non-human world have an upper limit, one that does not come close to explaining everything, let alone curing all disease and triumphing over death. Wauna, bereft of Mizora and gradually losing the vitality of her homeland (akin to anxieties seen in Hawthorne's "Rappaccini's Daughter" from 1844), dies in Zarovitch's arms. As Wauna accepts her death, Zarovitch is left with bitterness. Speculative Modernists knew that science is a powerful tool, but humanity is, for better *and* worse, lashed tightly and permanently to the non-human world.

News from Nowhere (1890) by William Morris depicts a utopia where people thrive alongside the non-human world. Especially in their agricultural pursuits, the people of future England lived in harmony with the natural world. Their work was their life, and they loved farming. The pleasure they got from the non-human world growing their crops and raising livestock reflected their deep connection to the whole of the world:

> England was once a country of clearings amongst the woods and wastes, with a few towns interspersed, which were fortresses for the feudal army, markets for the folk, gathering places for the craftsmen. It then became a country of huge and foul workshops and fouler gambling-dens, surrounded by an ill-kept, poverty-stricken farm, pillaged by the masters of the workshops. It is now a garden, where nothing is wasted and nothing is spoilt, with the necessary dwellings, sheds, and workshops scattered up and down the country, all trim and neat and pretty. For, indeed, we should be too much ashamed of ourselves if we allowed the making of goods, even on a large scale, to carry with it the appearance, even, of desolation and misery [Morris 245].

In this novel, William Guest, the protagonist who journeys into England's future, recognized that the world was, indeed, changing. In Guest's reality, England was "foul," "fouler," "ill-kept," and "pillaged." He recognized that the state of Industrialization he saw all around him must be temporary if the pastoral and green England of his childhood were to ever return. In his novel, Morris imagines a brighter future where the tools of science, specifically, a mastery of agriculture, would bring long-term happiness and contentment to all of humanity. Morris was not alone in proposing a very different future, one filled with hope that the tools of science would help humanity return to simpler—and better—times.

The continuing belief that humanity's knowledge would soon counteract the perils of humanity's dependence on the natural world would soon backfire. As the industrial revolution destroyed nature more efficiently and at greater speed, mankind began to believe that it was winning a "war" against nature—a war that we are now paying for in the twenty-first century.[2] Clare Winger Harris recognized the cavalier attitude modern science had for the environment during the Industrial age. She recognized that man's arrogance in this war would eventually cost him more than he realized. In her "The Miracle of the Lily" published in *Amazing Stories* in 1928, Harris wrote about the decision to destroy all plant life on the planet in the wake of a sudden attack by a growing insect population. Science had already developed a means to create artificial nutrients for human sustenance and so plant life was merely a harbor for man's deadliest enemy: the insect. In the year 2900, mankind ends its agriculture, and launches an all-out war on nature. Only one scientist, Professor Fair, suggests that this might be harmful to man in the long run, but he is put down as a "sentimentalist" who would hold on to the useless past.

Nearly a generation passes, during which the insects put up a fight, learning to eat humans and each other, but in the end succumbing to man's superior fire (and poison) power. A descendant tells about the last insect's death, and a further descendant tells of what man has lost:

> As I read back through the diaries of my sentimental ancestors I find occasional glowing descriptions of the world that was; the world before the insects menaced human existence. Trees, plants and flowers brought delight into the lives of people as they wandered among them in vast open spaces, I am told, where the earth was soft beneath the feet, and flying creatures, called birds, sang among the greenery [Harris 130].

But in the wake of their victory over the insects, mankind has become mechanical and drab. There is no waste anymore: everything is converted into its constituent elements and turned into food. Thanor writes in 2938:

> Is it not conceivable that man could destroy himself through excessive development of his nervous system, and give place for the future evolution of a comparatively simple form of life, such as the insects were at man's height of development? This, it seems to me, was the great plan; a scheme with which man dared to interfere and for which he is now paying by the boredom of existence [132].

A thousand years pass in drudgery until a further descendant, Nathano, finds among his great ancestors' legacy a receptacle containing seeds from long ago. After several tries—first he has to figure out where to find soil!—Nathano manages to grow a lily that sparks a mild interest in the drabs the humans have become in agriculture. For ten years, this new obsession among a few helps to reawaken the human soul. This newly recharged human race comes just in time as communications with other planets has just begun as well, and the news from Venus is that they are about to be exterminated by their own plague of tiny creatures. When Earth and Venus do establish video communications, they find out to their horror that Venus's reigning inhabitants are giant insects plagued by tiny humanoids.

This vision of humanity plagued by boredom because science's efficiency causes all suffering to cease seems more like a fear of success than an ecological warning, though. Harris doesn't warn against destroying all plant life because with it goes the soul of humanity, but rather that without struggle men will become bored. A renewed war with the insects will be just what humanity needs after a thousand years of strifeless living. Perhaps nature is meant to be more than just a place where mankind struggles to find sustenance, but also serves as a foil for human arrogance. If nothing else, nature gives humanity something to fight against.

By this point, as armies massed in Europe and life in cities was becoming intolerable, such unbridled optimism about the human/non-human relationship was increasingly the exception in Speculative Modernism and not the rule. *Ralph 124C 41+* (1925) by Hugo Gernsback depicts a world that has been thoroughly mastered by human ingenuity and incredible advances in science. People are happy, more or less, and the source of their happiness seems to arise from the advances in technology that make their daily lives a breeze. The bulk of the novel takes place in New York City in the year 2660. There are no references throughout the novel to any part of the cityscape that has not been paved, mastered, sterilized, and crafted by human ingenuity.

A brief history of food production is offered in the sixth chapter, and it tells the story of humanity erasing the non-human world's limits of agriculture. Key to this passage is the twin ideas of progress brought about by the intellectual power of the human mind and the inevitable arc toward human perfectibility at the expense of the non-human world:

> When, about the year 2600, the population of the planet had increased tremendously and famines due to lack of such essentials as bread and potatoes had broken out in many parts of the world, it was found vitally necessary to produce such necessities on a larger scale and with unfailing regularity. These farms became known under the term of Accelerated Plant Growing Farms and were located in every part of the world. The first (and now obsolete) European and African farms were built along the lines of the old-fashioned hothouses. The European farms were simply horizontal steel-latticed roofs, with ordinary glass

panes, permitting the sunlight to penetrate to the soil beneath. While covering huge acreages, they were not heated artificially, using only the sun's rays to accelerate plant growth. As compared with Nature's single crop of wheat or corn, two could be made to grow in the same season by means of these super hothouses [Gernsback].

Gernsback does in this paragraph what he does so well throughout the novel: he sees what is in front of him in 1911 and projects it forward at a dizzying rate until humans have remade the world according to their needs and wants. No longer is agriculture limited by the cycles of the season, day and night, and climate. Farmers can grow whatever they want whenever they want and at whatever speed they like.

The novel can be read as an extended meditation on what it means when human interests push back against the imperatives of the non-human world. What are *Homo sapiens* if not a species of animal walking the Earth, subject to the same immutable laws of hunger, conflict, scarcity, and death as every other living species? If Ralph is battling these "truths," if he is looking for a way past the idea that humans are constrained to live and die in a manner governed by instinct and the limits of our fragile bodies, then this novel, indeed, becomes the story of humanity transcending their limits. Early in the novel, as Ralph attempts to raise a dog from the dead, he muses along a similar vein:

If the experiment succeeded it meant the prolongation of human life over greater periods of the earth's history than had ever been possible. It meant that premature death except through accident would be ended. Would he succeed? Had he attempted the impossible? Was he challenging Nature to a combat only to be worsted? These thoughts obtruded themselves into his consciousness as he began the preparations for the great test of the afternoon [Gernsback].

As Ralph recovers from his own bout of space sickness, he describes his battle for survival in these terms: "He felt that Nature herself was punishing him for his daring assault upon her dominions. He had presumed to set the laws of Life and Death at variance, and this was the penalty, this living death" (Gernsback). Finally, when Ralph succeeds in thwarting the plot of the bad guys and rescuing his love, the theme reaches its apotheosis. Gernsback is not talking about crops or dogs. He is talking about a human life, and if Ralph can battle and triumph against death itself, then his triumph over the non-human world will be complete. Alice has been severely injured in the late stages of the novel, and even the best surgeon on Earth is having difficulty keeping her alive. Ralph, although he is badly injured, as well, uses a tool of learning, the Hypnobioscope, as a last, desperate effort to reactivate her brain. As Ralph does so, Gernsback invokes a motif he has employed several times during the novel, that all of human history has been a largely successful attempt by humanity to subdue the non-human world: "It was the last trench in his desperate combat with Nature. It was the supreme effort. It was the last throw of the dice in the game between Science and Death, with a girl as the stakes" (Gernsback). The final chapter explains Gernsback's curious title for the novel. If you say the title aloud, then it could be read as "one to foresee for one another."

The point is not about whether Ralph can or even wishes to "foresee" for others. It is more than that. Ralph is making it his business to help humanity transcend the limits placed on it by what has always been accepted by humanity, that we are born to live and die in a manner similar to other mammals: that we need to eat, are governed by the seasons, and will inevitably die sooner or later. This novel puts all of those concerns into sharp focus. Gernsback's vision—racist, sexist, and elitist as it is—is profoundly optimistic. The tools of human ingenuity will lift our species beyond the limits of our bodies, our genetics, and our physical capabilities.[3] The role of nature is not a steadily evolving idea in Speculative Modernism. Some voices hearken back to the preindustrial natural world of their childhoods. While Speculative Modernists do not agree on the role of nature, it is clear that questions about the human ability to control nature preoccupied them. The question moves from what *can* be controlled to what *should* be controlled.

There Are Things We Can Never Know: The Purple Cloud and the Limits of Science

Speculative Modernists of this era depicted worlds that were so far beyond the mastery of humans that there was simply no hope for humanity to fight back or even to survive if something went unexpectedly wrong with the climate or some other aspect of the human habitat. *After London*, the 1885 novel by Richard Jefferies that is introduced in our chapter "Utocalypse," depicts England in the years following an undefined natural catastrophe. It is clear that sea levels have risen drastically and human population has been reduced to almost nothing. The non-human world quickly reasserts itself by reclaiming what had once been cultivated; nature is at odds with human civilization; human works are rank and diseased; they do not survive on their own at all. On the other hand, the environmental scar left by the city of London has not healed even after several generations:

> Glancing behind him he perceived that the faint yellow mist had closed in and now encircled him. It came with two or three hundred yards, and was not affected by the wind, rough as it was. Quite suddenly he noticed that the water on which the canoe floated was black. The wavelets which rolled alongside

were black, and the slight spray that occasionally flew on board was black, and stained the side of the vessel. This greatly astonished and almost shocked him; it was so opposite and contrary to all his ideas about the Lake, the very mirror of purity. He leant over, and dipped up a little in the palm of his hand; it did not appear black in such a small quantity, it seemed a rusty brown, but he became aware of an offensive odour. The odour clung to his hand, and he could not remove it, to his great disgust. It was like nothing he had ever smelt before, and not in the least like the vapour of marshes [Jefferies 365–66].

The Earth is left to recover once human civilization has been erased. Jefferies's environmental awareness is strong; the idea that humanity is just one small strand in the web of life on Earth is one of the central themes of this novel pertinent to Speculative Modernism.[4] Like any other single species, if it goes away, other species will rise in its place to fill the niche in the ecosystem. Interestingly, the term "ecosystem" was not coined until roughly fifty years after Jefferies depicted the interlocking dependencies of life in England ("ecosystem").

M.P. Shiel's *The Purple Cloud* (1901) has been hailed as one of the great "last man" stories and has been cited as an influence by writers such as H.G. Wells and Stephen King. The novel tells the story of the last man on Earth, Adam Jeffson. When all of humanity is destroyed by the title catastrophe, Jeffson must contend to find a life's purpose in a world that seems to have been stripped of all meaning. He looks for salvation in all of advanced civilization's former institutions: banks, in communities, at home, in churches, in centers of government, and in other places, as well. Wherever he looks, he exposes these as temporary and impotent.

In conducting his search not only for other survivors but also for some meaning in this world without humanity, Jeffson nevertheless uses the final and most important tool in civilized humanity's toolbox, the scientific method.[5] He probes and tests each step along the way. He searches for truth using the best tool he knows about. The most profound question that motivates Jeffson as he travels the empty world looking for another survivor is what exactly happened to the world. What exactly killed everyone? It is not that it will make much of a difference to Jeffson. His pessimism and lack of hope have made him unable to think of a way forward out of despair.

The Purple Cloud can be read as a novel in which Shiel tests every possible institution of society and finds it lacking the permanence and objective meaning it had long asserted. Indeed, Jeffson finds a world in which everything means nothing in particular. He discovers this by using the one remaining reliable tool in his toolbox: the scientific method. The one question he cannot answer is, perhaps, the most pressing. He was driven to understand the cause of the extinction of humanity. His reliance on the scientific method gets him only part of the way toward an answer. He is able to learn what the toxin was not, but by the end of his search he feels as if he is no closer to an answer. Even the scientific method, the foundation of knowledge in the Western world for centuries, fails him, just as every other human institution did. Nevertheless, Jeffson's curiosity pushes him forward as he searches for clues, and his faith in the scientific method is unwavering throughout the first half of the novel.

As readers, we are also curious. Shiel seems to have had something specific in mind for this airborne toxin, some particular chemical. Throughout the novel, he provides many clues to the exact nature of the toxin. Although he never comes out and specifies the chemical process that killed all life, there may be enough clues here to make a good guess.[6] Jeffson is a man of science, not a scientist, but a firm believer in the scientific method. He is an educated man who has the tools and outlook to solve problems with skill and confidence. Shiel's world was filled with people like Jeffson. Indeed, Victorian society was built upon the idea that the world was knowable and nature could be mastered.[7] While Jeffson easily puts aside his faith in human institutions such as religion, love, politics, commerce, technology, and a host of other concerns of civilized world, he takes great pains to test the scientific method, the cornerstone of Enlightenment thinking and the foundation of all scientific inquiry.

By the end of the novel, despite all of Jeffson's skill in solving problems using the scientific method, he has come to the conclusion that there are definite limits to what even science can know. He grudgingly embraces a different way of knowing, one that is incompatible with the scientific method. By the end of *The Purple Cloud*, nothing remains of civilization. It is as if Jeffson has tested it all and found it wanting. In its place, Jeffson must, from the ground up, rebuild a new way for human civilization to organize itself. Shiel is one of the first Speculative Modernists to do it, and others followed his lead in later years in depicting the destruction of social and cultural institutions held sacred by British and American society.

Shiel is not the only early Speculative Modernist to destroy, or at least threaten extinction for, humanity. H.G. Wells did so several times, both in the present day in *The War of the Worlds* (1898) and in the distant future *The Time Machine* (1895). In both of those cases, the cause of the apocalypse was clear and unambiguous. Before the Modernist era, Jean-Baptiste Cousin de Grainville took his readers to the distant future where humans have become infertile and die out in his novel, *La Dernier Homme* (1805). Mary Shelley killed everyone with a plague in *The Last Man* (1826). Edgar Allan Poe waded into apocalyptic waters by crashing a comet into the Earth that removed all nitrogen from the atmosphere and thus caused a worldwide inferno in his short story "The Conversation of Eiros and Charmion" (1839). These stories were notable in that they posited familiar causes for the end of humanity. They gave us epidemics we already knew well. There was no real mystery to them because science, even at the time, understood them well. In Shiel's time, there was no shortage of catastrophe stories, a point illustrated by Roberta Scott and John Thiem, whose article on catastrophe fiction, including an annotated bibliography, is illuminating (Scott and Thiem). In it, they argue that "writers use the spectacle of modern civilizations undergoing the ordeal of destruction and its aftermath as a means of examining the strengths and fatal weaknesses of these civilizations" (Scott and Thiem 156). What distinguishes Shiel's end time is that the environment of the Earth goes haywire for seemingly no good reason, other than the dreamlike depiction of a volcanic eruption in the South Pacific. That makes Shiel's work align much more naturally with other early Speculative Modernists such as Richard Jefferies, whose masterwork *After London* wrecks the Earth's climate with no explanation or even speculation.

When it comes to Jeffson's investigation of the composition of the purple cloud, Shiel's deviation from hard and reliable science into baffling mystery is part of the point. The scientific method fails Jeffson just as every other institution of human civilization has. The inescapable conclusion in this case is that Shiel freighted his descriptions of the noxious gas in *The Purple Cloud* with enough science to make this particular apocalypse seem plausible. However, there is nothing known to our science even today that would act on a human population like the toxic nightmare did in *The Purple Cloud*. Like the Speculative Modernist that he was, Shiel did not feel compelled to wrap this story up in a neat little bow. The mystery at the heart of the novel persists. Was it a natural, chemical event? Was it a man-made chemical weapon? An experiment gone haywire? Or did it have a supernatural cause? There are no answers in the book.

If humanity does need a complete reset and if *The Purple Cloud* does end with a new Eve and Adam, then the novel reads hopefully. Ailise Bulfin, in the article "'One-planet-one-inhabitant': Mass Extermination as Progress in M.P. Shiel's *The Purple Cloud*," argues that this novel portrays an "idiosyncratic and extreme" (Bulfin "One" 1) vision of human progress. Her paper places the novel into its historical moment, a time characterized by the application of Darwin's ideas to the extermination of "inferior" races. She chronicles the intersection of colonial brutality with natural events such as epidemics and famine to show that Shiel's novel was part of the conversation about how superior races should have access to the entirety of the Earth by allowing or accelerating the extinction of "brutes" (Bulfin "One" 3). Bulfin's assertion is compelling, and the historical context she provides is fascinating, but the problem with this reading is that Jeffson, if he is the new Adam as Bulfin sees him, shows no signs of having the ability to do anything other than replicate what had come before. Given several generations, Jeffson's offspring might find itself right back where they started on an Earth teeming with injustice and "brutes" who are unfit to survive. Bulfin does not go far enough. Humanity does not die completely. Jeffson still draws breath. It is not the physical survival of humanity—or, more specifically, British imperial culture—that is at stake by the end of the novel. Jeffson survives, yes, but every idea he held about the world and truth has been undone. He and his descendants have been stripped of all but his biology. Even the way he ascertains knowledge about the world must undergo a fundamental change.

The Purple Cloud, therefore, is one of the foundational works of Speculative Modernism. It predates canonical Modernists by decades, and yet it does what they did who were hailed as visionaries. Once Jeffson is finished with his search for meaning in the world, every institution humanity had relied upon has been shattered. This novel perfectly illustrates the Speculative Modernist idea that the world around us is inherently unknowable. It stands in stark contrast to the utopians and even to catastrophe fiction writers who showed us floods, asteroids, and all manner of natural disasters. Those extinction-level events were understandable. Shiel's cloud, despite the best effort of a well-educated investigator, remains forever unknowable. Human ingenuity and resourcefulness has their limits. Shiel at least partly echoes Wells in *War of the Worlds* in that humanity's ability to master our world is incomplete and finite, and those gaps might cause us to be unable to react in time to avert annihilation.

Beyond This Place and Time: The Natural World Will Outlast Us

In 1859 Charles Darwin proposed a system of biological evolution, that the success of a species is based on its ability to adapt, and the world was altered permanently. This groundbreaking idea displaced humanity from the center of the universe, and writers of the years that followed imagined worlds that existed before mankind and ones that would continue after its end. Some of these writers gained critical acceptance, such as the poet, Gerard Manley Hopkins. Perhaps his most well-known poem, "God's Grandeur" (1887), speaks to this very idea:

> Generations [of man] have trod, trod, trod
> And all is seared with trade; bleared, smeared with toil
> And wears man's smudge and shares man's smell: the soil
> Is bare now, nor can foot feel, being sod.
>
> And for all this, nature is never spent; [199].

3. This Island Earth

Although Hopkins concludes his poem with the idea that the Holy Ghost will shine down on the world—thus playing counterpart to a godless world—that world will nonetheless continue after humanity has done its damage and expired. Speculative Modernists took up this theme and ran with it.

Just shy of the century's turn, H.G. Wells published *The Time Machine* (1895), one of the rare texts of speculative fiction that has become part of the literary canon. As such, there has been an extensive amount of analysis devoted to this foundational text,[8] but much of it has to do with the Time Traveller's theories on social and physiological devolution of the human species and the plausibility of its science. However, Wells's novella also contributes to the utopia/dystopia works of the late nineteenth century—and is an early entry in the "dying earth" themes of other Speculative Modernists—in providing a vision of a world that continues beyond humanity as it is today. According to *The Time Machine*, humanity is just one stop along the evolutionary path of nature. The human species will inevitably decline and disappear, but life will continue.

When the Time Traveller discovers the anthropoid life-forms of the Eloi and Morlocks in 802,701, he surmises that these species are descendants of humans. These "subspecies," he believes, are the result of achieving a human utopia and consequently losing our abilities, both physical and intellectual, due to lack of need:

> It is a law of nature we overlook, that intellectual versatility is the compensation for change, danger, and trouble. An animal perfectly in harmony with its environment is a perfect mechanism. Nature never appeals to intelligence until habit and instinct are useless. There is no intelligence when there is no change and no need of change. Only those animals partake of intelligence that have to meet a huge variety of needs and dangers.
>
> So, as I see it, the Upper-world man [Eloi] had drifted towards his feeble prettiness, and the Under-world [Morlocks] to mere mechanical perfection—absolute permanency [Wells *Time* 141–42].

It seems as though humanity had achieved perfection and devolved into the Eloi and Morlocks as a result of lack of competition or danger, although that idea might be in conflict with the existence of the predatory owl observed by the Time Traveller during his first days in the year 802,701. Here, the Time Traveller is rife with assumptions and apparently abandons scientific method through observation in favor of moral and social hyperbole. He casts humanity into a moral and social binary, and virtually neglects all other possible explanations (and life-forms).

Once he escapes the Morlocks, whom he "longed very much to kill" (Wells *Time* 130), the Time Traveller comes across what many critics assume to be a further devolution of the Eloi and Morlocks in the form of a "huge white butterfly" (145) and "monstrous crab-like creatures" (146), respectively, in the even more distant future. Not surprisingly, he cast them into the moral parallel he used before. His description of the crabs with "evil eyes" (146) is not very objective. This criticism can be explained by the layered narrative of the text, as many scholars have documented.

Once again escaping the horrors of devolution the Time Traveller presses forth into a future devoid of any remnant of crustacea or poisonous lichen, to a time of snow and desolation, progressing toward a red sun and an impending eclipse:

> A horror of this great darkness came on me. The cold, that smote to my marrow, and the pain I felt in breathing overcame me. I shivered, and a deadly nausea seized me. Then like a red-hot bow in the sky appeared the edge of the sun. I got off the machine to recover myself. I felt giddy and incapable of facing the return journey. As I stood sick and confused I saw again the moving thing upon the shoal [earlier dismissed as a rock] there was no mistake now that it was a moving thing—against the red water of the sea. It was a round thing, the size of a football perhaps, or, it may be, bigger, and tentacles trailed down from it; it seemed black against the weltering blood-red water, and it was hopping fitfully about [Wells *Time* 148].

Despite the glowing red sun and the climactic change experienced by the Time Traveller, this passage only seems to indicate the continuation of life and a turn in evolution. It can be argued that this hopping tentacled mass is not merely a recall back to the emergence of life from the oceans via Darwinian chronology, but a different trajectory altogether due to the level of intelligence found in cephalopods. Perhaps the experiment of humanity has failed, and—per Darwinian theory—the lichens, crustacea, and cephalopod biology has proven more adaptable to changing environmental conditions. According to the Time Traveller's theory, our quest for utopia has doomed humanity and our intellect had become an Achilles' heel.

In other voyages to the far future, William Hope Hodgson dreams of the end of the world in both *The House on the Borderland* (1908) and in *The Night Land* (1912). These are both stories about the end of existence, but, in the process of becoming extinct, individual humans somehow find the fulfillment of love. In *The House on the Borderland,* his main character wrestles first with demon creatures in his cellar, but in the second section of the book he witnesses the heat death of the solar system before returning home to be irretrievably lost to the demon creatures he was battling in the first section. This interlude focuses on the theories of William Thomson (known better for his discovery of "absolute zero" and as Lord Kelvin), who believed that the universe would continue to expand forever until there was not one particle within millions of miles of another. The authoritative biography of Lord Kelvin was published by Harold and Tiby Sharlin in 1990. They describe how Kelvin explored ideas about what he called "the heat death of the universe":

> I believe the tendency in the material world is for motion to become diffused, and that as a whole the reverse of concentration is gradually going on—I believe that no physical action can ever restore the heat emitted from the Sun, and that this source is not inexhaustible; also that the motions of the Earth and other planets are losing vis viva which is converted into heat; and that although some vis viva may be restored for instance to the earth by heat received from the sun, or by other means, that the loss cannot be precisely compensated and I think it probable that it is under-compensated [Sharlin 112].

Ideas such as Kelvin's were likely not far from Hodgson's mind and drove his thinking about the distant future, one version of which appears in *The House on the Borderland*.

The scene begins in his room after a particularly difficult day with the creatures from the pit below his house. He awakens to the whirring of his clock and the sudden onrush of day and then, just as quickly, night. At first, he is fascinated by the swift rising and setting of the sun and the quick passage of the seasons, but then he is horrified to discover that his beloved dog, Pepper, suffers the passage of time along with the world around him, while he remains an observer. When he discovers himself detached from his own dead and rapidly decaying body, he feels a sudden calmness and returns to his observations of the outside world. The sun dims and the earth slows in its progress, until our sun is consumed by the Green Star, which is, in turn, eclipsed by a Dead Sun at the center of the galaxy, or perhaps the universe:

> The huge bulk of the sun, rose high above me. The distance between it and the earth, grew rapidly less. Suddenly, the earth appeared to shoot forward. In a moment it had traversed the space between it and the sun. I heard no sound; but, out from the sun's face, gushed an ever growing tongue of dazzling flame. It *seemed* to leap, almost to the distant Green Sun—shearing through the emerald light, a very cataract of blinding fire. It reached its limit, and sank; and, on the sun, glowed a vast splash of burning white—the grave of the earth [Hodgson *House* 105].

With the earth disposed of, the sun would come next devoured by the Green Sun, which will later be consumed by the great Central Suns, which make up the Dark Nebula. In turn, each part of the immense galaxy is consumed by an even greater, darker, and more dead part of the universe. Hodgson uses this as a metaphor for love lost, and the ever-widening gulf between people—an apt metaphor for the Speculative Modernist period. Hodgson's vision of floating aimlessly through time and space as every object in the universe is slowly destroyed before his very eyes. The main character is snapped back to his own time after an encounter with a lost love one somewhere out beyond the edge of the universe at the end of time. Nothing is left; the universe has disintegrated, yet he encounters his love.

The Night Land has a similar theme: a roughly contemporary man falls in love with a woman who dies in childbirth, and his soul searches for her in the recesses of time during his dreams. At night, in his dreams, he discovers that he is a member of the last human outpost, an establishment doomed to fall to the creatures that live outside the protective sphere, which is currently failing. When he hears about a woman, whom the main character is sure is his departed wife from this previous lifetime, who needs his help, he runs to the outer limits of the protected area so that he can die in her arms. The world that Hodgson created here would inspire many generations of science fiction writers and their depictions of the last human outposts:

> And then, so it would seem, as that Eternal Night lengthened itself upon the world, the power of terror grew and strengthened. And fresh and great monsters developed and bred out of all space and Outward Dimensions, attracted, even as it might be Infernal sharks, by that lonely and mighty hill of humanity, facing at its end—so near to the Eternal, and yet so far deferred in the minds and to the senses of those humans. And thus hath it been ever [Hodgson *Night* 28–29].

The world has gone dark for two reasons: the sun itself has burned all of its own fuel, but still hangs there seemingly with its same density and gravitational pull, and tidal drag has slowed the earth's spin causing it—like Mercury—to have a face that always points toward the sun and one that always points away. In this far future, all that protects the last vestiges of humanity on a dying world is a great Earth-Current that acts as a barrier to all the monsters that lie outside of the Great Redoubt where the last humans live. But that Earth-Current grows weaker every year and as a result, the last outposts of human existence must all withdraw to the last home of the humans. Our hero, in his nightly dreams must rescue his true love from one of these outposts before the monsters can push through the last of the Earth-Current.

In both of these scenarios, the ending of the world—though monumental—plays out as metaphor for a man's own loneliness. The solitary life, empty of authentic connections to others, is a Modernist literary trope that was explored by T.S. Eliot in "The Love Song of J. Alfred Prufrock" (1915), in the character of Septimus Smith from *Mrs. Dalloway* (1925) by Virginia Woolf, and many others. The thought of a cold and callous universe that will simply one day fail us mirrors the end of a human life: no God or eternity is waiting beyond it. Yet, love, or perhaps the memory of love, provides some kind of reason to continue on to that distant point in time. Clark Ashton Smith gives us a glimpse at this deadened world, waiting for its own end, too, in his Zothique stories. The land of Zothique is all that is left of the Middle East and northeastern Africa. As Smith writes in "The Empire of the Necromancers" (1932), the first of the Zothique stories,

> Before the time of its telling, many epochs shall have passed away, and the seas shall have fallen in their beds, and new continents shall have come to birth. Perhaps, in that day, it will serve to beguile for a little the black weariness of a dying race, grown hopeless of all but oblivion. I tell the tale as men shall tell it in Zothique, the last continent, beneath a dim sun and sad heavens where the stars come out in terrible brightness before eventide [Smith "Empire" 315].

The failing world again reflects failing mankind and the hopelessness of an age. In the stories, men are driven back to primal magic and brutality, reverting into savagery, all due to the cold universe allowing a once great people to wither and die. Smith's stories are complex visions of this future realm under a dying star. They are full of regrets and misgivings, failed attempts at bettering one's life and cruel necromancers that fight for useless power in a desolate world. Always, though, there is Zothique—the last bit of land to remain above the oceans after the polar caps have melted away and everything is heated in the red star's light—that remains as the main character of the stories, haunting all of the other players and ruining their lives. Like the Green Star in Hodgson's *The House on the Borderland*, Zothique's star lies waiting for the passage of these pointless humans so that it can fulfill its death throes and rejoin the silent cold universe.

H.P. Lovecraft uses the landscape on occasion to act as a subtle reminder that mankind is not the only inhabitant of the Earth and that other beings await their turn at mastery of this tiny ball of dust alone in the depths of space. At the beginning of "The Dunwich Horror" (1928), Lovecraft allows us to imagine approaching the town of Dunwich:

> The trees of the frequent forest belts seem too large, and the wild weeds, brambles, and grasses attain a luxuriance not often found in settled regions. At the same time the planted fields appear singularly few and barren; while the sparsely scattered houses wear a surprisingly uniform aspect of age, squalor, and dilapidation. [...] When the road dips again there are stretches of marshland that one instinctively dislikes, and indeed almost fears at evening when unseen whip-poorwills chatter and the fireflies come out in abnormal profusion to dance to the raucous, creepily insistent rhythms of stridently piping bull-frogs[....] Once across, it is hard to prevent the impression of a faint, malign odour about the village street, as of the massed mould and decay of centuries. It is always a relief to get clear of the place, and to follow the narrow road around the base of the hills and across the level country beyond till it rejoins the Aylesbury pike [Lovecraft "Dunwich" 633–634].

Lovecraft sets his story of extra-dimensional beings and satanic rituals in this strange wasteland, and there is always the sense that the land itself is waiting for the human race to abandon its assault upon the land in the form of cultivation and tired ramshackle houses. In one of the unusually peaceful death scenes in the story, that of old Wizard Whateley, those whippoorwills chant in time to the old man's breathing as if waiting to catch his soul as it tries to fly by them. The old man even tells us that we will know if he escaped their clutches by their reactions after he breathes his last. "Yew'll know, boys, arter I'm gone, whether they git me er not. Ef they dew, they'll keep up a singin' an' laffin' till break o' day. Ef they dun't they'll kinder quiet daown like. I expeck them an' the souls they hunts fer hev some pretty tough tussles sometimes" (Lovecraft "Dunwich" 642).

In a place where the birds are just waiting for men's souls to leave their bodies, one cannot be unaware of the fact that Earth was here before mankind, and it'll be here long after as well. The idea did not originate with Lovecraft. Various versions of this were in the air at the time he was writing "The Dunwich Horror." American writer and influential environmentalist, John Muir, said it this way in 1916:

> This star, our own good earth, made many a successful journey around the heavens ere man was made, and whole kingdoms of creatures enjoyed existence and returned to dust ere man appeared to claim them. After human beings have also played their part in Creation's plan, they too may disappear without any general burning or extraordinary commotion whatever [Muir 140].

In all of the stories in this chapter, human life—bereft of God and romantic notions of an afterlife in this new Modernist era—is tied to a mortal universe. Perhaps *Homo sapiens* has an expiration date. Perhaps the entire universe does, as well. Whatever the case, stories about the ends of things—what came to be known as catastrophe fiction, or ideas about the heat death of the universe, or stories about the death of a single, alienated individual—became staples of Speculative Modernism.

Weaponizing Nature: Understanding the Non-Human World in Order to Destroy It

Speculative Modernists who came later, especially those intimately familiar with the gruesome reality of World War I, imagined humanity's worst impulses taking hold of these tools to wreak havoc on the non-human world. While humanity cannot know the universe in its entirety, we can develop tools to gain some mastery over our environment. Utopians imagined human ingenuity being used for the good of all. Speculative Modernists were less optimistic. They imagined the evil that humans were capable of being magnified by technology. This theme reached its apex at the dropping of the atomic bomb, but it had its foreshadowing in the late nineteenth and early twentieth centuries.

Robert Cromie's novel *The Crack of Doom* (1895) was his best-selling and most enduring work. Researcher and historian Bridget Hourican argues that it contains literature's first depiction of what plausibly might be an atomic explosion (Hourican). The protagonist is a man named Arthur Marcel, who stumbles upon and then joins a suicide cult comprised of gentlemen and ladies devoted to science. Instead of their own personal suicides, however, this group decides that the entire material universe is a mistake, that the Earth and all we know is nothing but an "etheric tumour" (Cromie 49). The material of the universe was best left uniformly simple, composed of ether and nothing more. When matter erupted from the nothingness, that is when the mistake happened. Herbert Brande, the leader of this cult, advocates nothing less that the re-etherization of all of the matter of the universe.

Brande first appears on a passenger ship that is crossing the Atlantic. He has time during the voyage from New York to Ireland to engage his fellow passengers on matters scientific, some of which are shocking. His casual announcement that "the universe is a mistake" (Cromie 1) for example, is at first treated as a joke by Marcel. The power of Brande's thorough knowledge about science and history made him a formidable man to argue with. Marcel, more intrigued by Brande's winsome sister than in Brande's ideas, spent as much time as he could with them during the second half of the voyage. The mystery of the secret society to which Brande belonged continued to draw Marcel closer. By the time they had reached Ireland, Marcel had convinced himself he needed to join in order to figure out how somebody so learned could have that nihilistic opinion about the entirety of the universe.

Marcel, the man who is trying to stop Brande, is an interesting counterpoint to Brande's disdain for all things material. When Marcel is confronted with a problem, his first instinct is to take a solitary walk in the woods to think it through. There is no Tintern-Abbey-like[9] inspiration to be found, but Marcel does seek communion of a sort with the non-human world: "I could not go indoors. A roof would smother me. Give me the open lawns, the leafy woods, the breath of the summer wind. Away, then, to the silence of the coming night. For an hour leave me to my thoughts. […] The resolution by which I have abided was formed as I wandered lonely through the woods" (Cromie 74). Notice the echo of Wordsworth's "I Wandered Lonely as a Cloud" in Marcel's reverie. Wordsworth's well-known poem is a Romantic reverie about the power of solitude in a non-human context. The speaker in the poem feels great kinship with daffodils, sparkling waves, and other beautiful sights. Marcel feels a similar release when, during his lonely walk through the woods, he is able to think clearly and accurately about Natalie, his love interest and also the sister of the universe-destroying maniac, Brande. Natalie will be joined at the hip to Marcel throughout the novel as she is torn between loyalty to her increasingly dangerous brother and love for Marcel, a man she sees as sensible and foolishly warmhearted.

Antagonist to Marcel is Natalie's brother, Herbert Brande, whose appreciation for the natural world would leave Wordsworth appalled. As justification for his plan to set off his apocalyptic bombs that would annihilate the Earth and possibly the entire solar system, thereby returning all matter, all life, to its original and pure components, he rails against the non-human world in seemingly direct response to an era of dreamers extolling the beauty and harmony of Nature. Moreover, Brande's attitude encompasses multitudes in that it anticipates Fascism, eugenics, and Sabina Spielrein's ideas about "the death drive," an idea she explored seventeen years later in her paper "Destruction as the Cause of Coming into Being" (1912). Many of those later Modernist voices either ignored anything outside of urban areas or recognized the chaos of the non-human world[10] and recoiled. Brande argues:

> [Nature] has no system, unless it be a *reductio ad absurdum*, which only blunders on the right way after fruitlessly trying every other conceivable path. She is not wise. She never fills a pail but she spills a hogshead. All her works are not beautiful. She never makes a masterpiece but she smashes a million "wasters" without a care. The theory of evolution—her gospel—reeks with ruffianism, nature-patented and promoted. The whole scheme of the universe, all material existence as it is popularly known, is founded upon and begotten of a system of everlasting suffering as hideous as the fantastic nightmares of religious maniacs. [...] Wholesale murder is Nature's first law. She creates only to kill, and applies the rule as remorselessly to the units in a star-drift as to the tadpoles in a horse-pond [Cromie 84–86].

There are seeds throughout Brande's philosophy of ideas that were later developed and popularized by Sigmund Freud in *Beyond the Pleasure Principle* (1920) and *Civilization and Its Discontents* (1930). If civilization restricts human freedom to act on individual instincts—especially when it comes to sex and violence—then the way toward maximum freedom is to eliminate society. The anarchists of Cromie's time, driven by a social philosophy that gained momentum during the second half of the nineteenth century, would have appreciated Brande's dismissive response to Romantic ideals. As the twentieth century dawned bloody and bleak, genre literature explicitly rejected that Nature is benevolent and beautiful. Decades later, mainstream literary Modernists works such as T.S. Eliot's *The Waste Land*, Virginia Woolf's *Mrs. Dalloway*, and Joseph Conrad's *Heart of Darkness* were hailed as innovations, and yet they followed with their characteristically claustrophobic pessimism the unacknowledged path that Speculative Modernists had long-since blazed.

Science is the cause of catastrophe in *Nordenholt's Million* (1923), the career-making novel by J.J. Connington. The story takes us to present-day London where men of science are trying to remake the world in their own image. One scientist in particular is a man named Wotherspoon, dismissed as a "dabbler" (Connington 2) by the narrator. Wotherspoon's ambition was to figure out a way to draw more life from the soil, to accelerate the cultivation and maturation process of food crops. Thereby, Wotherspoon hoped to hack nature itself and to use the tools of science to end scarcity, poverty, and malnourishment. He aims to do this by creating conditions of hyper-nitrification of the soil so that nitrogen, the major nutrient that all plants crave, is forever replenished and never runs out. Wotherspoon imagines a world of plenty, with plenty of statues devoted to the honor of Wotherspoon. Well, catastrophe literature being what it is, the dabbler's plan goes awry. His laboratory is struck by lightning and the nitrifying bacteria escapes out into London. Instead of replenishing the nitrogen in the soil, the lab-created and lightning-mutated bacteria remove all nitrogen from the soil. The blight spreads throughout England and then quickly across the globe rendering all soil incapable of sustaining plants. Soon all food stores are depleted, all land animals die, and civilization descends into chaos.

A wealthy industrial magnate named Nordenholt, however, sees what is coming and formulates a plan. He forces the government of the United Kingdom to accede to his wishes. He gathers five million people from all walks of life to establish "Nitrogen Areas" where coal is mined and converted to minerals that would replenish the fertility of the soil. Along with that effort, Nordenholt attempts to discover a cure for the bacteria. In this effort he is unsuccessful. He and his team also are looking for a more efficient and cheaper energy source than coal. The result sounds an awful lot like nuclear energy, which, in the early 1920s, was just a distant dream.[11] In this effort, after blowing up a few buildings and killing several teams of researchers, Nordenholt succeeds.

The bacteria were defeated not by any ingenuity on the part of Nordenholt's team of scientists, despite their best efforts. Instead, the bacteria simply run out of food. They removed the nitrogen, their one and only food source, from every bit of soil on earth, and they died. Nordenholt's stockpile of nitrogen was then reintroduced and civilization gained a new foothold in a mostly depopulated world. The ending, like so many of the racially troubling early speculative fiction stories, is depicted as a paradise once people with dark skin and "savage" ways were eliminated. *Mizora* is another illustrative example of this.

Nordenholt's Million is a novel where a scientist attempts to control nature only to have that experiment careen wildly out of control. In this way, it calls back to *Frankenstein* by Mary Shelley. For Connington, humanity will not be saved by anything it knows or does or invents. Instead, as in *The War of the Worlds*, all of human knowledge and science is ineffective against nature run amok. Nordenholt represents the combined knowledge of Western science and, although he is able to ruthlessly accomplish some of his survival goals, none of it would have mattered had not the bacteria run out of food and died of its own accord. Yes, in both *Nordenholt's Million* and *The War of the Worlds*, the tools of science are only useful when it comes to reestablishing an "improved" version of humanity on Earth. Self-annihilating hubris might make some believe they can "manage" the non-human world, but that way leads to extinction.

Conclusion

The Romantic poets urged us to leave the cities behind to enter the non-human world to have transcendent experiences. American Transcendentalist Henry David Thoreau urged us all to see the non-human world in near-religious terms, arguing that "in Wildness is the preservation of the world" (Thoreau "Walking" 609). Two decades later, the literary utopians idealized the agrarian lifestyle as a more pure and authentic way of life. For the first few generations of the Industrial Age, there was a clear distinction between urban and rural, between the polluted and bleak factory and mining towns and pristine farmland and wilderness. One, the human construct, was corrupt, unhealthy, and unsustainable. The other, the increasingly out of reach non-human world, was pure and innocent. It is no surprise that one was frequently compared to hell while the other was compared wistfully to the Garden of Eden.

By the late nineteenth century, writers who mixed science and the non-human world began to gain popularity. Two environmentalist writers in particular emerged who bridged the gap between the traditional Christian world view and the Modernist take on humanity's place in the world. In the United Kingdom, Richard Jefferies, who also dabbled in fiction with his landmark post-apocalyptic novel *After London*, published dozens of books and articles on environmental subjects. He became an influential presence for the growing environmental movement in the UK. Jefferies frequently published essays in the same magazines that published stories by H.G. Wells ("*After*"). Jefferies was beginning to see that the dichotomy defined by the Romantics and Transcendentalists no longer served him, and "as though hidden under Jefferies's marshes and weeds, is a complex desire for an alternative to industrial civilization—for a new world" ("*After*"). In the United States during the final two decades of the nineteenth century, John Muir gained great influence as a proponent of preserving undeveloped land, especially in the American West. He was instrumental in the passage of the law that created Yosemite National Park in 1890. He helped to establish the Sierra Club and advocated for laws to be passed for the purposes of preservation. He had the ear of powerful people from President Theodore Roosevelt on down. Muir,[12] according to the authoritative biography by Donald Worster, abandoned his belief in "the straight-laced dogma of traditional Christianity [...] Darwinism and science had transformed his thinking. [...] [H]e had no trouble accepting that our knowledge is partial and uncertain, or that humankind must make up rules by which it lives" (Worster 307). In a single generation, the conversation about environmental issues had been flipped upside down. It was into this rapidly changing world that Speculative Modernists raised their voices about humanity and its role as one of the many living things in the cosmos.

As the twentieth century dawned, Speculative Modernists questioned the idea that humanity lives in one place while "nature" is elsewhere. Instead, their new outlook asserted that the non-human world was not there for humans to master, nor was it possible for humanity, given our meager tools and brief lifespans, to control or even to understand the vast forces that operated oblivious to human needs or desires. These Speculative Modernists crafted stories in which human knowledge of the environment and the laws of nature were used by characters for destructive and selfish purposes. This era in literature saw a profound change in how stories depicted human relationship to the non-human world. People were neither headed toward harmony the way the Romantics and Transcendentalists dreamed, nor were not headed toward mastery the way utopians would have it. The non-human world just does not care about humanity—it is far too complex to understand, and it will outlive the human species by eons.

4

Worlds Beyond

> Thank God! there is always the Land of Beyond
> For us who are true to the trail;
> A vision to seek, a beckoning peak,
> A fairness that never will fail;
> A pride in our soul that mocks at a goal,
> A manhood that irks at a bond,
> And try how we will, unattainable still,
> Behold it, our Land of Beyond!
> —Robert Service, "The Land of Beyond" (1912)

Just as the nineteenth century was coming to a close, two pieces of literature were published that demonstrate the contradiction that haunted two of the great empires of the world: the United States, an emerging empire; and the United Kingdom, which was at its height. The first is Rudyard Kipling's poem "The White Man's Burden" (1899), as it reflects the perceived responsibility of the empire, the "superior" culture. The second is H.G. Wells's *The War of the Worlds* (1898), as it tells the story of the conquered, the culture that is to be eradicated. The conflict of these two ideas creates the foundation on which Speculative Modernism is built.

Though Kipling, himself, is a fringe Speculative Modernist, his poem reflects the first mindset, that of the expansionist empires of the past few centuries, exhorting its listeners to bravely bear the responsibility of civilizing conquered peoples. Kipling wrote it specifically in response to the end of the Spanish-American War and the first foray of the United States into overseas expansion in claiming the Philippines as a colony. The poem warns of the difficulties of this "burden"—the blood that must be shed in order to bring about this civilization—in terms of the noble conqueror who only seeks to aid the conquered. The fifth stanza reads:

> Take up the White Man's burden—
> And reap his old reward:
> The blame of those ye better,

> The hate of those ye guard—
> The cry of hosts ye humour
> (Ah, slowly!) toward the light:—
> "Why brought ye us from bondage,
> Our loved Egyptian night?" [Kipling 971].

This stanza (along with the first and the fourth) was read in United States Senator Benjamin Tillman's address in 1899, the same year the poem was written. He used the poem to call for the Senate to consider not going into a full-on war against the Philippines, but rather to set up a base there. He argued if, and only if the native population attacked, should the United States move to destroy them. He saw in the poem not just the call to bring "order" to non–Western European peoples, but also the warning of the cost of that expansionism. His desire to reach out to those he sees as less fortunate, his *noblesse oblige*, offers a hand of friendship to a nation that he claims we bought fair and square:

> We only want enough of your territory to give us a harbor of refuge, a naval station, the right to protect you from outside interlopers, and to get such commercial advantages as you of right ought to give us. Pass a resolution of that kind, and then if those people will not listen to reason and continue to fire on the flag, I for one will say the blood will be on their own heads [Tillman].

Guidance, as a parent to a child, is offered, but with just a hint of threat to make it clear that the empire will still rule.

Kipling's own science-fiction work includes stories about a global organization, called the Aerial Board of Control (or A.B.C. for short), that guides all air traffic[1] by the year 2000 with the added mandate "*and all it implies*" ("Night Mail" 17). By having one vast network that controls the skies, Kipling prophesied that a bureaucracy would bring the world to heel and eliminate the need for petty wars. In the first of the stories, "With the Night Mail" (1905), his A.B.C. would "confirm or annul all international arrangements and [...] find our tolerant, humorous, lazy little planet only too ready to shift the whole burden of public administration on its shoulders" (17). The British would bring serenity to the world through simple bureaucratic force. In the dispatches in the middle of the story, along with the weather and other notes about the shipping lanes, we hear about some of the last hold outs, the island of Crete, which has finally surrendered its government to the A.B.C. Even scientific experiments that might interfere with aerial travel fall under the jurisdiction of this Board. The lighting of cities, all kinds of commerce, even the declarations of war among countries are subject to the Board's approval. This is the way to civilize a world, the way to bring all nations together.

Wells examines the brutality of a war against a less technologically advanced society—this chapter's second mindset—in *The War of the Worlds*. In his first chapter, Wells writes about the Martians' desire for the planet Earth and all of its resources and how, as they have a much more advanced culture than that of Earth's, maybe they have a right to destroy the people they find:

> And before we judge them [the Martians] too harshly we must remember what ruthless and utter destruction our own species has wrought, not only upon animals, such as the vanished bison and the dodo, but upon its inferior races. The Tasmanians, in spite of their human likeness, were entirely swept out of existence in a war of extermination waged by European immigrants, in the space of fifty years. Are we such apostles of mercy as to complain if the Martians warred in the same spirit? [Wells *War* 280]

He advocates for a fairness in understanding the Martians' rapaciousness, since the English Empire had done no less when it was expanding to the four corners of the planet. Most important to Wells's argument, the British launched their campaign of genocide against the aboriginal Tasmanians in the nineteenth century to eliminate the resistance to British colonization. One could also note the implication of comparing the extinction of animals with the extermination of "inferior races." Genocide was often included in the rising discussion of racial purity, even among Speculative Modernists.[2] In *The History of Science Fiction*, Adam Roberts notes that "the arrival of the Martians and their mechanized brutalities are the symbolic forms Wells chose to explore a deeper set of concerns about the violence of Empire-building, and about the anxieties of otherness and the encounter with otherness that Empire imposes on the Imperial peoples" (148). Thus, *The War of the Worlds* serves as a double warning: not only for those who might eventually be conquered by a greater and more technological force, but for the imperialists who might be brought down by unexpected forces that protect these "inferior races."

These two ideas, the responsibility of bringing civilization to the uncivilized and the fear of having it brought to humanity, were frequently in conflict to the Speculative Modernists. The frontiers of this world were beginning to dwindle at the start of the twentieth century. The 1890 United States Census had declared for the first time that "[s]ettlement in the West remains very dispersed except for major, emerging urban centers. However, towns and cities occur regularly enough to disrupt the appearance of a clear, unbroken line separating the generally settled area from the frontier" (Census). By the end of the decade, the United States had won its first overseas war and was beginning to consider colonizing other parts of the world. At the beginning of the next century, the North and South poles would be visited by humans,[3] and air travel would begin in earnest. Speculative

Modernists took these real-world events and used them to ponder the conquering of other worlds.

This chapter examines the hopes and fears that these Speculative Modernist characters—be they intrepid explorers or bloodthirsty murderers—had for the continuing expansion of the human race, whether as a competitor seeking resources or as a dominant culture taking over the world. In the first section, "What Do We Really Have to Offer?," there is the question of what the conquerors have to offer the conquered. How, in fact, is the "superior culture" superior, and what really are its motivations? The plots and characters in this section focus mainly on how those who thought they were bringing civilization to the uncultured find in these so-called "inferior peoples" a mirror that questions their motivations, and even their own understanding of what being civilized is. The array of possibilities appears in works from the more traditional Modernist perspective in Joseph Conrad's *Heart of Darkness* (1899) and from the Speculative Modernist view in Wells's short story, "The Country of the Blind" (1904) to Edgar Rice Burroughs's *Tarzan of the Apes* (1912) and Charlotte Perkins Gilman's *Herland* (1915). These books examine, in very different ways, the concern over whose ways *are* better. More important, they ask what happens when the conquerors are not the ones with the better ways. Is there a moral imperative to adopt a more peaceful solution whether it conforms with one's understanding of reality or simply the imperative to win?

In some stories, both nations are depicted as conquerors. The second section, "They Want What We Want," looks at how Speculative Modernists saw the conflict of nations of equals on planets other than Earth. Sometimes the conquerors simply find beings like themselves who have the same issues of greed and desire that sent them on their travels. Wells's *The First Men in the Moon* (1901) addresses the conceit of the explorers who think they will only find inferior races in their travels, who think that those with different customs must lack their own motivations of greed and expansionism. In *A Princess of Mars* (1912), Edgar Rice Burroughs takes readers to Mars, or Barsoom as the natives call it, which becomes a surrogate world where our hero, John Carter, must watch as kingdoms wrestle each other. As an outsider, Carter finds it difficult to tell which side he should join. In *The Worm Ouroboros* (1922), E.R. Eddison brings his readers to Mercury on the wings of a bird to see that it is not as easy to distinguish good and evil from the outside, and how in the end, the struggle may be all there is.

Last, the third section, "'We're Down; We're Beat': Humanity's Defeat," addresses one of the most important and far-reaching fears of the Speculative Modernists that humans might be the "inferior" ones. Edward Bulwer-Lytton adapted Darwin's theory to wonder what the next step in evolution could be in *The Coming Race* (1871), postulating that humanity could be overrun as easily as the *Homo sapiens* overran the Neanderthals. Clark Ashton Smith's "The Dimension of Chance" (1932) and H.P. Lovecraft's "From Beyond" (1934) examine how beings from parallel universes might see humanity as inferior, or even worse, as prey.

The Speculative Modernists feared that, as the human race continues to expand, humanity may meet with more difficult foes than it had ever imagined. In traveling to other worlds, the danger is always that the explorers will find those who have achieved where they have failed, those who want what they want, or those who might be more powerful than they are. The Speculative Modernists provided opportunity for the conquering mentality to continue in many new forms. Roald Amundsen and others had taken us to the ends of the Earth in reality, but now it was time to ponder possible worlds beyond.

What Do We Really Have to Offer?

The Speculative Modernist authors sensed a great discontent, or as H.G. Wells called it in *The War of the Worlds*, "the great disillusionment" (1), and this profoundly affected the way they wrote about this era of European expansion and dominance, and the beginning of the "great wars" that would bring the world to the brink of annihilation. Writers such as Edgar Rice Burroughs, E.E. Smith, and E.R. Eddison sensed the potential for empire expansion, whether it be on this world or on others that space travel might bring closer in the twentieth century. They used the empires of their day to imagine the ones of tomorrow, and in many cases tried to warn against what the ever-expanding empires could become. While worlds to conquer may have seemed heroic at the beginning, the Speculative Modernists could see the war, deprivation, and destruction to which these heroics would lead.

The desire to extend the Empire dominated the European mentality during the nineteenth century, particularly under Queen Victoria and the British East India Trading Company. Economic and financial gain went hand in hand with European expansion. This was the core motivation behind the establishment and upkeep of Belgian stations along the Congo of Africa in Joseph Conrad's *Heart of Darkness*. Narrated by Marlow, but reported by an unnamed "I," the book unravels the madness that comes with displacement via the renowned Mr. Kurtz, the ivory trader with "unsound" methods, who is perhaps a stand-in for all of the European powers that have invaded the less technologically advanced areas of the world.

As a staple of the literary canon, *Heart of Darkness* rings with the spirit of Modernism and meaninglessness. However, it also has sections and passages that align more with H.P. Lovecraft and Edgar Rice Burroughs than Ezra Pound or Gertrude Stein. In the famous last lines whispered by Kurtz ("The horror! The horror!"), Conrad speaks to the emptiness and pessimism of the time. Yet it is his narrator that peers into the darkness of that abyss:

> This is the reason why I affirm Kurtz was a remarkable man. He had something to say. He said it. Since I had peeped over the edge myself, I understand better the meaning of his stare that could not see the flame of the candle but was wide enough to embrace the whole universe, piercing enough to penetrate all the hearts that beat in the darkness. He had summed up—he had judged. "The horror!" He was a remarkable man. After all, this was the expression of some sort of belief; it had candor, it had conviction, it had a vibrating note of revolt in its whisper, it had the appalling face of a glimpsed truth—the strange comingling of desire and hate [69].

It is only after Kurtz is displaced from his society and thrust into a new one, coming from Europe and "conquering" the Congo as a charismatic and philosophic white god, that he had "glimpsed truth"—a truth that was beyond Empire. Kurtz embraced this truth that Marlow could not accept. For however much Marlow admired and stood in awe of Kurtz, he was just as quick to dismiss him as being mad. Kurtz had the courage that Marlow did not.

In following his own reasoning and rationale (to which he so desperately clings), Marlow blames external forces for Kurtz's failings because he cannot accept that his world view is a house of cards. As he explains, "The wilderness had found him out early, and had taken on him a terrible vengeance for the fantastic invasion. I think it had whispered to him things about himself he did not know, things of which he had no conception till he took counsel with this great solitude—and the whisper had proved irresistibly fascinating" (Conrad 57). According to Marlow, it is the isolation that drove Kurtz mad. Yet, it is that very isolation, the escape from the false constructs of society, that allows Kurtz to glimpse the truth. This being too much for Marlow to process, he returns to that very society and even lies to Kurtz's intended, for the truth is too much to bear: "It would have been too dark—too dark altogether" (76). In returning to society, Marlow is more comfortable in believing the falsehood that empire is instead of facing the reality of what humans are in relation to "the whole universe." The ambivalence of conquerors, as both heroes to those to whom they would bring civilization while being so far from it themselves, mirrors the dichotomy of Wells and Kipling so well. Kurtz has used methods to collect the ivory that would certainly be considered uncivilized back in Europe. When Marlow looks into Kurtz's eyes, he sees the devastation that colonialism wreaks not only on the conquered, but on the conqueror as well. Critics of *Heart of Darkness* sometimes find it hard to decide whether this is a work that condemns colonialism or perpetuates it.[4]

Kipling's "burden" to bring civilization to those he deems less civilized does lend itself to a predatory ulterior motive that can so easily backfire. While the conqueror might think it reasonable to be rewarded for the "gift" of civilization, there will almost certainly be times when the conquered is not quite so forthcoming. Like Conrad's Kurtz, H.G. Wells's Nunez, in the short story "The Country of the Blind" (1904), learns that whether the English were right or not, the inhabitants of the conquered lands might not be open to the empire's perspectives of reality, and might demand that it is the conqueror who should change. While the story is built on the premise that the man with sight is right about the nature of reality, Wells also points out that the sighted man, Nunez, sees the opportunity of conquering the Country of the Blind, always repeating that proverb about how, in the Country of the Blind, the one-eyed man is king. He believes that his sighted ways are a better way to understand the universe: "I come from the great world—where men have eyes and see" (Wells "Blind" 623). This belief causes him to plot an overthrow of the people in this city. First, he tries telling them of all the wonders of sight, promising them all kinds of wonders if they will follow him, and when this is not enough to convince them, he considers violence. Even here, though, he is thwarted by his own civility. Nunez cannot bring himself to strike a blind man. Perhaps, in some way, this makes him more like Marlow in *Heart of Darkness*, rather than like Kurtz. Even though he is pressed, he prefers the illusion of his own cultured behavior, and this keeps him from truly dominating these people.

After a while, he finds himself doubting his own knowledge of the world: "blind philosophers came and talked to him of the wicked levity of his mind, and reproved him so impressively for his doubts about the lid of rock that covered their cosmic casserole that he almost doubted whether indeed he was not the victim of hallucination in not seeing it overhead" (Wells "Blind" 637). In his doubt he begins to settle in with these people, and to fall in love with a woman of their people, but the town elders and her own father will have none of it, as they are convinced that his eyes have made him an idiot. The villagers "grow angry at the idea of corrupting the race" (640). At last, the elders come up with a solution: they will remove the eyes that are so clearly corrupting his brain. He contemplates doing it for his love, but, in the end, he cannot surrender the very thing that informs his world, his sight.

At the conclusion of the story, Nunez runs off, after being faced with the choice of losing his eyesight entirely or being locked away as an insane man. For a brief moment, he nearly succumbs to the idea of surrendering his eyes in order to remain in this peaceful valley and to live a life with a woman with whom he has fallen in love. Wells's sympathy with the conquered races of man opens a door for the Speculative Modernists to imagine all sorts of worlds where the inhabitants would not make the conquerors welcome. In writing these stories Wells recognized the shared humanity with those whose ways seem either so primitive that they need saving or so advanced in their own scientific discovery that they've lost their empathy.

Wells is playing, in some ways, with Plato's "Allegory of the Cave" from *The Republic*. The main idea in the allegory is that most people can only glimpse the shadows of reality, but if a true philosopher were to ever come and show them the error of their ways, release them from their chains, and drag them out into the light of truth, their first impulse would be to kill the philosopher and demand their own world of shadows again. The spin that Wells and the Speculative Modernists put on this great dilemma is the question of whose world is in the light of truth and whose is in the cave of shadows may well rest upon who has control of the culture.

The Speculative Modernists realized that these intrepid explorers have nothing to offer the unconquered places, the undiscovered countries. They do not improve them with their presence, but, even worse, they learn nothing from them that can save the empire from collapse. At best, the war and struggle and conquering are just a distraction from man's ultimate trouble: the struggle is for nothing. The Speculative Modernists decided to test this theory out in the new places technology was opening up.

Edgar Rice Burroughs rejects the notion of the empire's improvement of the "uncivilized" in his the more than twenty novels of Tarzan. Although Burroughs's style is unremarkable in terms of character development and storytelling complexity, Tarzan exemplifies man reduced to his most primal instincts as a means of survival. In fact, he thrives under primitive conditions without the aid of technological advancements. He exhibits behaviors of primal man, equipped only with a knife (a remnant from his father, Lord Greystoke), and later, a rope noose fashioned from grass reeds. Yet, he thrives under savage conditions, an optimal combination of physical prowess and fundamental reasoning. He does this all without the social benefits of the English empire.

Where Burroughs comes up short with narrative sophistication, he excels in capturing the animalistic action in his tales of adventure. As has been argued, the plots of Tarzan novels are all very similar.[5] Their objective is not high literature, but entertaining stories for adolescents, and therefore they are appropriately packed with sequences of courageous action and outcast mentality. Despite the rather formulaic approach of plot structure, Tarzan does represent something very important. In his isolation, we get a glimpse of Tarzan as fundamental man. He portrays a simplistic morality in his childlike development, as seen in the first novel of the franchise, *Tarzan of the Apes* (1912):

> Tarzan of the Apes was no sentimentalist. He knew nothing of the brotherhood of man. All things outside his own tribe were his deadly enemies[....] And he realized all this without malice or hatred. To kill was the law of the wild world he knew[....] His strange life had left him neither morose nor blood-thirsty. That he joyed in killing, and that he killed with a joyous laugh upon his handsome lips betokened no innate cruelty. He killed for food most often, but, being a man, he sometimes killed for pleasure, a thing which no other animal does; for it has remained for man alone among all creatures to kill senselessly and wantonly for the mere pleasure of inflicting suffering and death [70].

Following this logic, as a creature of reason and biological prowess, man is a cruel thing—civilized or not. As Burroughs's narrator later explains, "Men were indeed more foolish and more cruel than the beasts of the jungle! How fortunate was he who lived in the peace and security of the great forest!" (126). Indeed, it is man that exhibits such cruelty, as Tarzan observes the murder of man by man, all for the sake of treasure.

Recalling the efforts of Joseph Conrad's *Heart of Darkness*, Burroughs thrusts civilized man into an unforgiving and inhospitable environment. Whereas Tarzan, despite his European heritage, is quite literally at home in the African jungle, the treasure hunters of the aristocratic class are unnerved (and unprepared) for the hostilities of nature. Lieutenant Charpentier, in an exchange with William Clayton, Tarzan's rival for Jane Porter and the Greystoke estate, says:

> [T]he other night as we lay in the jungle there [...] and those jungle noises rose and fell around us I began to think that I was a coward indeed. It was not the roaring and the growling of the big beasts that affected me so much as it was the stealthy noises—the ones that you heard suddenly close by and then listened vainly for a repetition of—the unaccountable sounds as of a great body moving almost noiselessly, and the knowledge that you didn't know how close it was or whether it were creeping closer after you ceased to hear it? It was those noises—and the eyes.
>
> "Mon Dieu! I shall see them in the dark forever—the eyes that you see, and those that you don't see, but feel; ah, they are the worst" [Burroughs *Apes* 181].

Men like Charpentier and Lieutenant D'Arnot (whom Tarzan rescued from "the blacks"—a jungle-dwelling tribe of cannibals) may be trained in the combat of civilized men, but are ill equipped to deal with the primeval forests of Africa. They have become too civilized, too dependent on being civilized, to adapt to their uncompromising environment. Only Tarzan can save them here. The question then is not only can they "save" Tarzan but also if they should.

Luckily, Jane Porter provides us with the variable needed to solve the equation. In a leap of narrative faith, Tarzan actually teaches himself how to read and write through the inspection of children's books left behind by his parents before their death at the hands of anthropoid apes. This is also how he acquired his famous knife. He then learns human speech from the aforementioned Lieutenant D'Arnot. Eventually, with the aid of D'Arnot, he gets introduced to European society in Africa at a military outpost. Now completely conversant in the language and decorum of civilized man, Tarzan elects to prove his prowess via a bet on whether or not he can kill a lion without the aid of a gun. According to Tarzan, it would not be a fair fight and "the pleasure of the hunt" would be reduced. It is here that readers get an explicit avowal of Tarzan's great conflict. Stripped naked per the fairness of the hunt:

> Tarzan had no sooner entered the jungle than he took to the trees, and it was with a feeling of exultant freedom that he swung once more through the forest branches.
>
> This was life! Ah, how he loved it! Civilization held nothing like this in its narrow and circumscribed sphere, hemmed in by restrictions and conventionalities. Even clothes were a hinderance and a nuisance.
>
> At last he was free. He had not realized what a prisoner he had been [Burroughs *Apes* 196].

At this point, Burroughs reaches beyond the appeal to boyhood fantasy and into commentary on the seeming pointlessness of civilization. Gore Vidal writes, "In its naïve way, the Tarzan legend returns us to that Eden where, free of clothes and the inhibitions of an oppressive society, a man can achieve in reverie his continuing need, which is, as William Faulkner put it in his high Confederate style, to prevail as well as to endure" (193). Tarzan of the Apes is better off than Tarzan, Lord Greystoke. Civilization has ruined the freedom that primal man enjoys. The "restrictions and conventionalities" of society are useless. Beyond that, they are damaging. Society is worse for them. Not even the fairy-tale version of love (via marriage to Jane) can supersede the call of the jungle for Tarzan. He knows where he is most himself. The Speculative Modernists knew that exploring these new worlds, while it may mean nothing in the history of empires, would do much to release the soul from too much civilization.

In these first few works, the Speculative Modernists have examined the question about what the "civilized" world may have to offer these "inferior cultures." What if, in fact, it was the "civilized" world that was the corruption and those they seek to conquer were the ones with the truth? Charlotte Perkins Gilman, in her novel, *Herland*, sends her three protagonists into the country they derisively call Herland when they hear the legends that this land is governed by, and made up of, only women. The narrator, Vandyck Jennings, sees himself as a level-headed scientist working with Terry O. Nicholson (a self-professed lady's man) and Jeff Margrave (a man who worships "his women" and puts them on a pedestal). Just like Nunez in Wells's story, who thinks he will be crowned king of the blind men in his valley, the three men discuss before they even confirm the existence of the country how they, by the mere fact of their masculinity, will easily seize control. Terry insists that there will be utter chaos as women could never work together and that their only technology will be in milling (as women have always been such good spinsters, they joke). Jeff insists that the place will be like a nunnery with an abbess. Terry even claims: "I'll get solid with them all—and play one bunch against another. I'll get myself elected king in no time—whew! Solomon will have to take a back seat!" (Gilman *Herland* 10). The men are making the mistake that women in a matriarchal society will react the same way to men as those they know from their homeland.

Just as the Speculative Modernists would see the need to tear societal constructs down and try to reimagine them, Gilman takes on the task of creating a society that is not just matriarchal, but actually has no men in it, taking out what she feels is the most important detriment to peace: men. Spontaneous parthenogenesis leads not only to there being no need for men, it also means that the society is built around love, rather than a collective need for security. Barbara H. Solomon, in her introduction to *Herland*, writes, "Gilman recognized that in America the rearing of children was a burdensome and isolating responsibility only of women. While the joys of motherhood were extolled and many expressed concern about the needs of children, the reality was that few resources were forthcoming and the sacrifices expected from mothers had no parallels in sacrifices of fathers" (xxix). Women, in the world Gilman creates, reproduce through a collective love of their society, which means that many of the institutions created in late-nineteenth-century American society are irrelevant. Formal education is unnecessary because of the love each woman has for every other woman in the society; the same is true for both religion and government. Without the concerns or fears produced by a society built on the usual kind of competitive procreation, the women can simply focus on building the perfect union. As a result, even nature falls under their sense of order and the women enjoy the fruits of a collective work ethic rather than a competitive one. Gilman emphasizes that the women of Herland are able to eliminate all of the woes produced in the current society simply by erasing the competitive nature that seems to follow men.

Unlike Mary Bradley Lane's *Mizora* (1880), Gilman sends three men to "discover" her women-run country, specifically men representing the privileged class, who see the conquering of lesser-developed nations or at least plundering them where they can as part of their privilege. They are well-provisioned and well-educated, but also more than a little mercenary, seeing in this wild country endless profit. They are drawn to Herland (as they will later dub it) because they find some extraordinary workmanship in some colored cloth that has accidentally floated downstream to them while they are in between plunders on the untraveled (and unidentified) continent and assumed they could exploit the labor of the women here and cheaply acquire the cloth to sell back home. However, the Herland natives toy with the men, being both more athletic and better able to deal with the nature of the area, keeping them locked up until they are willing to learn the women's language and ways. The men, after escaping for a while from their captivity and getting a chance to witness the culture a little more, realize that in the end, the women had allowed them their "escape" so that the women could learn more about them. Instead of them being kings, these men were merely playthings for these women. In all ways, these men are inferior to the women they thought to conquer. The women's sense of civilization far exceeds that of the world from which the men came.

Nature bows to these women and their ingenuity. The fields are well-ordered, although not farmed. The animals have lost their wildness—they've even taught the cats to not kill birds. All of nature's competitiveness is gone and just like the women, nature produces solely for the good of the society. The great revelation to the men is that all they ever thought of women and their habits was actually brought on by men and the competitive world women had come to know back at home. "Those 'feminine charms' we are so fond of are not feminine at all, but mere reflected masculinity developed to please us because they had to please us, and in no way essential to the real fulfillment of their great process" (Gilman *Herland* 60). Van begins to understand here that everything that he thought he knew about the nature of women had been created by men. What he understood to be women's preferences or behaviors were simply what men had dictated. The women of Herland, undefiled by man's competitive nature, were able to build a strong society without the pettiness and jealousies women had back in the men's society.

The Speculative Modernist tendency is to compare these cultures and to see what the would-be conquerors might have to offer. Gilman affords the men every opportunity to show their dominance, but one by one they succumb to the women of this land, even to falling in love with their captors. At one point, in the hopes of getting some dignity back, the men try to introduce their own customs—most notably monogamy, marriage, the church, and so on—to the Herland natives, only to find that they themselves have a hard time explaining the things they do. The women, respectful of all ideas, are game to try, but just never grasp the need for their man's protection or always being at their husband's beck and call. The women are not even sure why the men feel that they have to share a living space, which troubles each of them. Terry is "kicked" by his mate, Alima, when he tries to force her to have sex with him, and then is trussed up and carried off to prison. He feels ill-used by "his" woman, because she so easily rebuffs his need for dominance, and he demands to return home. The men think that the conventions of home will help to "civilize" the women, and again the women seem game to learn about the wider world. Instead, the men discover that it is those very conventions that keep their people, as a whole, unable to advance to the civilization of these women. The very premise of competition to be found in the capitalist society of England is what keeps it uncivilized when compared with the society of the women. The Speculative Modernist ideal of questioning and tearing down societal norms and expectations is at the heart of Gilman's *Herland*.

The women of Herland, in keeping an open mind, have gathered data about the world Jeff, Terry, and Van have described to them, and a few are interested in exploring all the knowledge from that world. They have done their best to learn what they can from the men, but they decide to go and see the world beyond their shores. The men are enjoined to not reveal the location of Herland until their emissary has returned and the women can decide if they want further congress with the world outside. Terry resists and promises to conquer the land the minute he gets home and gathers his resources, but eventually relents, and the men are sent home. The reader never gets to experience the Herlandian women in Europe or the ultimate decision about whether these extraordinary women will open their borders, but it is clear throughout the entire novel that Gilman feels that the men's world would be ripe for the conquering should these women ever deem it necessary. Luckily for the men, conquering was not in their nature.

Speculative Modernists ask those who seek to conquer what they have to offer. By challenging the hubris of the empire builders, these authors demonstrate that, leaving aside the grand speeches about carrying the "burden" of "civilizing" the wide world and acting as the standard bearers for truth and justice, the would-be conquerors of the world are really just barbarians grubbing for the resources that belong to others, no better than marauders at the gates of people who neither want nor need their civilization.

They Want What We Want

This section looks at what happens when the motivations of two cultures to expand meet head on. Perhaps, other beings—certainly other fellow humans—while foreign looking are not quite as foreign in motivation. By the early twentieth century, Europeans had encountered people all around the globe, and while certain specifics of politics, religion, or economics might have been radically different, the needs on a personal level were fairly universal: food, wealth, a peaceful working society. The Speculative Modernists wondered if the same would be true if the people of Earth encountered people off this planet. They wondered if humans would even be able to understand what drives alien civilizations, let alone deal with the differences of biology.

Not long after H.G. Wells had his Martians invade the Earth in *The War of the Worlds*, he sent his Earthlings off to discover what life was like on Earth's nearest neighbor in his *First Men in the Moon* (1901). Wells knew that, like in many of his other works, he was building on trends in science and literature that were already there. He even mentions Jules Verne's *A Trip to the Moon* (*De la Terre à la Lune* now generally translated as *From Earth to the Moon*) from 1865. Wells, however, would not even use the explosive kind of rocket he had used for the Martians in *The War of the Worlds*. This time, it is good old English ingenuity that would discover the way to block the radiation that creates gravity. The characters ponder if lead can block radioactivity, and certain kinds of glass can block ultraviolet radiation from the sun, why can't a substance, like the newly discovered element—helium—be found to block gravity.[6]

Speculative Modernists recognized that science seemed to thrive where commercial ventures could best take advantage of the new discoveries. Philosophical sciences like the further concepts of evolution did not really yield much in the way of capital success, whereas combustion engines, weaponry, and biological agents presented opportunities. The authors of this time recognized how these inventions would also go far in reordering society. Wells's genius, Mr. Cavor, meets up with the main narrator, Mr. Bedford, a failed businessman who is trying to become a writer, and after several awkward meetings decides to use Bedford as a sounding board for his frustrations in coming up with the substance that can block gravity. Together—although with Bedford mostly as a listener, positing ways that they could commercialize his discovery—they create the new substance, Cavorite, and prepare it for experimentation. Early in their association, Bedford asked Cavor what he intended to do with his antigravity machine, and Wells demonstrates clearly the difference between the scientific and business minds when discussing going to the moon. Bedford just can't see the value of going to the moon without someone to pay him for it; Cavor is just interested in new knowledge. The application of greed to science is a common trope among Speculative Modernists. Similar to what is seen in *Herland* and M.P. Shiel's *The Purple Cloud*, for all that people might try to convince themselves that they go on dangerous expeditions because they like to do difficult things, the desire for financial gain is always present.

Wells chronicles their preparations, their simple launch, and their arrival on the moon where they encounter the Selenites, who turn out to be essentially human-sized ants. Bedford is horrified, but Cavor recognizes that they have many similarities to humans—most notably they wear clothes and they build machines—and so works out a way to communicate with them. In giving us Bedford as a narrator, Wells provides the plot to the story; Bedford's emotions are of terror, hunger, greed, all the things with which the reader can connect. The scientist, however, makes many observations about how, despite their very alien appearance, the Selenites' motives match those of humanity.[7] Bedford notes over and over in the narrative that he wishes he had paid attention to all the science parts of the adventure so that he could re-create Cavor's invention for his own profits when he returns to Earth on his own, after being separated from Cavor.

Bedford's action-hero antics clash with Cavor's plan to get to understand the complex society of the Selenites. Like ants and other insects, they seem to have a hierarchical society where different body types indicate different roles in the society. Cavor realizes more and more they are sentient beings and wants to have further discussions with them, but Bedford finds that the low gravity makes the Selenites' bodies weak in comparison with his own muscle structure and he easily fights them off, discovering that he can generally kill them with one punch. He also makes the discovery that gold is quite abundant on the moon—they even use it in the making of his chains. After some struggles, Bedford retreats to their vehicle ready to return to Earth, only to find he has lost Cavor in the shuffle. He returns to Earth with enough gold to keep himself happy without the secret to Cavor's antigravity substance, and so seemingly ends the story.

However, after some time, Bedford is approached by a Dutch electrician, "who has been experimenting with certain apparatus akin to the apparatus used by Mr. Tesla in America,[8] in the hope of discovering some method of communication with Mars" (Wells *Moon* 525). Mr. Julius Wendigee informs Bedford that he has received certain communications from the moon concerning their visit. Six messages have been relayed from Cavor to the Earth, which amount to something of a warning. Wells essentially switches narrators from the failed businessman to the scientist, although he allows the first to continue a running editorial. Because Bedford, the businessman, controls the narrative, Wells demonstrates how easily scientific discovery can be coopted by greed.

Cavor manages to communicate with the Selenites and learns their history. He explains how each member of the Selenite society knows their place and their whole lives are geared toward fulfilling that destiny. "These beings with big heads on whom the intellectual labours fall, form a sort of aristocracy in this strange society, and at the head of them, quintessential of the moon, is that marvellous gigantic ganglion the Grand Lunar, into whose presence I am finally to come" (Wells *Moon* 538). Their society is so important to the Selenites that when there is no employment for the workers, they allow themselves to be drugged into unconsciousness and essentially stored in hibernation until they will once again be needed. Their lives are not their own.

Reminiscent of Jonathan Swift's *Gulliver's Travels* (1726), Gulliver's visit to the Houyhnhnms—an equine creature that is so far above man in cultivation that he finds it uncomfortable to be among humans again—in particular, Cavor expounds upon the Earthlings' way of life when he meets with the Grand Lunar, who is clearly interested in every single detail. The Grand Lunar is particularly interested when Cavor explains that all humans are the same bodily, asking about why, if that is the case, they don't all think alike. He is astounded by the fact that the Earth has many languages and cultures: "'You mean to say,' he asked, seeking confirmation, 'that you run about over the surface of your world—this world, whose riches you have scarcely begun to scrape—killing each other for beasts to eat?'" (Wells *Moon* 550). Wells knew the vulnerability of the Earth. Humanity's competitive nature would be fatal. Cavor, like Gulliver, begins to realize how awful humanity's way of life must sound to outsiders. He gets carried away with his own stories and realizes only in the end that he has given away humanity's weakness.

After this, there is more disruption in the messages, as if something or someone is blocking their transmission, particularly Cavor's last message in which he, first, admits to being a fool for telling the Grand Lunar everything, and, second, when he tries to send the chemical makeup for Cavorite. Then he is silent. Bedford understands the implication of what they have given to the Selenites. While he makes away with a bunch of gold, the Selenites are able to ferret out the way to Earth's destruction. Wells gives his Selenites, like his Martians, the desires that humans share, but he also gives them humanity's greed for power. The Speculative Modernists took up this warning in many of their depictions of alien life-forms. What drives humans to greed and corruption might also drive the beings they will have to contend with on the other side of the journey.

Just as Wells takes us to the Moon to explore human frailty with the Selenites, Edgar Rice Burroughs, in the first of his off-planet series, *A Princess of Mars* (1912), also delved into the motivations of his aliens to help us understand our own fracturing world. John Carter, an ex–Confederate soldier just looking to recoup what he lost by backing the wrong side in the Civil War, travels to Arizona with a fellow soldier and finds the gold that he's looking for, but his stake is right in the middle of Apache country. In trying to save his friend from an Apache attack, Carter is trapped in a cave where a mysterious gas paralyzes him and then transports him to Mars, where he finds himself in the middle of another clash of civilizations—the philosophical people of the noble floating city of Helium and the industrial Zodanga. Carter, whose wife and children were killed by Union soldiers in Richmond, Virginia, during the Civil War, rises through the ranks of a warrior species, the Tharks, who are essentially barbarians and not even considered as one of the civilizations on the planet. When Carter first encounters them, they are destroying eggs of their own species that have not hatched in their proper time. They are so brutal that all may challenge a Tharkian of rank in fight to the death in which the winner keeps all possessions of the loser. This may seem like less of a boon when it is realized that all the warrior may own is armor, weapons, and the furs that make up his bed. Carter, because of the extraordinary strength and agility on account of the gravitational differences between Earth and Mars, quickly defeats two challengers and immediately rises in the esteem of the other Tharks. It also earns him an opportunity to fall in love with Dejah Thoris, the princess of Helium (and the title character of the first book in the series).

Burroughs's choice of an ex-Confederate soldier and his decision to call the various races of the Martians by their color—the warrior race is made up of the Green Martians, while the noble masters of Helium are the Red Martians—creates a throwback to the antebellum South. However, the Speculative Modernist focus can be seen in Carter's motivation as an individual trying to reconcile his desire for love with society's seemingly endless desire for war and destruction. By removing all that might be familiar to an American—the remnants of the Confederacy, the conquering of the Old West, for example—Burroughs gives us the opportunity to see how individuals, torn by duty and prejudice, are battered by the conquering/conquered dichotomy. John Carter has been on the losing side of the intra-American wars in many ways, but his redemption comes in the intra-Martian wars as he not only becomes a hero, but regains the family he has lost. Perhaps this is the connection with the Confederacy as well: a dying culture that retains its old bigotries in the face of its own death is saved only when a soldier is able to unite those against whom the bigotry has been the strongest. John Carter unites the Green Martians to fight for the good Red Martians against the greedy Red Martians who would maintain the old ways. This can be summed up in the words of Dejah Thoris, Carter's new love: "Can it be that all Earth men are as you? Alone, a stranger, hunted, threatened, persecuted, you have done in a few short months what in all the past ages of Barsoom [Mars] no man has ever done: joined together the wild hordes of the sea bottoms and brought them to fight as allies of a red Martian people" (Burroughs *Mars* 200). Carter responds, "It was not I who did it, it was love, love for Dejah Thoris, a power that would work greater miracles than this you have seen" (200). Just like William Hope Hodgson's narrator in *The Night Land*, who finds that his Lady calls him even in the end times when the world is about to go dark for mankind, Carter's love for Dejah Thoris cuts through all of the heroism and violence of the Martian political landscape. Though Burroughs's story takes place on Mars, the motivations of the alien beings match those of humanity, and the resolution remains the same: love. Speculative Modernists recognized that there was no reason to assume that this would be different on other planets.

Meanwhile, on Mercury, E.R. Eddison's *The Worm Ouroboros* (1922) has a similar thesis about the people who reside there. In Paul Edmund Thomas's introduction to the 1991 edition, he assures us that Eddison—though writing among the great Modernist stars of his era: Stein and Joyce, and Pound, Lawrence, Woolf, and Eliot—is not at all a Modernist. Thomas alleges that the book is a throwback to the nineteenth century. He hedges:

> Nearly every generation has writers who look backward, who do not join their contemporaries in seeking new literary forms but rather take inspiration from older writers. E.R. Eddison is one of these. Eddison's literary work, though in some ways as modern as Eliot's or Pound's, belongs to the nineteenth century, to the aesthetics of the Pre-Raphaelites, of Swinburne, William Morris, Andrew Lang, and Walter Pater. [...] [*The Worm Ouroboros*] contains a strangely archaic and romantic story of heroic adventure on the planet Mercury. It has little in common with the modernist literature that dominated the decade [...] [Thomas xv–xvi].

However, Paul Edmund Thomas misses Eddison's use of this archaic style to make a connection for the Modernist era, an anchor to make a deeper point. While the language of Eddison's book is clearly archaic (Thomas uses as examples both the Middle English poem about Thomas the Rhymer that is included as a frontispiece and how Eddison has his characters spout off Shakespeare in places), the story often breaks the fourth wall through the use of a narrative observer named Lessingham, putting it firmly in the Modernist milieu. E.R. Eddison gives us a glimpse of the politics on Mercury, but he frames the story with Lessingham who starts off here on Earth and gets to witness the intrigue in the struggle between good and evil alongside a martlet, a little bird, who brings him to Mercury. For the first several chapters, the martlet instructs Lessingham (and thereby the readers) breaking the fourth wall, on who the good guys and the bad guys are because they are nearly indistinguishable without the guidance. Once the plot is set, though, the martlet leaves Lessingham and the readers to figure out the loyalties and the betrayals of the characters before them. The narrative choices are one of the important aspects that make this a Speculative Modernist text. The lines for why war is fought are not so clear, and war for its own sake is enough of a drive. It does not need to be about good and evil. Fighting for justice is not the only cause of war. Eddison adds this Modernist sensibility to the developments on Mercury.

Several times throughout the book, the characters act as though they are in a book and make references to the idea of being watched. The plots and subplots are inconsequential, except for the fact that the heroes are subject to Lessingham's approval. The reader is presented with the great Lords of Demonland, who seem so alike that in the Keith Henderson illustration for the 1926 Albert & Charles Boni edition they are drawn together and identically. They love the fight, the eternal struggle, and are bored in times of peace. At one point, Juss and Brandach Daha, two of the great lords, are informed of the betrayal of one of the countries they thought to be allies. Trapped now between the two armies, they discuss their strategies, but Juss pauses long enough to point out: "Thou fallest all of a holiday mood at the first scenting of this great hazard." Brandach Daha responds, "O Juss, thine own breath lighteneth at it, and thy words come more sprightly forth. Are not all lands, all airs, one country unto us, so there be great doings afoot to keep bright our swords" (Eddison 119). Then the men return to their strategies. The heroic Demons see the world as their own war zone to be used at any cost. They revel in having lands to conquer and in the danger of their mission. This hearkens back to Senator Tillman's address—particularly his inclusion of Kipling's poem—on the responsibility of the United States to bring order and democracy to the Philippines no matter the cost in lives of the natives.

However, it is the ending that strikes the most Modernist chord. The Witches are defeated; their treachery has been turned back on themselves and they have been thrown down. Gorice, the evil king, has only his beloved capital city of Carcë "black and smoking in ruin for his monument" (Eddison 382). Juss and Brandoch Daha and the other lords welcome an emissary from Zimiamvia, a country that we have been told is essentially a heaven on earth, to their own home. She offers them a boon for being the conquerors of Gorice and his Witches, and after a great deal of discussion, Lord Juss begins to understand what it is these lords of Demonland desire. He concludes: "[We] have flown beyond the rainbow. And there we found no fabled land of heart's desire, but wet rain and wind only and the cold mountain-side. And our hearts are a-cold because of it" (392). She asks how they can be so young and so bitter, and it is here he tells her what they all desire, the return of their enemies. However, his desire is more than just eternal war between the forces of the two countries. Instead, he asks her again for a dominion over his own fate:

> "Let me dream yet awhile. The double pillar of the world, that member thereof which we, blind instruments of inscrutable Heaven, did shatter, restored again? From this time forth to maintain, I and he, his and mine, ageless and deathless

for ever, for ever our high contention whether he or we should be great masters of all the earth? If this be but phantoms, O Queen, thou'st 'ticed us to the very heart of bitterness. This we could have missed, unseen and unimagined: but not now. Yet how were it possible the Gods should relent and the years return?" [396].

She prays, and it is granted by whatever powers there be. Paul Edmund Thomas explains this ending in his introduction as an invitation "to turn back to his first [page] and begin the adventure story again" (xlii). Surely there is something to the eternal quest, the never-ending story that remains from the ancient tales of Camelot and the fantasy stories of previous centuries. Yet, here it is the characters themselves asking this, making it a Speculative Modernist text. They have realized that there is nothing beyond this world—no eternity of peaceful remembrance of the brave deeds of the past, no loving glory for the heroes and damnation for the enemy. No rest for the weary soldier. Just death. At least if there was eternal struggle between Gorice and the lords of Demonland, there is something. Perhaps it is in the acceptance of war without end, the eternal struggle, that allows mankind to continue to be distracted from the meaninglessness of his own existence. Eddison's characters decide to embrace that. While Eddison's work might seem archaic, a throwback to a bygone method of storytelling, the truth is that he is a Speculative Modernist, through and through. By setting this story on another world, by recognizing that everything but the present moment is meaningless, E.R. Eddison is using twentieth-century methods to explore the disillusionment of the great wars.

In these stories, the Speculative Modernists are examining how the world has grown smaller, and that means the competition among nations is more imminent. For the previous four centuries, the world had been wide enough to accommodate the competitive European model of society. The countries clashed on the high seas or in the deep forests and jungles or anywhere else beyond their own homes. Modern technology, however, had shrunk the world again, and the great nations of the world were squaring off against each other with no thought of the damage they were doing to the countries they had colonized or people they had conquered. Speculative Modernists, by placing their stories on other worlds, could castigate or admonish their own societies with a plausible deniability in case their works hit too close to home.

"We're Down; We're Beat": Humanity's Defeat

H.G. Wells's fear of the rampaging monsters that could exterminate us like we were common roaches is the nightmare that lasted the whole

Speculative Modernist era—in both his book, *The War of the Worlds*, and its adaptation in the Orson Welles's Mercury Theatre production on Halloween Eve in 1938. In *The War of the Worlds*, our narrator encounters several different types of people as he flees the Martians. One of the last is an artilleryman, from whom we get the section's title (214). He has decided that mankind cannot win the war with the Martians, and so the humans must surrender for now in order to live to another day. The presumption of the novel is that those who can cross through the void of space must be technologically advanced and therefore a threat to us, as we would be to them. This terror stands the test of time, and maybe acts as a warning for those who would conquer others to think just a little bit about the conquered. His book was not the first, however, nor would it be the only one where biology would win the day. This section looks at some of those works that explore other existential threats to humanity. The warning should not only be for the monsters who would come with ray guns firing. There are plenty of other kinds of threats too. As the universe grows in the dimensions of time and space, so too do the number of threats humankind might face, and not all of them would simply be better fighters.

Edward Bulwer-Lytton's novel *The Coming Race* (1871) stands as a link between the travel stories like the medieval works *The Voyage of St. Brendan* (about 900) and *The Travels of Sir John Mandeville* (approximately 1357) as well as the parody adventures of Jonathan Swift's *Gulliver's Travels* and many others throughout the eras of exploration, with H.G. Wells and the Speculative Modernists. Bulwer-Lytton uses a first-person narrative to tell the story of an unnamed young American who is invited to help with an inspection of a very deep mine. When he tumbles down an extraordinarily deep shaft, he finds himself among a strange race of beings that live entirely underground called the Vril-ya. These beings are spiritually, technologically, politically, and in almost every other way superior to his fellow superterraneans. Within minutes of his discovery, the narrator is fed, housed, and educated through their superior mind control in the ways of their language and culture. Like many of the utopian novels both before and after *The Coming Race*, the narrator describes this perfect culture and compares it to his own through discussions with one or two of the beings set to be his guides.

The book is important to the Speculative Modernists for two great developments. The first is that this race is not only more just and efficient, but technologically superior as well. In fact, technology is what makes them who they are. The Vril-ya have discovered the secret of *vril*, the essence of all power. To this day, humans are in search of a unified field theory that can explain the basis of all forces that act upon physical bodies in this universe. Vril is the answer to that vision of unification. In that understanding lies the power to unlock every secret force in the universe from the immense destructive capability of "intra-atom energy" to the power of mind control and hypnotism. As one of the Vril-ya explains to the narrator:

> [T]he various forms under which the forces of matter are made manifest, have one common origin, or, in other words, are so directly related and mutually dependent that they are convertible, as it were into one another, and possess equivalents of power in their action. These subterranean philosophers assert that by one operation of vril, which Faraday would perhaps call "atmospheric magnetism," they can influence the variations of temperature—in plain words, the weather; that by operations, akin to those ascribed to mesmerism, electro-biology, odic force, etc., but applied scientifically, through vril conductors, they can exercise influence over minds, and bodies animal and vegetable, to an extent not surpassed in the romances of our mystics. To all such agencies they give the common name of vril [Bulwer-Lytton 22–23].

Vril can be used to induce sleep, control beings of a lesser nature to do one's bidding, to recharge a weary soul, to grow crops, and to make weapons of immense power that can destroy one's enemies with great ease. Luckily, the Vril-ya are highly evolved socially, in that they are mostly peaceful, and therefore the destructive power they could command rarely gets used for anything more than domestic issues.

They are, however, an expanding people that number in the millions for the moment. Their culture has undergone a time of great peace and, being intelligent about their subterranean resources, they try to spread out as much as possible so as not to tax any particular region too seriously. They live within the means that nature can grant them and so when they reach a certain population, they begin to populate new regions by clearing new tunnels underground. The dream of unlimited power wielded by philosophical rulers acts as both dream and nightmare for the Speculative Modernists, who witnessed the triumphs and failures of empire.

This leads us to the second important element of this book as to the rise of the Speculative Modernists, and that is the power of evolution, and the question of who will be those great leaders. At the time of *The Coming Race*'s appearance, Charles Darwin's book *On the Origin of Species* (1859) was only twelve years old. Bulwer-Lytton's book asks if compassion plays any role in evolution, a question that many overlooked upon first encountering the notion of evolution. The English had deemed themselves morally and socially more advanced than many of the peoples they encountered in their expansion around the globe. In so doing they also had decided that it was their right to determine the fate of those peoples, either through enslavement or eradication. Bulwer-Lytton's *The Coming Race* asks us to suppose what would happen if humanity, as a whole, encountered its betters.

One of the physical manifestations of the Vril-ya that best exemplifies that they are more advanced, evolutionarily, when compared with humans is their hands. Their thumbs are "at once longer and more massive" and their palms are "proportionally thicker than ours—the texture of the skin infinitely finer and softer—its average warmth greater" (Bulwer-Lytton 59). The daughter of his host, Zee, explains:

> With your slight formation of thumb [...] and with the absence of the nerve which you find more or less developed in the hands of our race, you can never achieve other than imperfect and feeble power over the agency of vril; but so far as the nerve is concerned, that is not found in the hands of our earliest progenitors, not in those of the ruder tribes without the pale of the Vril-ya. It has been slowly developed in the course of generations, commencing in the early achievements, and increasing with the continuous exercise, of the vril power; therefore, in the course of one or two thousand years, such a nerve may possibly be engendered in those higher beings of your race, who devote themselves to that paramount science through which is attained command over all the subtler forces of nature permeated by vril [Bulwer-Lytton 59].

Through the narrator's conversations with his guides—Zee and the son of the leader of the Vril-ya, Taee—he learns that the Vril-ya are most compassionate to any people who have attained their level of understanding of vril and who live in general by the codes and customs of peace. They are not concerned with varying philosophies, religions, skin color, or anything that the narrator explains separates the people who live above ground. However, they do deem that anyone who has not accomplished this level of proficiency in using vril powers must be treated as animals, and therefore they have no qualms extinguishing them if they became inconvenient. "Nations which, not conforming their manners and institutions to those of the Vril-ya, nor indeed held capable of acquiring the powers over the vril agencies which it had taken them generations to attain and transmit, were regarded with more disdain than the citizens of New York regard the negroes" (53). Their expansion will require that they remove those of the "lesser races" since they will never try to take resources from others who have attained the power of vril.

Taee explains about the lesser races, which the Vril-ya call Koom-Posh, those with some form of feeble government that is always in flux and always at war, and Glek-Nas, those who are simply barbaric—generally Koom-Posh after a generation or two—and he explains what must be done when encountering them:

> Sometimes, as it is, we take waste spots, and find that a troublesome, quarrelsome race of Ana [people], especially if under the administration of Koom-Posh or Glek-Nas, resents our vicinity, and picks a quarrel with us; then, of course, as menacing our welfare, we destroy it: there is no coming to terms of peace with a race so idiotic that it is always changing the form of government which

represents it. Koom-Posh [...] is bad enough, still it has brains, though at the back of its head, and is not without heart, but in Glek-Nas the brain and heart of the creatures disappear, and they become all jaws, claws, and belly [77].

Taee also demonstrates an amazingly simple weapon that he carries that has enough force to level an entire superterranean city in a second, all powered by vril. The narrator begins to see that any encounter with the Vril-ya will likely be devastating to his people. This realization anticipates Rudyard Kipling's poem "The White Man's Burden" (1899), which would spell this attitude out so clearly, but from the conqueror's perspective. There is no moral quandary here for the Vril-ya. Just as the English had no trouble removing those they deemed "lesser" from places they needed to colonize, the narrator should understand the Vril-ya's decisions to remove races that were holding them back.

The relationship the Vril-ya have with the "lesser races" becomes a personal problem for our narrator when both Zee and, later, the daughter of the leader of Vril-ya desire a romantic entanglement with him. The females of the Vril-ya are the ones who seek their mates, not the other way around. While our narrator at first finds this quite refreshing and talks about the importance of seeing all people as agents of their own freedom—both above and below the ground, regardless of race or gender—this becomes a serious issue for him. He is interested in forming a bond with the daughter of his host, and when he hears about the interest from the leader's daughter, he is momentarily seized by the idea of becoming a prince among the Vril-ya. This cannot be, his host tells him, because he is a member of a lesser species that would only weaken his people. His host would have no choice but to destroy him, which he would do—even though he seems to have a fondness for him—without any qualms, as it would be for the good of his people. The only trouble is that he cannot be released to return to his own people as he might warn them about the Vril-ya before they were ready to dispossess the sun-dwellers of their land and resources. In the end, Zee comes to his rescue and helps him to escape, but he is left with the sinking feeling that humans are in grave danger. The narrator concludes his book by explaining that he hopes his readers will choose to begin the long attenuation of their bodies and the bodies of their children to vril as he warns of the coming race in the final line of the book.

In his introduction to *The Coming Race*, Matthew Sweet explains that this book had quite an impact on the society of the Modernist period—how it affected everything from the use of electricity in spiritual support to the creation of the popular British meat paste, Bovril. He also talks about how it affected the ideologies of the day as well, among them

> Victorian readers who knew their Darwin and suspected industrialization might have thrown the processes of evolution into reverse; Edwardian readers

who knew how many Boer War recruits had been rejected on grounds of sickliness and wondered whether the nation didn't need a restorative shot of vril; occultists of the teens and twenties, with sons dead in the mud of France, praying for some sort of clear new dawn; the survivors of another war, hoping that Nazism might be explained by some supernatural force, rather than the self-pitying anti–Semitism that had been an everyday twentieth-century ideology well beyond the borders of Hitler's Germany [...] [Sweet xi].

By applying new theories of science and technology to the current state of affairs, Bulwer-Lytton's novel would help to create a whole range of ideas for the Speculative Modernists to play with: alien forces that were stronger than humans, as Wells would write about in *The War of the Worlds*; occult power sources; creative philosophies of interaction between nations; and the extreme racism, genocide, and eugenics that poisoned the early part of the twentieth century.

Alien life is not always something that grows apart from humanity but may already be competing with humanity in the same space. Throughout the nineteenth century and into the twentieth, science demonstrated that humans were not able to sense the entire universe on their own. X-rays, for example, had only been recently discovered in 1905. In "From Beyond," which was written in 1920, but not published until 1934, H.P. Lovecraft draws on the science of the day to propose that humanity does not have the capacity to see the monsters that are all around us right now. S.T. Joshi's note on the story includes a reference to Hugh Elliot's *Modern Science and Materialism* (1919) and indicates that the work of this philosopher-scientist inspired this story. One does not have to read far into Elliot's book to find the essence of "From Beyond":

> If then, all knowledge is based on sense-impressions, it is clear that our notion of the Universe is bound to remain for ever of the most incomplete possible character. Supposing we had a few more senses, how very different everything would appear! Supposing we had a hundred more or a thousand more, the Universe must appear different from anything now conceivable. To a being thus endowed, the philosophy of a mere human being must appear indeed primitive [Elliot 4].

Elliot combined the ideas of Materialism, a philosophy that focused on everything that can be made tangible, and T.H. Huxley's Agnosticism,[9] which he outlines as being the philosophy that even if humans had a million senses, we would still never have enough information to prove or disprove the existence of God, as well as a good many other ideas.

Lovecraft's Crawford Tillinghast has found the way to extend his senses, a machine that can excite the pineal gland. "'You have heard of the pineal gland? I laugh at the shallow endocrinologist, fellow-dupe and fellow-parvenu of the Freudian. That gland is the great sense-organ of organs—*I have found out.* If you are normal, that is the way you ought to get most of it.... I mean get most of the evidence from *beyond*'" (Lovecraft "Beyond" 117). The narrator, Tillinghast's rival, is shaken as he is suddenly able to see in the ultraviolet range and beyond that into a seemingly whole other universe that overlaps ours. Tillinghast has gone mad with the power of his discovery and torments the narrator, by forcing him to endure the monstrosities that exist in this deeper understanding of the universe.

Tillinghast, in his taunts, tells our narrator that these creatures that ebb and flow like jellyfish right in front of his eyes are nothing. Initially, Tillinghast warns against any movement, but now that our narrator can also see these creatures, he explains why he should not move a muscle:

> I have seen beyond the bounds of infinity and drawn down daemons from the stars.... I have harnessed the shadows that stride from world to world to sow death and madness.... Space belongs to me, do you hear? Things are hunting me now—the things that devour and dissolve—but I know how to elude them. It is you they will get, as they got the servants. Stirring, dear sir? I told you it was dangerous to move [Lovecraft "Beyond" 120].

Yet, that is all Lovecraft will give us. Our narrator shoots at the machine, destroying it, while the monsters that Tillinghast was hoping to bring down on our narrator attack and kill Tillinghast instead. When the police arrive, all they have is the crazy story of the nearly mad narrator, but once they verify that it was not the bullet that killed Tillinghast, they let him go. Now, however, our narrator will live the rest of his life tormented by the glimpse he had of the universe that exists all around us. Speculative Modernists certainly encourage the curious in their stories, but always with the caveat that the curious just might find what they are looking for.

This notion of the senses not being able to register everything there is to see in the universe haunts Speculative Modernists as it indicates how much else there is to discover. The evidence of the existence of these creatures suggests that it is impossible to fully understand the universe. The true terror is in Hugh Elliot's point about Agnosticism: with only five senses, nothing can be confirmed definitively about the universe.

Lovecraft's friend and fellow *Weird Tales* contributor, Clark Ashton Smith, also wrote about the universe that might exist superimposed over our own in both his "The Dimension of Chance" (1932) and "The Metamorphosis of the World" (1951). Though the second story's publication date does not fall quite within the time period for this book, through the many letters Smith wrote, we know that it was written between 1929 and 1930, only to have to wait twenty years before finding a home. Both of these stories are unusual in that they would mostly be classified as science fiction, rather than Smith's more usual turn at fantasy or horror. "The Dimension of Chance" begins in science fiction, but immediately descends into horror, which may explain its more immediate acceptance and publication. In his article "Visionary Star-Treader: The Speculative Writings of Clark Ashton Smith," Richard Bleier argues that "['The Dimension of Chance'] asks questions about the nature of time, space, and matter" (79). The story "presents a world in which everything is random, unique, and often hostile; it is administered by Masters, who rule by being able to forecast randomness" (79). While science fiction was not generally a part of Smith's oeuvre, these stories do express a very important feature of Speculative Modernism: the inability of humankind to fully understand the universe.

The American pilots, Morris and Markley, during a dogfight with the Japanese, are separated by a darkness that follows the terrible atom-crushing storm. Morris braves the chaotic universe to search for his friend. In his journey, he encounters two beings that come to be known to him as the Masters of Chaos:

> Both of them stood erect, and their conformation was vaguely human in its outlines, except for the enormous wings, ribbed and leathery as those of ancient pterodactyls, which hung half-folded at their backs. Their coloration was a dark, bituminous brown, verging upon ebon blackness in the wings, and lightening somewhat in their heads and faces. They were massively built, with a stature of eleven or twelve feet, and aquiline, sloping, hairless heads that denoted a large brain-capacity. No trace of ears could be detected; but two round, luminous, golden-yellow eyes were set far apart in their sphinx-like mouths and nostrils. Somehow they made Morris think of Satanic angels; but their aspect was not malign, and was wholly poised, aloof and dispassionate [Smith "Dimension" 89].

The description of the Masters of Chaos echoes the language of the description of the Vril-ya from *The Coming Race*: the stature and wings, the sphinx-like faces and nostrils, the darkness of their skin. Morris and one of the Masters of Chaos exchange histories through a simple touch. Morris sees how these creatures evolved to the point where they could control the chaos of this universe for a time, but how even these amazingly powerful beings were being slowly overmatched by "the beleaguering forces of cosmic anarchy" (90). The fact that evolution comes into the description again indicates some influence from *The Coming Race*. Morris, after initially being afraid of the Masters, realizes that they are not the threat, and that in time, all dimensions will have to face this cosmic anarchy, which will destroy everything.

These beings help Morris by carrying him away in their arms, flying through the tumult they have mastered for the moment, and arrive just in time to help Markley fend off their Japanese nemeses, shooting bolts of lightning at them and blowing them into dust. The Americans are returned to their rocket-plane and sent back through the blur to their own dimension, out of necessity losing all memory of what the Masters of Chaos have shown them, the existential threat that lies at the heart of all reality. Again, the Speculative Modernists were plagued by thoughts of the end of the universe, its simple dispersal into atoms stretched too far, but the thought of the very order that held this universe together being unraveled by a more immediate chaos is a true terror.

In Smith's "The Metamorphosis of the World," the Earth faces a much more local threat. A group of scientists are sent to explore a region of the Sahara Desert that seems to be suddenly producing a great deal of radiation, enough to kill everyone in the region and anyone who examines the damage with any proximity. Roger Lapham and a crack team of scientists explore the region from afar. Though they are more prepared than those surprised by the phenomenon, they also will succumb to radiation sickness. While he is sick, though, Lapham is able to make this summation: "It looks […] as if someone or something had blown up all the atoms in this part of the Sahara, and had then started a totally new process of re-integration and evolution, with the development of soil, water, minerals, atmosphere and plants such as could never have existed on the earth during any of its geological epochs" (Smith "Metamorphosis" 123). Lapham lives long enough to see this happen in regions all around the world and helps to discover a series of satellites that seem to appear over the affected regions at different times. His dying prediction, extrapolated from the information about the satellites, is that people from Venus are trying to turn the Earth into their world.

Though the concept of terraforming is credited to the Jack Williamson story "Collision Orbit," which appeared in *Astounding Science Fiction* in 1942, this is exactly what Smith is writing about in this story—just in reverse. The Venusians, rather than deal with adapting to the Earth's atmosphere and biosphere, have decided to change the Earth to meet the Venusians' needs. The story describes the panic and the refugee movement that forces the people of Earth to the poles, which have become somewhat habitable as the Venusians turn up the heat. In the end, though, the Venusians suffer the same fate as Wells's Martians, as they seem unprepared to survive our microscopic population. The humans, though greatly reduced in population will live on to fight for their freedom, but the Earth will remain a chaotic mess. Both of Smith's stories describe the Wellsian fear of beings more capable of dealing with the reality of the universe—a reality with which twentieth-century humans were only beginning to come to grasp, whether that reality be spacial, temporal, or interdimensional.

There are forces greater than any single being, culture, or species. The Speculative Modernists remind their readers time and time again that they are foolish to think of themselves as masters of any part of this universe. Any time people think that they have inched even a little closer to an understanding of the world around us, they must remember that they know so little, can sense so little, that the minute advance is quite nearly worthless. Humans are not conquerors; they are simply waiting for the more evolved creatures, or maybe the universe itself, to crush them.

Conclusion

While the writers of the Speculative Modernist era might be looking to the stars, or the depths of the oceans, or even the untraveled interiors of unyielding continents, humans go only to distract themselves from their own inevitable deaths. Exploring new worlds may begin as a heroic endeavor, but, whether the newcomers are the ones to civilize or the ones to be civilized, they all end up the same. Now that they had reached the limits of the world, humanity had no more distractions, no frontiers to challenge and to conquer. The Modernists saw only death and destruction as the various powers of the world fought over the dwindling space and resources of the world. The Speculative Modernists, however, offered more space, more resources, and perhaps, more time in which to find an answer to mortality.

The European expansion begun in the late fifteenth century had come full circle, and the powers of the world were at each other's throats once more. The Speculative Modernists saw an opportunity to begin that expansion all over again, this time in a limitless universe. They had the opportunity to think the expansion through, perhaps to learn from the mistakes of the first expansion. Their stories dwelled in the tension between the fear of Wells's conquerors and the responsibility Kipling's poem encouraged in the new would-be conquerors. By creating alien lands, like Barsoom, Demonland, and Herland, and imaginary peoples, like the Selenites, the Tharkians, and the Vril-ya, Speculative Modernists were able to explore the rapidly changing societies here on Earth at the end of the Victorian era and into the twentieth century. Authors could challenge the attitudes of empire confronting both England and the United States and examine carefully which attitudes might fail and which might succeed from a safe distance. With the past as a cautionary tale, humanity could proceed into the new century and try to learn from these errors so as not to just return to this same spot again and again.

While the Modernists felt the cruelty of a godless universe that enacted its judgment on living beings seemingly at random, Speculative Modernists were able to demonstrate how mankind had done the same,

4. Worlds Beyond   131

whether through the cruelty of Wells's Martians, the condescension of the Vril-ya, the simple oversight of the forces of chaos, or even the bacteria that grow in a drop of water. With other worlds, the Speculative Modernists could start the age of exploration all over again and correct the failings of the age here on Earth, giving those people opportunities to try out their approaches before the actual encounters might begin. Just as humanity was able to begin planning the next stages of evolution through its newfound understanding of genetics, it was also able to plan its expansion out into the universe. The Modernists lamented the state to which the previous ages of enlightenment and expansion had brought them; the Speculative Modernists tried to learn from and correct the errors that got us to that state as they prepared for the worlds beyond our own.

Organic life, though, might not be the only concern humankind would have to face. While the Selenites could breed their people for specific tasks and the Vril-ya could teach their bodies through the power of vril, Speculative Modernists saw in technology another force that could be tamed. In the next chapter, "Machinocracy," these writers address the notion that technology itself could be the force we have most to fear. Apart from devastating weapons and dangerous innovations that could lead to man's own helplessness, technology might be used to create humanity's own conquerors.

5

Machinocracy

> The machine is antisocial. It tends, by reason of its progressive character, to the most acute forms of human exploitation.
> —Lewis Mumford, *Technics and Civilization* (1934)

The second half of the nineteenth century brought about profound and widespread changes to life in both the United States and the United Kingdom. Specifically, technological developments made lives and livelihoods commonplace that would have been unrecognizable only a generation or two before. During this era, innovations in industrial processes created mass manufacturing that required labor, and so formerly agrarian populations relocated *en masse* to be near the higher-income jobs in factory cities and market hubs. The Gilder Lehrman Institute of American History reports that the share of national economic output and the number of people employed in agriculture both dropped precipitously during this era as the United States moved from being primarily agrarian to primarily urban, from agricultural to industrial (White). As powerful symbols of the ingenuity of the new America, Thomas Edison, the Wright Brothers, Alexander Graham Bell, and Henry Ford became national heroes during this era. In the United Kingdom, according to the BBC, "the material prosperity stemming from uncontrolled industrial and urban development came at a high environmental and social cost, causing urban squalor, despoiled landscapes, dislocated communities and jeopardised livelihoods" (MacLeod). As the century turned, children on both sides of the Atlantic who had grown up during these tumultuous times were now creating worlds on their typewriters that matched their disorienting realities, and a new kind literature sprang up, built on invention and the machines that were transforming daily life.

Early Speculative Modernists told stories about groundbreaking new technology that *A History of Modernist Literature* says "emphasized its capacity to combine order and peace with efficiency and productivity" (Gąsiorek 141). The rapid growth in technological achievements cast a mechanical spell. Especially in the early years of science-fiction literature, there was a strong current of machine-positive utopian thinking, presenting the view that humanity could and inevitably would invent its way out of injustice, poverty, bigotry, violence, and many other social problems. H.G. Wells frequently shared this optimism, and he argued in *A Modern Utopia* (1905) that the changes brought about in the Machine Age, typically defined as the years from 1880 to 1945, might be the cure for all of society's ills. His idea was that scientific innovation might show the way to a new age where humans would take their cue from the design of the machines to find more just and efficient ways of organizing society:

> The plain message physical science has for the world at large is this, that were our political and social and moral devices only as well contrived to their ends as a linotype machine, an antiseptic operating plant, or an electric tram-car, there need now at the present moment be no appreciable toil in the world, and only the smallest fraction of the pain, the fear, and the anxiety that now makes human life so doubtful in its value. There is more than enough for everyone alive. Science stands, a too competent servant, behind her wrangling underbred masters, holding out resources, devices, and remedies they are too stupid to use [73].

Wells suggested that the machines themselves provide the ideal model for social efficiency and justice and that humanity should attempt to organize themselves in imitation of them in order to mold and shape their world. Wells was not alone. Other Speculative Modernists played with similar ideas. Society was not perfect but perfectible, and with the limitless ingenuity of the human mind, any problem could be solved by engineering the right tool for the job. The first section of this chapter, "A Species in Distress: Machines Will Save Humanity," discusses the many literary forms that this optimistic outlook takes.

At the same time that technological innovation was being explored by writers of science fiction, writers in fantasy and horror explored a literary backlash against this new mechanized world by creating quasi-medieval worlds characterized by limited technology and no industrialization. The section titled "Sand in the Gears: Machines Can't Save Us," explores this idea. These writers recognized that the true path toward salvation was not along an assembly line, but into and through the stuff that lies beyond the ability to perceive it, what some call magic. Machines would not be the salvation of humankind, and to think they might is a fool's errand. Furthermore, Speculative Modernists of this era argued that machines were not simply inert tools, but that humanity had been fundamentally changed by the new machines. This was Wells's idea turned upside down. The newly mechanized society had caused a shift toward a new way of organizing human civilization. The changes wrought by the Machine Age were so profound, in fact, that the French philosopher Jacques Ellul, in his treatise *The*

Technological Society (1954), looked back at the first half of the twentieth century and stated:

> The machine, so characteristic of the nineteenth century, made an abrupt entrance into a society which, from the political, institutional, and human points of view, was not made to receive it; and man has had to put up with it as best he can. Men now live in conditions that are less than human. Consider the concentration of our great cities, the slums, the lack of space, of air, of time, the gloomy streets and the sallow lights that confuse night and day. [...] The machine took its place in a social milieu that was not made for it, and for that reason created the inhuman society in which we live [Ellul].

During the Speculative Modernist era, there is no shortage of stories in the genres as well as in mainstream literature that depict the limited possibilities for industrialized workers. *Metropolis*-like conditions[1] for the working class were not the exception, they were the rule. Some Speculative Modernists argued that machines could not save humanity, that the problems of society would remain no matter what machine or flashy new tool was invented.

Still other Speculative Modernists recast the machines that had been seen as possible saviors for humanity as dehumanizing technology that would cause the downfall of the human race. More and more often—especially between the world wars—stories were filled with machines that challenged humanity for supremacy. Moreover, these new machines allowed humanity's worst inclinations to express themselves, frequently with apocalyptic results. Even in science fiction, which frequently championed advances in technology, the "machine" was often seen as a negative force in stories as disparate as E.M. Forster's "The Machine Stops" (1909) and Aldous Huxley's *Brave New World* (1932). Adam Roberts calls the anti-mechanization characters of these stories "machine bashers" (Roberts 158). Wells showed readers the bleak future of a society bifurcated by heavy industry in *The Time Machine* (1895). Robert M. Coates demonstrated the gradual but ultimately extreme corruption of Charles Dograr in *The Eater of Darkness* (1926). The discussion continues even to today, with the familiar arguments that television, the internet, and mobile phones destroy social connections and rot one's brain. And it wasn't just the machines themselves that were pushing humanity in to the unknown. The changes brought about by social mechanization were also putting pressure on communities and individuals. Robert S. Levine argues that, during the Modernist era, "many intellectuals suspected that mass culture would create a robotic, passive population vulnerable to demagoguery" (674). Stephen Kern proposes that this drop in optimism tracks well with literary ages. Gothic and Victorian writers, he says, tended to look backward in time for answers to the profound questions of the day. Science-fiction writers of the Machine Age shifted that perspective completely and began to look toward the future to find meaning and to create civilization (Kern 94). Starting with a well-known example from the previous age, the philosophical gap between *Little Dorrit* (1857) by Charles Dickens—where his young title character longs "so ardently and earnestly" (573) for her former life even though it was filled with suffering and poverty—to Wells's *The Time Machine* (1895), a novel that looks all the way to the end of life on Earth, is immense. Nostalgia cannot help itself: it must be positive, almost by definition, even if memories of the sunny past are tinged with melancholy and regret. Speculative Modernist writers tend to look toward the future without the burden of nostalgia. Something was indeed different about the Machine Age, and the speculative writers of the era recognized it. Innovation arrived at such a breakneck pace that the ramifications were hard to understand, and humans at times felt swept up by forces they could neither comprehend nor control. The third section of this chapter, "Building the Perfect Gun: Machines Will Kill Us All," explores the movement toward technological pessimism.

Whole worlds were opening up with every delivery of magazines such as *Modern Electrics*, *The Thrill Book*, *Weird Tales*, and *Amazing Stories*. Although it was difficult to see it at the time, this era in science and speculative fiction profoundly changed the United States and the United Kingdom forever. As the Machine Age—sometimes called the Second Industrial Revolution—spread internal combustion, electrification, mass production, and radio everywhere, the seed of Speculative Modernism took root in sprawling industrial cities like London and New York. As in other areas that fall under the umbrella of Speculative Modernism, literary attitudes about technology ranged from the near-utopianism of the late-nineteenth century to nihilism, dystopianism, and negativity. The new machines that were invented and popularized during this era entered the minds of writers of fiction who, from these developments, extrapolated futures filled with wonders, and the reading audience could not get enough. Combined with innovations by Darwin, Einstein, Freud, Picasso, and others who overturned the widely accepted perception of the universe, the rise of the advanced, expensive, and powerful technology of the Machine Age was an important driving force for Speculative Modernism.

A Species in Distress: Machines Will Save Humanity

During the final two decades of the nineteenth century, Speculative Modernists expressed optimism about the Machine Age. They imagined bright futures filled with cures for deadly diseases, incredibly fast travel, and agricultural miracles. Some even imagined machines as new life-forms. Samuel Butler's "Darwin Among the Machines" (1863) is notable for its depiction of machines responding to the forces of natural selection described by Charles Darwin in *On the Origin of Species* (1859). Butler, who wrote about evolution and natural selection in the years immediately following the publication of Darwin's masterwork, shows the first stirrings of the Modernist influence on speculative fiction. Butler's fellow utopians were concerned with human society and the perfectibility of humanity, but, even at this earliest stage, Butler was already looking at the absurdity of these utopian social movements and thinking about a world after humanity has run its course:

> We refer to the question: What sort of creature man's next successor in the supremacy of the earth is likely to be. We have often heard this debated; but it appears to us that we are ourselves creating our own successors; we are daily adding to the beauty and delicacy of their physical organization; we are daily giving them greater power and supplying by all sorts of ingenious contrivances that self-regulating, self-acting power which will be to them what intellect has been to the human race. In the course of ages we shall find ourselves the inferior race. [...] Day by day, however, the machines are gaining ground upon us; day by day we are becoming more subservient to them; more men are daily bound down as slaves to tend them, more men are daily devoting the energies of their whole lives to the development of mechanical life. The upshot is simply a question of time, but that the time will come when the machines will hold the real supremacy over the world and its inhabitants is what no person of a truly philosophic mind can for a moment question [Butler "Darwin"].

Butler explored this idea in his novel *Erewhon* (1872). Machines, with their ability to adapt and evolve just like any other living thing, have been outlawed in Erewhon because some characters believed that the machines have feelings. Butler went on to argue in the final section of the novel, titled "The Book of the Machines," that there is reason to think that machines will evolve and replace humanity much faster than anyone thought possible. This insight into the limits of humanity and the potential for a world moving on after humanity has been surpassed is what makes *Erewhon* so important from a Speculative Modernist perspective.

Butler's work had some elements of satire in it, but, at the same time, there was a current of stories about machines for their own sake that contained no element of ridicule. Early Speculative Modernists emphasized the innocent coolness of a ray gun or a spaceship or any number of fantastic inventions over character development; these inventions became the subjects of a kind of science fiction that was almost totally devoid of social issues or their effect on human society. For about one hundred years, the American author and editor Edward Page Mitchell was unrecognized as a pioneer of science fiction, because, during his career in journalism, he published his stories anonymously and mostly in newspapers, not magazines devoted to fiction. Because of this, no one realized that they had been written by a single person until they were collected many decades later. Editor and scholar Sam Moskowitz, in his introduction to *The Crystal Man: Stories by Edward Page Mitchell* (1973), was the first to identify Mitchell as the single author of that array of previously unattributed stories. Among Mitchell's groundbreaking accomplishments, he is credited by Moskowitz as being the first to write stories about cryogenics, a way to make a person become invisible, a perfectly plausible faster-than-light transport, an electric computer inside the skull of a living person, and a machine for time traveling (Moskowitz ix–x)—two decades before H.G. Wells popularized the concept in *The Time Machine*. His stories could not have existed without the exciting new developments that the Machine Age was bringing to every city and town in United States and Britain. Mitchell's stories offer no ominous promises about dismal futures. Instead, they revel in the fun that can be had with all of these new gadgets.

In Mitchell's story "The Tachypomp" (1874), the protagonist is madly in love with a woman whose father is an eminent mathematician. In order to prove his worth to the skeptical father, this suitor must figure out a way to create a machine that travels a mile in six seconds, an unheard-of speed in those days. The protagonist falls asleep and dreams of an acquaintance who shows him a series of trains stacked vertically, each half as long as the one below it, each with another set of tracks on its roof. Once the bottom train begins to move forward along its track, the one above it begins to move forward along its track too. The one above that second train begins to move and the next one and so on. Stack the trains high enough, and you get a train surpassing the speed of light! Mathematics and engineering are depicted as wonderful and ethically simple toys by which men prove their worth or make their lives more manageable or enjoyable. Although these toys might allow an enterprising individual to wield great power to solve the world's problems, there is nothing more than a little healthy mischief possible if the tools are misused. Mitchell's view of the fantastic new technology was uncomplicated and wide-eyed. His stories exhibited an innocent fascination with the future and good humor as well. His attitude about the rapid and profound changes brought about by the Machine Age shared the optimism of his utopian contemporaries.

Similar to Mitchell's rapid-fire innovations, American writer and Modernist provocateur, Bob Brown, did all he could to shake the foundations of art and literature. During the early years of the twentieth century, he established his literary reputation and fortune in New York and Brazil. Between the world wars, he moved to Europe and befriended the crowd of expatriates in Paris that included Gertrude Stein, Kay Boyle, and other major figures of the Modernist era. Brown depicted the idea for the first ever e-reader, a now-ubiquitous piece of technology, in his book, *The Readies* (1930). (The title is not pronounced like "ready," but as in how the word "talk" is related to the word "talkies" which was the common slang for the new technology that allowed movies to have sound that synched to the action on the screen.) His machine would, as he envisioned it, revolutionize the act of reading by modernizing it. He wrote that letting the eye move across a page from word to word and line to line was hopelessly antiquated:

> The written word hasn't kept up with the age. The movies have outmanoeuvered it. We have the talkies, but as yet no Readies.
> I'm for new methods of reading and writing and I believe the up-to-date reader deserves an eye-ful when he buys something to read. I think the optical end of the written word has been hidden over a bushel too long. I'm out for a bloody revolution of the word.
> I don't mean maybe breakemup words I mean smashum [Brown 1].

In *The Readies*, the narrator dreams of somehow taking the words off the page and moving them into a realm where language is felt instead of simply read. He wants to take the rapid changes he sees everywhere else in his world and transform the act of reading as well, so that literature—words on the page—comes alive in ways that film brought photography to life (the brackets below appear in the original text):

> In our aeroplane age radio is rushing in television, tomorrow it will be a commonplace. All the arts are having their faces lifted, painting, [Picasso], sculpture [Brancussi], music [Antheil], architecture [zoning law], drama [Strange Interlude], dancing [just look around you tonight], writing [Joyce, Stein, Cummings, Hemingway]. Only the reading half of Literature lags behind, stays old-fashioned, frumpish, beskirted. Present day reading methods are as cumbersome as they were in the time of Caxton and Jimmy the Ink. Though we have advanced from Gutenberg's movable type through the linotype and monotype to photocomposing we still consult the book in its original archaic form as the only oracular means we know for carrying the word mystically to the eye. Writing has been bottled up in books since the start. It is time to pull out the stopper [Brown 28].

Using abbreviations such as RSVP and YMCA, the narrator argues that language can be drastically shortened without losing any meaning and that he could "read hundred thousand word novels in ten minutes if I want to, and I want to" (Brown 28). He proposes to accomplish this through the application of his Readies machine that would take language in a novel, for example, and break it down into more easily digestible, smaller, and fewer pieces. Brown is a fine example of the Speculative Modernist inclination to break down everything into its component parts and then reinvent new forms more suited to the times. He was early by a few generations, but with the rise of audio books, texting, social media, and e-readers in the past few decades, Brown was prescient.

The pulps in the 1920s and 1930s are filled with stories that all share an optimistic innocence about the shiny new technology that arrived in waves throughout this era. George Frederick Stratton's story, "Sam Graves' Gravity Nullifier," which appeared in 1929 in *Amazing Stories*, is typical of early science fiction's enthusiastic relationship with technology. In a canyon out west, a man named Sam Graves invents the titular work tool that allows for mining and other industrial activity to be carried on without the impediment of gravity. This is a huge breakthrough that allows the company's profits to soar. There is a battle over ownership of the idea and the machine, and then the story ends; plot is not the main attraction here. The depiction of the "gravity nullifier" is sufficiently specific to allow the reader to bathe happily in technojargon for a few paragraphs. In the story, there is not a scintilla of trouble with the technology. It has been invented, and it will be used to support the company that owns it. None of the other myriad possibilities for antigravity are even contemplated. Humanity invents flashy new technology to solve a problem, and those new machines serve humanity without complication. These stories abounded during the pulp era, but, at the same time, there were writers emerging and stories being published that pointed out the troubling and dysfunctional relationship that was developing between humanity and its inventions.

There are many stories throughout the Speculative Modernist era that emphasize the coolness of the gadgets that were being invented without giving much of a thought to the complications that might arise from ideas such as time travel, faster than light speed, and antigravity. Especially early in the era, it was enough just to be fun and fascinating, to put the nifty new tool into the hands of a hero and see the amazing things that happen. There was a sense of boundless optimism, as if the dream of the utopians was finally coming to pass. Humanity had the right ideas about making their collective future bright, and now the tools to accomplish those lofty goals were finally in the hands of the heroes of these stories. Soon thereafter, however, writers and readers began seeking more complexity in their stories. Technological innovation would not and could not change the stubborn social issues or solve eternal problems such as war, poverty, and disease. The stories changed in response to that demoralizing realization.

Sand in the Gears: Machines Can't Save Us

In mainstream literature, much of the social optimism of the late nineteenth-century utopians had ebbed after World War I. Literary

Modernism as we know it was well underway by then, with all of its pessimism and dystopian thinking. This change was especially profound when it came to the depictions of the power of technology to serve humanity. Speculative Modernists were way ahead of their much more well-known counterparts. Very quickly, they had moved from the breezy optimism of Edward Page Mitchell to a series of bleak futures where technology cannot come close to solving humanity's problems.

Indeed, there were already signs that a backlash against technology was beginning to build in Sir Arthur Conan Doyle's *The Doings of Raffles Haw* (1892). In this tale, a machine promises to save one man with one of the oldest dreams of science: it turns lead into gold. Raffles Haw, a young wealthy man stumbles across the long-lost secret of alchemy through modern chemistry simply by running electric current through various chemicals until one accidentally transforms entirely into another element. Once that barrier is broken, it is just a matter of trial and error until he comes up with the right chemical and the right amount of intensity of time and current to change lead into gold. He finds himself now able to produce approximately twenty-four thousand pounds sterling of gold in about twenty minutes of work. This allows him to not only solve all of his own problems, but all of the problems of the surrounding neighborhood, which he accomplishes anonymously at first.

Raffles Haw, though, discovers that he must use his wealth very carefully. First, he vows not to ruin anyone in his paying off debt. Second, he wants to prevent unscrupulous people from fulfilling their idle wishes rather than their fundamental needs. At the beginning of the book, he encounters the McIntyre family—Laura, Robert, and their father—who are suffering their own misfortunes. Robert is an idealist and a painter, who has the soul of an artist but not quite the talent of one, mainly because he is still young and trying to find his way. Haw is dressed like a common laborer when he first meets Robert and begins to ask him about what he thinks about all this new wealth that is suddenly pouring into their small town. Robert explains that he is no admirer of wealth, and when Haw presses him, he insists that all he wants to do is sell enough of his art to maintain a steady living but nothing more:

> "Art," said Robert, warming to the subject, "is her own reward. What mere bodily indulgence is there which money could buy which can give that deep thrill of satisfaction which comes on a man who has conceived something new, something beautiful, and the daily delight as he sees it grow under his hand, until it stands before him a completed whole? With my art and without wealth I am happy. Without my art I should have a void no money could fill" [Conan Doyle *Doings* 50–51].

Haw immediately hires him on to be one of his agents in dealing with contributing money all around the county to help people in all kinds of ways, from the personal level all the way up to the societal level. Haw takes Robert on a tour of his home which contains the modern miracle of a mechanism by which Haw can be in any room he wants to be with the press of a button. Haw shows Robert all his miracles, including in the end most of the miracle of the actual transmutation of lead into gold.

When Robert's father sets off to find out the mystery of Haw's wealth and to steal some of his gold, Haw has already had experience with greed of all sorts and so easily thwarts the old man's desire for money. What Haw does not see coming is that he has ruined Robert, as well. Robert, learning all that he has about Haw's amazing wealth, finds that he no longer has the drive or the desire to paint. His lavish scenes out of history seem a mere mockery when compared with what he accomplishes with Haw's magnificent machines. Robert wonders what painting can stand up to the good deeds to be done with the limitless power that those machines can provide. Haw destroys everything—his remaining wealth, the machine that created it, and even his own life—because he feels that there will never be a time when he can trust anyone or anything with this great wealth. He seems to sow only corruption, sloth, and greed with it, and so it is not something he wants to share with the world after all. In the end, it was not the wonderful machines that failed or threatened society, but the people who gained by them, and he could not foresee any fix for the greed of people.

There is a similar sentiment in Frank Stockton's "A Tale of Negative Gravity" (1895). Stockton, who is known best for "The Lady or the Tiger?" (1882), tells the story of a man who, in his spare time during his retirement, invents a way to "store centrifugal force" so that it acts as a counter to gravity. This invention allows him and his wife to carry heavy objects, including their own bodies, with very little effort. One might think that there would be many applications for this invention that would help humanity, from transportation to medicine and other fields, but the story explores none of those possibilities. The husband contemplates bringing the invention to the world, but his wife convinces him that they are happy as they were and that the invention will surely succeed to such a degree that their lives will be forever changed, and not for the better. Not only does he fear the future of his marriage, but his son, Herbert, is negatively affected by the wondrous invention, as well. The inventor has developed quite a reputation as "insane," "lunatic," and "deranged" (Stockton "Tale"). Herbert's future father-in-law, worried about his daughter, Janet, marrying into a family of maniacs, ends the engagement. When the inventor hears about this, his heart is broken. He goes to Janet's father and explains. After a demonstration, Janet's father is satisfied and the wedding is back on:

"My friend," I cried, with some excitement, "I have made up my mind on this subject. The little machine in this knapsack, which is the only one I now possess, has been a great pleasure to me. But I now know it has also been of the greatest injury indirectly to me and mine, not to mention some direct inconvenience and danger, which I will speak of another time. The secret lies with us three, and we will keep it. But the invention itself is too full of temptation and danger for any of us" [Stockton "Tale"].

A machine that would have improved the lives of humanity in inconceivable ways was placed into a drawer and forgotten about. There is a not a moment's consideration to the good or evil such a machine could help accomplish. The assumption here is that human society is more or less static and that if an innovation does not serve the status quo, it should rightly be tossed aside. Of primary importance is the happiness of relationships in a loving family. That is the thing that is prioritized over any fancy gadgets, no matter how useful:

There is a wonderful pleasure in tripping over the earth like a winged Mercury, and in feeling one's self relieved of much of that attraction of gravitation which drags us down to earth and gradually makes the movement of our bodies but weariness and labor. But this pleasure is not to be compared, I think, to that given by the buoyancy and lightness of two young and loving hearts, reunited after a separation which they had supposed would last forever [Stockton "Tale"].

For Stockton and many other writers in the post-utopian generation, machines and shiny new gadgets are fun, but they pale in comparison to the kind of excitement to be had by living a much simpler life free of the machines that were coming to dominate human society. The invention at the heart of Stockton's story resembles that in Stratton's "The Gravity Nullifier." Although they were published thirty-four years apart, these stories share the outlook that technology is simple and without complication. Stories with this central assumption remained popular throughout the entire Speculative Modernist era.

Growing right alongside those optimistic stories, however, came tales about the ambivalence toward humanity's amazing new inventions. During the first decade of the twentieth century, E.M. Forster published the novels *Where Angels Fear to Tread* (1905), *A Room with a View* (1908), and *Howards End* (1910), all best-selling and widely respected stories about class and race at the height of the British Empire. In 1909, he published a remarkable piece of science fiction, "The Machine Stops," which is the story of Kuno, a rebel who lives alone—as all humans do—under the surface of the Earth, his every need tended to by the "Machine." Each person watches what seems to be the equivalent of a combination of Facebook and Netflix while simultaneously communicating with each other via something closely resembling Skype (all in a story published in 1909!). People who seek out the physical company of others are considered suspect; people who travel to the surface of the planet are considered insane. Kuno's mother, Vashti, is content with her life, and he tries to break her out of her technology-abetted stupor. He is restless for an authentic experience, something that he cannot get from the Machine:

> Men made it, do not forget that. Great men, but men. The Machine is much, but it is not everything. I see something like you in this plate, but I do not see you. I hear something like you through this telephone, but I do not hear you. That is why I want you to come. Pay me a visit, so that we can meet face to face, and talk about the hopes that are in my mind [Forster 2].

The Machine is considered omnipotent and worshipped as a god, more or less. Humanity, in fact, has little else to do but to be docile and serve the Machine. When the Machine finally collapses (the title reveals the ending), the whole structure of human civilization collapses along with it.

E.M. Forster was not the only one sounding a warning about the machines in our midst. James Elroy Flecker published his first novel, *The Last Generation: A Story of the Future*, in 1908, a work that scholar and author Paul March-Russell called the "most cynical" example of texts about "the pathos of lingering apocalypse" (March-Russell 50) that were prominent at this time, a list that, for March-Russell, includes Wells's *The Time Machine* and T.S. Eliot's "The Hollow Men" (1925). Flecker published only two novels during a life cut short by tuberculosis. With his poetry, he was on the cusp of greatness. Flecker's death at such a young age in 1915 caused the poet and critic Alec Macdonald to remark in *The Fortnightly Review* that it was "unquestionably the greatest premature loss that English literature has suffered since the death of Keats" (Morra 34). His other novel, *The King of Alsander* (1914), is a fantasy set in a dreamlike kingdom. One can only guess about the prominent position Flecker might have taken in the speculative-fiction world had he lived longer.

The Last Generation: A Story of the Future is a science-fiction novel that is very much a response to the utopians. In it, not only has world peace been achieved through the imposition of a working-man's utopia onto the entire world, but every other "problem" facing humankind has been eradicated, most of them with machines. In short, humanity has achieved everything that we have ever dreamed of: "For centuries we endured the march of Civilisation [...] leading Humanity year by year along her glorious path. And, looking around them, the wise men saw the progress of civilisation, and what was it? What did it mean? Less country, fewer savages, deeper miseries, more millionaires, and more museums" (Flecker). Humanity has built "prodigious" and "splendid" buildings. All wars have been fought and won. In this story Flecker does what other Speculative Modernists do: he posits a future wherein all technology has run its course. Nevertheless, technological mastery has left a huge void in humanity's soul. The common people have triumphed over the elite and have established heaven on Earth. However, for all of the technological know-how of these future humans, they find that they now lack a reason for being and are "disappointed at the way in which human progress has been impeded, and at the impossibility of a continuous evolution of knowledge-accumulation, that they find no more attraction in life" (Flecker). The entire species decides to end it all by ceasing reproduction. It is decreed that no new children will be born and, if a child is born, that child and both parents will be killed. The current living people ride out their lifetimes in debauchery participating in the collective suicide of humanity. The novel ends with an anticipation of the cyclical nature of human civilization: "I saw the vast Halls and Palaces of men falling in slowly, decaying, crumbling, destroyed by nothing but the rains and the touch of Time. And looking again I saw wandering over and above the ruins, moving curiously about, myriads of brown, hairy, repulsive little apes. One of them was building a fire with sticks" (Flecker). When one falls, another doomed civilization is born. The destiny of that new civilization is to rise to greatness and then build tools powerful enough to destroy itself. Even during the Modernist period, Flecker's novel is notably cynical about the ambition of humanity to do great things with big ideas. The technology in this story worked exactly as its well-meaning designers intended, but it brought a raft of unintended consequences as well. These machines will lead to humanity's extinction by make people comfortable, bored, and, finally, apathetic.

It is not as if machines bring out the worst in humanity, the time traveler of John W. Campbell's oft-anthologized story "Twilight" (1934) argues. It is that machines give us precisely what we ask for that makes them so dangerous. Campbell is a towering figure in the history of speculative fiction in the United States. Despite his "crabby, malcontented views of science and society" (Berger *Machine* 191), his work as an editor of *Astounding Science Fiction* for over three decades allowed him to put his stamp on science fiction, fantasy, and horror. His sensibilities defined these genres and established clear boundaries, for better or worse, within which stories needed to exist in order to find room in the pages of his magazine.

In "Twilight," a traveler from the year 3059 hitches a ride and tells the story of his journey seven million years into the future. The few stragglers of humanity are still wandering the Earth as the perfect machines they created continue to maintain cities and towns with impeccable efficiency. In this future, disease, war, and other sources of pain and unpredictability have been all but eradicated. Humanity has eliminated all forms of life that had previously threatened human health, including harmful bacteria, predators, and other dangers. In the fulfillment of all of their desires, their lives become sterile and dull and, without challenges, they lose interest in everything that makes a life worth living:

> Can you appreciate the crushing hopelessness it brought to me? [...] And all the great city-structure throbbing and humming to the steady gentle beat of perfect, deathless machines built more than three million years before—and never touched since that time by human hands. And they go on. The dead city. The men that have lived, and hoped, and built—and died to leave behind them those little men who can only wonder and look and long for a forgotten kind of companionship. They wander through the vast cities their ancestors built knowing less of them than the machines themselves [Campbell "Twilight" 1067].

Campbell's story is a fine example of many stories during the Speculative Modernist era that call into question the mad rush toward the next greatest discovery. Humanity, in its desire to create technologies to make their lives wonderful, end up building their own elaborate, gear-and-piston prisons.

Speculative Modernists moved from the early optimism of Edward Page Mitchell and so many stories in the pulps to a feeling that while humanity had problems, machines were not the cure. Ambivalence became the watchword for a generation of writers. In a letter to the poet, Elizabeth Toldridge in 1935, H.P. Lovecraft speculated about the likelihood that machines would be the way for humanity to save itself from its inevitable extinction. He envisioned the advances in technology taking humanity down a path with only a few options. A stable society *might* be created with the help of machines. This outcome, Lovecraft opined, seems unlikely. Humanity could blow itself up, and the people who survive, if any, could start again in "barbarism": "One cannot yet tell whether a stable machine-culture will grow out of contemporary life without an intervening break, or whether the present fabric will explode & give place to a wholly new growth beginning with pastoral & agricultural barbarism amidst which the machine will be forgotten except as a subject of magical tales" (Lovecraft *Letters* 173–74). Lovecraft sees little hope in machines to make any difference in how humanity's lifespan plays out. In this letter, he discusses many possibilities for civilization to break down. He discovers none in which humanity can save itself no matter what fantastic new inventions appear. It seems that Lovecraft spoke for many Speculative Modernists in this letter, especially as the Depression raged across the world and Fascism gained momentum in Europe. The idea that humanity was doomed, and that technological innovations, no matter how superficially benign they appeared, would speed its demise, was not just a concern for Speculative Modernists. In 1939, on the brink of World War II, Bernard

De Voto, Pulitzer Prize–winning editor, author, and essayist, waded into the speculative-fiction realm:

> The race, you see, degenerates as it advances; all its miraculous metals, space ships, ray guns, and three dimensional telepathy are phenomena of decay. It treads the ordained way to extinction[....] Hope and belief have burned out, the nucleus has expanded, fate's equation has been factored to the last term. All movement is toward grayness, and life itself is degeneration [qtd. in Berger "Theories" 12].

In the speculative stories of this era, it is not just the war machines that will kill us all. The machines meant to make life "easier" and more "civilized" are the ones that will play a big role in humanity's undoing.

Building the Perfect Gun: Machines Will Kill Us All

Speculative Modernists have offered a gradually evolving vision of the role of machines in our lives and society. The late 1800s and early 1900s brought spectacular and shocking new inventions, and inventors themselves gained tremendous fame and acclaim. Speculative Modernist writers looked at their impact from all sides. Especially during the interwar years, they became disillusioned with the power of technology to change human lives for the better. After witnessing the horrors of trench warfare conducted with chemical weapons and on the way to Hiroshima and Nagasaki, a strong current in popular thought developed that argued that these new machines allowed humanity's worst instincts to manifest themselves in powerfully destructive ways.

Famed satirist Mark Twain entered into that conversation with his novel *A Connecticut Yankee in King Arthur's Court* (1889). The novel begins with boundless optimism about human innovation and the inclination to make use of it for the good of one and all. In the novel, Hank Morgan, a smart, ambitious, and enterprising man of the industrial age, is transported back to sixth-century England. He immediately begins to take charge, to reimagine that society as nineteenth-century New England. Morgan builds factories, electricity and telephone networks, and an industrial culture. Nevertheless, Morgan has trouble explaining a simple concept in economics to the assembled workers, and he is bewildered at their inability to understand: "Well, I was stunned; partly with this unlooked-for stupidity on his part, and partly because his fellows so manifestly sided with him and were of his mind—if you might call it mind" (Twain 229). He is able to herd these sheep toward the future, and things seem to be going well for a while. "Slavery was dead and gone; all men were equal before the law; taxation had been equalized" (Twain 278). Morgan is optimistic about his chances to drag humanity kicking and screaming into enlightenment, but his confidence is buffeted, especially near the end of the novel. He finds he is able to bully the people into doing what he tells them to do, but they just lack the ability to comprehend fully what he is talking about: "But no; you see I was an unknown person, among a cruelly oppressed and suspicious people, a people always accustomed to having advantage taken of their helplessness, and never expecting just or kind treatment from any but their own families and very closest intimates" (Twain 237). Unfortunately, people are who they are, and, no matter what futuristic tools he puts into their hands, the imagination of his fellow citizens limits their ability to see past their prejudices, fears, and superstitions.

The final battle between those who support Morgan and those who oppose him is what renowned scholar of nineteenth-century literature, Paul K. Alkon, calls "the nineteenth century science fiction's most disturbing image of industrialized warfare[....] Twain's intention was less prophecy than diagnosis of industrial civilization's darkest potentialities for self-destruction" (132). In the chapter "The Battle of the Sand Belt," Morgan's fifty men destroy the combined might of England's armed forces, some thirty-thousand knights and soldiers. Despite Morgan's optimism, it seems almost inevitable that the end result of the industrialization of sixth-century England would result in the deaths of thousands. Not only do the machines that Morgan brings with him not change English society and governance for the long term, but they allow the most destructive impulses of the men on both sides their most devastating expression. The technology brought to this era by Morgan—the machines common in late nineteenth-century New England such as trains, telephones, and gunpowder weapons—leave little room for human contact, human mercy, or simple charity. The machines dictate that those instincts are put aside. The machines in this novel draw out the worst in people and will lead, inevitably, to destruction. Worst of all, Morgan assumed that the machines would bring out a different frame of mind. Instead, these characters became more destructive versions of their previous selves.

In other stories, machines might not simply destroy. Some writers explored the idea that machines would serve to limit our freedom, to mechanize and enslave human society. H.G. Wells's novella "A Story of the Days to Come" was first serialized in 1897 and then again in 1928. The first chapter is titled "The Cure for Love." That title is a play on the funny old adage that "marriage is the cure for love." In Wells's novella, two young lovers, Elizabeth and Denton, defy the tight social stratification and get married. The woman's wealthy family disowns her, and the two lovebirds retreat to the completely depopulated countryside to live off the land. That does not go particularly well, and they are assailed by all manner of frightening events: dogs barking, cantankerous loners, a lack of any of the luxuries to which they had grown accustomed in the city. They decide to return to London and take brutal labor-intensive jobs under the surface of the city where the other laborers live. Wells had already explored this territory in *The Time Machine*, published two years earlier in 1895, which featured the Morlocks living under the surface of the future world in a mysterious industrial setting. Denton and Elizabeth, without family support, quickly run out of money and take jobs with the "Labor Company," which had begun as a sort of temporary employment agency but which had developed into the enforcement arm of the mandatory labor policies enacted by the government. This agency had "two or three hundred million clients" (Wells "A Story" 22) and ruled the underworld completely. These "serfs" were shackled to the machines that made the city above hum pleasantly for the wealthy minority of the population. Life below the city, where people serve the machines they built, "one thinks of one's work, one's little vexations and pleasures, one's eating and drinking and ease and pain. One lives, and one must die" (Wells "A Story" 24). The danger, as these Speculative Modernists saw it, was that machines would come to be the masters of humans, that humans would build them and then serve them.

Ten years later, the destructive power of machines was still on the mind of H.G. Wells. The hero of *The War in the Air* (1908) is an average man named Bert Smallwood. He is caught up in a planetary war that ends up destroying advanced human civilization. Tensions that had been festering between nations were allowed to explode into fatal conflict once the necessary advanced technology was introduced. First, the conquering Germans build a huge air force to attack the United States. At the same time, Japan and China are collaborating on a similar force that they launch simultaneously against the United States. New York City surrenders to the Germans, but the Germans bombard the city anyway. The Asians and Germans meet in the middle of the continent and debris rains down across the defeated United States. The Asians get the upper hand and the conflict devolves into a bloody ground war. War spreads as England, France, Spain, and Italy rush to match the air power of the Germans, while the American president distributes the schematics for a British flying machine that is far superior to what the Asians and Germans are using. War builds upon war, and humanity brings about its near-total annihilation. "And with the smash of the high and dangerous and splendid edifice of mechanical civilization that had arisen so marvellously, back to the land came the common man, back to the manure" (Wells *Air* 264). That is the overarching theme of this novel. Human genius will create the tools for humans to kill themselves. The novel ends with the shiny new gadgets and flying machines, inventions that had created both wonder and terror, forgotten as humanity reverts back to a preindustrial state. For Wells, there is no way for both humanity and advanced technology to coexist.

The sweeping advances in technology of the early part of the twentieth century do not improve the lives of the people in *The War in the Air*. In his *Science Fiction Studies* article, Steven Mollmann argues that Wells wrote *The War in the Air* as a warning about the dangers of unchecked advances in technology (20). He points out that the airships that wage the apocalyptic war are the perfect metaphors because they are "able to remove to such a distance that human bodies cease to exist as individuals who can be killed and become only aggregations, tactical groupings that can be destroyed[....] Without technological detachment, the moral authority their revolution requires could not exist" (22). These new machines allow humanity's worst impulses to come to the fore. It is war we want, societal suicide sooner rather than later. As Mollmann writes about the characters in *The War in the Air*, "high science only enables the worst aspects of humankind to flourish" (23). Throughout his career, Wells seems to have been of two minds about the effect of advanced technology on the future of humanity. On either chronological side of *The War in the Air* stand *A Modern Utopia* (1905) and *The Shape of Things to Come* (1933), two novels that posit human ingenuity and advanced machines as the path to peace and prosperity, even if it takes decades of bloodshed to get there.

Although primarily known (both celebrated and vilified) for his perspective on Empire and Imperialism, Rudyard Kipling dabbled in many areas of literature, and that includes flirtations with the fringes of topics inhabited by the Speculative Modernists. This includes his perhaps most famous work, *The Jungle Book* (1894). It also includes less celebrated shorter works such as "Mary Postgate" from 1915.

Set in the throes of World War I, "Mary Postgate" tells the story of an older woman who is the companion/caregiver to the senior Miss Fowler, and her adopted nephew, Wyndham (Wynn). As Wynn matures, he decides to enlist in the army, just as virtually every young man in England did. It was the noble and heroic thing to do, a chance to prove his worth. This is where the machines enter into the narrative. Fascinated with flying, Wynn enlists with the assignment of Flying Corps. Stationed thirty miles away, Wynn was able to visit home often to show off his knowledge of the latest airplane-related jargon. This was done not only to demonstrate his enthusiasm over the wondrous machines, but to also continually reassert his dominance over her. She had no choice but to play along. However, she did not have to for long. In one of his training exercises, young Wynn was "killed during a trial flight. Death was instantaneous" (Kipling "Mary" 340).

Kipling's story then takes an unexpected turn as both Mary and Miss Fowler feel next to nothing concerning Wynn's passing. Indeed, the two women know they should mourn, but do not feel the need to do so. When Mary asks if they "should wear mourning," Miss Fowler responds, "'Certainly not,' said Miss Fowler. 'Except, of course, at the funeral. I can't go. You will'" (Kipling "Mary" 341). Miss Fowler and Mary then proceed dispassionately to plan for the removal and burning of all of Wynn's possessions.

Mary ventures into town to purchase additional paraffin wax to aid in the burning, but gets interrupted by a tragedy wherein a child, Edna Gerritt becomes the victim of a silent air strike bomb from a German flyover. Apparently, the pilot cut his propellers to glide in and strike undetected. Then comes another, far more chilling turn from Kipling. Mary has now returned from town but has elected to keep the awful circumstances of Edna's death to herself for fear of riling Miss Fowler, who heard airplanes fly overhead a few hours prior. As Mary is burning Wynn's clothes and books in "the destructor," an open-air furnace constructed by Fowler herself, she comes upon the gruesome sight of a German pilot who somehow miraculously survived a fall from a plane by the aid of several tree branches. He was "a bareheaded man sitting very stiffly at the foot of one of the oaks. A broken branch lay across his lap, one booted leg protruding from beneath it. His head moved ceaselessly from side to side, but his body was as still as the tree's trunk" (Kipling "Mary" 347). It is through this encounter that readers finally get to see the real Mary Postgate.

Through an agonizing back-and-forth between the dying man and the emotionless caregiver via rough interpretations of German and English, the German pilot is pleading for a doctor and that Mary continually refuses, all the time armed with a pistol—what Kipling's narrator refers to as a "terrible machine" (Kipling "Mary" 348)—stating that she has seen the dead child over and over again. Mary Postgate allows the pilot to expire without aid and burns the last of Wynn's things. She then becomes transformed into a content woman at peace with herself.

What makes "Mary Postgate" an intriguing horror story is not only the chilling climax of the story, but that the machines are the pathways to death, whether it be those in the air that bring death from above or those that bring it by the pull of a finger. Like many Speculative Modernist stories of postindustrial war, machines are the enablers for humans to kill. They are not created to initiate life or joy, but to allow the worst instincts of humanity to become real. According to these types of tales, machines do not better mankind but only accelerate our destruction.

It was not just war that brought out the worst in people, however. Mathilde Roza, scholar on and biographer of Robert M. Coates, calls *The Eater of Darkness* (1926) "a hilariously misconstrued hurricane of happenstance, adventure and parody" (Roza 53). Science-fiction critic Floyd C. Gale has called the novel "the first surrealist novel in English" (Gale 119).[2] It was published by Contact Publishing Company, the home to Ernest Hemingway, William Carlos Williams, Ford Madox Ford, Ezra Pound, and H.D., among others (Roza 52). Coates went on to become the long-time and highly influential art critic for *The New Yorker*, but this novel came many years before that more conventional career move. He wrote this novel while living as an ex-pat in Paris running with Gertrude Stein and other canonical Modernists. In fact, it was Stein who helped *The Eater of Darkness* find its way into print. This novel is a landmark text in Speculative Modernism because it draws on trends that were happening at the time in mainstream literary Modernism in both the structure of the story—which is very, very different from the straightforward and linear storytelling favored by Hugo Gernsback—as well as in its writing style, which exemplifies the "playfully deconstructive mood" (Roza 53) favored by Stein and others who pushed the stylistic envelope. It is difficult to emphasize enough how different this novel is stylistically from the rest of speculative fiction at the time: "The sense of confusion is complete when the novel's narrator uses footnotes to reprimand Coates for his lack of control over his plot" (Roza 58). In terms of narratorial voice, point of view, character, chronology, and just about every other aspect of novel writing, this book smashes literary norms.

Charles Dograr, the protagonist of the story, is wholly corrupted by the technology of a machine that can kill from great distances. When he, lonely and recently arrived in New York City, meets his apartment house neighbor, he is looking for some companionship in a strange land. The neighbor, Picrolasis, a "retired professor of chemistry from a Western university" (Coates 63), has an apartment filled with strange scientific instruments; he is the classic mad scientist. He sits Dograr down in front of a strange machine with an eyepiece "lensed like the instruments of an optometrist" (27). This new invention is a tool by which anyone can peer into anyone else's life at whatever distance they want. Dograr peers into the eyepiece and marvels: "Successively (as the range increased), he followed the x-ray bullet through the wall of the opposite house—a chandelier—plaster ceiling—beams—rafters" (29). The machine allows Dograr to see in a straight line through the city, through people, buildings, cars, clothing, and anything else as his eyes travel along that straight line. This x-ray bullet allows a user to do more than simply observe, however. Once the range finds a subject of interest, a blast of electricity can be propelled directly to the subject. If it is applied to the brain, it kills instantly and with no trace at all.

When Dograr's line of sight, guided by Picrolasis, reaches the inside of the brain of a man who is sitting in his room reading a newspaper, Picrolasis commands Dograr to "close the switch!" (35). Dograr complies without much forethought. Instantly, the man reading the newspaper stiffens and then slumps to the floor dead. His brain has been "cooked like the contents of a crucible, set in an electric furnace" (59). Dograr's vision then returns along the same line of sight that it had just traveled until he is back in Picrolasis's apartment. Dograr is horrified. He flees the apartment into the city: "Charles walked to the curbstone and sat down and wept. 'Humanity! Humanity!' he cried. 'What is humanity that I should love it?' ... or fear it? ... or pity it? ... or—this came more slowly '—hate it?'" (47) He is distraught as a result of the experience and the growing realization that "I am a murderer!" (49). Up until this point in the novel, Dograr had been a relatively dull person. He had no interests or plans, it seemed, beyond wandering the streets of New York City, but with this act, made possible by Picrolasis's machine and Dograr's own lack of forethought, he propelled himself into insanity.

The story then spins wildly into realms of improbability that explode the genre conventions of science fiction, detective fiction, and romance. Through a series of coincidences, he is mistaken for a cousin of the victim and brought to the home where the man he murdered with the x-ray bullet lived. Dograr meets the victim's family—they call him "Cousin Herbert"—and develops a romantic relationship with the granddaughter of the deceased. Later, Picrolasis reveals his plan: stealing nineteen-million dollars using the x-ray bullet, buying a yacht, and escaping on the ocean to live a life of luxury, just him and Dograr. The lure of power and money is just too great for him to resist. What follows can only be described as the disintegration of Dograr's consciousness into thousands of genre tropes. The narrative unravels into scenes unconnected to the rest, chronology chopped up and shuffled. There is an absurd detective story, complete with disguises, secret codes, and layers of comic deception. There is a doomed romance. There is plotting and betrayal among thieves. There is a car chase near the end of the novel. By the end, the car is gone and Dograr is pursued through the New York City streets by an airplane that drops bombs on him as he runs for his life. At every turn, Dograr's well-being is threatened by machines, whether it be his conscience in the first murder that he commits or his actual physical safety in the final stages of the novel.

Technology in this novel corrupts; it takes what is inside us, the greed, jealousy, and selfishness, and magnifies it to outlandish proportions. In the first few pages of the novel, Dograr is restless and searching for something he cannot name. He is friendless and bored, too shy even to ask about how to find a job in New York. The ability to wield great power abetted by the machine is too seductive for him to resist, and he is thoroughly broken by the experience. His gradual fragmentation and dissolution do not stop him from aiding Picrolasis in planning and executing a bank robbery that leads to the novel's climactic scenes, and this dissolution is matched by the stylistic choices employed by Coates, especially late in the novel. As Roza remarks: "Coates employed incongruous literary styles, tones of voice, and dramatic incidents to capture the excitement and bewilderment generated by the contradictory and incompatible literary ideas afloat in Paris" (56). Dograr, in falling to Picrolasis's web of mass murder, shows exactly this kind of "excitement and bewilderment." For him, the world of New York City is fragmented and chaotic, and he cannot adapt successfully. The x-ray bullet allows Dograr's experiences to become disconnected from the physical reality of his body. The breakdown of Dograr's ability to interact with his environment is mirrored in the text of the novel itself, which begins more or less conventionally but soon starts to fragment and disintegrate, much like Dograr's ability to apprehend reality. *The Eater of Darkness* marks a clean break from the kind of speculative fiction favored by editors who preferred straightforward prose that told stories with minimal stylistic flourish, and that is what makes it a seriously underappreciated classic of Speculative Modernism.

Just as *The Eater of Darkness* was a movement toward experimentation in style, the collaborative novel, *Cosmos* (1934), was an experiment in authorship. Compiled by the editors of a fanzine, *Science Fiction Digest*, a true collaboration of established and amateur authors alike, the novel consists of seventeen chapters written by seventeen of the readers and writers of *Science Fiction Digest*. There were several well-known writers that contributed a chapter, including E.E. "Doc" Smith, A. Merritt, Francis Flagg, Raymond A. Palmer, and the legendary editor, John W. Campbell. Abner J. Gelula, however, was not one of the luminaries of the genre. In fact, up to that point, he was known much more as a fan and frequent letter writer to fantasy and science-fiction magazines. In addition to his contribution to *Cosmos*, he published a total of six stories in his lifetime, all during the 1930s. His chapter in *Cosmos* is titled "Menace of the Automaton," and it exhibits the kind of antipathy toward machines that was characteristic of the late Speculative Modernist period.

The story is set in the thirty-first century, a time when humans have easy lives because the automatons do every bit of tedious, dangerous, and physical work needed to keep human civilization going: "The entire system was based upon an illusion. Men had become content to permit things to continue their course under the continuous assurance that the Machines were designed for man and therefore were the slaves of man. But in practice it was different" (Gelula). The human protagonist, Alan Martin, receives a message from space warning him about the impending extinction of humanity. As he was listening to the message in amazement, his automaton, in an act completely out of character, destroys Alan's radio. Alan then begins to build the spaceship that will take him to a meeting on the moon of fellow biological beings intended to help humanity handle their automaton problem. The automatons sway public and government opinion against the journey:

> The cold reasoning, the unemotional logic of these calculating machines recognized that their hold on man would be broken should contact be made with other planets—planets that were ages ahead of Earth and whose wisdom had long since abolished the machines in forming a happier existence. Man would surely see the Utopian existence that machines made impossible, for the Automaton was the nucleus of a vicious circle—man fed the machine so the machine would feed man [Gelula].

The human team barely escapes with their lives, and the hold of the automatons on all of Earth is eventually broken in A. Merritt's chapter, titled "The Last Poet and the Robots." In the novel as a whole, there is a greater villain, something called "The Wrongness of Space," that is a much higher order of problem for humanity. It turns out that the tools of humanity are useless against this larger threat. The tools that humanity has created for itself actually contribute to its weakness. Humanity is ill-equipped for survival once the machines they build to make their lives easy and without pain change them into something easily squashed.

There was a messy chronological cause-and-effect sequence where the optimism of utopian thinking gave way to recognitions of the limits of science to improve human lives and then, finally, to the despair of the interwar period. Joseph E. Kelleam's short story, "Rust," which appeared in the October 1939 issue of *Astounding*, is a fascinating indictment of humanity's inability to wield powerful machines in the service of good. The story takes place in the distant future, long after humans have gone extinct. Three mechanical creatures are living out their days reminiscing about their misbegotten creation and the how they cannot escape their mandate to kill. Their world is filled with blown-up, mechanical war machines like themselves stacked atop human ruins.

The main character and the most functional of the three remaining machines, X-120, goes for a walk looking for something, anything, to make him happy. He is startled by a rabbit and, before he even knows what he is doing, he kills it. X-120 stares at the dead rabbit and "remorse and shame stole over him. He went on silently. Somehow the luster of the day had faded for him. He did not want to kill. Always he was ashamed, after the deed was done. And the age-old question went once more through the steel meshes of his mind: Why had he been made to kill?" (Kelleam 364). This is a central question that is asked by a host of Speculative Modernists. Humans discover the power of the atom, and its first use is as the most destructive weapon ever dreamed of. The Wright Brothers took to the air, but in fifteen years their invention was a war machine raining down death from above. Chemists uncovered the world's mysteries and then created mustard gas and other weapons of mass destruction. "Rust" takes this idea and runs with it: "In the haste of a war-pressed emergency, man had not taken the time to refine his last creation, or to calculate its result. With that misstep, man had played his last card on the worn gaming table of earth. That built-in urge to kill men in yellow uniforms had changed, ever so slightly, to an urge to kill—men" (365). Kelleam wonders if humanity is wise enough to handle ethically the fruits of its ingenuity. In "Rust," a story where the machines did exactly what they were designed to do and with apocalyptic consequences, the answer is a resounding and tragic no.

Finally, Clark Ashton Smith's year-5998 narrator in "The Great God Awto" (1940) rails humorously against the twentieth century's reliance on the automobile, a relationship the narrator compares to a god requiring endless human sacrifice. By this point, on the precipice of the atomic age, humanity's relationship to the machines they built has moved from heady optimism about the perfectibility of human society to a soul-crushing commitment to communal self-destruction. Smith's story is tongue-in-cheek, but it addresses the extent to which disillusionment with technology has saturated Speculative Modernism. The summation by the narrator at the end of Smith's tale tells the story of this chapter:

> Toward the end, it would seem that virtually the whole population must have belonged to the blood-mad priesthood. Going forth daily in the rituals of Awto, they must have turned their cars upon each other, hurtling together with the violence of projectiles. A universal mania for speed went hand in hand with a mania for homicide and suicide.
>
> Picture, if you can, the ever-mounting horror of it all. The nation-wide madness of immolation. The carnivals of bloody holidays. The highways lined from coast to coast with crushed and dismembered sacrifices!
>
> Can you wonder that this ancient people, their numbers decimated, their mentality sapped and bestialized by dire superstition, should have declined so rapidly? [Smith "Great" 192].

The words in this short section—"blood-mad," "mania," "homicide," "suicide," "horror," "immolation," "crushed," "dismembered," "decimated," "sapped," "bestialized"—communicate well the feeling most central to this story. Yes, it is a satire and there is certainly a lot to laugh about, but by the end, a helpless sadness and resignation is all that readers have left. When this story was published, Hitler's Final Solution was already well underway and the world was rapidly arming itself with new weapons only the cruelest imagination could invent. Five short years later, the nightmare of atomic war would become real, and the inevitable outcome seen in the annals of Speculative Modernism—and all of those stories about those shiny new gadgets—would be complete.

Conclusion

The period under discussion in this book—roughly 1880 to 1940—was an era of great technological innovation and advancement. Not only the elite but nearly everyone in the United States and the United Kingdom saw their lives changing drastically and quickly. Empires were falling, and machines showed the promise of a new day for humanity, an epoch where disease would be conquered, travel made easy, and prosperity would spread from border to border. Isaac Asimov defined science fiction as "that branch of literature which deals with the reaction of human beings to changes in science and technology" (92). If this is true, then it is no surprise that science fiction—along with the related genres of horror and fantasy—exploded onto the scene during these years. During the Machine Age, Speculative Modernists rejoiced in the amazing capability of the machines, worried that they would not be enough to save anybody and feared that machines would be the enablers of humanity's worst instincts. Their voices catalogued possibilities that mainstream Modernists only hinted at.

Although it was not a straight line of cause and effect throughout the Speculative Modernist era, enough textual evidence suggests that there might be a progression of thinking about the fabulous machines that were being invented and popularized during this era. Utopians and their ilk looked to these machines to help to perfect humankind, to give them the power to solve problems such as war, hunger, disease, and even death, itself. Soon thereafter, as the century turned and then when Archduke Franz Ferdinand took that fateful drive across Sarajevo, machines were already losing their luster. Speculative stories no longer placed machines front and center as saviors of humanity. Instead, they were just as limited as the people who designed, built, and operated them. Some stories took the added step of showing characters walking away from fabulous inventions after realizing that the machines responsible for their newfound wealth and power did not solve any of the problems they wanted to be solved. Finally, as one world war staggered toward the next, stories were published that showed humanity's technological ability far outstrips our ability to gauge the consequences of those machine-abetted actions. Changes to human society caused by technological innovations during this era were widespread and significant. Because they were talking about the implications of these innovations before anyone else and more often, it can be argued that Speculative Modernists were the most important chroniclers of and speakers for their times.

6

Divine Secrets

> "It is necessary," he said, "that I know whence and how I came; for how can one perform his duties unless able to judge what they are by the way in which he was intrusted with them? And what contentment can I have when I know not how long it is going to last? Perhaps before another sun I may be changed, and then what will become of the sheep? What, indeed, will have become of me?" Pondering these things Haïta became melancholy and morose.
> —Ambrose Bierce, "Haïta the Shepherd" (1891)

While the traditional powers had been mostly laid to rest, Speculative Modernists looked to the discoveries being made in the sciences, and began to guess at other powers that might lie behind the material world.[1] They went to the stars and pondered other worlds; they played with time and dimension using the newly discovered attributes of the physical world that had been dreamed of in earlier centuries, attributes that were now being verified as science got more and more precise with its calculations and reasoning.

Science was not the only field that was seeing an increase in public interest. The Speculative Modernists found supernatural (or perhaps preternatural) forces that lay open to the public now that the institutional churches—the monotheistic religions mainly—began to lose ground. Their prohibitions against pagan beliefs fell away, largely due to the intellectual movements at the end of the nineteenth century. During the latter half of the nineteenth century, funds from both private and governmental sources for libraries were made available on both sides of the Atlantic, allowing the public access to all kinds of thought. Science and mystical texts that had been largely unavailable to the public, began to resurface as private libraries were absorbed into public ones.

Christian writers throughout the nineteenth century attempted to reconcile the harsh realities of the industrial world with religious beliefs. Now at the end of the nineteenth century, Speculative Modernists, especially fantasy writers, were heavily influenced by the Scottish writer George MacDonald. MacDonald, who had been inspired by the German poet Georg Philipp Friedrich Freiherr von Hardenberg who wrote under the name Novalis, to look beyond the rational world into the spiritual realm. In Novalis's prose poem "Hymns to the Night," written in 1800 and translated by MacDonald in 1897, the poet explores the separation between the world in which he lived and the world to come and he sees Night as that transitional line. He seeks a connection with his dearly departed fiancée, but in the third section he describes a transforming experience:

> Away fled the glory of the world, and with it my mourning; the sadness flowed together into a new, unfathomable world. Thou, soul of the Night, heavenly Slumber, didst come upon me; the region gently upheaved itself; over it hovered my unbound, newborn spirit. The mound became a cloud of dust, and through the cloud I saw the glorified face of my beloved. In her eyes eternity reposed. I laid hold of her hands, and the tears became a sparkling bond that could not be broken. Into the distance swept by, like a tempest, thousands of years. On her neck I welcomed the new life with ecstatic tears [Novalis 12].

MacDonald himself would also connect to the world through this broad notion of love, primarily in two of his mystical works, *Phantastes* (1858) and *Lilith* (1895). That love is the real center of the universe is nothing new— Dante had written about it in his love for Beatrice in *La Vita Nuova* (1294) and in *The Divine Comedy* (1320)—but MacDonald and Novalis used this notion in a world of fractured religions, and, in both cases, this mysticism bordered on a description of magic that, though still based in his beloved Christianity, could incorporate the Celtic mythologies like the Arthurian legends, the Welsh *Mabinogion* (possibly written in the thirteenth century), and other pre–Christian works.

MacDonald's works of spirituality in a materialist world would inspire the Speculative Modernist writers, particularly writers of fantasy like C.S. Lewis, into the twentieth century. Lewis would go so far as to make Mac-Donald a character in his 1945 novel *The Great Divorce*, having him play Virgil to Lewis's Dante as he explored the cosmology of the afterlife.[2] The combination of spirituality and the new thoughts in science would drive the works authors like Charles Williams and Lewis into the next century, but this combination would also have repercussions among those who still retained their membership in the institutions of religion.

In the first decade of the twentieth century, Pope Pius X issued a decree, *Pascendi Dominici Gregis* (1907), warning specifically against Modernism, an attempt to bring the Christian faith into a twentieth-century understanding.[3] The Jesuit, Arthur Vermeersch, explained the Roman

Catholic Church's definition of "modernism" in the *Catholic Encyclopedia* in 1911 focusing on three main tenets: (1) that science, the State, private conscience, and the universal conscience should all be emancipated from the Church and the Church should not be able to limit any of these fields of study; (2) that all belief and thought should be in constant motion, "with an inclination to a sweeping form of evolution such as abhors anything fixed and stationary"; and (3) that all religions, particularly all forms of Christianity but also including atheism, are of the same value and therefore should reconcile with one another and see that their differences only lie in doctrine (Vermeersch). Most of the encyclical and the other statements against "modernism" defied the theological attempts to change the Catholic Church's stances on many of its policies toward science and philosophy, but this trickled down to literature and the arts in many places.

Intellectuals had already begun delving into divine secrets promised in ancient texts that were being recovered from private libraries. William Butler Yeats and the Golden Dawn, and Helena Blavatsky's Theosophists seemed to promise a scientific approach to the magical secrets of the Middle Ages. These and other secret societies sprang up in the intellectual communities, and allusions to them were written into fiction by writers like Somerset Maugham in *The Magician* (1908) and Aleister Crowley in *Moonchild* (1917). Rich people hosted séances and fortune-tellers mainly as a hope to escape the unsettling world that was developing in the run-up to World War I.[4] Some sought the roots of the Christian mystical tradition partly inspired by writers from the nineteenth century like the German mystical poet Novalis and the Scottish writer George MacDonald; some went beyond the Christian writers to the ancients like Lucretius and books ascribed to Hermes Trismegistus. Paracelsus and Cornelius Agrippa and other authors that had been buried in the Middle Ages by the Renaissance and the Enlightenment were revisited. The Tarot, most notably Arthur Waite's and Pamela Colman Smith's deck of cards published in 1909,[5] and other forms of divination became popular.

Inevitably, the interest in mysticism and magic (whether by charlatans and dilettantes or actual historians and theologists) began to trickle down into fiction. All the subgenres of fiction were affected by these endeavors. Magic and alchemy appeared in the works of fantasy writers such as Lord Dunsany; new theories about evolution and astrophysics combining new discoveries with ancient understandings about the universe fueled science-fiction stories; horror used the intrigue of the pre–Christian myths to create new legends of interdimensional gods and demons and their return to society in new forms. Speculative Modernism, almost in rebellion against the pope's concerns, seized the opportunity to update and modernize and retell the lost tales of previous centuries with a thought toward explaining the new realities after World War I.

At the time of the pope's encyclical, Evelyn Underhill became one of the foremost writers on Mysticism in general, and Christian Mysticism in particular. In her book *Mysticism: The Preeminent Study in the Nature and Development of Spiritual Consciousness* (1911), she argues: "Mysticism, like revelation, is final and personal. It is not merely a beautiful and suggestive diagram but experience in its most intense form. That experience, in the words of Plotinus, is the soul's solitary adventure: 'the flight of the Alone to the Alone'" (82). Underhill, who wrote about her interest in becoming a Roman Catholic after having been raised as an Agnostic, eventually decided that she could not commit to the Church because of the pope's encyclical against Modernism, mainly because of her interest in comparative religion and in mysticism.[6] Her own fiction, which was published in the years before the pope's condemnation, deals with a brand of Christianity that includes many things from outside the Catholic belief system. Most notably, she had included a form of reincarnation in her book *The Grey World* (1904) and her understanding of Christian mysticism both as a scholar and a fiction writer brought many works of dubious orthodoxy to light.[7] Underhill, like C.S. Lewis and Charles Williams, wrote challenging forms of Christian mysticism into their own brand of Speculative Modernism.

For the mystics of the late nineteenth and early twentieth centuries, the word "occult" simply means "hidden" in the sense that the real substance of the world was thought to be hidden beneath the layers of society and institutional belief that had been heaped on believers and thinkers since early times. The Hermetic Order of the Golden Dawn, founded in 1887, may be the most notable organization that studied the occult teachings of many different ancient cultures mainly because of its high-profile writers like William Butler Yeats, Arthur Machen, Algernon Blackwood, and Dion Fortune.[8] Yeats is the most canonized literarily of these authors, but Blackwood and Machen bring this study of the occult into Speculative Modernism. By combining the ancient rites of many traditions, these authors found a whole new foundation for their speculative fiction. Machen, who may have been a member of the Golden Dawn for the shortest time, was heavily influenced by his interest in the occult, and he found ways to combine this pursuit with scientific studies, which can be seen in his short story "The Great God Pan" (1894). Perhaps it was just this kind of questioning that worried the pope when it came to Modernism. Modernism opened the door to questioning all institutions, whether scientific or theological, and therefore allowed all things to be discussed equally, rather than starting from rationality and Christianity. The Speculative Modernists, cloaked in their fantasy worlds and tales of horror, were able to explore more deeply where this questioning might take us.

This chapter is divided into three sections, each devoted to the various literary responses to what one might find in their pursuit of divine secrets. In "The Benevolent Universe: Spiritual Rewards for the Speculative Modernist," though true access to the grand secrets was available only to the ones who would use this access for spiritual accomplishment, a sublime beauty was the reward. With understanding comes a peace that transcends the troubles of this world. In "Cruel Reality: Monsters Lurking Beyond the Veil," science opens the veil, but all it would show is the true horror that awaits on the other side, and for which societal and evolutionary constructs were built. In "The Neutral Universe: Our Truth Lies Within Ourselves," while finding an underlying reality that controls this one, one also finds that it has no interest in mere human beings. The caring must come from ourselves and not from some divine power. Those who can get beyond the veil gain no real material powers, but they do learn that the universe does not care.

This chapter looks at the way mysticism is translated by Speculative Modernists, who delved into the very personal union between humanity and the greater universe in its many forms, through science, through religion, and through the self. The Speculative Modernists had different ideas of what might be found when the veil was lifted and reality was revealed. While many thought of the mundane employment for scientific discoveries like electricity, speculative writers examined greater possibilities with implications that would change the way humanity interacted with the universe. By allowing science and religion to cross one another's boundaries, speculative writers found new ways to ask ancient questions.

The Benevolent Universe: Spiritual Rewards for the Speculative Modernist

In the late nineteenth century, *A Romance of Two Worlds* (1886) by Marie Corelli (the pseudonym for Mary Mackay) helped spark the imagination of those who wanted to find scientific legitimacy for religion, to bridge the gap between the two, and to start theosophy, a new science focused on religion. Corelli's work falls right in between the founding of Helena Blavatsky's Theosophical Society in 1875 and the founding of the Hermetic Order of the Golden Dawn in 1887, and carries with it the notion that religion could be studied in light of recent scientific discoveries, particularly the harnessing of electricity. Corelli is a difficult figure to pin down as far as Modernism goes. She was distinctly anti-modern in many senses, preferring notions that seem more appropriate in an earlier setting. Martin Hipsky, in talking about Corelli's work in general in *Modernism and the Women's Popular Romance, 1885–1925* says:

> As do so many of Corelli's fictions, these narratives figure spirituality in ways that are at once Christian-salvationist and idiosyncratically modern: romantic battles between good and evil are interfused with a metaphysical feminism, a defiant populism, and an idealistic rebellion against institutionalized masculine authority, whether it be that of the corrupt aristocracy, the calculating bourgeoisie, or the makers of cultural opinion [91].[9]

Scholars of the twenty-first century have recognized Corelli both as a feminist and an anti-feminist, a Modernist and a Victorian, a Christian who was willing to incorporate not only other religions, but science as well.

Corelli's novel argues that science does not disprove the tenets of religion, rather it is just another approach to the understanding of the universe. Michael H. Whitworth remarks in the coda to his essay, "Physics: 'A Strange Footprint,'" that "many commentators [of the 1930s] had expressed the belief that, at the very least, the scientific worldview was no longer a barrier to religious faith: at best, nature appeared to have recovered its miraculous qualities" (218). For the Speculative Modernists, science in many ways helped religion achieve its goals to prove the spiritual world and humanity's place in it. In Corelli's book, the unnamed main character is suffering from a malaise caused, in the story's estimate, by the harsh realities of a world turning away from religion. She is talked into taking a vacation on the French Riviera to escape a harsh English spring. There she meets an artist, Raffaello Celini, who recognizing her illness, introduces her to a new therapy based on electricity. She is sent to a doctor in Paris who has been experimenting with electricity and magnetism in order to prove the reality of the spiritual realm. While much of the story seems to be about the occult relationships the hero finds on her way to recovering her spirit, the author ties science into the mystical equation.

Corelli begins her novel with a prologue written by the unnamed protagonist in which she explains "[w]e live in an age of universal inquiry, ergo of universal scepticism" (*Romance* 15). The more wonders that are brought about through science in this age of miracles, the less people believe in miracles and therefore become more and more materialist. This materialism, she thought, would make it more difficult for people to believe in the immortal soul.

Corelli's main character in *A Romance of Two Worlds* travels through the world knowing that there is much more than the illusion of "reality." Her illness is more of an illness of the soul. She knows there must be more, but the world's cynicism comes crashing in on her, taking away her music and her soul. She recovers her health and more when Dr. Heliobas uses electricity to strengthen her body, which, in turn, helps her to grow her soul:

> "Electricity, mademoiselle, is, as you are aware, the wonder of our age. No end can be foreseen to the marvels it is capable of accomplishing. But one of the most important branches of this great science is ignorantly derided just now by the larger portion of society—I mean the use of human electricity; that force which is in each of us—in you and in me—and, to a very large extent, in Heliobas. He has cultivated the electricity of his own system to such an extent that his mere touch, his lightest glance, have healing in them, or the reverse, as he chooses to exert his power—I may say it is never the reverse, for he is full of kindness, sympathy, and pity for all humanity" [Corelli *Romance* 78].

In the final test of Heliobas's methods, the protagonist is released from her body and travels throughout the universe to the Central Sphere of Electricity from which all energy flows, and to which all energy is being returned. She ends up describing an early idea that presages the Big Bang Theory and perhaps predicts the theory of the ever-expanding and collapsing universe.[10] This journey is much like the journey William Hope Hodgson's hero of *The House on the Borderland* (1908) takes, but, in the end, Corelli's heroine is recharged and ready to face the world despite the loss of her dear friend Zara, whose death actually strengthens her belief in the world to come.

While Corelli's hero does talk specifically about Catholicism, she also tries to reconcile reincarnation into the understanding. On her journey to the center of the universe, she is given the opportunity to see why one of the souls tending the inhabited planets (it seems that most *are* inhabited) might give up their chance to return to the center in order to save the people on their specific planets. This is an idea that is taken up in C.S. Lewis's Perelandra series where all of the planets are connected, except that the Earth has somehow become disconnected from the others, mainly because its protective spirit has become inexplicably corrupted.

Speculative Modernism allows Corelli to take science and Christianity to new heights. She reconciles these new discoveries with the teaching of the Gospels. In her "Introduction to the New Edition" of *The Romance of Two Worlds*, she writes, "[T]he light of Science must be brought to bear on the New Testament, in which its glorious pages will grow bright with hitherto unguessed mystical meanings if humbly and prayerfully studied" (Corelli "Introduction" 10). She is able to transform both science and Christianity by creating a bridge between the Theosophists of the late nineteenth century with the mainstream Modernists, a bridge that would be both mocked and praised in the coming century. Her Dr. Heliobas is not unlike Somerset Maugham's Oliver Haddo, except of course that Haddo turns out to be evil and playing with forces he's not really able to control. The "magus" of the early twentieth century would be seen by the skeptics Corelli complains of as a fraud and a charlatan rather than as the compassionate healer Corelli creates. Corelli, herself, rails against the "so-called 'signs and wonders' of modern self-styled 'spiritualists' [that] are always contemptibly trivial in character, and vulgar, when not absolutely ridiculous, in display" (Corelli "Introduction" 9). She further complains that these fakers would take money for their spiritual remedies, and adds, "In this there is neither Christianity nor spiritualism" (Corelli "Introduction" 9). Other Speculative Modernists would try to reconcile the unease between science and spiritualism in the coming century, in order to use them both to further the understanding of the universe.

Corelli's book is generally referred to as a fantasy, perhaps in the same sense as George MacDonald's books were fantasies—that is to say, as journeys of discovery about the self—but it is clear that she was connecting recent scientific discoveries with her story to show how science can be incorporated into that sense of the fantastic. When *A Romance of Two Worlds* was published, the light bulb was only seven years old. Power stations were just being created and the thought of powering entire cities was still a way off. "Human electricity," Heliobas offers, however, has always been present, and just needed some cultivation in order to be consciously usable. He even demonstrates that he can use this electricity to communicate with his dog, to draw people of interest to him, to repel those with whom he has nothing in common, but mainly to broadcast his love in the form of a calming and healing presence. Victor Frankenstein would be lurking around behind the notion that somehow electricity could help bring dead tissue back to life, and in the world of scientists this goes all the way back to the first experiments with electricity to make a dead frog's legs move in 1760. Speculative Modernists would use spiritual explanations to try to make sense of all the new scientific discoveries that seemed to push man further and further from that great Central Sphere, whatever form it might take.

Corelli touches on the notion of reincarnation in her description of the narrator's journey through the universe. Reincarnation seems to hold a special place in this otherwise Christian description of being a way for unsettled souls, those who are not yet ready to use the electricity within themselves in order to reach out to God who sits in the Central Sphere. Chapters X to XIV contain the heart of Corelli's electric universe; Chapter XIV is actually a credo of this new form of Christianity, which Corelli refers to as her "Electric Creed." The credo is hard to sum up quickly, but it starts with a recasting of the Gospels. One of the main tenets is the connection between humans of spirit (or electricity) and God himself. Those who cultivate their inner electricity achieve perfection and union with the Central Sphere, while the usual sort of person, who maintains a little spirit, achieves a sort of Purgatory in which they are given time to cultivate their spirit in the outer rings of the Central Sphere. Finally, though, there are those who surrender their spirit:

> For instance, a man who is obstinate in pursuing ACTIVE EVIL can so retrograde the progress of any spiritual life within him, that it shall lack the power to escape, as it might do, from merely lymphatic and listless temperaments, to seek some other chance of development, but shall sink into the form of quadrupeds, birds, and other creatures dominated by purely physical needs. But there is one thing it can never escape from—MEMORY[....] Regarding the Electric Theory of Religion, it is curious to observe how the truth of it has again and again been dimly shadowed in the prophecies of Art, Science, and Poesy [Corelli *Romance* 233].

As a scientific description of the events of the Gospels, the Creed breaks down the events and descriptions of Christ's life as actual manifestations of electricity. Corelli, through this Creed, explains that the Virgin Mary was, in fact, a spiritual manifestation of this creative electricity and she points to many biblical passages to prove it. This would likely be the kind of writing to which Pope Pius X was referring in his encyclical against Modernism.

Evelyn Underhill, who used fantasy to explore her own religious interests, the author of *Mysticism*, is now celebrated by the Anglican and Episcopal Churches for bringing mysticism out of the Middle Ages and creating a "practical mysticism."[11] In her search for an understanding of the universe, she began to read the newly public manuscripts at the British Museum of medieval mystics. She was particularly drawn to the works of the lay mystics, like Richard Rolle and Margery Kempe, but she also uncovered the works of writers like Marguerite Porete (who would not be identified until mid-century) and Julian of Norwich. In so doing, she came across this same notion of the hierarchy of souls, and how some souls had a natural penchant to attain mastery of the spiritual connection with God. For many years, mainly because of the Pope's edict against Modernism, which included an indictment against women serving as priests, Underhill tried her hand at writing a fictional account of a new Christian mysticism.

Her novel *The Grey World* (1904) begins with a poor boy, growing up in West London, who is taken ill at the age of ten. Against doctor's orders his mother gives him a currant bun to enjoy, and his illness worsens, and he dies. That, however, is not the end of the poor boy's story. He is whisked into a Grey World, a world that sits next to, but cannot communicate with, the everyday world. His desire, though, for earthly things—that currant bun, for example—keeps him from the leaving the planet. Similar to what Corelli talks about in *A Romance of Two Worlds*, the boy's physical body is filled with the desire for earthly things and is dragged back to be reincarnated as another boy, Willie Hopkinson, but this time to a middle-class family. His father is described as a Materialist, one who lives by only what one's physical senses can reveal. Religion is seldom discussed around the house, but when the young boy is reminded of the Grey World, he can slip in and out of it. At first, his parents find him to be just a fanciful child, but by the time he is eleven, his father believes it is time to start behaving like a man. He has him shipped off to school where he learns about sports and science and languages, and so is distracted from his remembrance of the Grey World:

> He preferred his lying senses to his inconvenient perceptions, and became sedulous in the cricket field and wholesomely casual in class. On the day when Master Hopkinson learnt the "Psalm of Life" as an imposition, and repeated with smiling sincerity and unconcern, "Life is real! Life is earnest! And the grave is not its goal"; he was very nearly a normal boy. Education was doing its work. To take everything for granted, to grasp fringes and avoid fundamentals, to think only of the obvious, and to refuse to consider the unimportant incident called Death—these arts, in which our youngsters are so carefully instructed, Willie at last acquired, though perhaps less easily than his fellows [Underhill *Grey* 31].

The Speculative Modernists recognized that religion had served the function of distraction from the promised end of death, and that something needed to fill that place. Perhaps spiritualism could fill the void, but there had to be a way to make it palatable to the Modernist era. With disease and brutal wars, people were all too mindful of death, but this is what will bring Willie back to his thoughts of the afterlife.

Just as his father is about to introduce the boy to what in his Materialist eyes are the wonders of managing a factory, Willie is suddenly infected with scarlet fever and is reminded of that Grey World he left behind. In his recuperation, he decides that he would find a way out of that nightmarish middle world where nothing has any charm or color. Like Corelli's narrator after realizing the answer to her main question about the immortality of souls, he knows without a doubt the answer. Now it is up to him to figure what he can do with that knowledge. Underhill realizes that in this first stage of the understanding of the immortal soul, there is a danger of selfishness, an issue that Corelli's narrator hurdles quite easily in her love for Zara. Willie determines that the Grey World is for those who found their heaven only in earthly things, and he is going to try to defeat that. Underhill begins Willie's new quest by saying:

> To himself, he appeared more worthy of notice than at any previous stage of his existence; but unfortunately the fact that he had realized the illusory nature of life did not mitigate the distressing angles of his figure. Only a burning faith can

distinguish the philosopher under the veil of the hobbledehoy; the founders of new religions have generally been over twenty-one [Underhill *Grey* 43].

He is still a creature of the earth and drawn to earthly troubles. Burdened with supernatural knowledge at a young age, it is difficult for him to live a normal life without being labeled a "freak."

Willie is guided to the growing interest in spiritualism in London, with the hopes that he will meet others who understand the universe the way he does. When he locates a group called the Searchers of the Soul—perhaps modeled on Yeats's Golden Dawn—he thinks that he may have found that group, but instead he finds people who believe all kinds of things about the afterlife. They themselves have never experienced the Grey World. When he tells his story of the afterlife, the club members are happy to add it to the store of ideas, but they do not believe him straight away. He tries to correct their misunderstanding of his experience and realizes that they have no way of distinguishing his very real story from all the others. Underhill expresses her own frustrations with the Roman Catholic Church and other spiritual communities of twentieth-century London through Willie.

He meets Stephen Miller, however, who is described as "a man who sought dreams deliberately, as an artist; did not follow them blindly, as a fool" (Underhill *Grey* 50). Miller becomes a temporary solace for Willie as he finds a connection in him, a distrust of all the silly solutions the Searchers propound, but Miller has a different philosophy that focuses on beauty. At first, Willie thinks he is talking about some deep eternal beauty, but, in the end, finds that Miller is simply drawn to the idea of secular love and marriage. Underhill, like other Speculative Modernists, scorns the antiquated notion of beauty from the previous half century and portrays Willie's disappointment in his friend's conventional philosophy.

Willie does everything in his power to ignore the lurking Grey World, but time and again, he is drawn back to it. Willie also finds a woman who seems to love him among his fellow bookbinders, Mildred Brent. Initially, she is impressed by his skills in creating beautiful bindings for books, an art he takes up when his father deems him unfit to take over the family trade, and a skill he masters quite readily. However, he expresses his knowledge of the Grey World to her, feeling like he can finally open up to someone completely. She initially pretends to understand, but finds him to be quite unstable. When he continually tries to point out the inconsequentiality of this world, she can no longer stand him: "I won't have all my hopes and my ambitions poisoned, and made to seem not worth while. I've only one life as far as I know, and I claim it as a right to order it as I think best. I can't live it on your lines. You terrify me. I don't think you're quite alive in the human sense of the word" (Underhill *Grey* 121). She soon breaks off the marriage, to his relief. Here, Evelyn Underhill articulates the Speculative Modernist's struggle with reconciling spiritualism with modern life, and questions what marriage has become in the light of Materialism and Agnosticism.

When Willie's failing health and strange disposition begins to worry his friends, one of them suggests a trip to Italy to get him away from the cruelties of both his father and English society. Confused by his father's Materialism, his friends' ideas of beauty, and his own consciousness of the Grey World, he finds himself walking with a Franciscan monk, who shows him first the path of St. Francis, but even more astonishing to Willie, a painting created by a widow-recluse now living back in England. After hearing about how this woman found peace in art and after the death of her spouse, he decides to seek out this contemplative life. His journey, however, is interrupted by the death of his mother, which brings the Grey World back into full focus. He arrives at her bedside in time to see her die, regretting that he has never truly conveyed the pull of the Grey World to her. His mother's deathbed scene, in terms of the Speculative Modernist, is perhaps a foreshadowing of Wizard Whateley's monstrous deathbed scene in H.P. Lovecraft's "The Dunwich Horror" (1928). Willie is convinced that his mother's lack of character condemns her to the Grey World, just as the Whateley family sits waiting to see if the old man's soul will be caught by the whippoorwills that gather outside his window. Willie tries to tell her how to avoid the Grey World, but he is too late:

> He longed, as he had never longed for anything in his life, for the release of Mrs. Hopkinson from the Sorrowful Country. He was ready for a supreme sacrifice, forgetting altogether his cherished safety. His own future peace seemed a small price to pay for some surety of his mother's salvation.
> "Mother," he said, "be comforted! I'll find a way, I'll save you! There's a heaven here quite close, if only you would see it, only look at that" [Underhill *Grey* 159].

However, he can't save her. In his despair, with everything he learned in Italy forgotten, he is transported to the Grey World. While there, he manages to have a conversation with his departed mother. His trance is witnessed by the family, who find it disgraceful, and his hypnotic talk drives his sister to tears. Mr. Hopkinson tries to soothe her: "Death is a most distressing phenomenon, but unfortunately it's the rule of creation. No getting out of it, you know. We must resign ourselves. Mustn't expect Nature to preserve outworn material" (164). Like Willie's assertion about their mother in the Grey World, the Materialist notion of death does nothing to comfort her either. The only difference is that Willie's thoughts are closer to the truth.

Willie's own discovery is that his mother was never in danger for, just as he had found his art and the life of contemplation in Italy, his mother had found her bliss in the raising of her family and the love she had for her children. Her heaven was already forged for her. Her seemingly dull life was actually the key to heaven for her. She asks of him only one thing, and that is to remember her. Willie honors her request by finding the recluse he had heard about in Italy, Hester Waring, who has left society to live a contemplative life and to create her art. While his life choices are not popular among the people he leaves behind, he manages to find his own way in this world, which will help him establish his own part of the Grey World when he travels there.

Just like her fellow Speculative Modernist Marie Corelli, Underhill is attempting to bring the concept of Christian mysticism into the Modernist world, which seems so desolate. In finding her main character's voice, Underhill is seeking her own. After writing this book, Underhill spent the next few years looking for her own understanding of religion in this difficult time, trying out the mysticism of the Golden Dawn, the traditions of the Catholic Church, and the poetry of various mystical writers, but she always came up short. She struggled with reconciling her Christianity with the Modernist world for nearly forty years after the writing of *The Grey World*, and, in this struggle, she made herself into the mother of modern Christian mysticism and a doctor of the Anglican Church. Just like her poor Willie Hopkinson, she wrestled with the greater universe and found her own place in it.

Corelli's *A Romance of the Two Worlds* finds another direct connection to C.S. Lewis's Perelandra series, particularly in her description of the inhabited worlds that surround the Earth. In her journey to the Central Sphere of Electricity, the narrator of Corelli's *Romance* encounters life throughout the universe. She notices that there are spirits tending to each of the planets, and her guiding spirit explains that each spirit is working off its Purgatory by guiding the souls on the planet to God. They visit Saturn and find a world of humanoids that are both lofty of stature and radiantly beautiful, appearing almost as angels. The narrator's guiding spirit, Azul, explains how there are perfect worlds that passed the test of Adam and Eve and live in direct connection to the spirits of air that guard the planet and eventually to God himself. Azul tells her:

> "The three important differences between the inhabitants of this planet and those who dwell on Earth are these: first they have no rulers in authority, as each one perfectly governs himself; second, they do not marry, as the law of attraction which draws together any two of opposite sexes, holds them fast in inviolable fidelity; thirdly, there is no creature in all the immensity of this magnificent sphere who has ever doubted, or who ever will doubt, the existence of the Creator" [Corelli 177–78].

Earth is then one of the only inhabited planets that produces non-believers and those that are not connected through electricity to God. Lewis also takes up this discussion in *Out of the Silent Planet* (1938) and *Perelandra* (1943): first, when he has the spirit of Malacandra (Mars) tell the origin stories of life on each of the planets, and second, when he has Ransom, the hero, travel to Perelandra, or Venus, to help the newly formed creature there remain in their Eden.

Though it starts off as a science-fiction adventure with space travel and alien encounters, *Out of the Silent Planet* becomes Lewis's description of a cosmology. After all of the intrigue of arriving on Mars and trying to escape from his enemies, Ransom meets with the Oyarsa, the guiding spirit of Malacandra (Mars), and he hears the story of how Thulcandra (Earth) fell to a broken spirit, who isolated Thulcandra from the rest of the universe. In the Oyarsa's story, heaven is all around us at all times and every living being is connected one to another by an electricity of sorts. The worlds themselves are havens for the *hnau*—sentient mortal creatures that take different forms on different planets depending on whether their planet survived the first test of Maleldil, the spirit that drives all of reality, and whom the Oyarsa serve directly. The first test on Thulcandra would have been something like the parable told in the Adam and Eve story—everything is made for the *hnau*'s pleasure, except for one thing they must not indulge in. In the second book, *Perelandra*, the *hnau* of Venus live on a world of floating islands and their only prohibition is spending a night on a piece of fixed land. The Oyarsa of each world see that their *hnau* get proper assistance in surviving the test, but because Thulcandra's spirit was bent, there was no aid, and the people failed. The Oyarsa ends his story with a description of the aid given by Maleldil to the *hnau* of Earth, presumably in the form of the birth and death of Christ.

Lewis, like other Modernists, sees the impermanence of the world around him, but through this fantastic vision, which extends beyond the veil of reality, that impermanence loses its sting. When Ransom tells the Malacandrians of his fellow Earthling's plan to destroy all the inhabitants of Malacandra to conquer it for Earth, several of the Malacandrians say in response: "a world is not made to last forever, much less a race; that is not Maleldil's way" (Lewis, C.S. *Silent* 100). Lewis uses the death of one of the Malacandrians at the hands of the marauding humans to elaborate on his cosmology:

> Let it go hence, dissolve and be no body. Drop it, release it, drop it gently, as a stone is loosed from the fingers drooping over a still pool. Let it go down, sink, fall away. Once below the surface there are no divisions, no layers in the water yielding all the way down; all one and all unwounded is that element. Send it voyaging where it will not come again. Let it go down; the *hnau* rises from it.

6. Divine Secrets

This is the second life, the other beginning. Open, oh coloured world, without weight, without shore. You are second and better; this was first and feeble [131].

This universe, no matter which planet one is from, holds nothing for the spirit. The death of the Martian creature is to be celebrated in that he gets to travel onto the next world. Death, as seen by the Modernists, is something to be lamented, something that is unavoidable and renders everything meaningless. The Speculative Modernists, particularly the fantasy writers who follow MacDonald and Novalis, know that the meaninglessness of this world is vindicated in the uncovering of the divine secrets.

The second book in the series, *Perelandra*, directly addresses the Adam and Eve story. Ransom is brought to Venus (Perelandra) as an agent of the Oyarsa of that planet. One of the men, named Weston, who had carried him off to Mars in the first book has made his way to Venus this time and is attempting to corrupt the young Eve—known as the Green Lady—of that planet. Their one prohibition is that they must not sleep on the only fixed island and must dwell only on the floating islands of this ferociously hot world. Perelandra's Oyarsa implores Ransom to stand in opposition to Weston's corruption. In the middle of the book, Lewis gives the perfect Modernist rendition of the seduction of Eve by the Serpent, but this time there is a rebuttal in the form of Ransom.

Weston, as the Serpent, tells the Green Lady many facts about his own world, and how the great spirit of Maleldil made no prohibition about sleeping on the fixed land. By doing so, he suggests that Maleldil wants her to sleep on the fixed land, even though he has prohibited it, because he wants her to explore for herself. In a very persuasive dialogue, Weston leads the Green Lady to believe that Maleldil's words are meaningless in that their context indicates precisely the opposite of what they seem to mean. He convinces her that the prohibition Maleldil enjoined was a test to see if she could think for herself. By seeming to disobey him, the Green Lady would actually be doing Maleldil's will! Just as the Modernists would tear into the specific meaning of language, Weston is trying to do the same, thus muddying the poor innocent's understanding of her relationship with her God. This is a mirror of what was helping to create the despair in the Modernists—their understanding had been turned to meaninglessness. Lewis, through Ransom, offers another solution:

I think He made the one law of that kind in order that there might be obedience. In all these other matters what you call obeying Him is but doing what seems good in your own eyes also. Is love content with that? You do them, indeed, because they are His will, but not only because they are His will. Where can you taste the joy of obeying unless He bids you do something for which His bidding is the *only* reason? [Lewis, C.S. *Perelandra* 118].

The Green Lady responds,

> Oh, how well I see it! We cannot walk out of Maleldil's will: but He has given us a way to walk out of *our* will. And there could be no such way except a command like this. Out of our own will. It is like passing out through the world's roof into Deep Heaven. All beyond is Love Himself. I knew there was joy in looking upon the Fixed Island and laying down all thought of ever living there, but I did not till now understand [118].

Lewis provides an opportunity to explore the Modernist idea of meaninglessness, but turns it around so that there is a key to understanding, a divine secret that reveals meaning in the face of the chaos of the early twentieth century. This plays on Underhill's meaning of mysticism as well, the idea of surrendering ego in order to better understand one's place in the wide universe. Human senses reveal a world is just a cover for the spiritual reality. Like the characters of Underhill and Corelli, Lewis's human characters are limited by what they can sense, and the material world becomes all that they believe in. However, those who can see beyond the veil do not fear death. They welcome it because it allows them access to the heaven that is beyond this mortal realm. These Speculative Modernists combined the strange dichotomy of spiritual belief with the reality of war and death they found all around them. The symbols of the old religions needed an update if they were to confer to Modern people the comfort and spiritual understanding they were meant to provide. Corelli, Underhill, and Lewis made great strides in revealing the deeper message of Christianity through science, mystical wonder, and travel to other worlds.

Cruel Reality: Monsters Lurking Beyond the Veil

Another view that Speculative Modernists offered was that the constructs and symbols that undergird human society were put in place to protect humanity from knowing the madness of a chaotic universe. These protections manifest in religious and political beliefs that seem to create order, and in the weakness of our fallible senses which grants the ability to accept the chaos of the world. With no protecting gods and no limitations to human understanding of the universe, a Pandora's box of horrors awaits.

Arthur Machen's "The Great God Pan" discusses how science can help see the true world that lies behind normal life, but unlike in Corelli's or Underhill's stories, such revelations are not positive, and maybe one would wish that they remain unknown. The story is told as a series of incidents

6. Divine Secrets

over the course of two generations. They start with an experiment on the human brain, one that mirrors the real-life tests of Swiss psychiatrist Gottlieb Burkhardt. In 1888, Burkhardt performed the first "psychosurgery," defined by James L. Stone as "intentional damage to the intact brain for the relief of mental illness" (79), anticipating frontal lobotomies by nearly half a century. In Machen's story, an ingenious neuroscientist, Dr. Raymond, states that it is the physiology of the brain that keeps people from seeing the immortal world:

> [B]ut I tell you that all these things—yes, from that star that has just shone out in the sky to the solid ground beneath our feet—I say that all these are but dreams and shadows: the shadows that hide the real world from our eyes. There *is* a real world, but it is beyond glamour and this vision, beyond these "chases in Arras, dreams in a career," beyond them all as beyond a veil. I do not know whether any human being has ever lifted that veil; but I do know, Clarke, that you and I shall see it lifted this very night before another's eyes. You may think all this strange nonsense; it may be strange, but it is true, and the ancients knew what lifting the veil means. They called it seeing the god Pan [Machen "Great" 170].

Machen's view on science trying to explain religion seems more circumspect. Science's answers to the secrets of the universe can seem arrogant and reductive, and Dr. Raymond is a great example of that. The young woman, Mary, is a small price to pay to open the secrets of the universe, which he glibly calls "the Great God Pan" (179).

After a short operation on the teenager, Raymond and Clarke get to see what another sees when the veil is lifted. At first, Mary acts as if she is seeing a true wonder, but within a moment she begins to scream and does not stop until she is completely insane. From here on out the story is told from Clarke's point of view, mostly as he finds stories in the local newspapers and meets with people who seem to have some related issues. The stories are all about strange happenings, as if their experiment has loosed something from beyond the veil on the mortal world in the form of a human being that feeds on human emotion, particularly fear, and is good at ruining perfectly decent people. The odd thing is that without the connection of this particular experiment, a secret only Clarke and Dr. Raymond know, no one would ever notice how all of the ruined lives can be tied back to this one girl.

Clarke is drawn to discovering what the young test subject had seen, and while he proceeds with caution, he discovers more and more of these horrible stories of people who have seen "the Great God Pan." He first reads the tale of a young girl, Helen V., who travels into the forest near town every day and is sometimes seen talking to invisible creatures or beings. The child, who ends up playing with some of the other townspeople's children, introduces those children to her strange friends and the children begin to go insane. Then Clarke meets an old friend who has fallen on hard times. His friend claims that it is all on account of the woman he married who involved him in all sorts of strange rites that cost him his employment and most of his sanity. This woman eventually leads several men to commit suicide as well, just by showing them some things beyond that veil.

As Clarke gets more involved, he begins to recognize something about this woman. One of his friends, in the telling of the story, breaks off his narration and says:

> We know what happened to those who chanced to meet the Great God Pan, and those who are wise know that all symbols are symbols of something, not of nothing. It was, indeed, an exquisite symbol beneath which men long ago veiled their knowledge of the most awful, most secret forces which lie at the heart of all things; forces before which the souls of men must wither and die and blacken, as their bodies blacken under the electric current [Machen "Great" 232].

Machen, like C.S. Lewis in the last section, is tapping into that meaninglessness that the Modernists focused on, in both language and in the symbols of society that seem to offer protection, but in this case, the reason these meanings are hidden is because they have the capacity to drive one insane. There are secrets that humanity was not meant to understand, and in both Lewis and Machen the cause of not understanding is one's own brain. However, Machen's view seems to be that the brain is an important shield from these deeper meanings, these crueler realities beneath the surface, and that there is a great danger in tampering with them in the name of curiosity.

In the end, after many descriptions of the foul evil things this devil incarnate engages in throughout London, Clarke reconnects with Dr. Raymond, who describes what happens in his original test subject's last days. He tells how the addled young woman eventually gave birth to a child, who had an evil look about her, and how he raised her for a few years before giving her into the care of the people in the town by the forest. Clarke had accused Dr. Raymond of ruining the young woman's reason and driving her insane, all for his foolish theories about the immortal world. Raymond responds that, while he did indeed destroy a woman's happiness, his theories were not wrong: "It was an ill work I did that night when you were present; I broke open the door of the house of life, without knowing or caring what might pass forth or enter in" (Machen "Great" 242). Machen's story is a warning about those who attempted to enter into the study of the occult, even through scientific means. Unlike Corelli's tale of finding order and peace and love in the world beyond the veil, Machen tells of unspeakable horror of which man found a way to be ignorant in his ancient days. In that ignorance, people are able to live their mundane lives, raise families, and die peacefully. The danger of science, then, even from early on, is the danger of breaking down that barrier between the perceived world and the world beyond. Even in Corelli's vision, this world beyond is not for all people, and it is important to understand that freeing people of the chains of their own perception and sensitivity is not always a good thing.

In this same spirit, William Hope Hodgson found a way to combine the occult sciences with the cold, hard reason of a Sherlock Holmes in his Carnacki stories—nine all told. They first appeared in 1910 and presented a scientific response to the dangers that lurk beyond the veil. The stories range from deducible earthly solutions to strange deeper experiences with the great unknown, sometimes within the same story. Thomas Carnacki, who generally goes simply by his last name (readers find out his first name only because his mother appears in one of the stories), lives a life of adventure, solving hauntings for the most part, and then explaining the stories to his friends—Jessop, Arkright, Taylor, and the narrator, who unlike Holmes's Watson, never participates in the adventures except as a recorder and sometimes commentator on the adventure.

Carnacki's adventures always involve alleged ghosts, but do not always lead to the supernatural. As Carnacki himself reminds the reader in his tales, he likes to keep an open mind about the trials he undergoes, and so he is ready with earthly weapons as well as spiritual protection. For those who are more familiar with Holmes and Watson, they might be surprised when Carnacki whips out his trusted electric Pentacle—a pentagram with electric bulbs at each point instead of candles—which he sets up as protection against the creatures from the outer realms. Many times he has managed to undergo the onslaught of a creature from another dimension, or maybe an "ab-human" as he calls them in several of his stories, only to realize that to truly solve the case, he must step out of those protections. In the first two stories, "The Thing Invisible" (1912) and "The Gateway of the Monster" (1910), Carnacki is presented with age-old curses that he is able to solve, the former as a result of logic, the latter as a result of spiritual entryways to other dimensions, without too much danger to himself. Other stories turn out to be simply hoaxes perpetuated out of greed, using people's superstitions to keep them away.

The story that makes Hodgson's Carnacki Speculative Modernism is "The Searcher of the End House" (1910). By employing both mundane and spiritual solutions to the mystery, Hodgson allows his readers a brief look behind the veil. Simply put, Carnacki and his mother are plagued by literal bumps in the night—a rap on the upstairs banister and a mildewy smell that materializes every night after two a.m., which escalates to the slamming of doors, fishy footprints, and then finally physical manifestations of two ghosts. The first is a woman who appears to be searching for something, and the other is a naked child who appears to be running away from something. Carnacki gets his mother out of the way and engages a team of policemen who uncover a caper worthy of Scooby-Doo's gang: an old sea captain who becomes a fugitive of the law but wants to recover some lost treasure without getting caught by the new tenants who happen to be a ghost-hunter and his mother. That explains the mundane elements.

Carnacki, however, discovers that the terror he has undergone as part of the ruse, awakens him, the landlord, and several policemen to a different manifestation. The woman and the child seem to be part of an otherworldly play that is being performed at all times but can only be discerned in the heights of terror. Carnacki postulates, thanks to his reading of what he calls the Sigsand manuscript, that stillborn children are actually children whose spirits have been taken back at the last minute "by thee Haggs" as the manuscript states, and that what they experienced was a "primal Ego or Child's soul" that is trying to evade capture by the "Mother-Spirit" or these "Haggs":

> In other words, by certain Monstrosities of the Outer Circle. The thought is inconceivably terrible, and probably the more so because it is so fragmentary. It leaves us with the conception of a child's soul adrift half-way between two lives, and running through bye-ways of Eternity from Something incredible and inconceivable (because not understood) to our senses [Hodgson "Searcher" 231].

In this story, aside from the manifestations of the spirits themselves, Carnacki also experiences a shift in light, where he temporarily seems to enter this Outer Circle and so sees our world through their eyes. This mostly comes as a reversal of light and dark, in which Carnacki can suddenly see the objects of this world the way these spirits see them. He begins to understand that there is a whole other dimension of which mankind has no knowledge, and occasionally to which it is subject. This connects to Evelyn Underhill's Grey World and the horrifying universe from which we are protected by our own brains in both Machen's and Lovecraft's stories. Perhaps there is a good reason that human society occludes the "real" universe. This gives humanity the opportunity to stand in the face of these Monstrosities from the Outer Circle.

Alongside Machen and Hodgson is H.P. Lovecraft, arguably one of the most influential authors among the Speculative Modernists, especially concerning the weird tale. Writing an extensive catalog that can be compared directly to a nineteenth-century giant like Poe, Lovecraft is a colossus of the supernatural pulp stories emerging in the 1920s and 1930s. One aspect of Lovecraft's imaginative genius is that "those fixed laws of Nature" are limited by human understanding, which is not comprehensive. There are chasms full of unknown marvels, mysteries, and horrors that the human species has not yet stumbled across in its bumbling exploration of the world. In these abysses Lovecraft's cosmic fear most often lurks.

"The Call of Cthulhu" (1926) stands atop the impressive mountain of Lovecraft's influence and encompassing mythology. It is the story of the narrator, Francis Wayland Thurston, as he discovers some notes from his uncle, who had recently died at sea. After slowly unraveling the meaning behind the notes, he pursues the meaning of a mysterious sculpture which leads to the discovery of Cthulhu cults and eventually, to an additional manuscript by a deceased sailor, Johansen. Thurston comes to realize that Johansen inadvertently awoke and released the terrible and ancient monster but through the climactic and heroic ending, the monster was once again subdued in his deep-sea stronghold. There he remains, waiting for the stars to align once again and set in motion his ascension to rule the world, as he did so many vigintillions of years before man.

Lovecraft's horror is not limited to the monstrous descriptions of the chimeric cephalopod/dragon/human entity, nor its nearly unfathomable size. Instead, it is in the idea that Cthulhu has existed ages before man and will seemingly bring an end to man's era and continue onwards, a member of the "Old Ones" that populate the Lovecraftian universe. In addition, Cthulhu has been here all along, below the veil of the ocean—out of sight, out of mind, but always present:

> These Great Old Ones [...] were not composed altogether of flesh and blood. They had shape—for did not this star-fashioned [sculpture] prove it?—but that shape was not made of matter. When the stars were right, They could plunge from world to world through the sky; but when the stars were wrong, they could not live. But although They no longer lived, They would never really die. They all lay in stone houses in Their great city of R'lyeh, preserved by the spells of mighty Cthulhu for a glorious resurrection when the stars and the earth might once more be ready for Them[....] The time [for Cthulhu's return] would be easy to know, for then mankind would have become as the Great Old Ones; free and wild and beyond good and evil, with laws and morals thrown aside and all men shouting and killing and reveling in joy. Then the liberated Old Ones would teach them new ways to shout and kill and revel and enjoy themselves, and all the earth would flame with a holocaust of ecstasy and freedom [Lovecraft "Call" 367].

That great city, R'lyeh, is under the surface of the Earth's oceans. The past ages of the Older Ones have become virtually forgotten, but Their presence can still be felt and there are certain mentalities—called the "sensitive" ones that see Them in their dreams—and cults of worship that

> had always existed and always would exist, hidden in distant wastes and dark places all over the world until the time when the great priest Cthulhu, from his dark house in the city of R'lyeh under the waters, should rise and bring the earth

again beneath his sway. Some day he would call, when the stars were ready, and the secret cult would always be waiting to liberate him [366].

In slumber, Cthulhu and the other Old Ones inhabit our world. It is only through blind stumbling into a forgotten manuscript or lost idol do characters gain a glimpse of the cracks in their understanding of the world around them—that there is much more than they can begin to imagine. Unfortunately, the inability or outright refusal to acknowledge such a possibility keeps them in the virtual dark. Perhaps because of ego, these characters cannot allow for such a cosmic worldview. On the rare occasion when they are forced to reconcile those anomalies that do not align with their understanding of Nature, the result is horror, captured best in the last lines of the story: "Loathsomeness waits and dreams in the deep, and decay spreads over the tottering cities of men. A time will come—but I must not and cannot think!" (367).

Lovecraft's unnerving tale of supernatural infestation and regional haunting, "The Dunwich Horror" is set in Massachusetts, and the story unfolds with the lifespan of Wilbur Whateley, son of a malformed albino mother and a long-since disappeared father. The scorn of the entire town, the Whateleys are subjected to rampant rumor and superstition, isolating themselves outside of the rural village. Wilbur grows at an inhuman rate and teaches himself to read and write through ancient inherited texts from his suspect family line. This eventually leads him to an incomplete version of the forbidden *Necronomicon*, an arcane Book of the Dead.

In Wilbur's quest to track down the missing folios from his books, he is also attempting to resurrect an Old One, and a variety of suspicious tragedies occur in the village—everything from mangled livestock to the utter destruction of a residential home by an unseen force. Wilbur, now a giant at almost eight feet tall despite being an adolescent, is undone by a guard dog after an unsuccessful attempt at stealing a full copy of the *Necronomicon* housed at Miskatonic University. This is where Lovecraft reveals his atheism. Even the ones with knowledge and authority—both Wilbur Whateley and the scholars from Miskatonic University are left alone in the universe. S.T. Joshi writes in his introduction to *Against Religion*, "But it should be made clear that that cosmic vision is strictly dependent on Lovecraft's metaphysical—and, specifically, his atheistic—viewpoint. For in Lovecraft's universe, humanity is indeed alone in the cosmos" (xxv). The horror not only awaits the victims of the monstrous entities waiting to come back and reclaim earth; it also awaits those who would summon this chaos down on humanity. Wilbur, the sacrificing angel of the "Old Ones" perishes simply by the attack of a guard dog, not in the glorious return of the elder gods.

Lovecraft includes some familiar motifs in this story such as the hunting down of and researching a forbidden text that opens a gateway of sorts, but it is also reminiscent of Bierce's "The Damned Thing" in its emphasis on an invisible but very real monster. This time, the veil is only removed by a type of powder that renders the creature visible for a brief moment or two. However, that moment is the cause of madness in the one poor soul who looked upon it. It is also revealed in the pages of the *Necronomicon*:

> "Nor is it to be thought," ran the text as Armitage mentally translated it, "that man is either the oldest or the last of earth's masters, or that the common bulk of life and substance walks alone. The Old Ones were, the Old Ones are, and the Old Ones shall be. Not in the spaces we know, but *between* them, They walk serene and primal, undimensioned and to us unseen [...] of Their semblance can no man know, *saving only in the features of those They have begotten on mankind*; and of those are there many sorts, differing in likeness from man's truest eidolon to that shape without sight or substance which is *Them*. They walk unseen and foul in lonely places where the Words have been spoken and the Rites howled through at their Seasons" [Lovecraft "Dunwich" 645].

Although They can't be seen, they are here, and always have been. They defy human reconciliation with Nature, yet they are part of it—just not a familiar part. They are hidden (either by conscious or unconscious choice), but they exist nonetheless. Perhaps Armitage says it best: "It was—well, it was mostly a kind of force that doesn't belong in our part of space; a kind of force that acts and grows and shapes itself by other laws than those of our sort of Nature. We have no business calling in such things from the outside, and only very wicked people and very wicked cults ever try to" (667). Lovecraft warns of the insignificance of humanity, even for those who would betray humanity. These great forces do not even register humanity's existence. Lovecraft sums it up in a letter written in 1916 when he said that the human race was, "of no more importance in the annals of eternity and infinity than is the child's snow-man in the annals of terrestrial tribes and nations" (Lovecraft, *Against* 9). The monsters that exist in the universe are not waiting for humankind to get out of the way. Their timeline has nothing to do with humanity, and that is the true terror.

One of Modernism's tenets is to question the meaning of things—symbols, words, sounds, and so forth. Even in the vain attempts of occult societies such as Blavatsky's Theosophists or the Hermetic Order of the Golden Dawn to resurrect old meanings and ways, they discovered that the world had changed. Science was tearing down the old facades that had been built over centuries and millennia to keep the menace on the other side. Science, by asking questions and digging at the foundations of society, was opening those old barriers that kept the monsters at bay, the "real" forces that would in time destroy mankind anyway. If it weren't going to be actual monsters—the stuff of nightmares and old stories—it would be things like the heat-death of the universe or the sun ripping itself and everything around it apart. While science was hoping for some minor control of some of the local forces so that work could be done more efficiently or so that people could communicate more easily (both Corelli and Machen write frequently about the Atlantic cable that had just been laid for the telegraph), Speculative Modernists warned that they were playing with forces way beyond those simple conveniences.

The Neutral Universe: Our Truth Lies Within Ourselves

Speculative Modernists provide a third possibility on what lies beyond the veil. Perhaps the natural world is a non-personal place where no evil demons seek to crush humanity, no angels can be called on to help. There is only the individual who can make life a heaven or hell. While there might be a god or a devil or a heaven and hell, they are human inventions and they reward or punish according to man-made philosophies built upon the Judeo-Christian tradition. Speculative Modernists questioned whether humanity would benefit from living in their own creation and not worrying about the true nature of reality.

J.R.R. Tolkien has something to say about this veil between the worlds, but it was not something that he explored in his most famous tales, *The Hobbit* and *The Lord of the Rings*. In his short tale "Leaf by Niggle" (first published in 1945 but written in 1938), he tells of a poor artist who is desperate to create something from his own vision. He has started over and over, many times, and has never painted more than a few simple leaves. This tale involves neither the forces of magic or science or evil, just the simple artistry of painting. In Tom Shippey's introduction to Tolkien's *Tales from the Perilous Realms*, he says about this story, "It is generally accepted that this has a strong element of self-portrait about it, with Tolkien the writer—a confirmed 'niggler,' as he said himself—transposed as Niggle the painter" (Shippey x). This transformation allows us to simultaneously look at how Tolkien thought of himself, about his work, and about art in general.[12]

Niggle is a simple man trying to make his way through life, but he is constantly interrupted in his days of work by his neighbor, Parish, who always needs help with things—first minor repairs around the house, then help with his sick wife—and the only thanks he gets is that his neighbor does not tell him how awful he thinks his painting is. He becomes ill and after his recovery is forced to take a long journey, during which his house is ransacked for materials, including the canvas on which he was painting his leaf.

The veil is rent one night during his long convalescence—another link to Tolkien's own wounds and recovery. He hears two voices speaking about him: one voice lists all of his faults and explains how he could have done better both in this new place and his old home, while the second voice lists all that he has given up to help his neighbor and to complete his work here. They finally agree to release him to a new place, a heaven of sorts. Because he asks them about his neighbor before their plans for him, they send him to a place that essentially exists in his painting and allow him to live and work on that place for all eternity. He is reunited with Parish who explains that his own conversation with the two voices revealed Niggle's care for him and that had saved them both.

In the end, Parish participates in Niggle's creation, nurturing it and helping it to grow. Parish chides Niggle for never sharing this image with him and a guide responds: "He tried to tell you long ago, [...] but you would not look. He had only got canvas and paint in those days, and you wanted to mend your roof with them. This is what you and your wife used to call Niggle's Nonsense, or That Daubing" (Tolkien "Leaf" 308). Somehow in his earthly creations, he was making his own meaning out of the illness, war, and suffering he experienced. By his own art, he had forged his own heaven, one that was then suitable to admit other people, like his neighbor. This perspective connects Tolkien to Modernism writ large: "It was a shift in the focus of the arts to the subjective, from the object depicted or the story narrated to a vision, a state of mind and primal reaction, above all to the state of mind of the artist, whether it was comprehensible or not to anyone else" (Roberts, J.M. 324). Art and ingenuity, as the Speculative Modernists would have it, are what create meaning, even if it is only for oneself or one's friends.

Tolkien includes two short codas to his parable that drive home the limitations of art, and how personal art can be. The first is a discussion of various townspeople about all that remains of Niggle: one illustration of a leaf, torn off an old canvas that was used to patch Parish's roof. The second is a discussion between the voices that talks about the friendship between Parish and Niggle and how the place that Niggle had imagined ended up with the name Niggle's Parish. This short piece is tied to the other Speculative Modernist works in that it is a removal of the veil, a glimpse at the afterlife and the powers of the universe. There is no magic or science to it, unless you count the two mysterious voices that seem to have the bureaucratic power over life and death. It is also about artistry, the transience of the works people create and something about why people feel the need to create, even sometimes to the neglecting of societal demands and responsibilities. Again, the symbols here are important, and this story can be read in many different ways. The simplest form is that this is Tolkien's autobiography: a man who imagines an enormous world, and before he can even get one leaf painted or one tree in his forest constructed, he is shipped off to war. When he was finally freed, he was able to come home to create this enormous world he had already constructed in his imagination. At a very young age, Tolkien had begun creating the incredible world that his hobbits, elves, dwarves, men, dragons, orcs, etc., would inhabit and was shaping that world nearly to the day he died.

When the same two voices appear in the second coda, they talk mainly about how the area created by Niggle goes by the name Niggle's Parish as some sort of confusion of the two. They talk about how useful Niggle has been in creating his little world so that others can be more easily introduced to those mountains they had to climb. Niggle is recognized by the two voices as having done a service that he will not be remembered for either on Earth, as the first coda shows when the two men dismiss Niggle's achievements and derisively refer to him as a "silly footler" (Tolkien "Leaf" 310) whose work is largely destroyed in its repurposing to refurbish Parish's home, or in the afterworld.

This story does not have the power of Dr. Heliobas's electric elixir or the horror of Dr. Raymond's great god Pan, but it does share the lifting of the veil to see the worlds beyond the ordinary, no matter the reading. The real question was that of humanity and its role in this Modernist era. Tolkien's Gandalf may have said it most clearly when he tells Bilbo, "You are a very fine person, Mr. Baggins, and I am very fond of you; but you are only quite a little fellow in a wide world after all!" (Tolkien *Hobbit* 276). Tolkien seems to say in "Leaf by Niggle" that, while the role of art seems negligible in the midst of these catastrophic world wars, maybe his creations are what make him who he was, and, in creating his art, he is also carving out his own space in the uncaring universe.

On a lighter side, James Branch Cabell's *Jurgen* (1919) shows the neutral universe much more directly.[13] Jurgen travels beyond the veil of this reality to several key places in our legends and religions. He meets the heroes of the Round Table, he travels to various medieval sites where he displays his heroism, and he sleeps with powerful women (or at least "treats them fairly" as he says), raising his rank through his own cunning. He encounters Furies and Fates, gods and devils, each time escaping with a better honorific that most people are willing to accept.

Jurgen is condemned by his own unwillingness to submit to the Philistines' evil opinion of him and is sent to the regions of Hell. The only challenge the demons put forth is that he is not allowed to bring in any outside water. When he tells the demons that he is an emperor, they seem disappointed and tell him that they are all full up with emperors and kings and men of high degree. They ask him, prepared to be disappointed by the

6. Divine Secrets 183

answer, if he feels the need to be punished. Jurgen is astonished by the question, thinking like all people who fear Hell that that is the expected arrangement, but he is startled by the question, and he tells the demons:

> "No, I shall be quite satisfied even though you do not torture me at all."
> And then the mob of devils made a great to-do over Jurgen.
> "For it is exceedingly good to have at least one unpretentious and undictatorial human being in Hell. Nobody as a rule drops in on us save inordinately proud and conscientious ghosts, whose self-conceit is intolerable, and whose demands are outrageous."
> "How can that be?"
> "Why, we have to punish them. Of course they are not properly punished until they are convinced that what is happening to them is just and adequate. And you have no notion what elaborate tortures they insist their exceeding wickedness has merited, as though that which they did or left undone could possibly matter to anybody. And to contrive these torments quite tires us out" [Cabell 222].

Cabell is teasing his readers all the way through this section, warning them of the hubris that is required to create the notion of hell. Cabell has his representative of the uncaring universe, an omnipotent being named Koschei, create an entire race of beings—in this case, the demons—solely to torture Jurgen's forefathers for things nobody on Earth remembers.

On his way to meet Grandfather Satan, Jurgen encounters his own father being tortured in the flames, and the demons all start moaning about how this one is particularly tiresome and troublesome. After a short visit with Satan where he learns about Koschei and his love for human pride, Jurgen speaks to his father who is busy yelling at the little demons to throw more wood on his own pyre:

> "I think, myself, [...] you should be gentler with the boy. And as for your crimes, sir, come, will you not conquer this pride which you nickname conscience, and concede that after any man has been dead a little while it does not matter at all what he did? Why, about Bellegarde no one ever thinks of your throat-cutting and Sabbath-breaking except when very old people gossip over the fire, and your wickedness brightens up the evening for them. To the rest of us you are just a stone in the churchyard which describes you as a paragon of all virtues. And outside of Bellegarde, sir, your name and deeds mean nothing now to anybody, and no one anywhere remembers you. So really your wickedness is not bothering any person now save these poor toiling devils: and I think that, in consequence, you might consent to put up with such torments as they can conveniently contrive, without complaining so ill-temperedly about it" [Cabell 231].

The extraordinary thing here is how Jurgen recognizes what a bad guest his father is being to these poor devils. One's own personal guilt is not enough to waste everyone's time with this need for punishment. Even worse is the fact that his father is complaining that they are not torturing him enough! This universe does not care about the misdeeds in life; there is nothing we can do that is so big that the forces of good and evil must devise punishments, let alone an entire dimension of space devoted to punishment. Even the horrors of war, and the terrible things people do to their fellow people are soon lost in the wake of time. Hell, like Tolkien's heaven, is forged by and for human arrogance.

His last adventure is to go beyond the veil of the universe where he discovers Koschei himself, who can neither show love nor pride. The explanation for why he can't show pride is a heartbreaking idea for a writer, involving being locked in a room with only your own verses as companions. Koschei reveals that he was the cause of Jurgen's whole voyage through the universe, but nothing more. He took an unusual moment to converse with one of his very minor creations and that was all:

> Now, really, Jurgen, I remember our little meeting very pleasantly. And I endeavoured forthwith to dispose of your most urgent annoyance [his wife]. But I confess I have had one or two other matters upon my mind since then. You see, Jurgen, the universe is rather large, and the running of it is a considerable tax upon my time. I cannot manage to see anything like as much of my friends as I would be delighted to see of them. And so perhaps, what with one thing and another, I have not given you my undivided attention all through the year—not every moment of it, that is [Cabell 292].

When he expresses his dismay at this, Koschei tries to cheer him up, telling him that he is really impressed by his pride. "Do you consider, Jurgen, what I would give if I could find, anywhere in this universe of mine, anything which would make me think myself one-half so important as you think Jurgen is!" (292). He then offers to fulfill the reason for Jurgen's quest, the redeeming of his wife, but first he offers him any woman in the world and brings in a few just to be sure he knows what he might be missing. Jurgen insists on recovering his wife, and Koschei grants his beneficence with the final blow of charging Jurgen for taking care of his wife for a year.

Jurgen's view of his own importance is what creates his place in the universe. The creator has no interest in individual creations, and so Jurgen, who is so good at puffing up his own importance, discovers that this is really all he has. He stays true to himself when Koschei offers him any woman of his choosing by picking his own wife. She knows him so well, he reasons, and maybe that is enough in this enormous universe.

These Speculative Modernists recognized that divine imperative was not responsible for the troubles that beset humankind. With the old prohibitions against personal understandings of reality cast aside, individuals could create their own space out of the basic elements they found around them without repercussions from a vindictive force. Tolkien and Cabell recognized the great dilemma of the Modernist society: hanging on to the broken symbols of the past, without supplying one's own meaning, could lead to an utterly disastrous and uncomfortable existence. Tolkien's Niggle finds a way to build his own paradise, while Cabell's Jurgen discovers that without love and the ridiculous sense of one's own self-worth, the universe can be a very lonely and depressing place.

Conclusion

In 1584, Giordano Bruno proposed that the universe was much larger than anyone had realized to date in his *Of the Infinite Universe and Worlds*. At the beginning of his third dialogue in this treatise, he has one of his main characters, Philotheo, explain:

> "[The whole universe] then is one, the heaven, the immensity of embosoming space, the universal envelope, the ethereal region through which the whole hath course and motion. Innumerable celestial bodies, stars, globes, suns and earths may be sensibly perceived therein by us and an infinite number of them may be inferred by our own reason. The universe, immense and infinite, is the complex of this [vast] space and all the bodies contained therein" [302].

For this suggestion—and many others like it about the nature of God's creation—Bruno was burned to death in 1600. Bruno helped connect Copernicus to Galileo allowing the model of the solar system to be explored over the next three centuries, but the notion that those stars might harbor life would have to wait three-hundred years to be explored.

As the traditional and cherished models of the universe eroded, Speculative Modernists, now equipped with the evidence of an apparently infinite universe, found new ways of looking at all of that space in the night sky. In these three ways, then, Speculative Modernists uncovered the filmy veil of reality to show us what lurks underneath—sometimes the great joy of mystical union with the greater universe, sometimes the grievous horrors our distant ancestors hid from their descendants in the creation of society and a tolerable reality, and sometimes just another place to call home for good or ill. The Speculative Modernists were uniquely capable of this task because of the revolutions in the interface human consciousness had with the universe: religion and science, gruesome war and the promise of miraculous innovation, intercontinental communication and, perhaps, universal peace. Through science fiction, horror, and fantasy, rather than looking backward to humanity's difficult origins, these writers could reach beyond the rapid day-to-day changes to create a mythology that could give a new meaning to the seemingly cold universe. The patterns of the past needed an update, and these authors helped to shape that update throughout the first half of the twentieth century.

While the machines could help them to explore, humanity needed to open up their minds to the possibility that what was visible was only the beginning, the wrapping on a package that only shielded what lay within. They would need a connection to the heart of all that is that could only come with a new understanding, the key to which lay inside themselves. Three centuries of observation and scientific method were not enough to unlock all the secrets, so the Speculative Modernists reopened the old questions of magic and meaning available to them now that the constraints, like the ones that led to Bruno's execution, were starting to come loose. This, though, would take strong characters, ones that were not fettered by society and religion, etiquette and morality. In other times in the history of civilization, these people would be seen as outcasts and marauders, but were now precisely the ones humanity needed the most. These individuals are explored in the next chapter, "We Are Fortunately Flawed," and are exactly the kind of people who could wrestle with the divine secrets.

7

We Are Fortunately Flawed

>Beyond this place of wrath and tears
>Looms but the Horror of the shade,
>And yet the menace of the years
>Finds, and shall find me, unafraid.
>
>It matters not how strait the gate,
>How charged with punishments the scroll,
>I am the master of my fate,
>I am the captain of my soul.
>   —William Ernest Henley, "Invictus" [1888]

The Modernist era is often characterized and identified as a time period that witnessed the distrust and deconstruction of the societal and social pillars of the past due to an absence of meaning and purpose. It was a time that witnessed incredible shifts in virtually every aspect of culture, and literary developments were just as revolutionary as Cubism was to fine art or telephone and electric light were to domestic life. Ezra Pound and Gertrude Stein reimagined the language of poetry. Likewise, writers of fiction created fundamental shifts in narrative structure and chronology. Central to this chapter are the Speculative Modernist restructurings of character portrayal and development. Such changes mirrored the emergence of psychology, as discussed earlier with Sigmund Freud. In relation to fictional characters, American psychologist William James and French philosopher Henri Bergson[1] should be included in the discussion as well. In writings such as "What Pragmatism Means" (1906), James purported that individuals make their own realities, and truths are a matter of function (which distinguished them from facts). Bergson suggested that immediate experience and instinct are more instrumental to the construction of reality than rational thinking.[2]

The literary construct of character in the Modernist era differed from the self-reflection of George Eliot, the social constructs of Charles Dickens, and the colloquial appeals of Mark Twain. In his book *Out of Character: Modernism, Vitalism, Psychic Life*, Omri Moses states:

> These [Modernist] writers felt that overemphasis on personality limited the possibilities for imagining human beings because it prevented self-invention and enforced critical paradigms that looked for secret unmovable centers guiding and motivating behavior. To counter this, James, Stein, and [T.S.] Eliot tended to avoid ascribing to individuals any psychological quality that would encourage an act of interpretive penetration into a person's underlying character. They were sometimes perceived for this reason (erroneously, I would say) as taking a stand against character as such, so pervasive were—and are—the accounts that equate consistency with character [2].

He then goes on to examine how characters begin to act in accordance with specific situations and circumstances rather than rely on a moral grounding from previous literary eras and that "these characters think and act on the basis of attitudes that are not shaped in advance. In so doing, such characters make decisions that transform themselves as well as the objects of their actions" (2). Fictional characters move away from the societal expectations of behavior that were so prevalent in the nineteenth century and begin to reflect new ways of acting, reacting, and developing. The character heroes of Speculative Modernism wrestle with the dilemma of Modernism by exemplifying antisocial traits that allow them to thrive under such harsh conditions. Ego—a purposeful dismissal of the behavioral norms and customs of a now-meaningless society—and a desire for extreme violence enable these heroes to survive the doom of Modernism and provide the reading public with an escape from it. The Speculative Modernist idea of character was no longer tethered to expectations from classic literature where flaws are a character's downfall. New heroes thrived precisely because of the flaws.

However, the concept of the flawed character as hero did not begin with the early twentieth century. Looking back to nihilism of the middle to late nineteenth century, these ideas are taking root. Generally recognized to begin with the likes of philosophers Søren Kierkegaard and Friedrich Nietzsche, the concept of meaninglessness in relation to the ego of psychoanalysis can be seen in the foundations of nihilism. As individuals grow to reject societal standards and definitions, they begin to form their own perspective on the world around them and their place (or lack thereof) in it. If those individuals no longer recognize such a place and don't acknowledge an alignment with the meaning around them, they transition into forming their own—a world that makes sense to them and them alone. Such a shift might include spirituality, morality, sexuality/gender roles, epistemology, and political beliefs.

Nihilism is often associated with the Russian social revolution of the 1860s, but Nietzsche was the groundbreaker of the philosophy. He recognized that the world "as it ought to be" does not exist—that the illusions of society and meaning should not be understood as reality (Nietzsche 267). This is the central problem. As a solution to that problem, individuals become entrenched in their own reality, created by themselves and only for themselves, thereby rejecting any objective truth. Certain traits of nihilism can be seen in a variety of literature, so much so that it has become an archetype of fictional characters in the form of a Byronic Hero. Coined after Lord Byron and taking first shape in his closet drama *Manfred* (1816–1817) and his poem "Childe Harold's Pilgrimage" (1812–1818), the character is typically brooding, intentionally isolated, is motivated primarily by revenge (justified or not), and ultimately has a tragic end due to his own failings. Two iconic examples of such a character are Victor Frankenstein of *Frankenstein* and Captain Ahab from Herman Melville's *Moby Dick* (1851).

Complementary to nihilist philosophy, vitalism came into vogue during the turn of the century. This philosophy, one that loosely favors self-determination over a strict adherence to physical or chemical laws, can be seen in these new characters. "[W]riters such as [Henry] James, Stein, and T.S. Eliot wish to show not only how individuals change as they confront social reality but—because reality itself is only the sum of what we make of it—how the social sphere is open to change as individual agents access and modify it" (Moses 9). Characteristics of nihilism and vitalism would come to define some of the most influential characters of the late-nineteenth and early-twentieth centuries and exemplify many aspects of Modernism.

This chapter focuses on Arthur Conan Doyle's Sherlock Holmes, Edgar Rice Burroughs's Tarzan, science-fiction hero Buck Rogers, two fantasy heroes from Robert E. Howard (King Kull and Conan), and perhaps the first sword-and-sorcery heroine, Jirel, created by C.L. Moore, and how the apparent flaws of these characters—an alienation from society, an individual sense of order and morality, and a disregard for looking beyond the present, to name a few—are actually what saves them from the perils and pains of Modernist society as it fragments into oblivion. These characters all include traits of the Byronic Hero and nineteenth-century nihilism in their thought process, motivations, and actions. Their popularity in the Modernist era reveal the appeal of such perspectives in light of the meaninglessness that would come to define the era. While these characters demonstrate some nihilistic tendencies, Speculative Modernist heroes also step away from nihilism by creating a different worldview that protects them from Nietzsche's abyss. They endure, not as human perfection, but because of their behaviors and philosophies that society deems unfortunate at best and detestable at worst.

Sherlock Holmes: Ego and Ultra-Rationalism

One of the more acclaimed writers of speculative fiction, even among literary critics, is Sir Arthur Conan Doyle. Educated as a medical physician, Conan Doyle also had two stints with the Freemasons and was even a member of a well-known social club devoted to studies of the supernatural, The Ghost Club. However, history remembers Conan Doyle primarily for his literary creations, none more so than his novel *The Lost World* (1912) and the most famous detective of all time, Sherlock Holmes.

Sherlock Holmes exhibits personality characteristics that situate him outside of the social norms of society. In particular, his ego and thought process protects him from the trappings of British culture at the time. His unwavering sense of superiority acts as a shield against how meaningless the social customs of society are. He flaunts those customs, and this aligns him with the concepts underlying Speculative Modernism.

Holmes was a direct manifestation of Conan Doyle's worldview of justice. It is a common assumption that Holmes's primary motivation is to simply "solve" the puzzle of a crime, but it can be argued that the motivation to achieve justice is just as powerful—especially if one is to consider Holmes a reflection of Conan Doyle. In becoming almost obsessed with a sense of justice himself, Conan Doyle actually assisted in the reopening and further investigation of a criminal case in which he ultimately helped prove the innocence of a man sentenced to death for murder (Thompson). In his deductive abilities, Conan Doyle becomes Holmes. He employs Holmes's observational precision and adherence to the scientific method in order to solve a real-life crime and save a man's life.

Building on the detective fiction of Poe, the status of Conan Doyle's celebrated detective is at least equal to that of any fictional character of the Modernist period. First appearing in *A Study in Scarlet* (1887), Conan Doyle's character quickly found success with the critics. Conan Doyle went on to publish adventures of Sherlock Holmes in renowned monthly serials such as *Lipincott's* and *The Strand Magazine*. In fact, when Conan Doyle chose to resurrect his character due to prominent public displays of mourning Holmes's demise, and as Loren Estleman, the author of the introduction to *Sherlock Holmes: The Complete Novels and Stories, Volume 1*, says, it was an outpouring of grief over the loss of "justice and reason in a rising tide of incompetence and evil" at the turn of the century (xvi). Conan Doyle felt angered and limited by the success of Holmes. Conan Doyle was afraid of being trapped by the success and popularity of his character; he wanted to be recognized for the larger body of his work—work that included fantastic scientific journeys as well as a supernatural spiritualism that he often advocated for.

One of the more appealing aspects of Conan Doyle's detective fiction is the friendship that Holmes has with Dr. John Watson. Indeed, most of the Sherlock Holmes catalog is told through the narration of Watson. They are often at odds but typically supportive of each other. Estleman provides a compelling argument for the importance and significance of Watson, even though Holmes typically overlooks and dismisses him. Watson, however, may very well be an unreliable narrator. Watson's reporting is the only source of information about Holmes.

Despite Watson's adoration of Holmes, there are times when the narrator actually presents Holmes as not the idyllic and consummate professional detective, but as a flawed and sometimes vulnerable person. Where Holmes behaves as a superhuman rationalist who prides himself on his ability to observe details in order to piece together mysteries, he is susceptible to bouts of rampant egomania, cocaine use/abuse (although legal at the time), and intellectual vigilantism. One hardly needs to look beyond the first few chapters of the first Sherlock Holmes novel, *A Study in Scarlet*, to grasp the famed detective's shortcomings.

Watson provides some exposition to his own background as an ex-military physician who got shot on active duty and then fell sick with enteric fever. Being honorably discharged, he finds himself in London and in need of a roommate. In the very first encounter between Watson and Holmes—and indeed, between Holmes and the reader via Watson's first-person narration—readers come to understand Holmes as an eccentric that is susceptible to spells of melancholy and prefers isolation rather than companionship. His defining characteristic of arrogance reveals itself, even though he would later feign disinterest in such boastful recognition. Even before Holmes and Watson enter into the "get to know each other" dialogue, Holmes is ecstatic over a scientific discovery that allows authorities to test blood samples that are no longer fresh. In his self-congratulatory exuberance, Holmes makes a spectacle of himself and his accomplishments by placing a hand over his heart and ceremoniously bowing "as if to some applauding crowd conjured up by his imagination" (Conan Doyle *Study* 8). It is in this initial encounter that readers not only get a first glimpse into the relationship of Holmes and Watson, but also into the inner workings and motivations of Holmes's mind. Holmes's flare for the dramatic both protects and separates him from the larger society through people seeking his services but annoys Watson to no end. It is this mind, faults and all, that makes Holmes a Speculative Modernist hero. He is able to solve mysteries, deduce conclusions from the smallest observations, and make connections that most humans cannot make because they are otherwise occupied with the social and cultural awareness that prohibits such an extreme and unfiltered focus. Yet that very awareness and filtration civilized people value so much is rendered meaningless for Modernists. Holmes detaches himself from all of that, which allows him to operate in way that other people cannot.

Holmes's extraordinary ability of observation and deduction is necessarily balanced by the egomania, antisocialism, bipolar/autistic tendencies,[3] and substance use/abuse that appear in stories like *A Study in Scarlet*, *The Sign of Four* (1890), and *The Hound of the Baskervilles* (1901–2), and "The Adventure of the Engineer's Thumb" (1892). For as brilliant as he is, he is also socially inept and remarkably uncultured. Among Watson's famous list of Holmes's "limits" in Chapter 1 of *A Study in Scarlet*, is virtually no knowledge of literature or philosophy. Indeed, the only "culture" that Holmes enjoys (even validates) is the playing of the violin. Instead, Holmes thrives on physical sciences (aside from astronomy) and forensics. This plays to Watson's observation of his "cold bloodedness" (Conan Doyle *Study* 6). However, perhaps those cultural limits are his saving graces in the light of Modernist pessimism instead of damning qualities. Literature and philosophy typically educate and expand one's emotional worldview. For all of his brilliance, Holmes is distinctly lacking in qualities such as empathy, which are the subjects of the humanities. Apparently, this is by choice. By ignoring things like empathy and compassion, Holmes is able to imagine all possibilities, often arriving at solutions that everyone else cannot imagine. Once Holmes reveals his explanations, readers can follow his logic, but are unable to see it by themselves.

When Watson inadvertently disparages an article written by Holmes without realizing authorship, exclaiming, "'What ineffable twaddle!'" (Conan Doyle *Study* 16), Holmes reveals his justification for what knowledge he retains and what he chooses to ignore or quickly forget:

> I consider that a man's brain originally is like a little empty attic, and you have to stock it with such furniture as you choose. A fool takes in all the lumber of every sort that he comes across, so that the knowledge which might be useful to him gets crowded out, or at best is jumbled up with a lot of other things, so that he has difficulty in laying his hands upon it. Now that skillful workman is very careful indeed to what he takes into his brain attic[....] It is a mistake to think that that little room has elastic walls and can distend to any extent[....] It is of highest importance, therefore, not to have useless facts elbowing out the useful ones [13].

The cultural and social norms that are so important to Watson are "useless" to Sherlock Holmes. Holmes chooses to sift out such knowledge in favor of more scientific and forensic facts. To say that Holmes is brilliant is appropriate. To say that he is balanced, however, is not. He does not waste time or effort on the transience of society. This attitude is at the core of Speculative Modernism. He is shielding himself from the meaninglessness of social customs and restraints.

This selective knowledge lends itself to an almost-intolerable arrogance and egomania. While Holmes does indeed come off as brilliant, he is also rather distant. Part of this must be attributed to Watson's subjective narration mentioned earlier, but such bias is the only information that readers have to form an impression and evaluation. He readily dismisses Watson throughout the friendship, resulting in the catchphrase synonymous with the character, "Elementary, my dear Watson."[4] Watson is astounded by a Holmes deduction, but Holmes merely responds as if the method was rather simple:

> "Wonderful!" I [Watson] ejaculated.
> "Commonplace," said Holmes, though I thought from his expression that he was pleased at my evident surprise and admiration [Conan Doyle *Study* 21].

Holmes performs for an audience of one: himself. Likability is irrelevant to him. He sees himself as superior to virtually every being, as elucidated by his own evaluation: "'No man lives or has ever lived who has brought the same amount of study and of natural talent to the detection of crime which I have done'" (Conan Doyle *Study* 19). It is one thing to be the best, but another to call yourself the best. One can argue, in the vein of Speculative Modernism, that this egomania—in part—separates Holmes from the common ground of culture and society on its path to eventual ruin. It allows Holmes to distinguish himself from other famed detectives (which he categorically dismisses as little more than fools), but it also allows readers to do the same. In several ways, Holmes's egomania can be seen as a sort of shield against the doom of Modernism. In his belief that he is superior to everyone in matters that he is most concerned with, Holmes removes himself from society and holds himself accountable to only his own behavioral, emotional, and philosophical expectations.

Another misgiving of Holmes's that is related to his sense and belief of superiority is his justification to break laws—laws that he purports to defend—in order to solve the case at hand, and he even drags down Watson into the depths of criminality with him. This is made explicitly clear in "A Scandal in Bohemia" (1891), where Holmes enlists the assistance of Watson, but with a caveat. Holmes directly asks Watson, "'You don't mind breaking the law?'" and Watson replies, "'Not in the least.'" Holmes qualifies, "'Nor running a chance of arrest?'" and Watson responds, "'Not in a good cause'" (Conan Doyle "Scandal" 253). This is not the only instance of Holmes flaunting the law. It is not so much that Holmes deduces consistently through illegal activities, but despite his sense of justice, he is not bound to such confines if it suits his purposes. This is another instance of Holmes dismissing social norms and mores when it suits him even though he is working with authorities to enforce the law, a contradiction which is very comfortable for Speculative Modernist heroes.

Beyond his relationship with Watson, Holmes avoids any semblance of friendship or romantic entanglements at almost all costs. Likewise, Holmes is not above moral manipulation with women either. Because so many of his mysteries involve foibles of such entanglements, he purposefully distances himself from them in his own life. In "The Adventure of Charles Augustus Milverton" (1904), Holmes actually seduces and creates a false engagement with a woman, Agatha, in order to advance his case, not concerning himself in the least with her feelings. Holmes demonstrates irrational sexism as well, as evidenced by the dialogue between him and Watson in the *Sign of Four* (1890): "'I would not tell them [women] too much,' said Holmes. 'Women are never to be entirely trusted—not the best of them'" (Conan Doyle *Sign* 188). Upon Watson's announcement that he is engaged to Mary Morstan at the end of the novel, Holmes takes the opportunity to expound on his notions of love: "'love is an emotional thing, and whatever is emotional is opposed to that true cold reason which I place above all things'" (235). Excluding Watson, there is no room in the attic brain of Holmes for emotional attachment. In his superiority, his extraordinary ability to deduce, Holmes is alone. The rest of the world does not operate the way he does. He creates a reality based on facts and observations alone. During the Speculative Modernist era, a time of skepticism, pessimism, and perhaps even fatalism, Holmes's flaws allow him to rise above the flood, and that is, at least in part, why he is still fascinating. His ability to see the world unclouded by societal or cultural parameters and only recognize the cold truth of reality is unlike any other human. This makes him heroic, because humanity cannot attain this level of focus. It also makes him flawed, because he positions himself outside of humanity.

Tarzan: Natural Law and the Laws of Man

Running alongside Sherlock Holmes in terms of fame, influence, and longevity is Edgar Rice Burroughs's iconic character, Tarzan—although on entirely opposite ends of the societal spectrum.[5] His origins, described in the chapter "Worlds Beyond," enable Tarzan to move in and out of European civilization. Where Holmes is a culmination of scientific acumen, Tarzan is thrust into the primordial. As the protagonist of more than twenty novels by Burroughs dating from 1912 to 1936, Tarzan has distinguished himself as one of the most central archetypes in modern literature. Tarzan is a Speculative Modernist hero because of his preference for the uncivilized world. Despite learning to be a gentleman, he abhors the customs of civilization and yearns for the ephemeral existence of jungle life where past and future do not exist.

In a way, Tarzan recalls the motivations of Holmes. Tarzan employs and abides by his own sense of morality and justice. He kills when he needs to (either via direct challenge, revenge, or for food, although there are few exceptions to this), but Tarzan continuously attempts to do right by Jane, often in conflict with his own desires. As Tarzan says to Jane, "'I would rather see you happy than to be happy myself. I see now that you could not be happy with—an ape'" (Burroughs *Apes* 212). On the one hand, Tarzan is bound to Jane. On the other, he longs for his own freedom in the jungle. One can read this as a direct correlation: either he can have Jane's love and accept the rules of civilization or accept isolation and live happily in the jungle. Once Jane (reluctantly) rejects Tarzan, he goes back to the jungle. Tarzan retreats into the primeval, a reaction that most adolescent boys wish they could do when faced with similar circumstances. This is what makes him a speculative hero. Tarzan can switch worlds so easily, and the only thing that keeps him invested in the civilized world is his love for Jane. When that civilized world gets in the way of his love, he, like other Speculative Modernist heroes, rejects civilization in favor of isolation in the jungle.

The second novel of the Tarzan series, *The Return of Tarzan* (1915), continues this trajectory. On his way back to the jungle, he detours only to see his friend, naval officer Lieutenant Paul D'Arnot. Once he arrives in France, readers learn how civilized Tarzan, now in his early twenties, has become. He is miraculously refined in matters of custom, dress, language, and culture. However, he is also prone to blind fits of rage where he resorts to his primeval self. "'It is because I forget [...] that I am a civilized man. When I kill it must be that I am another creature'" (Burroughs *Return* 90). This recalls Stevenson's Jekyll and Hyde thirty years prior. Tarzan is learning the ways of man as well, discovering that wealth and status govern this way of "civilized" life: "his brief experience with civilization and civilized men had taught him that without money and position life to most of them was unendurable" (9). As Tarzan explains to D'Arnot:

> Jungle standards do not countenance wanton atrocities. There we kill for food and for self-preservation, or in the winning of mates and the protection of the young. Always, you see, in accordance with the dictates of some great natural law. But here! Faugh, your civilized man is more brutal than the brutes. He kills wantonly, and, worse than that, he utilizes a noble sentiment, the brotherhood of man, as a lure to entice his unwary victim to his doom [31].

Tarzan discovers what the Modernists were realizing. Civilization has created a world that takes readers farther and farther away from Tarzan's "great natural law," simply because either people are too egomaniacal or too fearful of the tenets of that law. That law does not concern itself with the past or future, but only the present. Tarzan and Holmes only concerned themselves with the here and now, much like Modernists such as William Carlos Williams and Virginia Woolf who used individual fragments and stream of consciousness in their writings. However, unlike the Modernists, these speculative heroes find security and not despair in the embrace of the present. For Holmes, it is a comfort in observational facts instead of the supernatural or superstitious. For Tarzan, it is the natural law of the jungle instead of the artificial law of civilization.

While in France, Tarzan is assigned a military position that requires him to travel to Algeria. Nicholas Rokoff, the arch-nemesis brother of Countess Olga de Coude who Tarzan befriends on the ship, follows Tarzan on assignment and makes several attempts to kill him and obtain military secrets. Now on his way to Cape Town, Tarzan meets Hazel Strong, best friend of Jane Porter. Rokoff follows him on the ship and eventually surprises Tarzan and throws him overboard, leaving him to drown in the open ocean. Tarzan manages to survive and swim to the shores of Africa, renouncing mankind for good. Similar to Holmes and other Speculative Modernist heroes, he retreats to a world that makes sense to him.

A treasure hunt for the gold hidden in the lost city of Opar brings Tarzan back into contact with Rokoff. In an interesting twist to the predictable path of Burroughs's adventures of Tarzan, the hero succumbs to the lure of gold in the ancient ruins of the African jungle. The lust for gold and wealth is not limited to civilized man. This is where the line between civilized and uncivilized becomes most thin and readers must then wrestle with Tarzan's dual nature. This city of sun worshippers is ruled by a high priestess La, who actually helps Tarzan escape from the city because he rescued her from the jealous blind rage of one of her subjects at the moment of Tarzan's sacrifice and because he is able to communicate with her through common language and is physically superior to her subjects.

Speaking to her in the primitive language of the Mangini, Tarzan learns that these sun worshippers are the last remnants of an ancient civilization that traces back to the epoch of "the mighty land that had [...] sunk into the sea" (Burroughs *Return* 173), and that their culture and biology have been devolving since. As she explains:

> "Slowly we have dwindled in power, in civilization, in intellect, in numbers until now we are no more than a small tribe of savage apes. [...] In time it will all be forgotten, and we will speak only the language of the apes; in time we will no longer banish those of our people who mate with apes, and so in time we shall descend to the very beasts from which ages ago our progenitors may have sprung" [173].

Fortunately for Tarzan, the males seem to have devolved more rapidly than the females and La becomes intrigued by the superior evolution of Tarzan.

This participation in racism was not uncommon among Speculative Modernists. Authors such as Lovecraft, Shiel, and H. Rider Haggard didn't rise above their racist tendencies and often used race to indicate value, couching them in vaguely Darwinian terms. Ideas about eugenics, discussed previously in the chapter "Worlds Beyond," became widespread during the Modernist era. Burroughs was no stranger to using these attitudes in his fictions.

Through an incredibly convenient shipwreck and miraculous survival on the open ocean along with Rokoff (going by the name of Thuran) who is now set to marry Hazel, Jane and William once again find themselves stranded in an unpopulated section of African shoreline. Jane is captured by the Oparian ape-men as they hunt for the refugee, Tarzan. Jane breaks off the engagement, citing her unrealized love for Tarzan, whom she believes to be dead at sea. Tarzan manages to once again enter the city of Opar and rescues Jane, but William eventually succumbs to fever and dies. In a moment of narrative reflective realization, Burroughs encompasses the Speculative Modernist world of Tarzan and Jane. "For a while both were silent—gazing into each others' [sic] eyes as though each still questioned the reality of the wonderful happiness that had come to them. The past, with all its hideous disappointments and horrors, was forgotten—the future did not belong to them; but the present—ah, it was theirs; none could take it from them" (Burroughs *Return* 213). There is a disengagement with the past, whose structures no longer apply, and a shielding of the future which is wrought with uncertainty. The only thing that matters to Tarzan and Jane is the here and now. It is the only thing knowable, the only thing real. In the true spirit of Speculative Modernism, Tarzan's idea of the great natural law governs.

According to the natural law and Tarzan's innate desire to do good and protect those he cares about must be engaged, and justice must be served. Yet Tarzan hedges his bets. When Tarzan reveals Thuran as Rokoff and learns how he let Clayton die without any attempt at saving his life despite the ability to do so, even Jane admits to Tarzan that he can be justified in Rokoff's dispatch: "'In the heart of the jungle [...] with no other form of right or justice [...] you would be warranted in executing upon this man the sentence he deserves'" (Burroughs *Return* 219). However, she reasons with him that such an action would be considered murder and that he would be arrested, thereby losing her again. Understanding this logic, Tarzan concedes and has Rokoff arrested by the ship's captain to be returned to France and sentenced.

Tarzan heads back to civilization with Jane and chooses his love for her over his love for the jungle. However, as readers know of the twenty-two remaining novels from Burroughs, the civilized life of John Clayton II Lord Greystoke does not take hold for very long, and Tarzan endures.

Buck Rogers: Future Perfect

On the surface, Buck Rogers does not fit in with the other Speculative Modernist heroes in this chapter. He is a team player who believes deeply in the ideals of the United States and he is willing to fight for his country, given the chance. On a closer reading, however, Rogers is anything but an unquestioning and disposable hero. Instead, Rogers fits the Modernist ethos perfectly. To be the kind of man he wants to be—to be the kind of American he wants to be—he needs to put significant distance between himself and the Depression-era United States. Rogers first appeared in the story *Armageddon 2419 A.D.* by Philip Francis Nowlan, which was in the celebrated August 1928 issue of *Amazing Stories*.[6] When readers first meet Rogers, he is unconscious in a cave and has been thus for five hundred years. Upon waking, he discovers that the United States as he knew it is gone:

> I awoke to find the America I knew a total wreck—to find Americans a hunted race in their own land, hiding in the dense forests that covered the shattered and leveled ruins of their once magnificent cities, desperately preserving, and struggling to develop in their secret retreats, the remnants of their culture and science and their independence [Nowlan].

The world is dominated by the "Hans," an Asia-based military and political force that rules absolutely. North America is covered by a forest, and so there are many places to hide. The remaining inhabitants have rebuilt their military and their infrastructure out of sight, mostly, of the Han warplanes. A rebellion is about to begin when Rogers introduces himself. He is a Modernist everyman, a veteran of World War I who now works with radioactive gases. When Han forces attack Rogers and his friends, Rogers contributes to their defense by shooting down one of the Han airships. He is accepted into the gang due to his military prowess and is finally made their leader. They strike a great blow against the Han forces, the rebellion is fully underway, and the story ends.

As a hero, Buck Rogers is the ideal American, with military experience and a broad and deep knowledge of all kinds of science, both theoretical and practical. It seems as if there is nothing he cannot do. He gladly joins the Wyoming gang and fits right in, subjugating his will to the will of the group. Rogers seems to lack the fierce individuality of the other heroes in this chapter, but that difference might be superficial. It is not as if he buys into the twentieth-century American way of life, rife with consumerism, wealth, and deep poverty. Instead, he has stumbled into what might be a nihilist's paradise. All of the structures—economic, religious, historical, cultural, racial, etc.—have been long forgotten. The only values remaining are strength, ingenuity, loyalty, and perseverance, and Rogers loves it. Late in the novel, he steps out of the narrative for a moment to lament what is to come once the Han overlords are vanquished. He sounds exactly like the Speculative Modernist hero:

> In later years I felt that there was a certain softening of moral fiber among the people, since the Hans had been finally destroyed with all their works; and Americans have developed a new luxury economy. I have seen signs of the reawakening of greed, of selfishness. The eternal cycle seems to be at work. I fear that slowly, though surely, private wealth is reappearing, codes of inflexibility are developing; they will be followed by corruption, degradation; and in the end some cataclysmic event will end this era and usher in a new one [Nowlan].

On the surface, Buck Rogers is the all–American hero fighting for the Constitution and the American way of life. Instead, he has seen the gradual breakdown of the ideal nation he has fought to preserve, and he thrives in the breakdown. Despite his seeming perfection as a hero, Buck Rogers exhibits a flaw in his rigidity. He is unable to accept any variance from his vision of reality. What happens to Buck Rogers when the fight for peace is over? Like the heroes in *The Worm Ouroboros*, he cannot fathom a world that no longer needs his heroism. For now, he can be the unfettered hero he was born to be.

King Kull: Governing by Axe

One of the staples of Speculative Modernism is the manipulation of linear chronology of eras. Conan Doyle was no exception to this, looking at the Lost World, nor was Burroughs with the Atlantean references in the city of Opar. Fellow adventure writer Robert E. Howard followed suit with his first fantasy publication, "The Shadow Kingdom" in *Weird Tales*, August 1929. Howard was noted for having a fondness for historical fiction, and it is where many of his supporters felt his best writing took place (Louinet "Introduction" xxi–xxii). His first fantasy protagonist, King Kull is Atlantean, "a violent brooder, a man of action" (Clute *Fantasy* 481), who has come to rule over the advanced civilization of Valusia before the Great Cataclysm that caused the land to sink into the sea, as outlined in "The Hyborian Age" (1938). Like other Speculative Modernist heroes, his flaw defines him. Kull straddles his universe, caught between the desire to rule and a people that actively fights against him due to his outsider status, a visceral present and a long forgotten, ancient past, and a governing rational mind and rage-fueled savagery. He is barbaric in nature, but governs with a civil hand. Although Kull has a bloodlust on the field of battle similar to Tarzan's bestial rage, he is measured and rational. King Kull is even willing to forgo racial rivalries and prejudices, something that Burroughs underscores in his fantasy works.

What makes Kull so compelling are his "meditations," and an inclination for self-reflection that was not part of the Tarzan formula. Where Tarzan acts or reacts more than reasons, Kull does the former only when "permitted" to do so; in "The Shadow Kingdom" Brule signals to Kull when it is time to rage by the simply saying "slay." However, Kull is just as likely to sit and think:

> And what, mused Kull, were the realities of life? Ambition?, power, pride? The friendship of man, the love of women—which Kull had never known—battle, plunder, what? Was it the real Kull who sat upon the throne or was it the real Kull who scaled the hills of Atlantis, harried the far isles of the sunset, and laughed upon the roaring tides of the Atlantean sea? How could a man be so many different men in a lifetime? For Kull knew that there were many Kulls and he wondered which was the real Kull [Howard "Shadow"].

Kull is at once an Atlantean barbarian and an existential philosopher. He questions his existence, his meaning, his motivations. While he defaults and even longs for action and battle, readers see the aftermath in his quiet meditative moments.

This inclusion of metaphysical reflection can be seen in Kull's second story "The Mirrors of Tuzun Thune" in the September issue of *Weird Tales* in 1929. In this short story, Kull is challenged by a wizard who is able to manipulate appearances of reality. He is forced to question the time and the universe as he knows it, and considers the possibility of alternate and parallel universes:

> At times he seemed on the point of discovering some vast, unthinkable secret. He no longer thought of the image in the mirror as a shadow of himself; the thing, to him, was an entity, similar in outer appearance, yet basically as far from Kull himself as the poles are far apart. The image it seemed to Kull, had an individuality apart from Kull's, he was no more dependent on Kull than Kull was dependent on him. And day by day Kull doubted in which world he lived; was he the shadow, summoned at will by the other? Did he instead of the other live in a world of delusion, the shadow of the real world? [Howard "Mirrors"].

By questioning the nature of reality and his very existence, Kull breaks new ground as a Speculative Modernist hero. He is greatly troubled by the possibility of multiple synchronous universes and cannot comprehend such complexities. Try as he might, he can only resort to what he knows and the comforts of familiar violence.

In Howard's final Kull story, "Kings of the Night" (1930), he brings Kull into the historical past of the Roman occupation of the British Isles and the character of Bran Mak Morn. Because Kull and Bran inhabit the same moment in time, Howard depicts time in a new light. In "Kings of the Night," as the Pictish faction seeks to ward off the oncoming siege from the Romans, they are in search of leaders who can guide them against such a formidable foe. A group of elders, including Bran Mak Morn, gather together to plan strategy. One of the elders, a wizard, reflects on the concept of time to Bran:

> "Who knows?" asked the wizard obliquely. "Time and space exist not. There was no past, and there shall be no future. NOW is all. All things that ever were, are, or ever will be, transpire *now*. Man is forever at the center of what we call time and space. I have gone into yesterday and tomorrow and both were as real as today—which is like the dreams of ghosts!" [Howard "Kings" 36].

Exposition of this nature recalls Burroughs's narration about time at the conclusion of *The Return of Tarzan*. However, Howard ups the ante and includes time travel as a way to enlist King Kull of Atlantis to help ward off the conquering Roman forces that are dismantling much of southern Europe. After winning the battle he had agreed to fight, Kull vanishes back into his own time. For Speculative Modernists like Howard, Kull's struggles over time reveal that time is just another flawed social construct. Kull can only view time on a linear basis.

Conan the Cimmerian: Blood on Steel

Conan's mentality warrants the spotlight in a discussion of heroes who thrive on what most people (including literary critics) would call character flaws. Conan's strength—both as an enduring character and a prototypical hero of Speculative Modernism—is his antiestablishment philosophy and unwavering loyalty to savagery and self-preservation in the face of monsters, magic, and man. Conan is most content when he slays, when he loves, when he lives. In living, Conan must seek adventure. Like Kull before him, Conan is not content with idleness. Even in ruling a kingdom, Conan ventures into the dark realms of adventure, and he is familiar with its fantastic elements. While not quite the level of influence and success as Holmes or Tarzan, Conan figures prominently in speculative fantasy. His run of influence has even outgrown Tarzan and currently enjoys prominent status in cinema, television, and comics. In terms of a cultural presence, Conan's imposing figure looms large.

Although Conan's heritage stems from Kull, he is most assuredly not an adaptation. In Conan, gone are the contemplations, meditations, anxieties, and doubts of King Kull. In this regard, Conan is very much in league with Holmes and Tarzan in confidence and almost superhuman ability. He is not Superman (who made his first appearance in 1938). He is not only a savage barbarian turned king, but also a thief, a womanizer, and a pirate. There is not a single instance where Conan feels any amount of guilt or remorse over this. He is his own man, an island unto himself.

In Howard's only true Conan novel (although first published in serial form) *The Hour of the Dragon* (1935), the hero finds himself ruling as King of Aquilonia, but is plotted against by heirs of the previous regime who resurrect an ancient wizard, Xaltotun, to dethrone and eliminate the Cimmerian. Even when confronted by the supernatural foe, Conan remains stoic:

> Conan glared at him unspeaking, feeling a chill along his spine. Wizards and sorcerers abounded in his barbaric mythology, and any fool could tell that this was no common man. Conan sensed an inexplicable something about him that set him apart—an alien aura of Time and Space, a sense of tremendous and sinister antiquity. But his stubborn spirit refused to flinch [Howard *Hour* 45].

In this example, one of many that fill the pages of the barbarian's chronicles, readers see the limitless courage of Conan, but Howard conveys this through his narration, not through the inner thoughts or dialogue of the protagonist. Unlike Holmes and Tarzan, Conan has no need to show off. As stated earlier, he is content to slay.

Yet, Conan is no idle king. Despite his savagery and seemingly simplistic philosophy, he is also remarkably conscientious about his people. He is able to look beyond personal prejudices according to races or religions of men. "Conan's was the broad tolerance […] and he refused to prosecute the followers of Asura or to allow the people to do so on no better evidence than was presented against them, rumors and accusations that could not be proven[….] 'Let men worship what gods they will'" (Howard *Hour* 95). While Conan is prejudiced, he does not act on that hatred. Instead, he tries to create a world that makes sense to him. Likewise, he refuses to be forced to abide by a world he despises. That world is the civilized one, antithetical to the Speculative Modernist hero's perspective.

Readers and fans have no doubts about who Conan is. He does not make any attempt at fitting into the social rules and customs of society and does not even acknowledge any type of law other than his own. In this way, he makes Holmes's and Tarzan's occasional indiscretions with the laws of civilization into nothing more than a buzzing fly that can easily be dispatched. Conan's only law is his own. Holmes is somewhat bound to law because he exists in society. He serves society's laws. Tarzan wants to obey the natural law but cannot because of his human ties and love for Jane Porter. As king, Conan longs for no such restriction:

> the awakening of old memories, the resurge of the wild, mad, glorious days of old before his feet were set on the imperial path when he was a wandering mercenary, roistering, brawling, guzzling, adventuring, with no thought for the morrow, and no desire save sparkling ale, red lips, and a keen sword to swing on all the battlefields of the world. Unconsciously he reverted to the old ways [Howard *Hour* 111].

This is the creed that Conan lives by and fights to maintain. Even more than Holmes and Tarzan, Conan exists outside of civilization. One of the pillars of such a civilization is a governing worldview, a belief in a larger meaning than Conan's creed, and he is always at odds with it: "This foul perversion [of man's desires embodied by Akivasha, a succubus] was the truth of that everlasting life. Through his physical revulsion ran the sense of a shattered dream of man's idolatry, its glittering gold proved slime and cosmic filth. A wave of futility swept over him, a dim fear of the falseness of all men's dreams and idolatries" (156). Even as king, Conan does not feel he fits into society. Civilization is the lie Conan sees that others cannot. His truth is a cold truth, not dissimilar to Holmes's although the means by which this truth is discerned is entirely different.

Holmes is ruled by reason that enforces the norms of late nineteenth-century London. Tarzan aligns himself with the natural law but is forced to contend with the laws of society. Kull, too, abides by those, despite his lust for battle and moments of savage rage. Although Conan has a faint ambition toward becoming a king, he does so almost by default. He does not aspire to lead. In actuality, Conan wants nothing more than to remove himself from humanity—aside from the pleasure he receives from women and the enjoyment of alcohol. As Howard explains in *Red Nails*, a novella first serialized in *Weird Tales* in 1936:

> The Cimmerian might have spent two years among the great cities of the world; he might have walked with the rulers of civilization; he might even achieve his wild whim some day and rule as king of a civilized nation; stranger things had happened. But he was no less a barbarian. He was concerned only with the naked fundamentals of life. The warm intimacies of small kindly things, the sentiments and delicious trivialities that make up so much of civilized men's lives were meaningless to him. A wolf was no less a wolf because a whim of chance caused him to run with the watchdogs. Bloodshed and violence and savagery were the natural elements of the life Conan knew; he could not, and would never, understand the little things that are so dear to civilized men and women [Howard *Red* 480].

One of the standout sections of this passage is "the sentiments and delicious trivialities" of civilized man. This can easily be read as wealth, social comforts, and love. The latter is where Conan is perhaps most flawed. The closest that Conan ever comes to a lasting relationship is with Bêlit in "Queen of the Black Coast" (1934). He becomes rather enamored with the pirate queen, and the feelings seem to be shared. Unfortunately, she dies at the hands of a fantastical creature and her corpse gruesomely hung at the bow of her ship. She is the closest Conan ever comes to a "true love" akin to Jane Porter for Tarzan, but that love is taken from him, and he quickly moves on to the next battle at hand.

However, that is not to say that Bêlit is Conan's only love. Indeed, Conan encounters many women who the Cimmerian enjoys physical liaisons with. One such woman is the princess Zenobia. Through the arc of *The Hour of the Dragon*, Zenobia and Conan rescue each other several time from the chains, swords, claws, and teeth of various foes. In the process, Conan vows to make Zenobia his queen once he regains the throne, but the novel ends before that can be accomplished. Conan is not meant to be monogamous. Likewise, he has no counterpart as Holmes does with Watson. He stands alone, even as king.

Jirel of Joiry: Darkness and Light

Both Conan the Barbarian and Jirel of Joiry—the first female counterpart to Conan, created by Catherine Lucille Moore (writing under the name C.L. Moore)—thwart societal expectations of what is acceptable behavior for the Speculative Modernist time period. Conan consistently foregrounds a simple philosophy of living only in the present and existing by his own sense of morality. Jirel, an early feminist character in the fantasy genre, breaks free from the shackles of patriarchal society and uses her physical prowess and sexuality to achieve power and enact revenge on her oppressors.

Capitalizing on Howard's success with Conan, C.L. Moore offers up a rather surprising wrinkle to the catalog with her story "Black God's Kiss" from the October 1934 edition of *Weird Tales*. In this story, Moore introduces the first sword-and-sorcery female protagonist, Jirel of Joiry. She is established as an equal in terms of ability and ferocity: "She was tall as most men, and as savage as the wildest of them" (Moore 39). In her article "'A Hot and Savage Strength': The Female Masculinity of C.L. Moore's Jirel of Joiry," Eileen Donaldson explains that "as a warrior, Moore's Jirel destabilizes stereotypes that were a staple of the genre, challenging readers to imagine that women could be physically and sexually aggressive, independent and also emotional and compassionate" (50). She is a fierce and powerful warrior, who happens to be female. Jirel aligns with other Speculative Modernist heroes as she subverts convention, largely through her actions as a warrior above all else. She not only uses her strength, bravery, and savagery in combat against patriarchal structures, but employs her sexuality to do so as well. She challenges conventions such as Christianity; she utilizes a mystical weapon acquired through fantastic means; she faces a world without literal and figural light. However, those characteristics can also be seen as flaws.

Moore's story is a tale of revenge, as Guillaume leads the conquering of Joiry and imprisons Jirel. However, before he does so, he forces a kiss upon her—thereby initiating her obsession to destroy him by any means necessary:

> Upon her mouth she felt the remembered weight of his, about her the strength of his arms. And such a blast of hot fury came over her that she reeled a little and clutched at the wall for support. She went on in a haze of red anger, and something like madness burning in her brain as a resolve slowly took shape out of the chaos of her hate. When that thought came to her she paused again, mid-step upon the stairs, and was conscious of a little coldness blowing over her. Then it was gone, and she shivered a little, shook her shoulders and grinned wolfishly, and went on [Moore 41].

This passage is important because it portrays the workings of Jirel's mind. What was nothing more than an unwanted kiss is described as a violation akin to rape. Guillaume's kiss was an assertion of dominance, an attack on Jirel's perceived vulnerability as a woman, an exercise in the patriarchal assumptions of sexism. It is because of all these associations that Jirel now has "a madness burning in her brain" (Moore 41). The cause of Guillaume's destruction turns out to be the acquisition of an unknown forbidden weapon of demonic origins.

Travelling down a secret tunnel under the prisoner's cell, Jirel enters into a journey that reads more like science fiction than epic fantasy. She is cast in darkness with labyrinthine tunnels and crevices that utterly disorient her amidst odd angles and shapes in the rock not produced or traversed by any human, reminiscent of the strange structures found on Lovecraft's R'lyeh. The disorientation, however, seems to stop once Jirel removes her necklace bearing a cross, a commentary on how Christianity blinds people to reality. Jirel's underground world is suddenly cast into ethereal light, and she undertakes a quest to find this magical weapon.

Navigating unfamiliar gravitational forces, voracious snapping monsters, and amphibious doppelgängers, Jirel reaches her destination—a black lake in which she was promised to find her weapon. Navigating the lake, she reaches the guardian of the weapon, "a semi-human figure, crouching forward with outthrust head, sexless and strange. Its one central eye was closed as if in rapture, and its mouth was pursed for a kiss" (Moore 59). Unable to resist the temptation, Jirel steals the kiss from this figure. Realizing her kiss is now poison, she ventures back to exact her revenge. After her return to the surface, she transmits her poison kiss to Guillaume but does not enjoy her revenge:

> She could not name it, but she saw it in his eyes—some dreadful emotion never made for flesh and blood to know, some iron despair such as only an unguessable being from the gray, formless void could ever have felt before—too hideously alien for any human creature to endure[....] Suddenly and blindingly it came upon her what she had done. She knew now why such heady violence had flooded her whenever she thought of him—knew why the light-devil in her own form had laughed so derisively—knew the price she must pay for taking a gift from a demon. She knew that there was no light anywhere in the world, now that Guillaume was gone [Moore 66–67].

Although Jirel does exact her revenge, she is not without regret. Donaldson contends that Jirel, is a type of black widow when she kills Guillaume, that she loves him but has to kill him. She is "the female warrior [and] is a sexual agent" (57). Jirel murders her antagonist with a poison kiss, not a biting sword.

Jirel, like the other Speculative Modernists heroes examined here, benefits from her apparent flaws. Her wavering of faith—the removal of her cross—allows her to gain the weapon she needs, but her affirmation of that faith enables her to return to the world she understands. Her physical ability and sexuality are the tools she uses to achieve her goal. She does not have to resort to one or the other. In enacting her revenge, she faces a world of personal darkness, a world she is entirely responsible for creating. Despite knowing that society is going to ostracize her, she chooses revenge even over love because that is who she is. Anyone who threatens her autonomy must face her wrath. She epitomizes the antithesis of society the Speculative Modernists often underscore in their works.

Conclusion

When religion, economics, and other institutions are revealed as mere social constructs created to artificially provide structure and meaning, society is left without a rudder on the turbulent sea of meaninglessness. Readers often turn to heroes during these points for inspiration. This is precisely what happened during the Modernist era. When rules of social decorum and traditional laws carried smaller and smaller relevance as the world lurched toward world wars, unique characters sidestepped "decency" and pursued what they alone felt is right and just. The reading public began to recognize how these characters were able to navigate such terrain because they exist outside of the social and cultural norms of society and civilization. Holmes is too arrogant and singular. Tarzan, Kull, and Conan have no trust in social or cultural norms and are subject to blood lust. Buck Rogers is almost too perfect (a fault that would come to plague Superman in DC Comics just a few years later). Jirel is too conflicted. These very faults that prevent them from being socially appropriate are the things that allow them to exist outside of a society. The hour of Yeats's beast is nigh. Characters like Conan are the only ones able to slay it.

The concept and construction of character underwent a shift in portrayal and development that matched the search for meaning in a meaningless world that was being experienced in the United Kingdom and the United States during the Modernist era. Since society could no longer remain consistent, characters could operate differently as well. They could contradict themselves and be impulsive in relation to specific situations. They could exist simultaneously in different roles within their narrative world. They were no longer bound by predetermined morality or ethics. It became clear that the world owed them nothing. As Stephen Crane posited in "A Man Said to the Universe":

> A man said to the universe:
> "Sir, I exist!"
> "However," replied the universe,
> "The fact has not created in me
> A sense of obligation" [99].

If the universe was under no obligation to individuals, then they had no loyalty to the universe and could operate under their own personal preferences. That is exactly what the heroes of Speculative Modernism do, and readers revere them for it.

The *fin de siècle* culture and upcoming era of Modernism dismantled the social institutions that kept the glue of culture intact. What were once binding constructs had become separate, crumbling fragments, and self-interest reigned. That possibility was too extreme and disheartening for people to accept as a new reality. From this void—this conflicting desire to believe in humanity but prepare for its ruin—the Speculative Modernist hero emerges.

These narratives enjoy a certain freedom that those who abide by society's customs and laws do not. As Howard articulates in one of his last Conan story arcs, "'Barbarism is the natural state of mankind,' the borderer said, still staring somberly at the Cimmerian. 'Civilization is unnatural. It is a whim of circumstance. And barbarism must ultimately triumph'" (Howard *Red* 499). That barbarism, whether it be cold calculation or merciless brutality, is what appealed to the Speculative Modernist audience and allowed for new and different heroes to be born.

Epilogue

> No good poetry is ever written in a manner twenty years old, for to write in such a manner shows conclusively that the writer thinks from books, convention and cliché, and not from life, yet a man feeling the divorce of life and his art may naturally try to resurrect a forgotten mode if he finds in that mode some leaven, or if he think he sees in it some element lacking in contemporary art which might unite that art again to its sustenance, life.
> —Ezra Pound, "Prolegomena" (1912)

One thing that can be learned from the authors discussed in this book is how deep their roots extend. The impact they made during their own era is still being felt in many ways in the writings of today. We want to end our story of Speculative Modernism by taking a short look at the impact this era had on the rest of the century, through a few different lenses, and how the publishers and producers would carry on the work started in this era that now seems so remote. What we discuss here is again in no way meant to be comprehensive. There are so many facets through which the Speculative Modernist writers have reached their audience that it will take several other books (and lifetimes) to recount those tales, to retrace all of those steps. It is important, however, to end this work with a little taste of how writers and readers have been granted this gift by an earlier generation in ways that are not always so clearly understood.

The Editorial Tastemakers

Science fiction, fantasy, and horror have an enduring appeal in part because they have been uniquely responsive to the dizzying rate of progress to which society in both the United States and the United Kingdom have needed to adapt in the past one-hundred-fifty years. During the Speculative Modernist era, capitalizing on the power of the pulp magazine industry, speculative fiction, along with other specialized genres, reached every corner of the United States and the United Kingdom by the start of World War II. The momentum established during the era has continued long after the period under scrutiny in our book.

At the turn of the century and without competition from film or television, Westerns, romances, railroad stories, boys' stories, sports, and other fiction genres proliferated on newsstands in the United States. A similar progression was slower to develop in the United Kingdom which "did not develop a body of specialist pulp magazines on the scale of the USA" ("Pulp"). In the United States, print production know-how, intense audience interest, near-universal literacy, and profound societal change collided to create this phenomenon. Although speculative fiction made up only a small part of overall pulp sales, the gradual spread of exclusively speculative fiction magazines allowed the genres to grow deep roots and flourish. Influential editor and scholar James Gunn argues: "The appearance of a magazine devoted to a single category, of genre, exerted a significant influence on the development of that genre, like building a hothouse for a single variety of flower or isolating a single bacterium in a petri dish and watching it multiply" (Gunn 15). At the helms of many of these new speculative fiction magazines sat an influential editor, whose preferences defined the genres.

These editorial tastemakers laid the groundwork for the success of speculative fiction that came during the era that is the focus of this book, for it was the editors who created the genre most directly. Starting with Frank Munsey's *Argosy* (1896) and continuing through Edwin Baird and Farnsworth Wright's *Weird Tales* (1923), Hugo Gernsback's *Amazing Stories* (1926), William Clayton's *Astounding* (1930), and many others, a series of powerful editors during the pulp era established a system whereby the tastes and preferences of a single person would drive the growth of an entire genre. Gernsback, John W. Campbell, and a small number of others exerted outsized influence on the development of science fiction, especially. Gunn claims, "What was SF then? Was it Vernian or Wellsian, fantastic or realistic, romantic or pragmatic, literary or scientific? It was all of these things, of course, at various times and sometimes at the same time; but as editors developed strength and skill and tastes, one aspect or another would predominate. As they did, the definition of SF was shaped" (Gunn "Gatekeepers" 16). As the decades advanced, the editors remained influential, but the imperatives changed along with the times.

The next generation of editors expanded the reach of speculative fiction magazines into the second half of the twentieth century. Audiences began to demand stories that delved deeply into the possibilities for psychological and ethical complexity in their characters and settings. John

Carnell edited *New Worlds* magazine starting in 1946, and "[b]y the late 1950s, authors such as [J.G.] Ballard, [Brian] Aldiss, John Brunner, and Harry Harrison were testing and breaking SF taboos in the magazine's pages" (Gunn *Encyclopedia* 330). Michael Moorcock took the reins in 1964 and brought with him a commitment toward bringing characters filled with human frailty and layered complexity into science fiction. Moorcock's goal as an editor, as he explained in the introduction to the *New Worlds* anthology, was to put his stamp on the genre:

> [I]t would specialise in experimental work by writers like [William] Burroughs and [Eduardo] Paolozzi, but it would be "popular," it would seek to publicise such experimenters; it would publish all those writers who had become demoralised by a lack of sympathetic publishers and by baffled critics; it would attempt a cross-fertilization of popular sf, science and the work of the literary and artistic avant garde [Moorcock "Introduction" 10–11].

He and his contemporaries—dubbed speculative fiction's "New Wave"— became the leading force in taking the hard-won gains of the Speculative Modernist era into the second half of the twentieth century.

By the end of the 1960s, the ideas that began to take hold during the Speculative Modernist era had reached their fullest possible bloom. It was as if for the first time the kind of experimentation in language and themes that was a key element for canonical Modernists had finally found their speculative fiction audience. Pursuing his own personal aesthetic, Moorcock would also publish some of J.G. Ballard's more experimental pieces, as well as the serial, *Bug Jack Barron*, by Norman Spinrad that Brian Aldiss says was so sexually explicit that *New Worlds* nearly lost its state funding after printing it (Aldiss 300). Authors such as Samuel R. Delany, Judith Merril, and Harlan Ellison pushed boundaries in diversity, language, character, and story structure. Gunn credits Moorcock's "liberalism" in aiding the New Wave of science fiction to reach new heights (Gunn *Encyclopedia* 330), something that the more conservative agendas of the Gernsback era never achieved.

Although speculative writers such as Isaac Asimov and Robert A. Heinlein were still publishing highly successful works devoid of complexity of character, others such as Samuel R. Delany, J.G. Ballard, and Joanna Russ were, as Michael Moorcock asserted, showing "that literate and humane sf and fantasy could be written" (Clute and Nicholls 823) and, not only written, but also published widely and became immensely popular among the reading public. By the middle of the century, complex characters were more readily acceptable. Characters such as Ursula Le Guin's Genly Ai, Stephen King's Carrie, Joanna Russ's Joanna/Jeannine/Janet/Jael, and Stephen R. Donaldson's Thomas Covenant became synonymous with the speculative genres. These characters live in different worlds—sometimes substantially so—but at their heart, they are filled with the kinds of frailties and vulnerabilities to which all human beings are subject.

The Book Publishers Who Made the Old New Again

Few of the Speculative Modernist writers we have studied in this book remain in publication from the time they first published their works to the present; H.G. Wells, J.R.R. Tolkien, and Ambrose Bierce are among the fortunate ones. Most authors, even very popular ones in their times, seem to fade after a time, and unless something wonderful happens relating to their work, vanish altogether. James Branch Cabell and Marie Corelli, for example, broke all kinds of sales records in their lifetimes, and both had careers spanning nearly fifty years, yet it is difficult to find many fans of either of them these days and harder to find print versions of their books. There are, however, a lucky few whose works are somehow revived, and most of these are on account of a devoted fan, or an enraptured editor. Perhaps, a grandparent leaves a lucky child a load of old books, or an ancient library housing priceless treasures is cleared out to make way for new books. Generally, it is all about the timing.

For many of the books discussed in this volume, the process has involved several revivals, aided by a lot of luck. A good example of a writer who could easily have vanished is H.P. Lovecraft. While Lovecraft had found the perfect home for most of his stories in *Weird Tales*, first edited by Edwin Baird and then Farnsworth Wright, he never found a more stable home in a published collection of his work during his lifetime. Lovecraft's writing would have disappeared with the pulp on which it had been published except for a young devotee who founded the publisher, Arkham House, solely in order to publish *The Outsider and Others* (1939), a collection of his writings. August Derleth, a fellow *Weird Tales* contributor who corresponded with Lovecraft, along with Donald Wandrei, his partner at Arkham, managed to keep Lovecraft's writing in print until it could reach a wider audience, and find new popularity in the fantasy boom of the 1960s and 1970s.

August Derleth took it upon himself to not only publish Lovecraft's collected works, but even tried his hand at finishing off some of the fragments Lovecraft left behind after he died in 1937. In 1974, three years after Derleth's death, a collection of "collaborations" called *The Watchers Out of Time* appeared from Arkham, with a foreword by Derleth's daughter, April Derleth. She writes of her father's relationship with Lovecraft:

Derleth and Lovecraft never did meet each other; theirs was strictly an epistolary friendship. And it was out of this extensive correspondence that a genuine mutual respect developed. [...] When Lovecraft died in 1937, Derleth was one of the few to recognize him as a prominent figure in the domain of supernatural horror. That recognition was to develop into a quasi-obsession ... a personal commitment to see that Lovecraft's obsession (supernatural horror) would be contained between hardcovers [viii].

Though August Derleth brought forth many works of his own, among them the great Solar Pons detective stories, his enduring legacy is the preservation of Lovecraft's writing and the founding of a publisher who would deal strictly with the stranger fiction of the original *Weird Tales* days.[1] In the 1970s, his works would reach a wider audience in the Ballantine Adult Fantasy paperback editions. Arkham House also helped to preserve some of the authors in our study: Clark Ashton Smith, Algernon Blackwood, and William Hope Hodgson, among the most prominent.

While much of the fantasy literature boom of the later twentieth century can be attributed to the arrival of J.R.R. Tolkien's masterwork, *The Lord of the Rings*, which was originally published in three volumes in 1954–1955, the real surge would come in the middle of the next decade when the volumes appeared in the United States first in Ace paperbacks and then in the authorized Ballantine editions in 1965. Ballantine's success with these books caused a demand for more works like them. Jamie Williamson's *The Evolution of Modern Fantasy* chronicles how from 1965 to 1968, Ballantine published other Tolkien titles, like *The Tolkien Reader* (1966) and *Smith of Wooton Major and Farmer Giles of Ham* (1969), along with authors like the Tolkien-inspirer E.R. Eddison, and Tolkien-inspired Peter Beagle. Williamson writes:

> Enter Lin Carter. A younger writer who had begun to publish sword and sorcery, including Conan spin-offs in collaboration with [L. Sprague] de Camp, during the mid–1960s, Carter approached Betty and Ian Ballantine in 1967 with a proposed book on Tolkien. This was accepted and published as *Tolkien: A Look Behind the Lord of the Rings* in early 1969. One of the chapters, "The Men Who Invented Fantasy," gave a brief account of the nonpulp fantasy tradition preceding Tolkien, which dovetailed with their editions of Eddison, [Mervyn] Peake, [David] Lindsay, and Beagle. Sensing a good source for editorial direction, Ballantine contracted Carter as "Editorial Consultant" for their subsequent Ballantine Adult Fantasy Series, which commenced in spring 1969 [Williamson].

Carter's Ballantine Adult Fantasy series produced sixty-five volumes from 1969 to 1974, and while it was never a big money maker for Ballantine, it preserved so many of the authors of fantasy that predated and were contemporaries of Tolkien, among them James Branch Cabell, Arthur Machen, George MacDonald, and Clark Ashton Smith. Lovecraft would also be republished by Ballantine in the 1970s with particularly lurid covers, and the cheap price helped draw in readers.

Fortunately, there have been many series and book editors who have found time throughout the last half a century to revive Speculative Modernist authors. In the writing of this volume, we found series like Brian Stableford's Greenhill Science Fiction & Fantasy series, David Hartwell's science-fiction series for Gregg Press, the Centipede Press Library of Weird Fiction, and the Night Shade Books editions of both William Hope Hodgson and Clark Ashton Smith. Editors like S.T. Joshi have helped produce editions of Lovecraft, M.P. Shiel, Hodgson, and many more, while editors like Ellen Datlow have helped to open the door for twenty-first-century authors to respond to Lovecraft's writings. Joshi writes of Lovecraft:

> The history of Lovecraft's reputation—his initial rejection by Edmund Wilson and others as a pulp hack; the championing of his work by Derleth, Fritz Leiber, and George T. Wetzel; the revolution in scholarship as a result of the work of such critics as Dirk W. Mosig and Donald R. Burleson; and his final acceptance as a canonical author with the publication of his work in Penguin Classics and the Library of America—would make an interesting chapter in the evolution of literary taste [Joshi *Lovecraft* xiii–xiv].

Thanks to Joshi and other editors, many of the Speculative Modernists have survived to be examined and reexamined by each successive generation, sometimes finding new audiences to charm.

In some cases, the scrutiny has called into question the underlying messages of these works. American author Charles Saunders sought to recast the racism of Speculative Modernist writers and published fantasy short stories and novels that "reimagined the white worlds of Tarzan and Conan with Black heroes and African mythologies in books that spoke especially to Black fans eager for more fictional champions with whom they could identify" in the 1970s and 1980s (Genzlinger). In the twenty-first century some of the earlier works, particularly Lovecraft's writings, have caused backlashes against their racist and sexist themes. Victor LaValle's *The Ballad of Black Tom* and Matt Ruff's *Lovecraft Country* address Lovecraft's racism. Peter Jackson's film versions of *The Hobbit* attempted to incorporate more female main characters. Though some Speculative Modern works have reprehensible underpinnings, new authors and readers continue to find inspiration in their own understanding of these works.

Conan as Chronicle

The influence of Speculative Modernist writers continued well past their origins, and their characters realized new successes and audiences

Epilogue 215

through a variety of new formats. Robert E. Howard's Conan is an illustrative example of this. Howard had only a decade of publishing success before his suicide in 1932 and only four years of his most famous creation. However, one does not have to look far to see that Conan is still an active aspect of popular and literary culture today nearly a century later.

After the publication of Howard's first Conan novel, *The Hour of the Dragon* (1936), tales of the Cimmerian appeared sporadically in speculative magazines covering all three genres in the 1950s. In the same decade, Gnome Press released a retitled version of Howard's novel, now under the name *Conan the Conqueror*. Due to its success, Conan collections in hardcover followed suit under editor L. Sprague de Camp. De Camp would later coauthor numerous Conan pastiches with Björn Nyberg, carrying Conan through the 1950s and into the 1960s with Lancer Books.

Surviving the science-fiction craze of the mid-century, Conan found new audiences in different mediums with a comic book adaptation from Marvel Comics in the 1970s. *Conan the Barbarian* (1970), written by Roy Thomas with artwork by Barry Windsor-Smith, launched a highly successful run that helped Marvel outpace their top rival, DC Comics, throughout the decade. Comic arcs Savage Tales and Giant-Sized Conan (1974–1975) would popularize Howard's character from decades earlier even more. Just as in the Modernist period, Conan's barbarity seemed to fit perfectly with a decade plagued by presidential impeachment, a highly controversial war, a hangover from the Civil Rights movement, and widespread drug use. Civilization was in decay; Conan found new audiences.

Comic book readers and fans alike finally had visual representations of Conan beyond the incredibly influential cover art of Frank Frazetta. Conan lived in both color from comic storyboards and black-and-white from newspaper strips. It was now time for the small and big screens. The Conan influence was on full display with the Saturday morning cartoons, *Thundarr the Barbarian* (1980–81)[2] and *Blackstar* (1981).

The largest gateway into popular culture for Howard's character was the blockbuster film *Conan the Barbarian* (1982), directed by John Milius and funded by Dino De Laurentiis, with a screenplay by Milius and Oliver Stone. The film also introduced Arnold Schwarzenegger to the big screen,[3] being chosen for his physical similarities to the famous Frazetta paperback covers. The film, which also featured Hollywood heavyweights James Earl Jones and Max von Sydow, combined episodes from the comic series as well as from Howard's original works (specifically, "A Witch Shall be Born" [1934] and "The Tower of the Elephant"). Although critics and Howard aficionados would judge the film with mixed results, audiences filled the theaters, earning top spot in its opening weekend and going on to gross well over $68 million.[4] The film was so successful that it generated a sequel,

Conan the Destroyer (1984). Unfortunately, the sequel suffered from a poor script and a recut PG rating that reduced much of the graphic violence of its predecessor.

During the 1970s and 1980s, Conan pastiches were heavily circulated through Lancer/Ace Books and Bantam Books. Reprints from tales originally published in *Weird Tales* were being produced by Berkley/Medallion. Tor became the major publisher of Conan pastiches by Robert Jordan, Steve Perry, Leonard Carpenter, and John Maddox Roberts through the 1980s and into the 1990s. Conan was also introduced to new audiences through video games and role-playing games like *Conan: Hall of Volta* (1984) and *GURPS Conan* (1986). Following the massive popularity of *He-Man and the Masters of the Universe* (1983) (which was, in part, modeled after Conan),[5] Howard's lead character finally got his own cartoon in 1990 and a toy line soon followed.

In 2004, McFarlane Toys launched a series of highly realistic figures based directly on Howard's characters. As the artist stated in an interview with Dark Horse Comics, "We just followed the words of Robert E. Howard himself. Howard was an incredibly descriptive writer and he often loved to linger on detailed descriptions of not only his characters but also the lush worlds they lived in" and that "[h]is stories are the foundation upon which we built our toy lines" ("McFarlane"). Those words of Howard generated a 2011 film reboot, *Conan the Barbarian*, starring Jason Mamoa. While Howard fans and critics applauded Mamoa's appearance and portrayal as being much more in line with the original stories (as opposed to Schwarzenegger looking more like Frank Frazetta's Conan book covers), the film lacked the impact of the Milius film in both cultural influence and commercial success. Nonetheless, Conan remains omnipresent through seven decades after Howard wrote his last tales of high adventure.

Without the revival of interest—and the heroic efforts of editors, filmmakers, and other creatives in making Speculative Modernist texts available to future generations—it is hard to say whether we would still know about many of the authors mentioned in this volume. Thanks to the internet and the burgeoning digitization of century-old books and magazines, readers can unearth more gems from this boundless genre of speculative fiction and the Speculative Modernists who helped make it a literary movement.

Chapter Notes

CHAPTER 1

1. In the inaugural issue of *Amazing Stories* in April 1926, Hugo Gernsback coined the term "scientifiction" for what soon became known as science fiction: "There is the usual fiction magazine, the love story and the sex-appeal type of magazine, the adventure type, and so on, but a magazine of 'Scientifiction' is a pioneer in its field in America. By 'scientifiction' I mean the Jules Verne, H. G. Wells, and Edgar Allan Poe type of story—a charming romance intermingled with scientific fact and prophetic vision. (...) But with the ever increasing demands on us for this sort of story, and more of it, there was only one thing to do—publish a magazine in which the scientific type of story will hold forth exclusively (Gernsback, "A New," 3).

2. Gary Westfahl is the authority on all things Gernsback, and he presents a well-rounded portrait of this complex man in *Hugo Gernsback and the Century of Science Fiction* (2007).

3. For example, it would not be until 1920 that women in the United States were permitted the right to vote with the ratification of the 19th Amendment, although non-white Americans had to wait decades longer for true access to the ballot. For more on this tumultuous era, read these two anthologies of primary sources from the era: *Treacherous Texts: An Anthology of U.S. Suffrage Literature, 1846–1946* (2011) edited by Mary Chapman and Angela Mills and *Suffrage Days: Stories from the Women's Suffrage Movement* (1996) edited by Sandra Stanley Holton.

4. For more about the Hoover administration, see the following biographies: *Herbert Hoover in the White House: The Ordeal of the Presidency* (2017) by Charles Rappleye and *Hoover: An Extraordinary Life in Extraordinary Times* (2017) by Kenneth Whyte. Both offer insights into the character of the leader who coined the term "rugged individualism."

5. In the United Kingdom, the Defence of the Realm Act (1914) began regulating drug trafficking. Two years later, the sale of psychoactive drugs was banned by Regulation 40B. See this site for more history: http://ww1centenary.oucs.ox.ac.uk/body-and-mind/drugs-and-dora-2/. In the United States, the Food and Drug Administration began the identification and control of drugs in 1906. For more on the history of drug control in the United States, https://www.fda.gov/about-fda/history-fdas-fight-consumer-protection-and-public-health.

6. Shakespeare's *The Tempest*, referenced in the title *Brave New World*, depicts the civilized drunkards' fascination with the "savage" Caliban. The "Noble Savage" emerged as an archetype in the eighteenth century and a literary fixture in James Fenimore Cooper's Leatherstocking Tales, most specifically *The Last of the Mohicans* (1826). Cooper correlated this figure directly to Native Americans. Joseph Conrad also used the term "savages" to indicate indigenous and non-civilized Africans in *Heart of Darkness* (1899).

7. After a century's long fight in Britain, the Representation of the People Act (1918) enfranchised women over 30 years old who owned a minimum requirement of property. In 1928, all women over the age of 21 regardless of property ownership were granted the vote by the Representation of the People (Equal Franchise) Act. *Literature of the Women's Suffrage Campaign in*

England (2004), edited by Carolyn Christensen Nelson, is an anthology of primary sources—plays, songs, stories, essays—from the 1890s until about 1920 that chronicles the struggle for women's suffrage in the United Kingdom.

8. An early draft was serialized in 1927 *The Recluse*. A revised and serialized edition appeared in *The Fantasy Fan* from 1933 to 1935. The full text was first published in *The Outsider and Others* in 1939.

Chapter 2

1. Examples of developments from such disciplines are genetic inheritance that extends Darwin's theories, wireless telegraphy/Hertzian radio waves (1880s), man's first flight from the Wright Brothers (1903), Walter Pater's re-imaginings of aesthetics as living in that specific moment in time of creation (1868), and Psychoanalysis via Sigmund Freud (1896). For a more inclusive and explanatory history of developments in Modernism, please see *The Cambridge History of Modernism* edited by Vincent Sherry (2016) and James Gunn's *Alternate Worlds: The Illustrated History of Science Fiction* (1975).

2. Doubling, used as a synonym for "Doppelgänger," refers to a "recurrent motif in Gothic and horror literature, mostly in the nineteenth century, ultimately coming from the anthropological belief in an innate duality of man [… and is] an archetype of otherness and narcissistic specularity indissolubly linked to the individual" (Ballesteros González 119), in addition to signifying the conflict of colonial allegiances to authors, especially Canadian-American and Irish-British authors.

3. Sigmund Freud theorized the Oedipal Complex in his book *The Interpretation of Dreams* in 1899. Stevenson's *The Strange Case of Dr. Jekyll and Mr. Hyde* predates Carl Jung's theories on archetypes of the Self in *On the Nature of the Psyche* (1947) by more than half a century.

4. For an excellent source on Gothicism in literature, see Andrew Smith's *Gothic Literature* (2013). For Gothicism in a larger context, see David Punter's *The Edinburgh Companion to Gothic and the Arts* (2019).

5. The study of magnetism has an extensive history dating back to the ancient world. However, the revelation that magnetism and electricity were actually related fields came in 1873 with James Clerk Maxwell's "A Treatise on Electricity and Magnetism." This, in part, led to Albert Einstein's Theory of Special Relativity in 1905.

6. The foundations of psychology began in the mid-nineteenth century with Wilhelm Wundt (the Psychology of Consciousness) in Germany and Herbert Spencer (the Psychology of Adaptation) in England. These schools of thought would be followed up by Freud (Psychoanalysis). Please see *A Brief History of Modern Psychology* (2018) by Ludy T. Benjamin Jr., for a more detailed explanation on the history of psychology.

7. Please see Talia Schaffer's article "'A Wilde Desire Took Me': The Homoerotic History of Dracula" (Schaffer).

8. Many articles and books have been written about what Dracula represents. For instance, Christopher Bentley writes about sexuality and Dracula in his chapter "The Monster in the Bedroom: Sexual Symbolism in Bram Stoker's *Dracula*" (Bentley). Likewise, Patricia McKee discusses symbolism in Stoker's novel in "Racialization, Capitalism, and Aesthetics in Stoker's *Dracula*" (McKee).

9. Mary E. Braddon's "Good Lady Ducayne" (1896) and Florence Marryat's *The Blood of the Vampire* (1897) are earlier, but lesser-known examples. However, Braddon's tale is more aligned with the exploits of Elizabeth Báthory than that of a traditional vampire and Marryat's novel about a psychic vampire was generally viewed as an inferior version of *Dracula*, published in the same year.

10. The narrator in "The Yellow Wallpaper" is diagnosed as having hysterical tendencies, a condition commonly assumed of womanhood at the time of publication.

11. The epistolary novel was a popular form of literature throughout the nineteenth and into the twentieth centuries. Famous examples include *Frankenstein* and *Dracula*, but the form was not limited to horror alone. *Lady Audley's Secret*, written by Mary Elizabeth Braddon and serialized in 1862, also enjoyed tremendous popularity.

12. In her argument, Dunbar examines how society has never held more belief in the realities of ghosts than it does now (at the turn of the century), and that ghosts are

no longer simply the moral agents of the traditional form but often lack a specific purpose.

13. For more about the relationship between canonical Modernism and spiritualism, please see Helen Sword's *Ghostwriting Modernism* (2002).

14. Detective fiction was an emerging category of genre literature, much like science fiction, fantasy, and horror. Generally beginning with Edgar Allan Poe and his "tales of ratiocination" with "Murders in the Rue Morgue (1841) and the first appearance of detective C. Augustine Dupin (Sova, xi), the genre progressed with Wilkie Collins in England and in Anna Katherine Green in the United States. Conan Doyle's Sherlock Holmes led the genre into the "golden age" of the early twentieth century.

15. Natural histories saw an increase in popularity throughout the nineteenth century, as did museums and displays of private collections of menageries, aviaries, and botanical gardens. In particular, the study of entomology became especially popular among the middle classes ("David Young").

16. Once a reader understands the trick of the ending, the name Crocker takes on added humorous significance. Croak, in Crane's time, had acquired the connotation of something that was about to give way, something decrepit, something feeble ("crock, v.4"). The crucial meal had been prepared in a vessel resembling a crock pot. The word "crock" has the same origin as the word "croak," which in Crane's time was in wide use as a slang term for the act of dying ("croak, v."). Interestingly, given the parodic nature of this "ghost" story, crock did not gain its meaning as "a lie" until the middle of the twentieth century when disparaging phrases such as "crock of sugar" (and their variants) began appearing ("crock, n.1.").

17. Interestingly, Bierce, Dawson, and Atherton were all regular contributors to *The Argonaut*, an influential California newspaper published during this era.

18. Machen might have had some help at the start. David Clarke, in his *Folklore* article, chronicles rumors that swirled about the Battle of Mons in the days immediately following. Clarke's research did not reveal a definitive source, however. Machen was among the first to spread the story among folks back home (Clarke 153).

CHAPTER 3

1. The terms non-human and nonhuman are used interchangeably neither in our book nor in academia in general. The hyphenated non-human is used almost exclusively in ecocritical context, and, for the purposes of this chapter, one that has more than a little bit of an ecocritical bent, the spelling non-human will be used. In other contexts in this book—most often in the chapter "Shadows at the Turn"—the unhyphenated form "nonhuman" will be used. See the seminal guide, "Defining Ecocritical Theory and Practice," a publication of the Association for the Study of Literature and the Environment.

2. One excellent resource is *The Human Relationship with Nature* (2000) by Peter H. Khan, Jr. There are many, many other books on this subject by some of the leading lights of environmental literature, including Rachel Carson, David Quammen, Alan Burdic, Dave Foreman, Vandana Shiva, and others.

3. Stories about genetics became popular with the reading public through H. G. Wells's *The Island of Dr. Moreau* (1896).

4. The nascent field of ecology was just getting underway during the early part of the twentieth century. In fact, the first full-length textbook on ecology was published in 1905 by Frederic Clements, *Research Methods in Ecology*. In this book, Clements was the first to posit a very science-fiction-like idea: that plant communities—even forests as a whole—function like a single organism that progresses through a life cycle like any other organism.

5. At this time, there was no consensus on a definition for "scientific method," although the term was used widely. Nevertheless, the generally accepted meaning of the term at the time tracked closely with the rigorous, experimental nature of Jeffson's search for scientific truth. At the term's peak usage during the 1920s—in other words, at the heart of the literary era under study in this book—more than three percent of all science books had the phrase "scientific method" in their titles (Thurs 309). *Wrestling with Nature: From Omens to Science* (2011), edited by Peter Harrison, Ronald Numbers, and Michael H. Shank, is a thorough history of the meaning of the

word "science" from ancient Mesopotamia through the present day.

6. It might be worth noting here that the ethics of the use of chemical weapons in warfare was discussed deeply during the time that Shiel was composing *The Purple Cloud*. One landmark international agreement signed in 1899 was the "Declaration concerning the Prohibition of the Use of Projectiles with the Sole Object to Spread Asphyxiating Poisonous Gases," which was ratified at the Hague Convention of 1899. This meeting and the agreements that sprang from it were among the first statements about the limits of warfare, especially as the development of destructive new technologies, including the use of poison gas, advanced at a rate that had never before been seen in human history. This convention produced rules about warfare that "have become part and parcel of customary international law" (Dinstein 10).

7. A fascinating collection of primary sources about the history of science as it was known in the nineteenth century is contained in the book *Nineteenth Century Science: An Anthology* (2000). The table of contents reveals the century's incredible array of discoveries in mathematics, geology, astronomy, biology, physiology, physics, and many other avenues of inquiry.

8. The Norton Critical Edition of *The Time Machine* (2008) contains many useful essays. Additional analysis can be found in *H. G. Wells's The Time Machine: A Reference Guide* (2004) by John R. Hammond.

9. "Lines Written a Few Miles above Tintern Abbey, on Revisiting the Banks of the Wye during a Tour, July 13, 1798" is the 1798 poem by William Wordsworth that is one of the foremost and influential examples of English literary Romanticism.

10. Not all canonical Modernists ignored what happened outside of the city limits, however. Howard J. Booth's study of nonurban Modernist writers includes close attention to E. M. Forster, D. H. Lawrence, and William Faulkner, three Modernists "whose main subject was not the city" (700). These writers, Booth asserts, "found forms and styles not only to register the elements—new, old, diverse, at times contradictory—present in modern, non-metropolitan locations but also to explore what might emerge from such simultaneity" (713).

11. Although theorized for decades, often in science-fiction stories, the first successful nuclear reactor was created as part of The Manhattan Project and was activated for the first time in 1942. The use of nuclear power to generate electricity for communities first occurred during the 1950s.

12. In addition to his political and environmental advocacy, John Muir was also a highly influential nature writer. His book, *My First Summer in the Sierra* (1911), has become a standard in the field.

Chapter 4

1. While this focuses mainly on dirigible traffic, Kipling adds in the burgeoning aeroplane traffic as well. Kipling preferred the dirigible and in his work predicted it would be the mainstay because of the carrying capacity. The first Europe-to-America dirigible flight was made by the H. R. A. 34 from July 2 to July 13, 1919. In a footnote in the published logs of the journey, Air Commodore Edward Maitland noted that Kipling had guessed correctly that the entry point for a westward bound airship to the American Continent would be Trinity Bay. "Mr. Kipling, to celebrate this coincidence, gave the writer a signed copy of his book and, in return, received the actual volume we carried on board, inscribed with the signatures of all the crew" (Maitland 65).

2. Eugenics was a prevalent topic in literature, film, and government policies of the early twentieth century. Speculative Modernists contributed to this conversation, especially Edward Bulwer-Lytton, H. G. Wells, and Hugo Gernsback. For more information, refer to Martin S. Pernick's *The Black Stork* (1996) and *The Oxford Handbook of the History of Eugenics* (2010).

3. Traveling to the North Pole was the work of centuries, and even today claimants to the throne of being first to the pole are in dispute. The first undisputed trip to the North Pole was made by Roald Amundsen and his 15-man crew on May 12, 1926. Amundsen also conquered the South Pole 15 years earlier on December 14, 1911.

4. For deeper discussion of this confusion and about European colonialism, see *Colonialism in Joseph Conrad's Heart of Darkness* (2012), edited by Claudia Durst Johnson.

5. See "Tarzan Revisited" by Gore Vidal

in *Esquire*, May 14, 2008. Vidal points out that while Burroughs's plots for these books are not widely varied, his skill lies in creating action scenes. Vidal explains that this is why readers (almost exclusively males, he claims) came back again and again and why there are more than twenty sequels.

6. French astrophysicist Pierre Jules Janssen and English astronomer Norman Lockyer are credited with the discovery of helium, thanks to the use of the spectroscope to observe the sun in 1868. Italian physicist Luigi Palmieri identified the element on Earth in 1882. For a more complete story, see "How Scientists Discovered Helium, the First Alien Element, 150 Years Ago" (2018) by Lorraine Boissoneault.

7. *The Cambridge Companion to Science Fiction* (2002) links the books Wells wrote between 1895 and 1901 (starting with *The Time Machine*) to the works by C. H. Hinton collected in 1886 in a book called *Scientific Romances*. Hinton was a mathematician who was trying to imagine new dimensions through various thought experiments. "Wells's time machine became the first of a series of facilitating devices that opened up the further reaches of time and space to a kind of rational enquiry that had previously been severely handicapped by its reliance on obsolete narrative frameworks" (24). Wells created these scientific romances in order to play with these new ideas from science the way Hinton used the developments in mathematics.

8. Nikola Tesla (1856–1943), inventor and sometime employee, sometime rival of Thomas Edison, is probably most famous for his development of the use of alternating current (AC). By the writing of *The First Men in the Moon*, Tesla had already developed "Tesla coils," a wire that was powerful enough to send and receive radio signals. He could well have invented a way to communicate with people on Mars.

9. T. H. Huxley, grandfather of Aldous Huxley, coined the term "agnosticism" to describe his thoughts on beliefs with no evidence one way or the other. In 1860, in a correspondence with Charles Kingsley, who had written a consoling note about the death of his son, Huxley took up the notion of immortality: "I neither deny nor affirm the immortality of man. I see no reason for believing in it, but, on the other hand, I have no means of disproving it" (Huxley 357).

CHAPTER 5

1. Fritz Lang's *Metropolis* (1926) is set in a futuristic urban environment and features a stark division between plutocrats and the exploited working class. For an excellent collection of essays about this film, see Michael Minden's *Fritz Lang's Metropolis: Cinematic Visions of Technology and Fear* (2009).

2. There are many excellent books about the surrealist period in visual art, especially painting. One literary resource is the anthology *The Surrealism Reader: An Anthology of Ideas* from the University of Chicago Press (2015). It contains primary texts from surrealists from about 1920 through the 1990s, and it places the movement into its historical and cultural context.

CHAPTER 6

1. Scientists such as William Thomson (Lord Kelvin) were making wild predictions about science across many fields. Thomson's theory on the heat-death of the sun has already been discussed. In his letters, he also expressed his belief that aeronautical aviation would not advance much beyond balloons, that there was probably less than four or five centuries' worth of free oxygen remaining on Earth, and that the Earth was about twenty to forty million years old. Science, while promising a much richer universe as far as space, also made many dire predictions about the fate of that universe.

2. In his spiritual biography, *Surprised by Joy* (1955), Lewis writes about reading MacDonald's *Phantastes*: "It is as if I were carried sleeping across the frontier, or as if I had died in the old country and could never remember how I came alive in the new. For in one sense the old country was exactly like the old. I met there all that had already charmed me in Malory, Spenser, Morris, and Yeats. But in another sense it was all changed" (99).

3. The encyclical assails the very nature of Modernism, claiming that the vilest part of this condition is that it pretends to try, through the use of philosophy, belief, theology, history, criticism, apologies, and reform to recover the truth about the universe and hides behind Agnosticism, the inability to know an answer that lies beyond man's senses for sure. Pius warns that these

people are not only outside of the Church or among the laity, but even among priests. The pope writes in the section entitled "The Gravity of the Situation": "Finally, and this almost destroys all hope of cure, their very doctrines have given such a bent to their minds, that they disdain all authority and brook no restraint; and relying upon a false conscience, they attempt to ascribe to a love of truth that which is in reality the result of pride and obstinacy" (Pius).

4. One of the great chroniclers of nineteenth- and early twentieth-century spiritualism is Sir Arthur Conan Doyle, who published *The History of Spiritualism* (1926), a two-volume set that tells the history of mediums and accounts of the afterlife as related by spirits as described from Emanuel Swedenborg's (1688–1772) writings until the end of World War I. The bulk of the accounts are from the half-century before publication of the work.

5. This deck was originally published as the Rider-Waite deck. In 2009, Pamela Colman Smith was acknowledged for her role as the artist for the cards with a change in the name of the deck the Smith-Waite Tarot Centennial Edition Deck. In Stuart R. Kaplan's introduction to *The Artwork & Times of Pamela Colman Smith* (2009), he writes, "Many people feel that adequate credit has not been given to the artist since the deck's name refers to Rider & Company, the original publisher, and Arthur Edward Waite, who authored *The Pictorial Key to the Tarot*" (3).

6. See *The Life of Evelyn Underhill: An Intimate Portrait of the Groundbreaking Author of* Mysticism (2003) by Margaret Cropper for a full explanation of the relationship Underhill had with the Roman Catholic Church.

7. The Middle English *Mirror of Simple Souls*, for example, which was translated by Evelyn Underhill in 1910, was later discovered to be the work of Marguerite Porete, who was burned at the stake in 1310 for her writing.

8. See *Talking to the God: Occultism in the Work of W. B. Yeats, Arthur Machen, Algernon Blackwood, and Dion Fortune* (2015) by Susan Johnston Graf. Graf's study makes important connections between the writings of these authors and their interest in the occult.

9. Hipsky's work also describes Corelli's popularity and how she helped change the market for books. "Corelli benefited hugely from the sudden decline of the circulating libraries in 1894–95; during the years that followed, enjoying more direct access to her hundreds of thousands of buying readers, she became remarkably prolific, publishing nine novels in the first decade of the twentieth century alone. For a good part of that time, she was one of Britain's best-selling novelists."

10. Georges Lemaître, a French Catholic priest and astronomer, did not propose his theories of how an expanding universe would have originated at a singular point until 1927, forty years after Corelli's novel was published. This was the same decade in which several astronomers demonstrated that the universe was expanding.

11. She is listed as a spiritual writer and celebrated on June 15 in the Anglican and Episcopal calendars.

12. In a letter to Caroline Everett on June 24, 1957, Tolkien admits that this story "arose from my own pre-occupation with *The Lord of the Rings*, the knowledge that it would be finished in great detail or not at all, and the fear (near certainty) that it would be 'not at all'" (*Letters* 257).

13. Michael Swanwick, in his 2007 monograph *What Can Be Saved from the Wreckage? James Branch Cabell in the Twenty-First Century*, writes: "It is hard to imagine today the magnitude of James Branch Cabell's fame in the early part of the last century. Cabell's books were Mark Twain's chief reading in the great humorist's declining years. Theodore Roosevelt received him at the White House. The occultist Aleister Crowley harried him with fan letters. H. L. Mencken was his advocate. A symphonic tone poem based on Cabell's Jurgen debuted at Carnegie Hall in 1925. Sinclair Lewis, accepting the Nobel Prize for Literature in 1930, mentioned him as one of a number of writers who might reasonably have won it." This book rose to prominence thanks, in part, to the attempts to censor it in 1922 for being lewd and lascivious, as described by Swanwick. Cabell wrote a piece called *The Judgment of Jurgen*, which explains his side of the story allegorically.

Chapter 7

1. William James was a prominent psychologist, philosopher, and educator during

the late nineteenth and early twentieth century. He founded the American Society for Psychical Research in 1884 and was the first person to offer psychology as an academic course. In addition, he taught Gertrude Stein during her education at Harvard. Henri Bergson was a close friend of William James and a significant contributor to continental philosophy (see William R. Schroeder's *Continental Philosophy. A Critical Approach* from 2005).

2. For more on Bergson's ideas please consult the *Stanford Encyclopedia of Philosophy* (2021).

3. Although it has been argued by critics and fans alike, any diagnosis remains unofficial and subjective. In relation to this chapter, it is not being suggested that such a diagnosis is a "flaw," but only a possible aspect to Holmes's character sketch. Please see Sonya Freeman Loftis's article "The Autistic Detective: Sherlock Holmes and his Legacy" in *Disabilities Studies Quarterly*, Volume 34, Issue 4 (2014) for further analysis on Holmes and his connection to autism.

4. This quote was never actually stated by Holmes in any of Conan Doyle's stories. The closest Conan Doyle comes to using this phrase is in "The Crooked Man" (1893), where Holmes calls his counterpart "my dear Watson" and then soon follows that with "Elementary" (Conan Doyle "Crooked" 645).

5. Similar to Conan Doyle's Sherlock Holmes and detective fiction as category of genre fiction, adventure fiction was also becoming very popular with mass literacy during the mid-nineteenth century, and then especially in the pulps.

6. Gary Westfahl devotes an entire chapter of his book *The Rise and Fall of American Science Fiction, from the 1920s to the 1960s* to this single issue, a collection he said "changed everything" (21). Science fiction to this point was staggering along and might have soon found itself consigned to the scrapheap of literary history. Then, in this issue, not only did Buck Rogers make his first appearance, but the first installment of the seminal space opera, E. E. Smith's *The Skylark of Space*, was also published, "helping to inaugurate the reign of full-grown, interstellar space opera in U.S. sf" (Clute "Science Fiction" 880).

Epilogue

1. *Weird Tales* ceased publication from 1954 but was restarted in 1988. It is now titled *Worlds of Fantasy & Horror*.

2. The trio of Thundarr, Ookla the Mok (a bipedal cross between a lion and a bear), and Princess Ariel (who is also a sorceress) may be the inspiration behind the protagonists in Ralph Bakshi's animated feature film *Fire and Ice* (1983). Bakshi collaborated with Frazetta on the film. Thundarr, Ookla, and Ariel appear to have a direct parallel to Bakshi's Larn, Darkwolf, and Teegra.

3. Schwarzenegger appeared as the lead role in the independent film *Hercules in New York* (1970) and then again in the bodybuilding/Mr. Universe documentary *Pumping Iron* (1977). Additionally, the film also gave composer Basil Poledouris has first major hit through his Wagnerian orchestral score.

4. This figure does not include home video release, which generated even more success, bringing the gross total over $300 million (Sammon 107).

5. The *He-Man and the Masters of the Universe* cartoon was to serve as a half-hour long commercial for a new "'fantasy Make Believe' [sic]" toy line from Mattel and the generic male action figure that Roger Sweet, a Mattel executive, said in a memo "would be oriented toward Fr[a]zetta type figures possibly combined with parts Conan, Flash Gordon, and Star Wars" (12).

Works Cited

"After London; or, Wild England." *Environment & Society Portal*, www.environmentandsociety.org/mml/after-london-or-wild-england.

Aldiss, Brian. *Trillion Year Spree*. Athaneum, 1986.

Alkon, Paul K. *Science Fiction Before 1900: Imagination Discovers Technology*. Twayne, 1994.

Asimov, Isaac. "How Easy to See the Future!" *Natural History*, vol. 84, no. 4, 1975, p. 92.

Atherton, Gertrude. "The Striding Place." *American Fantastic Tales: Terror and the Uncanny from Poe to the Pulps*. Edited by Peter Straub. The Library of America, 2009, pp. 232–237.

Bairoch, Paul. *Economics and World History: Myths and Paradoxes*. University of Chicago Press, 1995.

Ballesteros González, Antonio. "Doppelgänger." *The Handbook of the Gothic*. Edited by Marie Mulvey-Roberts. NYU Press, 2009, p. 119.

Balmer, Edwin, and Philip Wylie. *When Worlds Collide*. Frederick A. Stokes Company, 1933.

Barrett, Mike. "Mostly in Shadow: The Work of Mary Elizabeth Counselman." *New York Review of Science Fiction*, vol. 21, no. 8 [248], Apr. 2009, pp. 1, 4–5.

"Battle of Mons." *Encyclopædia Britannica*, Encyclopædia Britannica, Inc., www.britannica.com/topic/Battle-of-Mons-1914. Accessed 16 August 2019.

Beerbohm, Max. "Enoch Soames: A Memory of the Eighteen-nineties." *Treasury of the Fantastic*. Edited by David Sandner and Jacob Weisman. Tacyon, 2001, pp. 668–695.

Bellamy, Edward. *Looking Backward, 2000–1887*. Project Gutenberg. www.gutenberg.org/files/624/624-h/624-h.htm. Accessed 18 February 2019.

Ben-Tov, Sharona. *The Artificial Paradise: Science Fiction and American Reality*. University of Michigan Press, 1995.

Bentley, Christopher. "The Monster in the Bedroom: Sexual Symbolism in Bram Stoker's Dracula." *Dracula: The Vampire and the Critics*. Edited by Margaret L. Carter. UMI Research Press, 1988, pp. 25–34.

Berger, Albert I. *The Magic That Works: John W. Campbell and the American Response to Technology*. Borgo Press, 1993.

———. "Theories of History and Social Order in Astounding Science Fiction, 1934–55." *Science Fiction Studies*, vol. 15, no. 1 [44], Mar. 1988, pp. 12–35. EBSCOhost, search.ebscohost.com/login.aspx?direct=true&AuthType=ip,uid&db=mzh&AN=1988060792&site=ehost-live&scope=site.

Best, Gary Dean. *The Politics of American Individualism: Herbert Hoover in Transition, 1918–1921*. Greenwood Press, 1975.

Bierce, Ambrose. *Can Such Things Be? Tales of Horror and the Supernatural*. The Citadel Press, 1974.

———. *The Collected Writings of Ambrose Bierce*. Ameron House, 1946.

———. "The Damned Thing." *Can Such Things Be? Tales of Horror and the Supernatural*. The Citadel Press, 1974, pp. 139–147.

———. "Haïta the Shepherd." *Can Such Things Be? Tales of Horror and the Supernatural*. The Citadel Press, 1974, pp. 147–152.

———. "One Summer Night." *Can Such Things Be? Tales of Horror and the Super-

natural. The Citadel Press, 1974, pp. 36–37.

Blackwood, Algernon. "The Transfer." *Blood Thirst: 100 Years of Vampire Fiction*. Edited by Leonard Wolf. Norton, 1997, pp. 80–89.

Bleiler, Everett Franklin. "M.P. Shiel, 1865–1947." *Science Fiction Writers: Critical Studies of the Major Authors from the Early Nineteenth Century to the Present Day*. Edited by Everett Franklin Bleiler. Scribner's, 1982, pp. 31–37. *EBSCOhost*, search.ebscohost.com/login.aspx?direct=true&AuthType=cookie,ip,cpid&custid=s5805083&db=mzh&AN=1982071501&site=ehost-live&scope=site. Accessed 9 August 2019.

Boissoneault, Lorraine. "How Scientists Discovered Helium, the First Alien Element, 150 Years Ago." *Smithsonian Magazine*. Aug. 17, 2018. https://www.smithsonianmag.com/history/how-scientists-discovered-helium-first-alien-element-1868-180970057/.

Booth, Howard J. "Non-Metropolitan Modernism: E. M. Forster, D. H. Lawrence, and William Faulkner." *The Cambridge History of Modernism*. Edited by Vincent B. Sherry. Cambridge University Press, 2017, pp. 700–16.

Botting, Fred. *Gothic: The New Critical Idiom*. Routledge, 1996.

Broad, Katherine. "Race, Reproduction, and the Failures of Feminism in Mary Bradley Lane's *Mizora*." *Tulsa Studies in Women's Literature*, vol. 28 no. 2, 2009, pp. 247–266. *Project MUSE* muse.jhu.edu/article/393356.

Bronfen, Elisabeth. "Death." *The Handbook of the Gothic*. Edited by Marie Mulvey-Roberts. NYU Press, 1999, pp. 113–116.

Brown, Bob. *The Readies*. Roving Eye / Bad EMS, 1930. E-book, Connexions, 2009.

Bruno, Giordano. "On the Infinite Universe and Worlds." Translated by Dorothea Waley Singer as an appendix to *Giordano Bruno His Life and Thought*. Henry Schuman, 1950, pp. 225–378.

Bulfin, Ailise. "'The End of Time': M.P. Shiel and the 'Apocalyptic Imaginary.'" *Victorian Time: Technologies, Standardizations, Catastrophes*. Edited by Trish Ferguson. Palgrave Macmillan, 2013, pp. 153–177. *EBSCOhost*, search.ebscohost.com/login.aspx?direct=true&AuthType=cookie,ip,cpid&custid=s5805083&db=mzh&AN=2013421203&site=ehost-live&scope=site. Accessed 3 February 2019.

———. "The Natural Catastrophe in Late Victorian Popular Fiction: 'How Will the World End?'" *Critical Survey*, vol. 27, no. 2, 2015, pp. 81–101. *EBSCOhost*, search.ebscohost.com/login.aspx?direct=true&AuthType=ip,uid&db=mzh&AN=2016390475&site=ehost-live&scope=site. Accessed 3 February 2019.

———. "'One-Planet-One-Inhabitant': Mass Extermination as Progress in M. P. Shiel's *The Purple Cloud*." *Trinity College Dublin Journal of Postgraduate Research*, vol. 7, 2008. https://www.academia.edu/2127809/_One-planet-one-inhabitant_Mass_Extermination_as_Progress_in_M._P._Shiel_s_The_Purple_Cloud_ P. 1–15. Accessed 9 August 2020.

Bulwer-Lytton, Edward. *The Coming Race*. London: Hesperus Classics, 2007.

Burleson, Donald R. "On Mary Elizabeth Counselman's 'Twister.'" *Studies in Weird Fiction*, vol. 15, 1994, pp. 16–18.

Burroughs, Edgar Rice. *A Princess of Mars*. *The Martian Tales Trilogy*. Barnes & Noble, 2004, pp. 3–218.

———. *The Return of Tarzan*. Ballantine Books, 1963.

———. *Tarzan of the Apes*. Ballantine Books, 1963.

Butler, Samuel. "Darwin Among the Machines." New Zealand Electronic Text Centre. https://web.archive.org/web/20060524131242/http://www.nzetc.org/tm/scholarly/tei-ButFir-t1-g1-t1-g1-t4-body.html. Accessed 9 August 2020.

———. *Erewhon*. Project Gutenberg, http://www.gutenberg.org/files/1906/1906-h/1906-h.htm. Accessed 6 June 2020.

Cabell, James Branch. *Jurgen*. Dover, 1977.

Campbell, John W. *The Mightiest Machine*. Ace, 1972.

———. "Twilight." *Science Fiction: Stories and Contexts*. Edited by Heather Masri. Bedford/St. Martins, 2009, pp. 1052–68.

Carter, Paul A. *The Creation of Tomorrow: Fifty Years of Magazine Science Fiction*. Columbia University Press, 1977.

Chesterson, G. K. *Heretics*. The Bodley Head, 1950.

Clareson, Thomas D. "The Emergence of American Science Fiction, 1810–1915; a Study of the Impact of Science upon American Romanticism." 1956. University of Pennsylvania, PhD dissertation.

Clarke, David. "Rumors of Angels: A Legend of the First World War." *Folklore*, vol. 113, no. 2, Oct. 2002, pp. 151–173. *EBSCOhost*, doi:10.1080/0015587022000015293. Accessed 26 February 2019.

Clute, John, and John Grant. *The Encyclopedia of Fantasy*. St. Martin's Griffin, 1999.

Clute, John, and Peter Nicholls. *The Encyclopedia of Science Fiction*. Orbit, 1999.

Coates, Robert M. *The Eater of Darkness*. Capricorn, 1959.

Cole, Sarah. *Inventing Tomorrow: H.G. Wells and the Twentieth Century*. Columbia University Press, 2020.

Collier, John. *Tom's A-Cold*. Macmillan, 1933.

Conan Doyle, Sir Arthur. "The Adventure of Charles Augustus Milverton." *The Return of Sherlock Holmes*. Project Gutenberg. https://www.gutenberg.org/files/108/108-h/108-h.htm. Accessed 22 June 2020.

———. "The Crooked Man." *Sherlock Holmes: The Complete Novels and Stories, Volume 1*. Bantam Classics, 1986, pp. 644–662.

———. *The Doings of Raffles Haw*. Greenhill Books, 1986.

———. "A Scandal in Bohemia." *Sherlock Holmes: The Complete Novels and Stories, Volume 1*. Bantam Classics, 1986, pp. 239–263.

———. *Sherlock Holmes: The Complete Novels and Stories, Volume 1*. Bantam Classics, 1986.

———. *The Sign of Four. Sherlock Holmes: The Complete Novels and Stories, Volume 1*. Bantam Classics, 1986, pp. 121–236.

———. *A Study in Scarlet. Sherlock Holmes: The Complete Novels and Stories, Volume 1*. Bantam Classics, 1986, pp. 3–120.

Connington, J.J. *Nordenholt's Million*. Penguin, 1946.

Conrad, Joseph. *Heart of Darkness*. 3rd ed. Norton, 1988.

Corelli, Marie. "Introduction to the New Edition." *A Romance of Two Worlds*. New York: Grosset & Dunlap, 1887.

———. *A Romance of Two Worlds*. New York: Grosset & Dunlap, 1887.

Counselman, Mary Elizabeth. "The Three Marked Pennies." *The Prentice Hall Anthology of Science Fiction and Fantasy*. Edited by Garyn G. Roberts. Prentice Hall, 2003, pp. 120–125.

Cox, Michael, and R.A. Gilbert, eds. Introduction. *Victorian Ghost Stories: An Oxford Anthology*. Oxford University Press, 1992, pp. ix–xx.

Crane, Stephen. "The Black Dog." www.archive.org/stream/short_ghohor_008_librivox/crane_black_dog_djvu.txt. Accessed 9 August 2020.

———. "The Short Stories of Stephen Crane." *A Companion to the American Short Story*. Edited by Alfred Bendixen and James Nagel. Wiley-Blackwell, 2010.

———. *Stephen Crane Complete Poems*. Edited by Christopher Benfey. Library of America, 2011.

———. *Stephen Crane: Letters*. Edited by R. W. Stallman and Lillian Gilkes. New York University Press, 1960.

Crawford, F. Marion. "The Blood Is the Life." *American Fantastic Tales: Terror and the Uncanny from Poe to the Pulps*. Edited by Peter Straub. The Library of America, 2009, pp. 286–301.

———. "The Upper Berth." *The World's Greatest Horror Stories*. Edited by Stephen Jones and Dave Carson. Barnes & Noble, 2004, pp. 211–228.

"croak, v." *OED Online*, Oxford University Press, December 2019, www.oed.com/view/Entry/44617. Accessed 28 Jan. 2020.

"crock, n.1." *OED Online*, Oxford University Press, December 2019, www.oed.com/view/Entry/44653. Accessed 28 Jan. 2020.

"crock, v.4." *OED Online*, Oxford University Press, December 2019, www.oed.com/view/Entry/44662. Accessed 28 January 2020.

Cromie, Robert. *The Crack of Doom*. Digby, Long, and Co., 1895.

Crossley, Robert. "The First Wellsians: *A Modern Utopia* and Its Early Disciples." *English Literature in Transition, 1880–1920*, vol. 54, no. 4, 2011, pp. 444–469. *EBSCOhost*, ezproxy.uwc.edu/login?url=http://search.ebscohost.com/login.aspx?direct=true&AuthType=cookie,ip,cpid&custid=s5805083&db=mzh&AN=2011581723&site=ehost-live&scope=site. Accessed 16 March 2020.

Daly, Nicholas. "Art and Its Others I: The Aesthetics of Technology." *The Cambridge History of Modernism*. Edited by Vincent B. Sherry. Cambridge University Press, 2017, pp. 404–421.

"David Young: Acquiring the Friedrich Tippmann Collection." lib.ncsu.edu.

2020. https://www.lib.ncsu.edu/archived exhibits/tippmann/victorian.html. Accessed 11 Jan. 2020.

Dawson, Emma Francis. "An Itinerant in the House." *American Fantastic Tales: Terror and the Uncanny from Poe to the Pulps*. Edited by Peter Straub. The Library of America, 2009, pp. 238–254.

de Camp, L. Sprague. *Lovecraft: A Biography*. Doubleday, 1975.

"Defining Ecocritical Theory and Practice: Defining Ecocritical Theory and Practice Sixteen Position Papers from the 1994 Western Literature Association Meeting Salt Lake City, Utah—6 October 1994." *Association for the Study of Literature and the Environment*, https://www.google.com/url?sa=t&rct=j&q=&esrc=s&source=web&cd=&cad=rja&uact=8&ved=2ahUKEwjv1OS0wpfuAhVLX60KHXVeAOAQFjAAegQIAxAC&url=https%3A%2F%2Fwww.asle.org%2Fwp-content%2Fuploads%2FASLE_Primer_DefiningEcocrit.pdf&usg=AOvVaw117YPwGinXqQy3zvNxyaoJ.

de Grainville, Jean-Baptiste Cousin. *La Dernier Homme*. Gallica, https://gallica.bnf.fr/ark:/12148/bpt6k83202k/f10.pleinepage.langEN. Accessed 16 March 2020.

Derleth, April. Foreword. *The Watchers Out of Time and Others* by H. P. Lovecraft and August Derleth. Arkham House, 1974, pp. vii–ix.

Dickens, Charles. *Little Dorrit*. Overlook Press, 2008.

Dinstein, Yoram. *The Conduct of Hostilities under the Law of International Armed Conflict*. Cambridge University Press, 2009.

Donovan, Josephine. *After the Fall*. Penn State University Press, 1989.

_____. *Feminist Theory*. Ungar, 1985.

Du Bois, W. E. B. "The Comet." *Dark Matter: A Century of Speculative Fiction from the African Diaspora*. Edited by Sheree R. Thomas. Warner Books, 2010, pp. 4–18.

Dunbar, Olivia Howard. "The Shell of Sense." *American Fantastic Tales: Terror and the Uncanny from Poe to the Pulps*. Edited by Peter Straub. The Library of America, 2009, pp. 326–336.

"ecosystem, n." *OED Online*, Oxford University Press, December 2019, www.oed.com/view/Entry/59402. Accessed 23 January 2020.

Eddison, E. R. *The Worm Ouroboros*. Ballantine, 1962.

Elbert, Monika. "Mirrors, Sickrooms, and Dead Letters: Wharton's Thwarted Gothic Love Plots." *Women's Studies*, vol. 46, no. 8, 2017, pp. 803–826.

Eliot, T. S. "The Waste Land." *Norton Anthology of English Literature: The Twentieth and Twenty-First Centuries*. Edited by Stephen Greenblatt, Norton, 2018, pp. 659–673.

Elliot, Hugh Samuel Roger. *Modern Science and Materialism*. London: Longmans, Green and Co., 1919.

Elliott, Emory, and Cathy N. Davidson. *The Columbia History of the American Novel / Emory Elliott, General Editor; Associate Editors: Cathy N. Davidson*. Columbia University Press, 1991.

Ellul, Jacques. *The Technological Society*. Translated by John Wilkinson, https://archive.org/stream/JacquesEllulTheTechnologicalSociety/Jacques%20Ellul%20-%20The%20Technological%20Society_djvu.txt. Accessed 9 August 2020.

Estleman, Loren D. "On the Significance of Boswells." Introduction. *Sherlock Holmes: The Complete Novels and Stories. Volume 1* by Arthur Conan Doyle. Bantam Classics, 1986, pp. vii–xviii.

Fadiman, Clifton. Introduction. *Can Such Things Be?* by Ambrose Bierce. The Citadel Press, 1974, pp. 5–13.

Fedorko, Kathy A. *Gender and the Gothic in the Fiction of Edith Wharton*. University of Alabama Press, 1989.

Fernihough, Anne. *D.H. Lawrence: Aesthetics and Ideology*. Cambridge University Press, 1993.

Firchow, Peter Edgerly. *The End of Utopia: A Study of Aldous Huxley's A Brave New World*. Bucknell University Press, 1984.

Fitch, Eric L. "How Green Was My Utopia? A Reflection on William Morris's *News from Nowhere*, H G Wells's *Men Like Gods*, and Ernest Callenbach's *Ecotopia*." *Wellsian: The Journal of the H. G. Wells Society*, vol. 19, 1996, pp. 30–35. EBSCOhost, ezproxy.uwc.edu/login?url=http://search.ebscohost.com/login.aspx?direct=true&AuthType=cookie,ip,cpid&custid=s5805083&db=mzh&AN=2002871456&site=ehost-live&scope=site. Accessed 1 March 2020.

Flecker, James Elroy. *The Last Generation:*

A Story of the Future. www.gutenberg.org/files/32769/32769-h/32769-h.htm. Accessed 9 August 2020.

Forster, E.M. "The Machine Stops." *Oxford and Cambridge Review,* November 1909. https://www.ele.uri.edu/faculty/vetter/Other-stuff/index.html. Accessed 14 August 2020.

Freeman, Mary E. Wilkins. "Luella Miller." *Blood Thirst: 100 Years of Vampire Fiction.* Edited by Leonard Wolf. Norton, 1997, pp. 69–79.

_____. "The Shadows on the Wall." *The World's Greatest Horror Stories.* Edited by Stephen Jones and David Carson. Barnes & Noble, 2004, pp. 249–262.

Fumagalli, Maria Cristina. "Representing the World Instead of Reproducing It: M. P. Shiel's *The Purple Cloud.*" *ARIEL: A Review of International English Literature,* vol. 33, no. 1, Jan. 2002, pp. 63–82. *EBSCOhost,* search.ebscohost.com/login.aspx?direct=true&AuthType=cookie,ip,cpid&custid=s5805083&db=mzh&AN=2004533792&site=ehost-live&scope=site. Accessed 16 April 2020.

Fussell, Paul. *The Great War and Modern Memory.* Oxford University Press, 1975.

Gale, Floyd C. "*Galaxy*'s 5 Star Shelf." *Galaxy Science Fiction,* August 1960, pp. 117–121.

Garbee, Elizabeth. "Pulp Sci-Fi's Legacy to Women in Science." *Slate,* 16 Nov. 2015, www.slate.com/technology/2015/11/pulp-science-fictions-legacy-to-women-in-science.html. Accessed 9 August 2020.

Gąsiorek, Andrzej. *A History of Modernist Literature.* John Wiley & Sons, 2015.

Gelula, Abner J. *Chapter 9—Menace of the Automaton by Abner J. Gelula.* 22 Nov. 2014, www.cosmos-serial.com/cosmos-the-serial/chapter-9-menace-of-the-automaton-by-abner-j-gelula/. Accessed 9 August 2020.

Genzlinger, Neil. "A Black Literary Trailblazer's Solitary Death: Charles Saunders, 73." nytimes.com. 2021. https://www.nytimes.com/2021/01/21/books/charles-saunders-dead.html?referringSource=articleShare. Accessed 24. Jan. 2021.

Gernsback. Hugo. "A New Sort of Magazine." *Amazing Stories,* April 1926, p. 3. *Internet Archive,* Experimenter Publishing Co., archive.org/details/AmazingStoriesVolume01Number01/page/n3/mode/2up.

_____. *Ralph 124C 41+.* E-book, Gutenberg, www.gutenberg.org/files/60944/60944-h/60944-h.htm. Accessed 9 August 2020.

Gilman, Charlotte Perkins. *Herland and Selected Stories.* Penguin Books, 1992.

_____. "The Yellow Wallpaper." *Literature: A Pocket Anthology.* 6th ed. Edited by R.S. Gwynn. Pearson, 2015, pp. 56–68.

Graf, Susan Johnston. *Talking to the Gods: Occultism in the Work of W. B. Yeats, Arthur Machen, Algernon Blackwood, and Dion Fortune.* SUNY Press, 2015.

Greenfield, Patricia. "The Changing Psychology of Culture From 1800 Through 2000." *Psychological Science,* vol. 24, no. 10, 2013. https://www.researchgate.net/publication/255706530_The_Changing_Psychology_of_Culture_From_1800_Through_2000.

Griffin, Angela M., and Judith H. Langlois. "Stereotype Directionality and Attractiveness Stereotyping: Is Beauty Good or is Ugly Bad?" *Social Cognition,* vol. 24, no. 2, 2006, pp. 187–206.doi:10.1521/soco.2006.24.2.187

Gunn, James. "The Gatekeepers." *Science Fiction Studies,* vol. 10, no. 1 [29], Mar. 1983, pp. 15–23. *EBSCOhost,* search.ebscohost.com/login.aspx?direct=true&AuthType=ip,uid&db=mzh&AN=1984027238&site=ehost-live&scope=site. Accessed 16 June 2020.

Hardy, Thomas "The Darkling Thrush." *The Norton Anthology of English Literature. The Major Authors. Volume 2.* 10th ed. Edited by Stephen Greenblatt. Norton, 2019, pp. 1049–1050.

_____. "Hap." *The Norton Anthology of English Literature. The Major Authors. Volume F.* 8th ed. Edited by Stephen Greenblatt. Norton, 2006, pp. 1848–9.

Harris, Clare Winger. "The Fate of the Poseidonia." *The Prentice Hall Anthology of Science Fiction and Fantasy* by Garyn G. Roberts. Prentice Hall, 2003, pp. 501–514.

_____. "The Miracle of the Lily." *Amazing Stories,* April 1928, pp. 48–55.

Hawthorne, Nathaniel. "Young Goodman Brown." *The Dark Descent.* Edited by Edward G. Hartwell. Tor, 1987, pp. 132–141.

Hipsky, Martin. *Modernism and the Women's Popular Romance in Britain, 1885–1925.* Ohio University Press, 2011.

Hodgson, William Hope. "The Gateway of the Monster." *The Collected Fiction of William Hope Hodgson, Volume 2:*

The House on the Borderland and Other Mysterious Places. San Francisco, Night Shade Books, 2004, pp. 159–176.

———. *The House on the Borderland. The Collected Fiction of William Hope Hodgson, Volume 2.* Night Shade Books, 2004, pp. 1–134.

———. "The Night Land." *The Collected Fiction of William Hope Hodgson, Volume 4.* Night Shade Books, 2005, pp. 1–389.

———. "The Searcher of the End House." *The Collected Fiction of William Hope Hodgson, Volume 2: The House on the Borderland and Other Mysterious Places.* San Francisco: Night Shade Books, 2004, pp. 209–232.

———. "The Thing Invisible." *The Collected Fiction of William Hope Hodgson, Volume 2: The House on the Borderland and Other Mysterious Places.* San Francisco, Night Shade Books, 2004, pp. 137–158.

Holland, Owen. "Spectatorship and Entanglement in Thoreau, Hawthorne, Morris, and Wells." *Utopian Studies*, vol. 27, no. 1, 2016, pp. 28–52. *Project MUSE*, muse.jhu.edu/article/611963. Accessed 6 July 2020.

Homer. *The Homeric Hymns.* Trans. Charles Boer. Swallow, 1970.

Hoover, Herbert. "Address on the 150th Anniversary of the Battle of Kings Mountain." *The American Presidency Project.* https://www.presidency.ucsb.edu/documents/address-the-150th-anniversary-the-battle-kings-mountain. Accessed 21 January 2021.

Hopkins, Gerard Manly. "God's Grandeur." *Poetry: An Introduction.* 6th ed. Edited by Michael Meyer. Bedford/St. Martin's, 2010, p. 199.

Hourican, Bridget. "Reading between the Lines: Why Sci-Fi Sometimes Gets It Right." *Technology Ireland*, 2007.

Howard, Robert E. "Beyond the Black River." *Project Gutenberg.* 2013. http://www.gutenberg.org/files/42254/42254-h/42254-h.htm. Accessed 7 August 2020.

———. "Cimmeria." *The Coming of Conan the Cimmerian.* Ballantine Books, 2003, p. 1.

———. *The Hour of the Dragon: The Essential Conan.* Edited by Karl Edward Wagner. SFBC Fantasy, 1998, pp. 1–192.

———. "The Hyborian Age." *The Coming of Conan the Cimmerian.* Ballantine Books, 2003, pp. 381–398.

———. "Kings of the Night." *Bran Mak Morn: The Last King.* Random House, 2005, pp. 31–75.

———. "The Mirrors of Tuzun Thune." *Weird Tales*, September 1929. Project Gutenberg Australia. http://gutenberg.net.au/ebooks06/0603481h.html. Accessed 20 June 2020.

———. "'The Phoenix on the Sword' (First Submitted Draft)." *The Coming of Conan the Cimmerian.* Ballantine Books, 2003, pp. 353–374.

———. "The Phoenix on the Sword." *The Coming of Conan the Cimmerian.* Ballantine Books, 2003, pp. 353–374.

———. "The Queen of the Black Coast." *The Coming of Conan the Cimmerian.* Ballantine Books, 2003, pp. 119–149.

———. *Red Nails: The Essential Conan.* Edited by Karl Edward Wagner. SFBC Fantasy, 1998, pp. 427–632.

———. "The Shadow Kingdom." *Weird Tales*, August 1929. Project Gutenberg Australia. http://gutenberg.net.au/ebooks06/0603491h.html. Accessed 20 June 2020.

———. "The Tower of the Elephant." *The Coming of Conan the Cimmerian.* Ballantine Books, 2003, pp. 59–81.

Howells, William Dean. *A Traveler from Altruria.* Project Gutenberg. http://www.gutenberg.org/files/8449/8449-h/8449-h.htm. Accessed 19 Feb. 2019.

Huxley, Aldous. *Brave New World.* Harper Perennial, 2006.

Huxley, Thomas Henry. *The Major Prose of Thomas Henry Huxley.* University of Georgia Press, 1997.

James, Edward, and Farah Mendlesohn. *The Cambridge Companion to Science Fiction.* Cambridge University Press, 2013.

James, M. R. "The Ash-Tree." *Count Magnus and Other Ghost Stories.* New York: Penguin Books, 2005, pp. 37–50.

———. "Preface." *More Ghost Stories.* E-book, Delphi Classics, 2017.

Jefferies, Richard. *After London, or, Wild England.* Cassell, 1885.

Johnson, Claudia Durst. *Colonialism in Joseph Conrad's Heart of Darkness.* Greenhaven Press, 2012.

Jones, Stephen, and Dave Carson, eds. *The World's Greatest Horror Stories.* Barnes & Noble, 2004.

Joshi, S.T. "Introduction." *Against Religion* by H. P. Lovecraft. Sporting Gentlemen, 2010.

_____. Introduction. *The Complete Fiction by H. P. Lovecraft* by H. P. Lovecraft. Barnes & Noble, 2008, pp. ix–xiv.

_____. Introduction. *Count Magnus and Other Ghost Stories* by M.R. James. New York: Penguin Books, 2005, pp. vii–xviii.

Joyce, James. "Araby." *Dubliners*. Penguin, 1984, pp. 29–35.

Kaplan, Stuart R., and Lynn Araujo. *The Artwork & Times of Pamela Colman Smith*. U.S. Games Systems, Inc., 2009.

Kapur, Akash. "The Return of the Utopians." *The New Yorker*, 26 Sept. 2016, www.newyorker.com/magazine/2016/10/03/the-return-of-the-utopians. Accessed 5 Jan. 2021.

Kauffman, Frank. "Barbarism Ascendant." *Conan Meets the Academy: Multidisciplinary Essays on the Enduring Barbarian*. Edited by Jonas Prida. McFarland, 2013, pp. 35–50.

Keep, C.J. "Cross-Dressing at the End of Time: Orientalism and Apocalypse in M.P. Shiel's *The Purple Cloud*." *Revue Frontenac Review*, vol. 10–11, 1993, pp. 129–49. EBSCOhost, search.ebscohost.com/login.aspx?direct=true&AuthType=cookie,ip,cpid&custid=s5805083&db=mzh&AN=1994071052&site=ehost-live&scope=site. Accessed 12 June 2020.

Kelleam, Joseph E. "Rust." *Astounding Science Fiction*, October 1939. *Fighting the Future War: An Anthology of Science Fiction War Stories, 1914–1945*. Edited by Frederic Krome. Routledge, 2012, pp. 360–67.

Kern, Stephen. *The Culture of Time and Space: 1880–1918*. Harvard University Press, 1983.

Kipling, Rudyard. "Mary Postgate." *Best Short Stories of Rudyard Kipling*. Signet Classics, 1987, pp. 336–350.

_____. "The White Man's Burden." *The Norton Anthology of English Literature*. 8th ed. Volume 2. Edited by Stephen Greenblatt. Norton, 2006, pp. 1821.

_____. "With the Night Mail." *Collected Stories*. Everyman's Library, 1994, pp. 649–678.

Lane, Mary E. Bradley. *Mizora*. Gregg Press, 1975.

Lepore, Jill. "Wonder Woman's Unwinnable War." *The New Yorker*, 2 June 2017. https://www.newyorker.com/culture/cultural-comment/wonder-womans-unwinnable-war. Accessed 10 August 2020.

Levine, Robert S., ed. *The Norton Anthology of American Literature. Volume II: 1865–the Present*. Shorter 9th ed. Norton, 2017.

Lewis, C.S. *Out of the Silent Planet*. Macmillan, 1965.

_____. *Perelandra*. Macmillan Publishing Co., 1976.

Lewis, R.W.B. Introduction. *The Collected Short Stories of Edith Wharton* by Edith Wharton. Scribner's, 1968.

Lewis, Wyndham. "Manifesto." *Blast: A Vorticist Journal*, vol. 1, 1914, pp. 11–44.

Linthicum, Kent. "Dancing on a Volcano: Subverting Catastrophe in M.P. Shiel's *The Purple Cloud*." *Nineteenth-Century Contexts*, vol. 40, no. 2, May 2018, pp. 149–163. EBSCOhost, search.ebscohost.com/login.aspx?direct=true&AuthType=cookie,ip,cpid&custid=s5805083&db=mzh&AN=2018395316&site=ehost-live&scope=site. Accessed 19 January 2020.

Loftis, Sonya Freeman. "The Autistic Detective: Sherlock Holmes and his Legacy." *Disabilities Studies Quarterly*, vol. 34, no. 4, 2014. https://dsq-sds.org/article/view/3728/3791. Accessed 5 February 2021.

Louinet, Patrice. "Hyborian Genesis." *The Coming of Conan the Cimmerian* by Robert E. Howard. Ballantine Books, 2003, pp. 427–452.

_____. Introduction. *The Coming of Conan the Cimmerian* by Robert E. Howard. Ballantine Books, 2003, pp. xix–xxv.

Lovecraft, H. P. *Against Religion*. Sporting Gentlemen, 2010.

_____. "The Call of Cthulhu." *H.P. Lovecraft. The Complete Fiction*. Barnes & Noble, 2010, pp. 355–379.

_____. "The Dunwich Horror." *H.P. Lovecraft. The Complete Fiction*. Barnes & Noble, 2010, pp. 633–667.

_____. "From Beyond." *H.P. Lovecraft. The Complete Fiction*. Barnes & Noble, 2010, pp. 115–120.

_____. *Letters to Elizabeth Toldridge and Anne Tillery Renshaw*. Hippocampus Press, 2014.

_____. "On the Trail of the Weird and Phantastic: The Weird Work of William Hope Hodgson." *The Phantagraph*, February 1937, pp. 3–8. https://imgur.com/a/Fg0ea#xL9SKAn.

_____. "The Shadow out of Time." *H.P. Lovecraft. The Complete Fiction*. Barnes & Noble, Inc., 2010, pp. 948–998.

_____. "Supernatural Horror in Literature." *H.P. Lovecraft. The Complete Fiction.* Barnes & Noble, 2010, pp. 1041–1098.

Luckhurst, Roger. "Modern Literature and Technology." *The British Library,* The British Library, 23 June 2016. www.bl.uk/20th-century-literature/articles/modern-literature-and-technology. Accessed 9 August 2020.

Lundie, Catherine A., ed. *Restless Spirits. Ghost Stories by American Women 1872–1926.* University of Massachusetts Press, 1996.

Machen, Arthur. "The Bowmen." *Collected Fiction.* Edited by S.T. Joshi. Hippocampus, 2019, pp. 14–17.

_____. "The Great God Pan." *The House of Souls.* Alfred A. Knopf, 1923.

MacLeod, Christine. "Britain as Workshop of the World." *BBC History Trails: Victorian Britain,* 18 Sept. 2014, www.bbc.co.uk/history/trail/victorian_britain/industry_invention/britain_workshop_world_02.shtml. Accessed 1 January 2021.

Maitland, E. M. *The Log of H. M. A. R34: Journey to America and Back.* Hodder and Stoughton, 1921.

March-Russell, Paul. *Modernism and Science Fiction.* Palgrave Macmillan, 2015.

Mayer, Jed. "A Darker Shade of Green: William Morris, Richard Jefferies, and Posthumanist Ecologies." *Journal of William Morris Studies,* vol. 19, no. 3, 2011, pp. 79–92. EBSCOhost, ezproxy.uwc.edu/login?url=http://search.ebscohost.com/login.aspx?direct=true&AuthType=cookie,ip,cpid&custid=s5805083&db=mzh&AN=2013140240&site=ehost-live&scope=site.

McDowell, Margaret B. "Edith Wharton's Ghost Stories." *Criticism,* vol. 12, 1970, pp. 133–52.

"McFarlane Toys Talks Conan." darkhorse.com, 2021. https://www.darkhorse.com/Interviews/1216/McFarlane-Toys-Talks-Conan. Accessed 24 Jan. 2021.

McKee, Patricia. "Racialization, Capitalism, and Aesthetics in Stoker's *Dracula*." *Novel: A Forum on Fiction,* vol. 36, no. 1, 2002, pp. 42–60.

McKitterick, Christopher. "John W. Campbell: The Man Who Invented Modern Fantasy and the Golden Age of Science Fiction." *Argentus,* vol. 11, 2011, pp. 22–25.

McLean, Steven. "'The Fertilising Conflict of Individualities': H. G. Wells's *A Modern Utopia,* John Stuart Mill's *On Liberty,* and the Victorian Tradition of Liberalism." *Papers on Language and Literature: A Journal for Scholars and Critics of Language and Literature,* vol. 43, no. 2, 2007, pp. 166–89. EBSCOhost, ezproxy.uwc.edu/login?url=http://search.ebscohost.com/login.aspx?direct=true&AuthType=cookie,ip,cpid&custid=s5805083&db=mzh&AN=2007580867&site=ehost-live&scope=site. Accessed 11 May 2020.

Miles, Robert. "Radcliffe, Ann (1764–1823)." *The Handbook of the Gothic.* Edited by Marie Mulvey-Roberts. New York University Press, 1999, pp. 76–83.

Minden, Michael. *Fritz Lang's Metropolis: Cinematic Visions of Technology and Fear.* Camden House, 2009.

Mitchell, Edward Page. *The Crystal Man; Landmark Science Fiction.* Doubleday, 1973.

"The Modern Library's Top 100 Nonfiction Books of the Century." *The New York Times,* https://archive.nytimes.com/www.nytimes.com/library/books/042999best-nonfiction-list.html.

Mollmann, Steven. "Air-Ships and the Technological Revolution: Detached Violence in George Griffith and H. G. Wells." *Science Fiction Studies,* vol. 42, no. 1 [125], Mar. 2015, pp. 20–41. EBSCOhost, doi:10.5621/sciefictstud.42.1.0020. Accessed 16 July 2020.

Moorcock, Michael. Introduction. *New Worlds: An Anthology.* Edited by Michael Moorcock. Thunder's Mouth Press, 2004.

_____. "Putting a Tag on It." *Amra,* vol. 2, no. 5, 1961, p. 15.

Moore, C. L. "The Black God's Kiss." *The Sword & Sorcery Anthology.* Edited by Jacob Weisman and David G. Hartwell. Tachyon Publications, 2012.

Morgan, Monique R. "Madness, Unreliable Narration, and Genre in *The Purple Cloud*." *Science Fiction Studies,* vol. 36, no. 2 [108], July 2009, pp. 266–283. EBSCOhost, search.ebscohost.com/login.aspx?direct=true&AuthType=cookie,ip,cpid&custid=s5805083&db=mzh&AN=2009026256&site=ehost-live&scope=site. Accessed 23 January 2020.

Morra, Irene. *Verse Drama in England, 1900–2015: Art, Modernity, and the National Stage.* Bloomsbury, 2016.

Morris, William. *News from Nowhere and*

Selected Writings and Designs. Penguin, 1987.

Moses, Omri. *Out of Character: Modernism, Vitalism, Psychic Life*. Stanford University Press, 2014.

Moskowitz, Sam. "Lost Giant of American Science Fiction—A Biographical Perspective." Introduction. *The Crystal Man; Landmark Science Fiction* by Edward Page Mitchell, Doubleday, 1973, pp. ix–lxxii.

Motard-Noar, Martine. "From Persephone to Demeter: A Feminist Experience in Cixous's Fiction." *Images of Persephone*. Edited by Elizabeth T. Hayes. University of Florida Press, 1994.

Murphy, Timothy S. "Labor of the Weird: William Hope Hodgson's Fantastic Materialism." *Science Fiction Studies*, Vol. 46 Issue 2, July 2019, p. 225–249.

National Center for Biotechnology Information. PubChem Database: Hydrogen Cyanide. www.pubchem.ncbi.nlm.nih.gov/compound/Hydrogen-cyanide. Accessed 1 June 2019.

Nietzsche, Frederich. *The Will to Power. An Attempted Transvaluation of All Values*. Volume I. Books I and II. Trans. By Anthony M. Ludovici. Project Gutenberg. https://www.gutenberg.org/files/52914/52914-h/52914-h.htm. Accessed 2 August 2020.

Novalis. "Hymns to the Night." *Novalis: Hymns to the Night, Spiritual Songs*. Trans. George MacDonald. Temple Lodge Books, 1992.

Nowlan, Philip Francis. "Armageddon 2419 A. D." *Amazing Stories*, vol. 3, no. 5, August 1928. *Internet Archive*, www.archive.org/details/Amazing_Stories_v03n05_1928-08_ATLPM-Urf/page/n3/mode/2up. Accessed 9 August 2020.

Ostroff, Hannah S. "How the 19th-Century Bicycle Craze Empowered Women and Changed Fashion." Smithsonian Stories. 17 May 2018. https://www.si.edu/stories/19th-century-bicycle-craze. Accessed 20 January 2021.

Partington, John S. "The Death of the Static: H. G. Wells and the Kinetic Utopia." *Utopian Studies*, vol. 11, no. 2, 2000, pp. 96–111. *EBSCOhost*, ezproxy.uwc.edu/login?url=http://search.ebscohost.com/login.aspx?direct=true&AuthType=cookie,ip,cpid&custid=s5805083&db=mzh&AN=2000060438&site=ehost-live&scope=site. Accessed 23 January 2020.

———. "*The Time Machine* and *A Modern Utopia*: The Static and Kinetic Utopias of the Early H. G. Wells." *Utopian Studies: Journal of the Society for Utopian Studies*, vol. 13, no. 1, 2002, pp. 57–68. *EBSCOhost*, ezproxy.uwc.edu/login?url=http://search.ebscohost.com/login.aspx?direct=true&AuthType=cookie,ip,cpid&custid=s5805083&db=mzh&AN=2002651690&site=ehost-live&scope=site. Accessed 3 January 2020.

Phillips, Terry. "The Discourse of the Vampire in First World War Writing." *Vampires: Myths and Metaphors of Enduring Evil*. Edited by Peter Day. Brill/Rodopi, 2006.

Pius X. *Pascendi Dominici Gregis*. Libreria Editrice Vaticana. http://www.vatican.va/content/pius-x/en/encyclicals/documents/hf_p-x_enc_19070908_pascendi-dominici-gregis.html, 1907. Accessed 25 June 2020.

Plotz, John. "Speculative Naturalism and the Problem of Scale: Richard Jefferies's *After London*, after Darwin." *Modern Language Quarterly: A Journal of Literary History*, vol. 76, no. 1, Mar. 2015, pp. 31–56. *EBSCOhost*, ezproxy.uwc.edu/login?url=http://search.ebscohost.com/login.aspx?direct=true&AuthType=cookie,ip,cpid&custid=s5805083&db=mzh&AN=2015391368&site=ehost-live&scope=site. Accessed 29 March 2020.

Poe, Edgar Allan. "The Conversation of Eiros and Charmion." *The Complete Tales and Poems of Edgar Allan Poe*. Barnes and & Noble, 2007, pp. 330–334.

———. "The Facts in the Case of M. Valdemar." *The Complete Tales and Poems of Edgar Allan Poe*. Barnes and & Noble, 2007, pp. 721–728.

"Pulp." *SFE: The Science Fiction Encyclopedia*, www.sf-encyclopedia.com/entry/pulp.

Ragland-Sullivan, Ellie. *Jacques Lacan and the Philosophy of Psychoanalysis*. University of Illinois Press, 1986.

Raine, Anne. "Ecocriticism and Modernism." *The Oxford Handbook of Ecocriticism*. Edited by Greg Garrard. Oxford University Press, 2014, pp. 98–117.

Rainey, Lawrence S. *Modernism: An Anthology*. Blackwell, 2011.

Rappleye, Charles. *Herbert Hoover in the White House: The Ordeal of the Presidency*. Simon & Schuster, 2017.

Reid, Robin. *Women in Science Fiction and Fantasy*. Kindle ed. Sexual Identities, 2016.
Riquelme, John Paul. "Oscar Wilde's Aesthetic Gothic: Walter Pater, Dark Enlightenment, and *The Picture of Dorian Gray*." *Modern Fiction Studies*, vol. 46, no. 3, 2000, pp. 611–631.
———. "Toward a History of Gothic and Modernism: Dark Modernity from Bram Stoker to Samuel Beckett." *Modern Fiction Studies*, vol. 46 no. 3, 2000, pp. 585–605.
Roberts, Adam. *The History of Science Fiction*. Palgrave Macmillan, 2007.
Roberts, J.M. *Twentieth Century. The History of the World, 1901–2000*. Viking, 1999.
Roellinger, Francis X. "Psychical Research and 'The Turn of the Screw.'" *The Turn of the Screw* by Henry James. Edited by Robert Kimbrough. Norton, 1966, pp. 132–142.
Romney, Rebecca. "The Skeptic's Guide to Sherlock Holmes: Twenty-five facts about the detective." *Baker Street Journal*, vol. 65, no. 4, Winter 2015, pp. 6–15.
Roth, Phyllis A. "Suddenly Sexual Women in Bram Stoker's *Dracula*." *Dracula* by Bram Stoker. Edited by Nina Auerbach and David J. Skal. Norton, 1997, pp. 411–421.
Roza, Mathilde Helene. *Following Strangers: The Life and Literary Works of Robert M. Coates*. University of South Carolina Press, 2011.
Sammon, Paul M. *Conan the Phenomenon*. Dark Horse Books, 2007.
Sargent, Lyman Tower. "Themes in Utopian Fiction in English Before Wells." *Science-Fiction Studies*, vol. 3, 1976, pp. 275–82. *EBSCOhost*, ezproxy.uwc.edu/login?url=http://search.ebscohost.com/login.aspx?direct=true&AuthType=cookie,ip,cpid&custid=s5805083&db=mzh&AN=1976102526&site=ehost-live&scope=site. Accessed 3 August 2019.
———. *Utopianism a Very Short Introduction*. Oxford University Press, 2010.
Schaffer, Talia. "'A Wilde Desire Took Me': The Homoerotic History of *Dracula*." *Dracula by Bram Stoker*, edited by Nina Auerbach and David J. Skal. Norton, 1997, pp. 470–482.
Scott, Roberta, and Jon Thiem. "Catastrophe Fiction 1870–1914: An Annotated Bibliography of Selected Works in English." *Extrapolation*, vol. 24, no. 2, 1983, pp. 156–169.
Seeley, Tim, and Steve Seeley. *The Art of He-Man and the Masters of the Universe*. Dark Horse Books, 2015.
Segal, Howard P. *Future Imperfect: The Mixed Blessings of Technology in America*. University of Massachusetts Press, 1994.
Shanks, Jeffrey. "Hyborian Age Archaeology: Unearthing Historical and Anthropological Foundations." *Conan Meets the Academy*, edited by Jonas Prida. McFarland, 2013, pp. 13–34.
Sharlin, Harold I., and Tiby Sharlin. *Lord Kelvin, the Dynamic Victorian*. Pennsylvania State University Press, 1979.
Shelley, Mary. *The Last Man*. The Hogarth Press, 1985.
Sheppard, Richard. "Modernism, Language, and Experimental Poetry: On Leaping over Banisters and Learning How to Fly." *Modern Language Review*, vol. 92, no. 1, Jan. 1997, pp. 98–123. *EBSCOhost*, doi:10.2307/3734688. Accessed 9 January 2020.
Shiel, M. P. *The Purple Cloud*. Gregg Press, 1977.
Sidomak, Curt. "The Eggs from Lake Tanganyika." *The Prentice Hall Anthology of Science Fiction and Fantasy*, edited by Garyn G. Roberts. Prentice Hall, 2003, pp. 495–501.
Singley, Carol J., and Susan Elizabeth Sweeney. "Forbidden Reading and Ghostly Writing: Anxious Power in Wharton's 'Pomegranate Seed.'" *Women's Studies*, vol. 20, no. 2, 1991, pp. 177–203.
Smith, Clark Ashton. "The Dimension of Chance." *The Collected Fantasies, Vol. 4: The Maze of the Enchanter*. Night Shade Books, 2009, pp. 75–94.
———. "The Empire of the Necromancers." *A Rendezvous in Averoigne*. Arkham House, 1988, pp. 315–325.
———. "The Great God Awto." http://www.eldritchdark.com/writings/short-stories/88/the-great-god-awto. Accessed 9 August 2020.
———. "The Metamorphosis of the World." *The Collected Fantasies, Vol. 1: The End of the Story*. Night Shade Books, 2015, pp. 117–140.
———. *A Rendezvous in Averoigne*. Arkham House, 1988, pp. 315–325.
Smith, Thorne. *Topper*. New York: Pocket Books, 1926.

Solomon, Barbara H. "Introduction." *Herland and Selected Stories* by Charlotte Perkins Gilman. Signet Classics, 1992, pp. xi–xxxi.

Solomon, Eric. *Stephen Crane from Parody to Realism*. Harvard University Press, 1971.

Sorrentino, Paul. "The Short Stories of Stephen Crane." *A Companion to the American Short Story*. Edited by Alfred Bendixen and James Nagel. Wiley-Blackwell, 2010.

⸺. *Stephen Crane: A Life of Fire*. The Belknap Press of Harvard University Press, 2014.

Sova, Dawn B. "Introduction." *The Complete Tales and Poems of Edgar Allan Poe*. Barnes & Noble, 2007, pp. ix–xv.

Spielrein, Sabina, et al. *The Essential Writings of Sabina Spielrein: Pioneer of Psychoanalysis*. Routledge, 2019.

Squires, John D. "Publications and Revisions of M.P. Shiel's *The Purple Cloud*." *New York Review of Science Fiction*, vol. 19, no. 3 [219], Nov. 2006, pp. 13–15. *EBSCOhost*, search.ebscohost.com/login.aspx?direct=true&AuthType=cookie,ip,cpid&custid=s5805083&db=mzh&AN=2006300588&site=ehost-live&scope=site. Accessed 7 December 2019.

⸺. "Shiel's Liquid Air Engines in *The Purple Cloud*." *New York Review of Science Fiction*, vol. 22, no. 4 [256], Dec. 2009. *EBSCOhost*, search.ebscohost.com/login.aspx?direct=true&AuthType=cookie,ip,cpid&custid=s5805083&db=mzh&AN=2010300433&site=ehost-live&scope=site. Accessed 30 June 2019.

Stableford, Brian. "The Black and White Mystery of *The Purple Cloud*." Introduction. *The Purple Cloud* by M.P. Shiel. Tartarus Press, 2004, pp. v–xv.

⸺. "Ecology." *The Encyclopedia of Science Fiction*. Edited by John Clute and Peter Nicholls. Orbit, 1999, pp. 365–366.

Stephens, Paul. "Bob Brown, 'Inforg': The 'Readies' at the Limits of Modernist Cosmopolitanism." *Journal of Modern Literature*, vol. 35, no. 1, 2011, pp. 143–164. *EBSCOhost*, search.ebscohost.com/login.aspx?direct=true&AuthType=ip,uid&db=mzh&AN=2012381417&site=ehost-live&scope=site. Accessed 5 June 2019.

Stevenson, Robert Louis. *The Strange Case of Dr Jekyll and Mr Hyde*. Edited by Richard Dury. Edinburgh University Press, 2004.

Stockton, Frank. "My Translatophone." *John Gayther's Garden and the Stories Told Therein*. Project Gutenberg. www.gutenberg.org/files/22737/22737-h/22737-h.htm#IX. Accessed 9 August 2020.

⸺. "A Tale of Negative Gravity." *Full-Reads*, www.fullreads.com/literature/a-tale-of-negative-gravity/. Accessed 1 July 2020.

Stoker, Bram. *Dracula*. Edited by Nina Auerbach and David J. Skal. Norton, 1997.

Stone, James L. "Dr. Gottlieb Burkhardt—The Pioneer of Pyschosurgery." *Journal of the History of Pyschosciences*, vol. 10, no. 1, 2001, pp. 79–92.

Stone, Leslie F. "Out of the Void." *Amazing Stories*, vol. 4, no. 5, August 1929, pp. 440–455.

Stratton, George Frederick. "Sam Graves' Gravity Nullifier." *Amazing Stories*, vol. 4, no. 5, August 1929, pp. 465–469.

Straub, Peter, ed. *American Fantastic Tales: Terror and the Uncanny from Poe to the Pulps*. The Library of America, 2009.

Sussman, Herbert L. *Victorians and the Machine the Literary Response to Technology*. Harvard University Press, 1969.

Suvin, Darko. "Victorian Science Fiction, 1871–85: The Rise of the Alternative History Sub-Genre." *Science Fiction Studies*, vol. 10, no. 2 [30], July 1983, pp. 148–169. *EBSCOhost*, search.ebscohost.com/login.aspx?direct=true&AuthType=ip,uid&db=mzh&AN=1984023790&site=ehost-live&scope=site. Accessed 1 June 2019.

Svitavsky, William L. "From Decadence to Racial Antagonism: M.P. Shiel at the Turn of the Century." *Science Fiction Studies*, vol. 31, no. 1 [92], Mar. 2004, pp. 1–24. *EBSCOhost*, search.ebscohost.com/login.aspx?direct=true&AuthType=ip,cpid&custid=s5805083&db=mzh&AN=2004700131&site=ehost-live&scope=site. Accessed 29 June 2020.

Sweet, Roger. "Idea Disclosure." *The Art of He-Man and the Masters of the Universe* by Tim Seeley and Steve Seeley. Dark Horse Books, 2015, p. 14.

Taylor, Jesse Oak. "The Novel after Nature, Nature after the Novel: Richard Jefferies's Anthropocene Romance." *Studies in the Novel*, vol. 50, no. 1, 2018, pp. 108–133. *EBSCOhost*, ezproxy.uwc.edu/login?url=http://search.ebscohost.com/login.aspx?direct=true&AuthType=

cookie,ip,cpid&custid=s5805083&db=mzh&AN=2018301844&site=ehost-live&scope=site. Accessed 10 June 2020.

Thomas, Helen. "Sir Arthur Conan Doyle Once Helped Clear an Innocent Man of Murder." *Smithsonian Magazine.* 22 May 2015. https://www.smithsonianmag.com/smart-news/sir-arthur-conan-doyle-investigates-180955379/. Accessed 2 August 2020.

Thomas, Paul Edmund. Introduction. *The Worm Ouroboros* by E. R. Eddison. Dell Fantasy, 1991, pp. xv–xlii.

Thoreau, Henry David. *Walden. The Portable Thoreau.* Revised edition. Edited by Carl Bode. Penguin, 1981, pp. 258–572.

———. "Walking." *The Portable Thoreau.* Revised edition. Edited by Carl Bode. Penguin, 1981, pp. 592–630.

Thurs, Daniel P. "Scientific Methods." *Wrestling with Nature: from Omens to Science.* Edited by Peter Harrison et al. University of Chicago Press, 2011, pp. 307–35.

Tillman, Benjamin. "Address to the U. S. Senate." February 7, 1899. http://nationalhumanitiescenter.org/pds/gilded/empire/text7/tillman.pdf. Accessed 9 August 2020.

Tolkien, J.R.R. *The Hobbit.* Houghton Mifflin Harcourt, 2007.

———. "Leaf by Niggle." *Tales from the Perilous Realm.* Houghton Mifflin Harcourt, 2008.

———. *The Letters of J.R.R. Tolkien.* Selected and edited by Humphrey Carpenter. Houghton Mifflin, 1981.

Trott, Nicola. "Lewis, Matthew (1775–1818)." *The Handbook of the Gothic.* Edited by Marie Mulvey-Roberts. New York University Press, 1999, pp. 54–57.

Twain, Mark. *A Connecticut Yankee in King Arthur's Court.* Signet/Penguin, 1963.

Underhill, Evelyn. *The Grey World.* Scriptoria Books, 2014.

———. *Mysticism: The Preeminent Study in the Nature and Development of Spiritual Consciousness.* Image Books, 1990.

"Urban Settlement." *Encyclopædia Britannica,* Encyclopædia Britannica, Inc., www.britannica.com/place/United-Kingdom/Urban-settlement.

Vermeersch, Arthur. "Modernism." *The Catholic Encyclopedia.* Vol. 10. New York: Robert Appleton Company, 1911. 2 Jan. 2021. http://www.newadvent.org/cathen/10415a.htm.

Vidal, Gore. "Tarzan Revisited." Esquire Classics, 1 December 1963. https://classic.esquire.com/article/1963/12/1/tarzan-revisited. Accessed 11 August 2020.

Weinbaum, Stanley. "A Martian Odyssey." *The Prentice Hall Anthology of Science Fiction and Fantasy.* Edited by Garyn G. Roberts. Prentice Hall, 2003, pp. 556–574.

Wells, H. G. "The Country of the Blind." *The Country of the Blind and Other Stories.* www.freeclassicebooks.com/H.G.%20Wells/The%20Country%20of%20the%20Blind.pdf, 609–648. Accessed 9 August 2020.

———. *The First Men in the Moon. H. G. Wells: Seven Novels.* Barnes & Noble, 2006, pp. 407–553.

———. *Men Like Gods.* Grosset & Dunlap, 1922.

———. *A Modern Utopia.* Penguin, 2005.

———. "A Story of the Days to Come, Chapter I." *Amazing Stories,* April 1928, pp. 6–25.

———. *The Time Machine.* Broadview, 2001.

———. *The War in the Air.* Penguin, 2005.

———. *The War of the Worlds.* The New York Review of Books, 1960.

Westfahl, Gary. *Hugo Gernsback and the Century of Science Fiction.* McFarland, 2007.

———. *The Mechanics of Wonder: The Creation of the Idea of Science Fiction.* Liverpool University Press, 1998.

———. *The Rise and Fall of American Science Fiction, from the 1920s to the 1960s.* McFarland, 2019.

Wharton, Edith. "Afterward." *American Fantastic Tales. Terror and the Uncanny from Poe to the Pulps.* Edited by Peter Straub. The Library of America, 2009, pp. 386–413.

———. *"Artemis to Actaeon" and Other Verse.* Scribner's, 1909.

———. *The Collected Short Stories of Edith Wharton.* Volume 2. Scribner's, 1968.

———. *The Ghost Stories of Edith Wharton.* Scribner's, 1973.

———. *The Letters of Edith Wharton.* Edited by R.W.B. Lewis and Nancy Lewis. Scribner's, 1988.

———. "The Pomegranate Seed." *Scribner's,* vol. 51, no. 3, 1912, pp. 284–91.

———. *The Writing of Fiction.* Octagon, 1970.

Wheeler, L. Kip. "Modernism." Literary Vocabulary. https://web.cn.edu/kwheeler/lit_terms.html. Accessed 9 August 2020.

White, Richard. *The Rise of Industrial America, 1877–1900*. The Gilder Lehrman Institute of American History, www.gilderlehrman.org/history-resources/essays/rise-industrial-america-1877-1900.

Whitehead, Alfred North. "The Concept of Nature." *Project Gutenberg,* https://www.gutenberg.org/files/18835/18835-h/18835-h.htm#Page_99. Accessed 9 August 2020.

———. *Science and the Modern World*. Free Press, 1967.

Whitworth, Michael H. "Physics: 'A Strange Footprint.'" *A Concise Companion to Modernism*. Edited by David Bradshaw. Blackwell, 2003.

Whyte, Kenneth. *Hoover: An Extraordinary Life in Extraordinary Times*. Vintage Books, 2018.

Wilde, Oscar. "The Canterville Ghost." *The Works of Oscar Wilde*. Paragon, 2000, pp. 193–214.

Williamson, Jamie. *The Evolution of Modern Fantasy: From Antiquarianism to the Ballantine Adult Fantasy Series*. E-book, Palgrave Macmillan, 2015.

Witchard, Anne. "Purple Clouds and Yellow Shadows: Sickly Vapours and Perilous Hues at the Fin-de-Siècle." *Lord of Strange Deaths: The Fiendish World of Sax Rohmer,* edited by Phil Baker and Antony Clayton, Strange Attractor, 2015, pp. 41–78. *EBSCOhost,* search.ebscohost.com/login.aspx?direct=true&AuthType=cookie,ip,cpid&custid=s5805083&db=mzh&AN=2017140708&site=ehost-live&scope=site. Accessed 30 June 2020.

Wolf, Leonard, ed. *Blood Thirst. 100 Years of Vampire Fiction*. Oxford University Press, 1997.

Womack, Ytasha L. *Afrofuturism: The World of Black Sci-Fi and Fantasy Culture*. Lawrence Hill Books, 2013.

Wordsworth, William. "I Wandered Lonely as a Cloud." *Poetry: An Introduction*. 6th ed. Edited by Michael Meyer. Bedford/St. Martin's, 2010, p. 663.

Worster, Donald. *A Passion for Nature: The Life of John Muir*. Oxford University Press, 2011.

Wosk, Julie. *Women and the Machine: Representations from the Spinning Wheel to the Electronic Age*. Johns Hopkins University Press, 2001.

Yaszek, Lisa. "Leslie F. Stone." *The Future Is Female*. http://womensf.loa.org/leslie-f-stone/. Accessed 9 August 2020.

Yeats, William Butler. "The Second Coming." *The Norton Anthology of English Literature Volume F, 8th ed. The Twentieth Century and After*. Edited by Jon Stallworthy and Jahan Ramazani. Norton, 2006, pp. 2036–2037.

Index

Adam and Eve 29, 170–171
"The Adventure of Charles Augustus Milverton" 194
"The Adventure of the Engineer's Thumb" 192
Afrofuturism: The World of Black and Sci-fi and Fantasy Culture 29
After London 11, 18–19, 34
Against Religion 178
Agnosticism 160, 168, 221n9
Agrippa, Cornelius 159
Aldiss, Brian 211
Alkon, Paul K. 147
"Allegory of the Cave" 109
Alternate Worlds: The Illustrated History of Science Fiction 218n1
Amazing Stories 1, 23–24, 31, 135, 139, 198, 210, 217n1
Amundsen, Roald 106, 220n3
Apocalypse 11
"Araby" 11
archaeology 38
The Argonaut 219n17
Argosy 210
Arkham House 213
"Armageddon 2419 A.D." 198–199
The Artwork & Times of Pamela Colman Smith 222n5
Asimov, Isaac 156
Astounding Science Fiction 144, 154, 210
Atherton, Gertrude 64–65

Baird, Edwin 210, 212
Bairoch, Paul 76
Bakshi, Ralph 223ch8n2
The Ballad of Black Tom 214
Ballesteros-González, Antonio 218n1
The Battle of Dorking 16
Beerbohm, Max 27
Bellamy, Edward 18
Benjamin, Ludy T. 218n6

Benjamin, Walter 20
Bentley, Christopher 218n8
Bergson, Henri 187
Best, Gary Dean 31
"Beyond the Black River" 40
Bierce, Ambrose 67–69, 157
"Black God's Kiss" 204
The Black Stork 220n2
Blackstar 215
Blackwood, Algernon 63–64, 160
Blavatsky, Helena 159, 161
Bleier, Richard 128
The Blood of the Vampire 218n9
Boissoneault, Lorraine 221n6
Booth, Howard J. 220n10
Botting, Fred 47
Braddon, Mary E. 218n9, 218n11
Brave New World 32–34, 134, 217n6
A Brief History of Modern Psychology 218n6
Broad, Katherine 80
Bronfen, Elizabeth 48
Brown, Bob 137–139
Browning, Todd 52
Bruno, Giordano 185–186
Bulfin, Ailise 89
Bullfinch's Mythology 38
Bulwer-Lytton, Edward 105–106, 122–126
Burroughs, Edgar Rice 105, 109, 117–119, 194–197
Butler, Samuel 136
"By This Axe I Rule!" 36
Byronic hero 189

Cabell, James Branch 3, 182–185, 212
"The Call of Cthulhu" 177–178
The Cambridge Companion to Science Fiction 221n7
The Cambridge History of Modernism 218n1
Campbell, John W. 144, 211
Carnacki, Thomas 64, 175–176

239

Carnell, John 210–211
Carter, Lin 213–214
Catholic Encyclopedia 159
Census, United States, 1890 104
Chesterton, G.K. 40–41
"Childe Harold's Pilgrimage" 189
Christianity 12–13, 157–160, 164–166, 167, 169–170, 172, 205
Clarke, David 219n18
Clayton, William 210
Clements, Frederic 219n4
Coates, Robert M. 134, 150–153
Cole, Sarah 22
Collier, John 34–35
Collins, Wilkie 219n14
Colonialism in Joseph Conrad's Heart of Darkness 220n4
"The Colour Out of Space" 24
"The Comet" 28–30
The Coming Race 16
Conan 13, 16, 36–40, 189, 201–204, 206–207, 214–216
Conan Doyle, Sir Arthur 140–141, 190–194, 219n14
Conan the Barbarian 215
Conan the Destroyer 216
A Connecticut Yankee in King Arthur's Court 146–147
Connington, J.J. 99–100
Conrad, Joseph 98–99, 105–108, 217n6
Continental Philosophy. A Critical Approach 223ch7n1
Cooper, James Fenimore 217n6
Corelli, Marie 161–166, 169–170, 175, 212
cosmic horror 25, 35–36
Cosmopolitan 21
Cosmos 153–154
Cox, Michael 43, 57
Crane, Stephen 65–66, 207
Crawford, Francis Marion 54–57
Crockett, Davy 31–32
Cromie, Robert 97–99
"The Crooked Man" 223ch7n4
Cropper, Margaret 222n6
Crowley, Aleister 159
The Crystal Man: Stories by Edward Page Mitchell 137
Cubism 5, 187

Daly, Nicholas 76
"The Damned Thing" 179
Dante 158
Darwin, Charles 76, 89, 90, 92, 101, 105, 123, 136, 197, 218n2

"Darwin Among the Machines" 136
Dawson, Emma Frances 49
"Defining Ecocritical Theory and Practice" 219n1
de Grainville, Jean Baptiste Cousin 88
Derleth, April 212–213
Derleth, August 212–213
De Voto, Bernard 145
Dickens, Charles 135
Disabilities Study Quarterly 223ch7n3
The Divine Comedy 158
Doctor Faustus 28
The Doings of Raffles Haw 140–141
Donaldson, Eileen 204
doppleganger 50–55, 74, 205, 218n2
Dracula 10, 43, 46, 51–55, 64, 218n7
The Dream of X 10, 25
Du Bois, W.E.B. 28–30
Dunbar, Olivia Howard 57
Dunsany, Lord 159
"The Dunwich Horror" 168, 178
dystopia 16, 17, 32, 140

The Eater of Darkness 134, 150–53
Eddison, E.R. 105–106, 119–121
The Edinburgh Companion to Gothic and the Arts 218n4
Elbert, Monika 72
Eliot, T.S. 7, 94, 98–99, 143
Elliot, Hugh 126
Ellul, Jacques 133–134
"Enoch Soames" 10, 27, 36
Erewhon 16, 17, 136
Estleman, Loren 190–191
eugenics 220n2
evolution 136, 144, 196
The Evolution of Modern Fantasy 213

Fadiman, Clifton 67
The Fantasy Fan 218ch1n8
Fire and Ice 223chEn2
The First Men in the Moon 221n8
Fleckner, James Elroy 143–144
Forster, E.M. 134, 142–143
Fortune, Dion 160
Frankenstein 16, 189, 218n11
Frazetta, Frank 216
Freeman, Mary E. Wilkins 52–54, 60
Freud, Sigmund 43, 98, 187, 218n1, 218n3, 218n6
Fritz Lang's Metropolis: Cinematic Visions of Technology and Fear 221ch5n1
From the Earth to the Moon 8

Index 241

Garby, Lee Hawkins 1
"The Gateway of the Monster" 175
Gelula, Abner J. 153–154
Genzlinger, Neil 214
Gernsback, Hugo 23–25, 31, 84–86, 210, 217n1
ghosts 55–73, 175–176, 190, 218n12
Ghostwriting Modernism 219n13
Gilbert, R.A. 43, 57
Gilman, Charlotte Perkins 53, 105, 111–115
"Good Lady Ducayne" 218n9
Gothic 42–50, 134, 218n4
Graf, Susan Johnston 222n8
"The Gravity Nullifier" 142
Great Depression 31, 34
The Great Divorce 158
"The Great God Awto" 155
"The Great God Pan" 160, 172
Green, Anna Katherine 219n14
Greenfield, Patricia 76
The Grey World 160, 165–169
Griffin, Angela M. 50
Gunn, James 210

"Haïta the Shepherd" 157
Hammond, John R. 220n8
"Hap" 11
Hardy, Thomas 46
Harlem Renaissance 30
Harris, Clare Winger 83–84
Hawthorne, Nathaniel 82
He-Man and the Masters of the Universe 216, 223chEn5
Heart of Darkness 217n6
Henderson, Keith 120
Henley, William Ernest 187
Herbert Hoover in the White House: The Ordeal of the Presidency 217n4
Hercules in New York 223chEn3
Herland 10, 111–114
The Hermetic Order of the Golden Dawn 159–161, 169, 179
Hinton, C.H. 221n7
Hipsky, Martin 162
A History of Modernist Literature 132
The History of Spiritualism 222n4
The Hobbit 1, 180, 214
Hodgson, William Hope 25–27, 64, 92–95, 119, 163, 175–176
"The Hollow Men" 143
Holmes, Sherlock 190–194, 223ch7n3
Holton, Sandra Stanley 217n3
Hoover, Herbert 31, 217n4
Hoover: An Extraordinary Life in Extraordinary Times 217n4

Hopkins, Gerard Manley 90–91
The Hound of the Baskervilles 192
The Hour of the Dragon 202, 204, 215
Hourican, Bridget 97
The House on the Borderland 26, 163
"How Scientists Discovered Helium, The First Element, 150 Years Ago" 221n6
Howard, Robert E. 36–40, 199–204, 207, 214–216
Howard's End 142
Howells, William Dean 21
Hugo Gernsback and the Century of Science Fiction 217n2
The Human Relationship with Nature 219n2
Huxley, Aldous 32–34, 134
Huxley, T.H. 126–127, 221n9
Hyborian Age 36–40, 199
"Hymns to the Night" 158

imperialism 40, 102–106, 114, 121–125, 149
industrialization 10, 15, 75–101, 132, 147
The Interpretation of Dreams 218n3
Inventing Tomorrow: H.G. Wells and the Twentieth Century 22
"Invictus" 187
The Island of Dr. Moreau 219n3

James, Henry 44–45
James, M.R. 60–63
James, William 187
Janssen, Pierre Jules 221n6
Jefferies, Richard 19–20, 86–87, 100
Jirel of Joiry 189, 204–206
Johnson, Claudia Durst 220n4
Joshi, S.T. 61, 126, 178, 214
Journey to the Center of the Earth 8
The Judgment of Jurgen 222n13
Julian of Norwich 165
The Jungle Book 149
Jurgen 1, 182–185

Kaplan, Stuart R. 222n5
Kelleam, Joseph E. 154–155
Kelvin, Lord (William Thomson) 92–93, 221ch6n1
Kempe, Margery 165
Kern, Stephen 134–135
Khan, Peter H., Jr. 219n1
King Kull 36, 189, 199–201, 203, 206
The King of Alsander 143
"Kings of the Night" 200–201
Kipling, Rudyard 102–103, 107, 125, 149–150

Lady Audley's Secret 218*n*11
"The Lady or the Tiger?" 141
Lane, Mary E. Bradley 79–82, 112
Lang, Fritz 221*ch*5*n*1
Langlois, Judith H. 50
The Last Generation: A Story of the Future 143–144
The Last of the Mohicans 217*n*6
LaValle, Victor 214
"Leaf by Niggle" 180–182
Le Fanu, Sheridan 51–52
Lemaître, Georges 222*n*10
Levin, Ira 53
Levine, Robert S. 134
Lewis, C.S. 158, 163, 169–172
Lewis, Matthew 47–48
Lewis, Wyndham 77
The Life of Evelyn Underhill: An Intimate Portrait of the Groundbreaking Author of Mysticism 222*n*6
Lilith 158
"Lines Written a Few Miles Above Tintern Abbey, on Revisiting the Banks of the Wye During a Tour, July 13, 1798" 220*n*9
Literature of the Women's Suffrage Campaign in England 217*n*7
Little Dorrit 135
Lockyer, Norman 221*n*6
Loftis, Sonya Freeman 223*ch*7*n*3
London 19, 135, 165, 203
Looking Backward 18
The Lord of the Rings 180, 213, 222*n*12
The Lost World 190
"The Love Song of J. Alfred Prufrock" 13
Lovecraft, H.P. 24, 35, 61, 63, 95–96, 106, 126–127, 145, 169, 176–180, 212–214
Lovecraft Country 214
Lucretius 159
Lugosi, Bela 52

Mabinogion 158
Macdonald, Alec 143
MacDonald, George 158–159, 221*ch*6*n*2
Machen, Arthur 69–70, 160, 172–175
Machine Age 133, 135, 137, 156
"The Machine Stops" 134, 142–143
The Magician 159
Maitland, Edward 220*n*1
"A Man Said to the Universe" 207
Manfred 189
March-Russell, Paul 143
Marryat, Florence 218*n*9
Martians 15, 32, 170–171
"Mary Postgate" 149–150

Maugham, Somerset 159, 163
Maxwell, James Clerk 218*n*5
Mayer, Jed 20
McFarlane Toys 216
McKee, Patricia 218*n*8
Mechanics of Wonder 24
Metropolis 134, 221*ch*5*n*1
Middle Earth 11
Mirror of Simple Souls 222*n*7
"The Mirrors of Tuzun Thune" 200
Mitchell, Edward Page 136–137, 140
Mizora 17
Moby Dick 189
Modern Electronics 23–24, 135
A Modern Utopia 23, 133, 149
Modernism and the Women's Popular Romance, 1885–1925 162
Mollmann, Steven 149
Moonchild 159
Moorcock, Michael 211
Moore, C.L. 204–206
Morris, William 20, 82–83
Moses, Omri 187–189
Moskowitz, Sam 137
"The Moth" 1
Mrs. Warren's Profession 5
Muir, John 96, 101, 220*n*12
Munford, Lewis 132
Munsey, Frank 210
"Murders in the Rue Morgue" 219*n*14
Murnau, F.W. 51
Murphy, Timothy S. 26
My First Summer in the Sierra 220*n*12
mysticism 157, 160, 165, 169, 172
Mysticism: The Preeminent Study in the Nature and Development of the Spiritual Consciousness 160, 165

Narnia 13
Nelson, Carolyn Christensen 218*ch*1*n*7
New Worlds 211
New York City 12, 25, 30, 135, 137, 148, 151–153
The New Yorker 151
News from Nowhere 20–21
Nietzsche, Friedrich 188–189
The Night Land 26
nihilism 188–189
1984 32
Nineteenth Century Science: An Anthology 220*n*7
nonhuman 11, 42–101, 219*n*1
Novalis (Georg Philipp Friedrich Freiherr von Hardenberg) 158–159
Nowlan, Philip Francis 1, 198–199

Index

Of the Infinite Universe and Worlds 185
Old Ones 177–179
On the Nature of the Psyche 218*n*3
On the Origin of the Species 136
Out of Character: Modernism, Vitalism, Psychic Life 187
Out of the Silent Planet 170
The Outline of History 38
The Outsider and Others 212, 218ch1n8
The Oxford Handbook of the History of Eugenics 220*n*2

Palmieri, Luigi 221*n*6
Paracelsus 159
Partington, John S. 22–23
Pascendi Dominici Gregis 158
Pater, Walter 42–43, 218*n*1
Perelandra 13, 163, 169–172
Pernick, Martin S. 220*n*2
Phantastes 158, 221ch6n2
"The Phoenix on the Sword" 37–39
"Physics: A Strange Footprint" 162
Pius X 158–159, 165
Plato 109
Poe, Edgar Allan 48–49, 219*n*14
Polidori, John 51
The Politics of American Individualism 31
Porete, Marguerite 165
Pound, Ezra 209
"Prolegomena" 209
psychoanalysis 5, 218*n*6
Pumping Iron 223chEn3
Punter, David 218*n*4
The Purple Cloud 30, 86–90, 115, 220*n*6

"The Queen of the Black Coast" 39

"Racialization, Capitalism, and Aesthetics in Stoker's *Dracula*" 218ch2n8
Radcliffe, Ann 47
Ralph 124C 41+ 12, 23–25, 32
The Readies 138
The Recluse 218ch1n8
Red Nails 203, 207
Research Methods on Ecology 219*n*4
The Return of Tarzan 195–197, 201
Richardson, Maurice 43
Riquelme, John Paul 42–44
The Rise and Fall of American Science Fiction, from the 1920s to the 1960s 223*n*6
The Rite of Spring 5
Roberts, Adam 104, 134
Roberts, J.M.: *The Twentieth Century* 7
The Rock 15

Roellinger, Francis X. 44–46
Rogers, Buck 1, 16, 189, 198–199, 207
Rolle, Richard 165
A Romance of Two Worlds 161–165, 169
Romanticism 43, 76, 220*n*9
A Room with a View 142
Roosevelt, Theodore 101
Roth, Phyllis 43
Roza, Mathilde 150
Ruff, Matt 214
"Rust" 154–155
Rymer, James Malcolm 51

"Sam Graves' Gravity Nullifier" 139, 142
Sargent, Lyman Tower 17–18, 25, 34
Saunders, Charles 214
"A Scandal in Bohemia" 193
Schaffer, Talia 218*n*7
Schroeder, William R. 222*n*1
Science Fiction Digest 153
The Science Fiction Encyclopedia 34
scientific method 87–90, 186, 190
Scientific Romances 221*n*2
Scott, Roberta 89
"The Searcher of the End House" 175
"The Second Coming" 37, 39
Segal, Howard P. 79
"The Shadow Kingdom" 199
"Shadow Out of Time" 35
Shakespeare, William 217*n*6
Shanks, Jeffrey 38
The Shape of Things to Come 7, 22, 149
Sharlin, Harold 92–93
Sharlin, Tiby 92–93
Shelley, Mary 88, 100
Sherlock Holmes 13, 189–195, 201–202
Sherlock Holmes: The Complete Novels and Stories, Volume 1 190
Sherry, Vincent 218*n*2
Shiel, M.P. 30, 86–90, 115, 220*n*6
Shippey, Tom 180
The Sign of Four 192, 194
The Skylark of Space 1, 223*n*6
Smith, Andrew 218*n*4
Smith, Clark Ashton 94–95, 106, 127–130, 155
Smith, E.E. "Doc" 1, 106
Smith, Pamela Colman 159, 222*n*5
Smith, Thorne 72–73
Smith of Wooten Major and Farmer Giles of Ham 213
Solomon, Stephen 66
The Souls of Black Folk 28
Spielrein, Sabrina 98
Spinrad, Norman 211

Stableford, Brian 77, 214
Stanford Encyclopedia of Philosophy 223ch7n2
Stevenson, Robert Louis 50–51
Stoker, Bram 43, 51–52, 54
"A Story of the Days to Come" 147–148
The Strange Case of Dr. Jekyll and Mr. Hyde 195, 218n3
Stratton, George Frederick 139
A Study in Scarlet 190–192
Suffrage Days: Stories from the Women's Suffrage Movement 217n3
Surprised by Joy 221ch6n2
surrealism 5, 150, 221ch5n2
The Surrealism Reader: An Anthology of Ideas 221ch5n2
Suvin, Darko 16
Swanwick, Michael 222n13
Swedenborg, Emanuel 222n4
Sweet, Matthew 125–26
Sweet, Roger 223Ch8n5
Swift, Jonathan 117, 122
Sword, Helen 219n13
sword-and-sorcery 36, 189, 199–205

"The Tachypomp" 137
"A Tale of Negative Gravity" 141–142
Tales from Perilous Realms 180
Talking to God: Occultism in the Work of W. B. Yeats, Arthur Machen, Algernon Blackwood, and Dion Fortune 222n8
Tarot 159, 222n5
Tarzan 13, 109–111, 189, 194–197, 199, 201–202, 206
Tarzan of the Apes 194
"Tarzan Revisited" 220n5
Technics and Civilization 132
The Technological Society 133–134
The Tempest 217n6
terraforming 129
Tesla, Nikola 221n8
Thiem, John 89
"The Thing Invisible" 175
Thomas, Paul Edmund 119
Thoreau, Henry David 75, 100
The Thrill Book 135
Through the Eye of the Needle 21
Thundarr the Barbarian 215
Tillman, Benjamin 103
The Time Machine 22, 33, 134–135, 137, 143, 148, 220n8, 221n7
The Time Machine: A Reference Guide 220n8
Tolkien, J.R.R. 180–182, 213–214
The Tolkien Reader 213
Tom's A-Cold 34–35

"The Tower of the Elephant" 36, 40, 215
A Traveler from Altruria 21
Treacherous Texts: An Anthology of US Suffrage Literature 217n3
"A Treatise on Electricity and Magnetism" 218n5
Trismegistus, Hermes 159
Twain, Mark 146
The Twentieth Century 7
"Twilight" 144–145

Underhill, Evelyn 160–161, 165–169
utopia 15, 17, 19, 22, 24–25, 27, 34–36, 41, 135–136, 139
Utopianism 17

Vermeersch, Arthur 159
Verne, Jules 115
Vidal, Gore 220n5
La Vita Nuova 158
vitalism 187–189

Waite, Arthur 159
Walpole, Horace 46–48
The War in the Air 148–149
The War of the Worlds 11, 22
"The Waste Land" 7, 39
The Watchers Out of Time 212
Weird Tales 36, 135, 199–200, 203–204, 210, 212–213, 216, 223ch7n1
The Well at the World's End 21
Welles, Orson 122
Wells, H. G. 1, 7, 22–23, 88, 90–92, 100, 105–109, 115–117, 121–122, 133, 143, 147–149, 219n3
Westfahl, Gary 24, 217n2, 223n6
Wharton, Edith 70–72
What Can Be Saved from the Wreckage? James Branch Cabell in the Twenty-First Century 222n13
Where Angels Fear to Tread 142
Whitehead, Alfred North 77–78
Whitworth, Michael H. 162
Whyte, Kenneth 217n4
Wilde, Oscar 42–43, 57, 66–67
"'A Wilde Desire Took Me': The Homoerotic History of Dracula" 218n7
Williams, Charles 158
Williams, Tennessee 52
Williams, William Carlos 196
Williamson, Jack 129
Williamson, Jamie 213
"A Witch Shall Be Born" 215

Wolf, Leonard 51
Womack, Ytasha 29
"Woman in a Hat" 5
Woolf, Virginia 60, 94, 98–99, 196
Wordsworth, William 220n9
World War I 10, 13, 16, 21, 27, 31, 34, 35, 40, 139, 149, 151, 160
World War II 145, 155, 198, 210
Worlds of Fantasy & Horror 223chEn1
The Worm Ouroboros 105, 119–121, 199
Worster, Donald 101

Wrestling with Nature: From Omens to Science 219n5
Wright, Farnsworth 210, 212
Wundt, Wilhelm 218n6

x-ray 151–152

Yeats, W.B. 37, 64, 159, 160
"The Yellow Wallpaper" 218n10

Zuleika Dobson 27

www.ingramcontent.com/pod-product-compliance
Lightning Source LLC
Chambersburg PA
CBHW030324020526
44117CB00030B/1093